You Belong to Christ

You Belong to Christ

*Paul and the Formation of Social Identity
in 1 Corinthians 1–4*

J. BRIAN TUCKER

PICKWICK *Publications* · Eugene, Oregon

YOU BELONG TO CHRIST
Paul and the Formation of Social Identity in 1 Corinthians 1–4

Pickwick Publications
An Imprint of Wipf and Stock Publishers
199 W. 8th Ave., Suite 3
Eugene, OR 97401

www.wipfandstock.com

ISBN 13: 978-1-60899-676-6

Cataloguing-in-Publication data:

Tucker, J. Brian.

    You belong to Christ : Paul and the formation of social identity in 1 Corinthians 1–4 / J. Brian Tucker.

    xiv + 332 pp. ; 23 cm. Includes bibliographical references and index.

    ISBN 13: 978-1-60899-676-6

    1. Bible. N.T.—Corinthians, 1st, I-IV—Criticism, interpretation, etc. 2. Bible. N.T.—Corinthians, 1st, I-IV—Social scientific criticism. 3. Group Identity—Biblical teaching. I. Title.

BS2675.2 T85 2010

Manufactured in the U.S.A.

To Amber

Contents

Acknowledgments

I WOULD LIKE TO express my sincere gratitude to Dr. William S. Campbell, my doctoral supervisor, mentor, and friend during my studies at the University of Wales, Lampeter, UK. His graciousness, timeliness, and passion for Pauline studies modeled for me the importance of a life of balanced scholarship and research. Furthermore, I would like to express my thankfulness to Dr. Kathy Ehrensperger, my secondary doctoral supervisor for her insightful questions, desire for evidence, and unfailing support throughout my research program. I would like to thank Dr. Andrew D. Clarke and Dr. Paul Middleton for their recommendations and criticisms, though the shortcomings that remain are of course my own responsibility. I would like to thank Dr. K. C. Hanson and Dr. Chris Spinks at Wipf and Stock Publishers for their advice in the preparation of this manuscript. I would like to thank my faculty colleagues at Moody Theological Seminary–Michigan for their critical dialogue and patient encouragement. I would like to express my gratitude to Laura Hunt for her tireless efforts in bringing this manuscript to completion.

I want to thank my family for their unwavering support. I love and appreciate my parents, Joseph and Ann Tucker, for believing in me and helping me to fulfill God's call on my life. To my sisters, Kimberly, Julie, and to both of their families, thank you for modeling Christ-likeness in our relationship. I also want to thank my four beautiful, intelligent, and godly daughters, Ashley, Alexandria, Annaliese, and Abigail, for being amazing Christ-followers, I love you all. Richard and Carol Goode, thank you for all your support and for allowing me to be part of your life via marrying your daughter. And to Amber, you have been amazing, indescribable, and the perfect partner with whom to live, love, raise children, and serve the Lord. Your hard work, kindness, support, and excellent academic abilities make you a rare combination and I thank God for you everyday (Prov 31:10–12). I love you.

J. Brian Tucker
April 2010

Abbreviations

ANTC	Abingdon New Testament Commentaries
ASCSA	American School of Classical Studies at Athens
ABD	*Anchor Bible Dictionary*
AGJU	Arbeiten zur Geschichte des antiken Judentums und des Urchristentums
ANRW	*Aufstieg und Niedergang der römischen Welt*
BDAG	Danker, F. W., W. Bauer, W. F. Arndt, and F. W. Gingrich. *Greek-English Lexicon of the New Testament and Other Early Christian Literature*. 3rd ed. Chicago, 2000
BDB	Brown, F., S. R. Driver, and C. A. Briggs. *Hebrew and English Lexicon of the Old Testament*. Oxford, 1907
BDF	Blass, F., A. Debrunner, and R. W. Funk. *A Greek Grammar of the New Testament and Other Early Christian Literature*. Chicago, 1961
BECNT	Baker Exegetical Commentary of the New Testament
Bib	*Biblica*
BibInt	*Biblical Interpretation*
BIS	Biblical Interpretation Series
BETL	Bibliotheca Ephemeridum Theologicarum Lovaniensium
BibSac	*Bibliotheca Sacra*
BNP	*Brill's New Pauly*. Edited by H. Cancik and H. Schneider.
BNTC	Black's New Testament Commentaries
BTB	*Biblical Theology Bulletin*
BZ	*Biblische Zeitschrift*
CBQ	*Catholic Biblical Quarterly*

CBR	*Currents in Biblical Research*
CIL	*Corpus Inscriptionum Latinarum*
CTR	*Criswell Theological Review*
DPL	*Dictionary of Paul and His Letters.* Edited by G. F. Hawthorne and R. P. Martin. Downers Grove, 1993
EDNT	*Exegetical Dictionary of the New Testament.* Edited by H. Balz and G. Schneider. ET. Grand Rapids, 1990–1993
EKKNT	Evangelisch-Katholischer Kommentar zum Neuen Testament
EvQ	*Evangelical Quarterly*
ExpT	*Expository Times*
FRLANT	Forschungen zur Religion und Literatur des AT und NT
GPBS	Global Perspectives on Biblical Scholarship
GR	*Greece and Rome*
GRBS	*Greek, Roman and Byzantine Studies*
HALOT	*The Hebrew and Aramaic Lexicon of the Old Testament.* Edited by L. Köhler, W. Baumgartner, and J. J. Stamm. Translated and edited under the supervision of M. E. J. Richardson. 5 vols. Leiden, 1994–2000
HRCS	Hatch, E. and H. A. Redpath. *Concordance to the Septuagint and Other Greek Versions of the OT.* 2 vols. Oxford, 1897. Suppl., 1906. Reprint, 3 vols. in 2, Grand Rapids, 1983
HTKNT	Herders theologischer Kommentar zum Neuen Testament
HTR	*Harvard Theological Review*
HTS	Harvard Theological Studies
IBC	Interpretation: A Bible Commentary for Teaching and Preaching
ICC	International Critical Commentary
ILLRP	Inscriptiones Latinae Liberae Rei Publicae
JAAR	*Journal of the American Academy of Religion*
JBL	*Journal of Biblical Literature*

JBV	*Journal of Beliefs and Values*
JETS	*Journal of the Evangelical Theological Society*
JSNT	*Journal for the Study of the New Testament*
JSNTSup	Journal for the Study of the New Testament Supplement Series
JTS	*Journal of Theological Studies*
LNTS	Library of New Testament Studies
L&N	*Greek-English Lexicon of the New Testament: Based on Semantic Domains.* Edited by J. P. Louw and E. A. Nida. 2nd ed. New York, 1989
LCL	Loeb Classical Library
LSJ	Liddell, H. G., R. Scott, and H. S. Jones. *A Greek-English Lexicon.* eds.
M&M	Moulton, J. H., and G. Milligan. *The Vocabulary of the Greek Testament Illustrated from the Papyri and Other Non-Literary Sources.* London, 1930. Reprint, Peabody, MA, 1997
NA27	Nestle-Aland, *Novum Testamentum Graece* 27th ed.
Neot	*Neotestamentica*
NICNT	The New International Commentary on the New Testament
NIDNTT	*New International Dictionary of New Testament Theology.* Edited by C. Brown. 4 vols. Grand Rapids, 1975–1985
NIGTC	New International Greek Testament Commentary
NovT	*Novum Testamentum*
NovTSup	Novum Testamentum Supplements
NTS	*New Testament Studies*
OCD	*Oxford Classical Dictionary*
OED	*Oxford English Dictionary*
OLD	*Oxford Latin Dictionary*
PCPS	*Proceedings of the Cambridge Philological Society*
PTMS	Princeton Theological Monograph Series
RB	*Revue biblique*

RIC	*Roman Imperial Coinage.* C.H.V. Sutherland
SBL	Studies in Biblical Literature
SBLDS	Society of Biblical Literature Dissertation Series
SBLSP	*Society of Biblical Literature Seminar Papers*
SCT	Self-Categorization Theory
SIT	Social Identity Theory
SNT	Studien zum Neuen Testament
SNTSMS	Society for New Testament Studies Monograph Series
SNTW	Studies of the New Testament and its World
TDNT	*Theological Dictionary of the New Testament.* Edited by G. Kittel and G. Friedrich. Translated by G. W. Bromiley. 10 vols. Grand Rapids, 1964–1976
TynBul	*Tyndale Bulletin*
WBC	Word Biblical Commentary
WUNT	Wissenschaftliche Untersuchungen zum Neuen Testament
ZNW	*Zeitschrift für die neutestamentliche Wissenschaft und die Kunde der ältenKirche*

Introduction

THE ACCEPTED READING OF the Pauline discourse downplays variability and replaces it with a universalistic discourse in which difference is not allowed to continue. It emerges from an uncritical acceptance of the progress and forward movement of "Christianity" from Jerusalem to Rome and sees no continued relevance for Jewish identity within the Christ-movement. William S. Campbell, on the other hand, argues that Jewish identity continues to be relevant within the Christ-movement, as do other social identities. Campbell is convincing with regard to the continuation of Jewish identity for Jewish Christ-followers. However, can the same be said for Greek or Roman social identities, which have a different ideological basis than Israel's scriptures? This is the concern for this present study: is there evidence, specifically in 1 Corinthians 1–4, that Paul equally saw the continuation of gentile social identity "in Christ"? If so, what are the implications of such a reading of Paul?

This introductory chapter will uncover the object, describe the limits, and discuss the approach to be followed in this book. Then, it will review the scholarly debate concerning the cause of the conflict/opposition that Paul addresses in 1 Corinthians 1–4 and offer another possible organizing concept to help explain the divisions in Corinth. Finally, it will introduce Warren Carter's framework for discerning the way a text seeks to form social identity in its auditors.

THE OBJECT OF THIS BOOK

This study on 1 Corinthians 1–4 examines the way Paul sought to form the social identity of the Christ-followers in Corinth. The research proceeds from an understanding of social identity based on the Social Identity Theory (SIT) of Henri Tajfel and the Self-Categorization Theory

(SCT) of John Turner and is informed by an understanding of Christ-movement identity which follows William S. Campbell.[1] Archaeological, epigraphic, numismatic, and literary artifacts are used in order to demonstrate that civic identity in the Roman colony of Corinth, understood as a subset of social identity, was in transition in the first century and that this may account for the difficulties Paul addressed in 1 Corinthians.

This book argues that some in Corinth were continuing to identify primarily with key aspects of their Roman social identity rather than their identity "in Christ" and that this confusion over identity positions contributed to the problems within the community. Paul seeks to re-align the positions within the Corinthians' identity hierarchy in order to produce an alternative community with a distinct ethos. This approach uniquely asserts that previous social identities are relevant and not extraneous "in Christ." The tensions within the community are thus over conflicting understandings concerning the social implications of the gospel received from Paul.

The argument begins by addressing further introductory issues in this first chapter. Then chapter two provides a rationale for using Social Identity Theory and a theoretical description of the concept from the field of social psychology. Chapter three discusses two approaches within Pauline studies with regard to the social identity of the early Christ-movement in order to support the approach taken in this book. Chapter four provides evidence for the transitional nature of civic identity in Roman Corinth and argues that this is a plausible background for the difficulties Paul addresses in 1 Corinthians. Chapters five through nine provide a social-scientific reading of 1 Corinthians 1–4 in order to demonstrate that Paul was seeking to form social identity and to show the way contemporary social-scientific theory may provide insights into the processes that are expressed in the text. Chapter five delineates the foundation and framework for social identity, while chapter six reveals a lack of salient "in Christ" social identity within the ἐκκλησία in Corinth. Chapter seven studies the cognitive aspects of identity and the way external forces may impact identity salience both negatively and positively. Chapter eight continues the exegetical study of 1 Corinthians 1–4 and brings to the fore the importance of a sense of belonging within a salient community. Paul's identity and strategy of social identity formation are

---

1. Tajfel 1972; Turner 1987; Campbell 2006a.

made evident in chapter nine. The final chapter summarizes the findings of this book.

THE LIMITS OF THIS BOOK

A study such as this requires certain boundaries within which to proceed. The exegetical portion of this book will be limited to a social-scientific reading of the way Paul addresses the problem of Roman social identity in 1 Corinthians 1–4. Thus, it will not address all of the exegetical issues in 1 Corinthians 1–4 and many scholarly debates will be bracketed out. However, it will give sufficient attention to the aspects of Paul's argument that are most relevant for understanding the way his line of reasoning forms social identity and for substantiating a particularistic understanding of Christ-movement[2] identity in an extended portion of text outside of Romans and Galatians.[3] So, lexical, grammatical, and syntactical issues will be highlighted when relevant, and evidence from the historical context as well as elements of various social-scientific theories will be integrated in order to provide a plausible reading of the text.

This also raises the question, What is social identity? We will use Henri Tajfel's definition of social identity, which is "that *part* of an individual's self-concept which derives from his [sic] knowledge of his [sic] membership of a social group (or groups) together with the value and emotional significance attached to that membership."[4] One of the aims of this book is to provide a description of social identity in general as well as an assessment of its application within Pauline studies.[5] Often, scholars use the term identity in a generic way, not realizing the poten-

---

2. "Christianity" as a separate religion did not occur until after the time of Paul. Thus, in order to avoid conflating later Christian identity from the second and third centuries with what was occurring during the time of Paul, we will use the term "Christ-movement" to describe the Pauline communities (MacDonald 1988: 11; Horrell 1993: 86; Ehrensperger 2007: 182 n.12). Horrell (2008: 185–203) has recently questioned the use of Pauline Christianity; however, his arguments are based on his understanding of the development of Christian identity which differ from the approach argued for in this book. See further p. 10 n. 45.

3. One of the aims of this book is to see the way a particularistic approach to identity (evident in the letters addressed to Rome and Galatia) might be substantiated in the letter written to those in Corinth, which addresses a different set of social issues.

4. Tajfel 1978b: 63 emphasis original; Esler 2003a: 20. The implications of this definition are discussed on p. 41.

5. This will occur in chaps. 2 and 3. See Börschel 2001: 12.

tial for equivocation. Identity is used within philosophy to explore the consistency of the self over time. It is used in psychology as a descriptor of personal identity. It is used within sociology with a focus on social identity. Finally, it is used within Pauline studies to describe the relationship between Jewish and gentile[6] identity with regard to the Christ-event and its soteriological or anthropological implications. This book focuses on the way social identity illuminates theological identity; it is not concerned with the philosophical questions nor primarily with individual psychological concerns, though they may intersect this research, especially in relation to Paul's identity.[7]

QUESTIONS OF METHOD

The discussion of method that follows responds to specific criticisms that are relevant to this book and is not a comprehensive defense of social-scientific criticism.[8] The word identity is a modern invention,[9] and this study could therefore be accused of engaging in a semantic anachronism by discussing the role of social identity in the formation of the early Christ-movement.[10] Social-scientific criticism as a method for interpreting the Bible is still a debated issue; it lacks, for example, a clear, agreed-upon method.[11] John Elliott describes the exegetical

6. The difficulty in translating τὰ ἔθνη relates to contemporary conceptions that "Gentile" is an "ethnic term equivalent and opposite to Jews" (Campbell 2006a: 12). Thus, in this book, "gentile" will, following Campbell, not be capitalized when it translates τὰ ἔθνη. At times, however, τὰ ἔθνη will be rendered as "the nations" which emphasizes the Roman imperial understanding of τὰ ἔθνη (see Lopez 2008: 4–7).

7. Brawley (2005: 19–20; 2007: 109–11) provides a useful survey of the philosophical approaches to identity in the context of Pauline studies. Cf. Berger 2003: 28–29.

8. This has already been provided by others, e.g., Elliott 1993; Barton 1995: 61–89, 1997: 277–89; Garrett 1992: 89–99; Martin 1999: 125–41; Schmidt 1989: 115–32; DeNeui 2008: 7–35. One example which is not addressed here is the concern over foundational or ideological differences with regard to the social-sciences in comparison with theology (Barton 2005: 754; Holmberg 2004: 271). It should be noted that specific questions of method are also addressed at relevant points. For example, there is an extended explanatory rationale at the beginning of chapter two, which addresses concerns about the inclusion of contemporary research into identity.

9. *OED* 620. But see Brawley 2005: 17.

10. Nguyen's recent work, which is addressed below, has somewhat ameliorated this concern (2008a: 10–51).

11. Scroggs 1980: 166; Clarke 1993: 3–6. Tidball (1984: 20–21) offers other difficulties which include sparse "evidence"; "models [that] simplify reality"; "theories" which are untestable; and problems associated with "parallelomania." Lawrence (2005: 15)

method used here as "that phase of the exegetical task which analyzes the social and cultural dimensions of the text and of its environmental context through the utilization of the perspectives, theory, models, and research of the social sciences."[12] This study uses historical-critical tools and social-scientific analyses to understand more clearly the group dynamics and the social implications of 1 Corinthians 1–4.[13]

Scholars who have researched the Corinthian correspondence have recognized that it contains significant material regarding the social setting of the early Christ-movement and is thus particularly suited to social-scientific analysis.[14] These scholars, however, differ about the ways this material is to be evaluated and understood. Social historians focus on Jewish,[15] Greek, or Roman[16] texts and artifacts to establish the context for understanding the setting of the Christ-movement.[17] Social theorists

---

suggests researching "with humility, in order to cast fresh light on, rather than dictate or presume to wholly understand patterns" as a way through some of these difficulties.

12. Elliott 1993: 7.

13. Kee describes group analysis as one of the main areas of concern for social-scientific approaches to New Testament interpretation (1989: 32, 43–50). Elliott (1993: 53) notes "a group-identifying function" inherent in texts (see DeNeui 2008: 35).

14. Adams 2000; Birge 2002; Butarbutar 2007; Chester 2003; Chow 1992; Clarke 1993, 2000, 2006, 2008; Dutch 2005; Ebel 2004; Fotopoulos 2003; Horrell 1996; Litfin 1994; Marshall 1987; Martin 1995; May 2004; Meeks 1983a; Meggitt 1998; Nguyen 2008a; Økland 2004; Pickett 1997; Pogoloff 1992; Robertson 2001; Strüder 2005; Theissen 1982; Welborn 2005; Winter 2001, 2002a.

15. The translation of 'Ιουδαῖοι as "Jews" or "Judeans" has been the focus of significant scholarly attention over the last twenty-five years (Schwartz 2007: 3). Esler opts for "Judean" while Campbell and Schwartz prefer "Jew" and Johnson Hodge transliterates it "*Ioudaioi*" (Esler 1998: 4; 2003a: 12; Campbell 2006a: 12; Johnson Hodge 2007: 15). This book, while paying clear attention to the post-Shoah environment in which this research is undertaken, will normally translate 'Ιουδαῖοι as "Jews" (Ehrensperger 2004: 16; Schwartz 2007: 4, 23).

16. When the term "Greco-Roman" is employed in this book, it should be recognized that the overarching cultural context of life in the first century CE was Roman, though there was, to a certain extent, a mutually beneficial context of Roman power and Greek cultural identity (Whitmarsh 2001: 20, 249; Jossa 2006: 10; Sugirtharajah 2002: 24). Because of the interpenetration of these cultural dynamics this book may alternate between "Greco-Roman" as well as "Greek and Roman" (Ostenfeld 2002: 5; Pratt 2008: 7; Arafat 1996: 92–97). Also, its use is not intended to obscure the Jewish context in which Paul's identity and line of reasoning were formed (Acts 21:39; 22:26–28; Clarke 2002: 108; Geiger 2002: 242; Gruen 2002: 214). Winter (2001: 245) rightly notes that in Corinth, Roman and not Greek culture prevailed.

17. E.g., Judge 2008; Winter 2001; Clarke 1993; Asher 2000; Nguyen 2008a; DeNeui 2008.

rely on resources from various social-scientific theories to provide insight into the significance of the evidence that is uncovered from both
texts and material remains.[18] These approaches are sometimes set against
one another and understood as competing scholarly frameworks. Since
this book proceeds from a combination of social theorists' and social
historians' perspective, a few observations should be made concerning
this issue.[19]

Social theorists are sometimes accused of anachronistically employing theories developed in a later context and read back into another
setting for which the theory holds no warrant. Edwin Judge's approach
to the social distinctives and context of the earliest Christ-movement
relies on papyrological, textual, and inscriptional evidence while dismissing a significant explanatory role for contemporary social-scientific
models. He argues that these models were developed much later and in a
context foreign to that of the Roman Empire.[20] Thus, he insists that New
Testament scholars should resist using the results of "modern sociology"
until their findings can be validated through a type of "painstaking field
work" that is all but impossible when dealing with ancient cultures. He
concludes that those who employ these methods are engaging in "the
sociological fallacy."[21]

Social-scientific theories may be utilized cautiously after the historical context is established by the rigorous application of social histori-

18. E.g., Esler 1998; Horrell 1996; Malina 2001; May 2004; Adams 2000. This does
not imply that the first group does not employ contemporary theories; they sometimes
do, but in a limited fashion (Nguyen 2008a: 1–2). The work of the Context Group is
notable here (Pilch 2001).

19. Holmberg (2004: 267–68) places "Gerd Theissen and Wayne Meeks" in this combination social theoretical and social historical group and describes this approach as a
"mediating position" characterized by "a much more tentative use of social theory" in
an "eclectic and piece-meal" fashion (Meeks 1983a: 6). This characterization may be
challenged in that the integration of various approaches does not imply eclecticism or
a general disregard for method. Also, Meeks and Theissen approach the Pauline corpus
from a moderate functionalism (see Horrell 2009: 7).

20. Judge 1980: 210–17; Barton (2005: 754) notes, concerning the findings of sociological and anthropological approaches, that they "may draw attention (working
by analogy) to significant features of biblical and early Christian social dynamics that
might otherwise go unnoticed." This is not meant to diminish the level of incommen-
surability between the first century context and the contemporary context, only to note
that there may be analogous features based on the shared human experience (see Clarke
2008: 6 and Garrett 1992: 89).

21. Judge 1980: 210; Holmberg (2004: 255–59) offers an extensive discussion concerning this issue.

cal methods.[22] Andrew Clarke argues that the problem Paul addresses in 1 Corinthians 1–6 is a misunderstanding concerning the nature and practice of leadership within the ἐκκλησία.[23] Specifically, Clarke demonstrates that some had brought "secular" leadership practices into the ἐκκλησία and thus Paul writes to correct their misapplication of "worldly" leadership concepts.[24] Clarke uses inscriptional, onomastic, numismatic, and literary sources to establish the socio-historical context for 1 Corinthians 1–6 and then provides an exegetical analysis that supports his contention that the nature and practice of leadership were contested in Corinth. He concludes that leadership within the ἐκκλησία should "not rely on boasting or social status to create reputation, not to establish a popular following by recourse to the law-courts, and not to rely on a reputation carved out by oratorical prowess or patronal respect. This constitutes an inverting of the world's views of leadership."[25]

This study follows many of the general contours of Clarke's work and seeks to extend it by the application of SIT/SCT and a particularistic understanding of Christ-movement identity. For example, Clarke recognizes problems related to leadership within the community while this study focuses on the group dynamics that may have given rise to those problems and locates the exigence in a misunderstanding over the way the Corinthian Christ-followers' Roman social identity was transformed "in Christ."[26] In other words, Clarke argues that there is no place for these concepts in the "church" while this work contends that there was a misunderstanding concerning how these same notions were to function in a reprioritized way within the community (1 Cor 7:20).[27]

22. Winter 2001: xiii–xiv.

23. This book will normally leave ἐκκλησία untranslated in order to avoid implying an institutionalized understanding of "church" which would not be in view at this early stage in the Christ-movement (Horsley 1997: 208–9; but see Clarke 2000: 12–19). The idea of "community" is a close English approximation for ἐκκλησία, which emphasizes "shared belief" and "common identity," an emphasis that is also evident in Diog. Laert. 8.41, cited in BDAG 303. For stylistic reasons, at times, "church," "assembly," or "community" may be employed, and "house-church(es)" may also be used when addressing scholarly discussions concerning actual meeting places and should not be understood as an equivocation (cf. McCready 1996: 59–73; Elliott 2008b: 97–116).

24. Clarke 1993: 6 n. 25; 2000: 49.

25. Clarke 1993: 125.

26. Clarke 1993: 101–5.

27. Winter (2001: 263) suggests that Paul had in mind "the use not the abuse of this present life."

Clarke's approach follows that of Judge with regard to the use of sociological theories and adopts a contextually qualified universalistic approach to identity. This is seen in Clarke's essay entitled "Jew and Greek, Slave and Free, Male and Female" where he concludes that Paul's "greetings" are "presented in such a way as to transcend all ethnic, social and gender barriers."[28] However, it does not follow that Clarke completely dismisses the continued relevance of cultural and ethnic identity in Paul's letters. With regard to those in Rome, Clarke remarks that "Paul's response is not to ride roughshod over such distinctives, but to recognize cultural diversity within these groups."[29] In *Serve the Community and the Church*, Clarke recognizes that Christ-movement identity emerged within the nexus of the "Jewish and Greek philosophical and theological tradition" as well as "the complex and multi-cultural world of the early Roman empire" and thus these contexts continue to impact and be relevant for communal life.[30] So, it may be proper to view Clarke's approach as a contextually qualified universalistic understanding of Christ-movement social identity.[31]

Clarke's primary concern with the use of contemporary social-scientific theories is that they often do not take into consideration the historical situation of the text and thus result in unhistorical readings.[32] We concur with Clarke in this regard; however, the solution is not to reject the use of social-scientific theories but to apply them dialogically in the context of exegetical and historical research. This will provide the language to address the contemporary context in which a text is read, while also giving a historically plausible basis for that reading. The binary nature of Clarke's argument leads to the conclusion that "secular" concepts should not be used in the practice of leadership within the ἐκκλησία.[33] However, this may be too stark, and an exegetical and social-scientific investigation of 1 Corinthians 1–4 may offer another possibil-

28. Clarke 2002: 123.

29. Clarke 2002: 111.

30. Clarke 2000: 1–2.

31. The differing approaches to Christ-movement identity will be discussed beginning on p. 61.

32. Clarke 1993: 3–7, 132.

33. Legitimation is an important issue for leadership, and Clarke (1993: 126) concludes that the "basis of legitimation is thus contrary to that of the surrounding Greco-Roman society."

ity. Clarke rightly discerns "secular" practices in the ἐκκλησία; however, this may be the result of Paul's teaching that previous social identities "in Christ" continue to be relevant (1 Cor 7:17–24).[34] Thus, Paul writes in 1 Corinthians 1–4 to align practices with the social implications of the gospel, which will in turn impact communal practices and Roman social identity within the ἐκκλησία. What are these social implications? For this we turn to the work of Raymond Pickett.

Pickett argues in a fashion similar to Clarke that "Greco-Roman ideals and values continued to have a stronghold in the Corinthian congregation," and this is the reason for the "repeated contrasts" between their former "pagan identity"[35] and the new identity "in Christ."[36] However, Pickett understands Paul to be engaged in "secondary socialization" with regard to the existing social identities of those following Christ. In this understanding of social identity, Paul is not seen to be ignoring existing identities but rather reconfiguring the "discrepancy between social and baptismal identity."[37] The significance is that those existing social identities are the framework from which the Pauline mission may be extended throughout the Roman Empire and in which they seek to "live out their Christian calling."[38]

Pickett's research reveals a potential weakness in Clarke's approach. Social identities are an important part of communal life for Paul. In other words, Clarke understands the problem in Corinth to be a relatively small group of social elites who had sought to bring in "secular" concepts of leadership into the "church," a move that was rejected by Paul.[39] However, it may be that Paul had taught the Corinthians concerning the continuing importance of their previous identity, but because of issues of cultural translation and possibly a misunderstanding related to baptism they had misapplied Paul's teaching on this important subject (1 Cor 5:9–10; 7:17–24; 9:19–22).[40]

---

34. Wenham 1997: 137–41.

35. Clarke (2002: 111) connects this identity with Paul's use of ἔθνη in 1 Cor 12:2.

36. Pickett 1997: 32.

37. Picket 1997: 33, 101–2, 213.

38. Pickett 1997: 91, 99.

39. Clarke 1993: 130.

40. The thought here is that if passages such as Gal 3:28, 1 Cor 12:13, Col 3:11 are part of a baptismal formula, one could conceive of a situation in which questions would emerge with regard to the continuing significance of these social categories within the

Pickett is correct to note the social significance of the "word of the cross" and that previous social identities were part of Paul's concern; however, he, too, envisions a universalistic understanding of Christ-movement identity.[41] For example, he writes that being "in Christ" "brought into sharp relief the question of the efficacy of the believer's previous historical identity and the social forces which shaped it."[42] Thus, he rightly recognizes the impact that previous identities were having on communal life in Corinth; however, for Pickett, the problem is that the Corinthians were not living out the social implications of the cross, which he interprets as the subversion of "human categories of distinction."[43] While Paul's stance is that these distinctions are salvifically insignificant, they continue to impact communal life and are to be reprioritized "in Christ."

Social-scientific theories may furnish language to describe phenomena in the text that then provide insight into the way the text may be appropriated in a new context.[44] Henry Nguyen argues that *persona* functions as an ancient equivalent for the concept of social identity and thus may be studied to understand more clearly Paul's rhetoric and the way the Corinthian Christ-followers[45] were employing this concept in "their conception of Christian identity."[46] Nguyen compares the use of *persona/prosōpon* in the works of Valerius Maximus, Epictetus, and Paul. He concludes that by adding the modifier "social" in front of *persona* one may understand Paul to be addressing a preoccupation with the superficial aspects of one's social identity in a manner similar to that of the

---

Christ-movement. Pickett (1997: 213) understands these distinctions to be "subverted by the death of God's Son." Clarke (2000: 123) describes these verses as a reflection of Paul's "theology of inclusiveness."

41. Pickett 1997: 103.

42. Pickett 1997: 98.

43. Pickett 1997: 122.

44. Barton 2005: 753.

45. This book will employ "Christ-follower" rather than describing members of the Christ-movement as "Christians"; χριστιανός is used only three times in the NT (Acts 11:26; 26:29; 1 Peter 4:16) and does not become a key term of self-designation before the second century when Ignatius employs it (Eph 11:2; Magn 4:1; Trall 6:1; Horrell 2007: 364; Campbell 2006a: 12). In the Corinthian correspondence, Paul employs "in Christ" language as his preferred group designation (1 Cor 1:12; 3:23; 15:23; 2 Cor 10:7). See n. 2 p. 62.

46. Nguyen 2008a: 130.

other two authors.[47] With the exception of Marcel Mauss, his approach does not overtly employ contemporary identity studies, but his move to include "social" in front of *persona* provides a possible model for the combining of these two approaches.[48] Nguyen's work is a continuation of Judge with regard to social identity. His rejection of contemporary sociological theories might explain Nguyen's reticence with regard to their usage. Thus, *Christian Identity in Corinth* studies the social location and relations of the early Christ-movement but provides language that may be used to further study contemporary dynamics similar to those within the text that this book examines, thus extending the work of Judge, Winter, Clarke, Pickett, and Nguyen by the application of tools from social-scientific criticism. In this way it follows the suggestion of Bruce W. Winter that after the "proto-sociological" work has been completed, social theorists might apply the findings of the work of social historians.[49] Nguyen's work provides an important first step in the study of early Christ-movement social identity in Corinth;[50] however, a study that combines the resources of the social history and social theory approaches remains to be done.[51] That is what this book hopes to accomplish with regard to the issue of social identity in Roman Corinth.[52] But which approach offers a way forward, maintaining the historical locatedness of the social historian's approach while avoiding anachronisms and mirror-reading?[53]

47. Nguyen 2008a: 5–9; e.g., Nguyen (2008a: 3) points to "rank and status."

48. Mauss (1938: 263–81) discusses issues related to personhood in antiquity as compared to selfhood in the modern era.

49. Winter 2001: xiii; Clarke 1993: 5.

50. I would suggest that Nguyen's approach emphasizes the resources of social history while this book emphasizes the resources of social theory; however, neither approach fully neglects the other.

51. In chapter four, this book brings to the fore the importance of the idea of transitional civic identity as a part of Roman social identity within the interpretive framework of the New Testament. Also, it is hoped that this book contributes to the ongoing discussion concerning how a particularistic approach to Christ-movement identity may be sustained outside of Romans and Galatians.

52. We recognize that at this stage in the Roman Empire there was no one stable Roman social identity; rather, it was highly contextual and differed based on various group memberships.

53. See Barclay (1987: 73–93) concerning the problems with mirror-reading. In DeNeui's (2008: 35) study on Pauline metaphors, he argues that because not enough background work has been done on those metaphors he has chosen "social-historical

Philip Esler, a member of the Context Group, and David Horrell wrote a series of articles debating the way sociological models should be employed within social-scientific biblical interpretation.[54] Esler's approach is structured around the use of sociological models to help understand the rhetoric of a text and to more accurately answer questions concerning its function.[55] Horrell, in another recent essay, is critical of the approach represented by Bruce Malina, another member of the Context Group. Horrell argues that the exclusive reliance on models is not warranted in that some leading practitioners within the social sciences (e.g. Grace Davie and David Sutton) rely on approaches that do not cohere with Malina's exclusive model-based approach.[56]

This book generally follows Horrell's approach[57] which allows themes to emerge from the text and then seeks to apply the categories from modern theories, be they psychological, sociological, or anthropological, to provide language by which to answer questions in a contemporary context.[58] In other words, understanding issues of social identity

---

description." However, he (2008: 35) insightfully notes that "this approach is not intended to deny that the application of social-scientific theory and modeling can produce useful results." With regard to the social and group dynamics in 1 Corinthians 1–4 significant work has been done, and thus it may be useful to apply social theories to the findings of others to see if further insight may be gained.

54. Esler 2002: 107–8; Horrell 2000b: 84–86. Holmberg (2004: 267–69) also provides an excellent analysis of the Esler/Horrell debate.

55. Esler (2002: 112) rejects the claim that his exegetical conclusions are based on models and not on the actual textual data itself. See Garrett's (1992: 96–97) discussion of Malina and Neyrey with regard to the imposition of models that avoid ethnocentric readings. See Holmberg's (1990: 12–14) warnings concerning the use of models whether explicit or implicit.

56. Horrell 2009: 14.

57. We should note one area where we disagree with Horrell. He claims that there is no significant distinction between the work of social historians and social theorists; however, this downplays the distinctive manner in which scholars such as E. A. Judge, B. Winter, and A. Clarke approach the interpretive task as compared to social theorists such as P. Esler, W. S. Campbell, and K. Ehrensperger. These approaches can be combined; however, it is too stark to suggest, as does Horrell (2009: 17), that "there is no sustainable distinction to be drawn."

58. Adams 2000: 23–38; Horrell 2000b: 83–105; Esler 2002: 107–13. It should be noted that with regard to the chosen theoretical framework, this book uses Social Identity Theory which is drawn on by Esler rather than Giddens' Structuration Theory which is used by Horrell (Esler 1998, 2003a; Horrell 1996). Sugirtharajah (2002: 12–13) provides an introduction to the issues of method related to postcolonial analysis, while Ehrensperger (2004: 39–42) provides the same from a feminist perspective. In some

construction within the early Christ-movement does not rely on any one theory of social identity but cautiously reads the Pauline discourse in 1 Corinthians informed by various theoretical approaches. As Kathy Ehrensperger rightly concludes, "Contemporary theories can provide an illuminating perspective and shed light on aspects of the fragmentary discourse of the Pauline epistolary conversation which would otherwise go unnoticed."[59] So the method applied in this book pays attention to the social context in both its exegetical and historical details as well as the contemporary setting in which this study is undertaken.[60]

The explicit use of social-scientific theories assists the researcher in making clear for the reader which theoretical framework is being utilized.[61] Likewise, feminist scholars have stressed the importance of making clear one's research assumptions for the benefit of the reader.[62] Thus, this book is supported by three presuppositions that influence the manner in which it is carried out. First, Paul is understood to be thoroughly embedded in Judaism. The various expressions of second Temple Judaism serve as the proper interpretative framework for understanding the way Paul reasoned and deployed his mission to the nations. The approach of this book coheres well with those identified as "beyond the new perspective on Paul."[63] Paul is not understood as an abstract Christian theologian but as a Jewish teacher, primarily of gentiles, who is immersed in the Jewish symbolic universe as practiced among the diaspora communities of the Roman Empire. Second, Roman imperial ideology is Paul's primary interlocutor. Paul, as a continuing member of the synagogue community, was not attacking a works-oriented, legalistic Judaism. Instead, Paul's main concern was the formation of the Christ-movement around the Mediterranean basin. The principal hindrance to communal stability was the pretentious Roman Empire, as expressed through provincial governors and local collaborators. It was most dif-

---

ways, Garrett (1992: 98) anticipates the approach followed by this book in calling for "sustained theoretical reflection" on "the interface between sociological study and various forms of literary criticism."

59. Ehrensperger 2007: 3.

60. Holmberg (2004: 270) provides a helpful warning that "models or theories cannot substitute for evidence, by filling in gaps in the data" and "historically based models can turn a guess into an educated guess, but no more."

61. Elliott 1993: 36–59.

62. Ehrensperger 2004: 13.

63. Zetterholm 2009: 127–63.

ficult, if not impossible, to separate religious from political power, and thus Roman imperial ideology served as a primary concern for Paul in fulfilling his mission.[64] Third, a particularistic approach to social identity is understood as Paul's ideological position.[65] Paul did not set out to obliterate Jewish identity, or gentile identity for that matter. He understood social and cultural identities to be vital to the fulfillment of his mission, as long as they did not contradict God's commands (e.g., immorality, idolatry, cultural boasting, or unscriptural patterns of thinking). This view is in stark contrast to the understanding of Paul as one who sought to transcend the particularities of Judaism for an egalitarian vision of humanity, often at the expense of the "so-called" parochial concerns of Judaism. These three presuppositions guide the research for this book.[66]

PREVIOUS APPROACHES TO 1 CORINTHIANS 1–4

Scholarship dealing with 1 Corinthians 1–4 often focuses on the issues of behavior evident in the text and thus sees the problem in Corinth primarily in terms of ethics.[67] Recent scholarship—while recognizing that this component is present—notes that there appear to be broader communal problems, those dealing with community ethos. The genesis of such problems is described variously as: external teachers presenting a different message, Gnosticism, Hellenistic-Judaism, differing leadership styles, or the elevation of sophists.[68] These reconstructions all address key components of the text, but there is no consensus concerning the source of Paul's opposition[69] in 1 Corinthians 1–4. However, there is a

64. Lopez 2008; Elliott 2008a; Yeo 2008; Finney 2005; Oakes 2005; Swancutt 2001; Horsley 2000, 2008; Williams 2000; Wright 2000; Georgi 1992.

65. Runesson (2000: 142–44) discusses issues related to particularism and universalism within the earliest Christ-movement.

66. I will substantiate these presuppositions throughout this book.

67. Robertson and Plummer 1911: 12. The history of scholarship has also focused too much on conflict to explain Paul's argument. If the early Christ-movement had been experiencing an overwhelming amount of conflict it is doubtful if it would have survived. Also, there is a tendency to describe Paul's rhetoric in terms that are too stark, especially in relation to prevailing cultural values.

68. Thiselton 2000: 1–56.

69. Asher (2000: 36) has convincingly argued that scholarly reconstructions of opposition in Corinth are unnecessary for understanding Paul's rhetorical purposes in writing to the Corinthian Christ-followers. This book follows Asher to the extent that it downplays the role of opposition in its reconstruction of the rhetorical exigence in 1 Corinthians 1–4.

third component that needs be included in this discussion—identity.[70] Identity salience "in Christ" leads to proper ethical choices within the community of Christ-followers, which results in an ethos distinct from that of Roman imperial ideology,[71] which Paul understood to be passing away (1 Cor 2:6–8). It is the balance of all three of these (i.e., identity, ethics, and ethos) that provides an understanding of Paul's strategy and mission in writing to the Corinthian Christ-followers.

The Parties in Corinth as Theological Opposition

A review of the scholarly reconstructions of Paul's opposition and its relationship to the situation in 1 Corinthians 1–4 begins with "Die Christuspartei" written by F. C. Baur in 1831. He understood the conflict in Corinth to be related to the competing missions between Peter and Paul. He developed his approach through his understanding of what occurred in the Antioch event (Gal 2:1–10) and an analysis of the parties mentioned in 1:12.[72] This led him to conclude that the four parties mentioned in 1:12 were actually divided into two factions which mirrored the conflict within early Christianity. The factions included those who supported the Pauline mission (i.e., Paul and Apollos groups) of a law-free gospel and those who supported the Petrine mission (i.e., the Cephas and Christ group), which required gentiles to maintain key markers of Jewish identity. Thus, for Baur, the conflict for Paul in Corinth was primarily with Judaism and Jewish Christ-followers. Recently, Odell-Scott has argued for a modified Baurian framework in which the Christ party includes James and the earthly family of Jesus.[73] While Baur's reconstruction is possible, it tends to over-emphasize conflict within the early Christ-movement and as Lütgert noted,[74] it imports the results of the Antioch event into the situation in Corinth.[75] The tension in Corinth

70. Van der Watt 2006: 4–6; Robertson 2001: 4–6.

71. Gilbert 2004: 237.

72. Baur 1831: 76 [136].

73. Odell-Scott 2003: 73.

74. Lütgert 1908: 42.

75. Baur's approach rests on three premises. (1) Paul was attempting to vindicate his apostleship in 1 Corinthians (and 2 Corinthians for that matter) against those who argued that he had not followed Jesus during his earthly ministry; (2) The Christ party consisted of Jewish Christian opposition to the Pauline mission, normally focused on issues of Jewish identity (e.g., circumcision) but in Corinth on apostolic claims; (3) The Christ party and the Cephas party were a united front against Paul's mission in Corinth.

was not the same as in Rome or Galatia nor does the Christ-movement need to define itself in terms that reflect negatively on Judaism.[76]

Lütgert argued that Paul's opponents were from the "enthusiasts" (*Schwärmer*) who emphasized "gnosis" in Corinth.[77] This group elevated their own charismatic experiences. They believed that the knowledge those experiences produced was more acute than the teaching they had received from Paul.[78] Schmithals notes, however, that Lütgert never made it clear how a disparate group of "pneumatics" received the descriptor of "Christ people" nor offered a plausible "explanation for" the development "of the Gnostic preaching in Corinth."[79] Schmithals finds in Corinth a "heresy" that "involved a well-defined Christian Gnosticism."[80] This,

---

The first premise may be questioned; just because Paul discusses his apostleship it does not follow that his apostleship was being attacked. This is a central node in Paul's identity hierarchy and discussion of it should not be seen as *prima facie* evidence that it was being questioned. Furthermore, Baur's case requires the collation of references from 2 Corinthians where it appears that Paul's apostleship was challenged; however, when the references from 1 Cor 1–4, 9 are assessed independently from 2 Corinthians, Baur's claim is significantly weakened. The second premise may also be questioned. Baur never adequately explains the way the existing so-called Judaizing issues, such as circumcision, developed *de novo* as concerns for apostolic authority. Similar to the previous assessment, Baur's strongest arguments for this premise occur in 2 Corinthians; however, the rhetorical exigence between the two letters is too dissimilar to support such a crucial assertion. The third premise is also open to question. As noted by Baur himself (1831 [2003]: 303), there is lack of textual support for the claim that these two parties refer to one group.

76. Adams and Horrell 2004: 15; Campbell 2006a: 15–17.

77. Lütgert 1908: 43–62, 79–82. Bultmann (1947: 180–81) understood the opponents as "pre-Christian gnostics," as did Käsemann (1942: 33–71). Godet (1898: 77) concluded they were proto-Gnostics. Reitzenstein (1927: 62) argues that the Gnosticism present was from Paul and not the Corinthians. Dunn (1995: 27–45) provides an excellent summary of many of the background issues related to 1 Corinthians 1–4. Mihaila (2006: 134–80) offers a substantial review of the social and rhetorical background of 1 Corinthians 1–4.

78. Lütgert (1908: 76, 86) effectively removed the ethnic implications from Baur's approach, though Schlatter and Käsemann, whose critiques of Baur were similar to Lütgert's, retained the view that Jewish issues were part of the Corinthian problem (Schlatter 1914: 68; Käsemann 1942: 33–71; Barrett 1968: 44; Goulder 2001: 47). Many scholars still follow the general contours of Lütgert's approach. Thiselton provides a summary of these (2000: 126, 131). Conzelmann sees in the background of the groups "the pneumatic Christology of exaltation" (1975: 34). Barrett follows T. W. Manson and describes this group in a manner similar to proto-Gnostics (1968: 45).

79. Schmithals 1971: 121–22 [GT 1956].

80. Schmithals 1971: 151.

for Schmithals, was the only opponent that Paul was combating in the Corinthian correspondence.[81] Wilson and Theissen have questioned the existence of Gnosticism this early in the first century, but in dismissing the Gnosticism hypothesis they acknowledged that there was at least some kind of *"gnosis"* in Corinth.[82] Recent work on Gnosticism discounts its impact on the situation in Corinth while Clarke has made a strong case that theological opposition is not in view at all.[83] Paul's opposition in Corinth was not primarily theological; in this Baur and Lütgert were wrong. However, others question whether there were actually parties or factions in Corinth.

Lack of Parties and Lack of Theological Reasons for Opposition

F. C. Baur's reconstruction of the Peter and Paul parties in Corinth was also critiqued by Munck, who argued that there were no parties in Corinth rather internal strife based on personal preferences for teachers.[84] The problems in Corinth were not Jewish in nature but related to the Corinthians' Roman environment, especially as it relates to sophistry and wisdom. The Corinthians understood the gospel as wisdom, their leaders as wisdom teachers, and themselves as wise persons who had accepted this wisdom as evidenced by their new life and the spiritual gifts over which they were also boasting and "bickering."[85] Clarke follows Munck and concludes that the Corinthians "were aligning themselves behind their favourite leaders with the result that there was disagreement and distinction."[86] Clarke also sees "a personality cult" rather than theological differences in the Corinthian situation.[87] Nguyen follows

81. Schmithals 1971: 118. Wilckens originally argued for a view similar to Schmithals, although recently he has argued for a type of Jewish-Gnostic teaching (1997: 508).

82. Wilson 1982: 112; 1972: 65–74; Theissen 1982: 132–36.

83. Clarke 1993: 90; Winter 2002a: 245; Cousar 1993: 90–102; Martin 1995: 71; Adams 2000: 94. Cf. Campbell 2006a: 9–13; Thiselton 1978: 526; Kuck 1992: 161–62; Brown 1995: xix; Schrage 1991: 244; Munzinger 2007: 70–71.

84. Munck (1959: 136; 138–39, 140) also concludes, "we therefore know nothing at all from 1 Corinthians about these two 'factions,' the Paul faction and the Cephas faction." Zahn (1909: 282), fifty years earlier, remarks, "nothing could be more erroneous than to suppose either in Paul's thought, or in fact, the Church was divided into four factions or even sects."

85. Munck 1959: 154.

86. Clarke 1993: 91.

87. Clarke 1993: 92.

closely the work of Munck and Clarke here but extends their work by the inclusion of the idea of social *persona*.[88]

Strüder also rejects the idea that there were parties in Corinth and that Paul created slogans as "his own illustration of what people in Corinth might have said."[89] This does not mean that there were no actual groups who were quarrelling. Paul's slogans prepare the reader for "Paul's solution to the authority problem in 3, 22–23."[90] Paul's rhetoric was meant to emphasize the superiority of Christ as compared to any other human authorities or personal preferences.[91] Munck's understanding of a Greek sophistic background is followed by Fee, while Winter builds on Munck's general understanding of the Corinthian situation.[92] Winter also recognizes, however, that Munck relied too much on the later work of Philostratus and that he lacked a way of arguing that key terms in 1 Corinthians 1–4 were sophistic and not theological.[93] Winter argues that the Second Sophistic as a movement had its beginnings in the first century CE, which strengthens Munck's argument.[94] He diverts, however, from Munck and argues that the divisions in the community were between the Paul and Apollos parties and related to the disparity in their public speaking abilities.[95] Winter understands Paul's opponents to be "adherents to the sophistic tradition."[96] Overall, this approach has the most to commend it, and this book follows Munck's approach with the correctives provided by Clarke and Winter. However, these scholars do not fully consider the role of social identity in the communal disagreements, though Nguyen's recent work comes close. Nguyen's focus is on

88. Nguyen 2008a: 136–38.

89. Strüder 2003: 448.

90. Strüder 2003: 450.

91. Strüder 2003: 450–51.

92. Fee 1987: 64–65 n. 79; Winter 2002a: 9–11.

93. Winter 2002a: 10.

94. Winter 2002a: 4. Pogoloff (1992: 65) rejects the idea of the Second Sophistic in the first century, while Whitmarsh (2004: 146–48) correctly connects it with first century CE oratory.

95. Winter 2002a: 176–78. Cf. Munck 1959: 143–44; Konradt 2003: 181–214; Nguyen 2008a: 137.

96. Winter 2002a: 246, see also 223. Schnabel (2006: 82) understands Paul to be addressing „die Frage der Parteiungen und Loyalitätsbekundungen, sowie den Inhalt der apostolischen Verkündigung."

the personal aspects of social identity while this book is concerned with its corporate dimension.

Greco-Roman Rhetoric as the Cause of Opposition

Litfin researches the context and impact of rhetoric on Paul's preaching in Corinth.[97] He concludes that there were two parties: "those who aligned themselves with Paul, and those who aligned themselves with others against Paul."[98] Those aligned against Paul, in Litfin's estimation, were those who had decided that Paul's speaking was not up to the standards of eloquence they had come to expect and thus had declared "their independence from him."[99] Litfin's contribution is in the way he makes clear the expectations for eloquence within Greco-Roman rhetoric.[100] The focus on the Greek and Roman context of wisdom is also seen in the work of Pogoloff who brings to the fore the role that eloquent speech played in the "tensions between urban/rural" groups as well as "Roman/ Greek identity."[101] He understands the tension in Corinth to be related to status and the way it is reinforced by rhetoric.[102] He understands the division to be between those who follow Paul and those who follow Apollos, a view that is rejected by Schnabel.[103] Pogoloff employs the resources of both rhetorical criticism and the new rhetoric[104] to complete his research and brings to the fore the importance of the rhetorical situation in understanding the exigence in Corinth.

Mitchell on the other hand employs rhetorical criticism to produce a study that emphasizes the Roman political significance of Paul's cor-

---

97. Litfin 1994: 244.

98. Litfin 1994: 184–85.

99. Litfin (1994: 187) actually follows Dahl (1967: 322) in this regard.

100. His general approach is followed by Hays 1997: 22–24; 1999: 112; Bullmore 1995: 6–9; Winter 2002a: 14.

101. Pogoloff 1992: 127.

102. Pogoloff 1992: 273.

103. Schnabel (2006: 80) contends that „Dass Apollos selbst in der korinthischen Gemeinde einen Konflikt provoziert hat, ist eher unwahrscheinlich: Paulus erwähnt Apollos immer nur wohlwollend (3,4.5.6.22; 4,6; 16,12; Tit 3,13), und es gibt keinerlei Belege für die Annahme, dass Apollos in Korinth eine problematische „Weisheitstheologie" eingeführt hat."

104. Perelman and Olbrechts-Tyteca 1969: 21, 191–92, 411–59; see particularly their discussion of dissociative arguments.

respondence.[105] She understands the groups in Corinth as political factions and believes Paul is writing to restore unity within the community (1 Cor 1:10). The political significance of the factions in Corinth is also clear in the work of Welborn. Following Weiss, Welborn does not see disparate theological views as the problem but rather the likelihood that they will act like everyone else in the culture (1 Cor 3:3).[106] By this he means that the community is in the process of dividing based on economic and status categories (1 Cor 1:16). The primary concern for Paul is the group claiming an elite understanding of wisdom.[107] More recently Welborn shifts the focus from the political context to the theatrical context and argues that Paul's appropriation of "the fool" in 1 Corinthians 1–4 was done in order to distance himself from the demands for rhetorical brilliance and eloquence among the Corinthians.[108] Dunn argues that Welborn downplays the "theological" aspects of the situation; however, separating political and religious realities in antiquity is not always possible.[109] This group of scholars provides significant insight into the role that rhetoric played in Corinth, and this book builds on their work to suggest that the rhetorical practices associated with Roman imperial ideology were of concern for Paul, not just eloquent speech in general.[110]

---

105. Mitchell (1991: 65–67, see also 23) importantly argues that 1 Corinthians is a unified document and an example of deliberative rhetoric.

106. Welborn 1987b: 88; Weiss 1910: 15–16. Mitchell (1991: 85) critiques Welborn's use of these constructions and argues that there is a lack of evidence for the political usage.

107. The leaders of these factions, in Welborn's (1987b: 96–98, 102–3) estimation, were local leaders using the name of "renowned figures" to establish their "power" claims.

108. Welborn (2005: 13, 102) also argues for a partition theory approach to 1 Corinthians and understands 1 Corinthians 1–4 as a separate document. Cf. Schmithals 1971: 90–96; Jewett (1978: 389) includes 1:1—6:11 as part of letter C, with letter A being 1 Cor 11:2-34, and letter B including 2 Cor 6:14—7:1 + 1 Cor 6:12-20 + 1 Cor 9:24—10:22 + 1 Cor 15:1-58 + 1 Cor 16:13-24.

109. Dunn 1995: 43. See Clarke (2000: 5–7) and Price (1984: 71) for a discussion of the political and religious realities in antiquity.

110. Rhetorical practices associated with Roman imperial ideology will be discussed on p. 92.

Hellenistic-Jewish Wisdom as a Contributing Factor

The combination of rhetorical criticism[111] and an emphasis on the political context of Corinth is central to the work of Horsley. He focuses on the religious context of wisdom within Hellenistic-Judaism (e.g., Wisdom of Solomon and Philo) as the cause for much of the difficulties evident in Corinth.[112] Pearson argues for the Hellenistic-Jewish background of ψυχικός and πνεῦμα terminology primarily in relation to Gen 2:7. The findings of his study then are applied to the two groups in Corinth: the πνευματικοί who were living an elevated existence through the "cultivation of wisdom" and the ψυχικοί who were not.[113] Horsley recognizes the difference "between apocalyptic Judaism (located primarily in Palestine) and the Hellenistic-Jewish religion focused on Sophia (Logos)" as the point of conflict between the rhetorical vision of Paul and those in Corinth.[114] Horsley's work is an important reminder concerning the Jewishness of the early Christ-movement as a context for the gentile mission; however his contention that Paul was intensively subversive and sought to establish an alternative society is too stark.[115] In some ways this book tempers Horsley's approach.

Davis seeks to extend the work of Pearson and Horsley by researching Jewish wisdom literature from the "early post-Biblical" period (e.g., Sirach, Qumran, and Philo) and argues that some in Corinth were seeking wisdom from Torah while Paul understood wisdom to have its basis in Christ-crucified.[116] For Davis the opponents in Corinth are those seeking spiritual fulfillment through Torah.[117] The pursuit of wisdom by means of Torah is also affirmed in the work of Joachim Theis who notes that Paul re-positions this viewpoint and understands himself to be a "teacher of wisdom" (*Weisheitslehrer*) proclaiming the "word of the

111. Horsley 1998: 28; 2000: 88.

112. Horsley 1998: 35. Horsley (2004: 3–4) takes the view that "from Paul's first long argument . . . [he] opposes his gospel to the Roman rulers and the imperial order." Horsley rightly combines the political and theological issues.

113. Pearson (1973: 12–39) also ties in the τέλειοι and νήπιοι to refer to these groups. Cf. Horsley 1998: 60–61. Horsley follows Pearson closely in relation to 2:13–14.

114. Horsley 2008: 88 [1980: 51]. Horsley's 2008 compilation gathers his foundational articles from the 70's and 80's. See Hvalvik 2005: 123–43.

115. Horsley 2008: 75; Horsley 1997: 209. This is addressed further on p. 124.

116. Davis 1984: 5, 94.

117. Davis 1984: 131.

cross" (*Weisheitsverkündigung*).[118] It is difficult to see a polemic against Torah in 1 Corinthians 1–4, and Davis' lack of a consideration of the context of Roman Corinth limits the usefulness of his work.[119]

Goulder, though arguing from a Baurian framework, understands the Jewish wisdom background to be related to the Peter group in Corinth.[120] For Goulder "the central issue in chs. 1–4 was the substance of the gospel: was it the word of the cross that brought salvation, or was it the torah?"[121] Jeffrey Lamp understands Paul to be transforming the Corinthians' understanding of the Jewish wisdom traditions by recentering them upon Christ, who as true wisdom is the only means by which to live a spiritual life.[122] For Lamp the issue is not the gospel but "the proper exercise of wisdom in the social relations of the community."[123] Baur's argument that the conflict between Paul and Peter is behind all the problems in the Corinthian correspondence is unconvincing. Lamp's work does hold promise in explaining the continuity between Jewish wisdom traditions, Paul's teaching, and his "christocentric understanding of wisdom" as "consonant with Jewish wisdom traditions."[124] Lamp's findings, however, are limited to explaining Paul's argumentation because, as Munck noted, Paul says it is the "Greeks" who "seek wisdom" (1 Cor 1:22).[125] There is no clear evidence that the predominantly gentile Christ-movement in Corinth was pursuing Jewish wisdom concepts; however, it is possible that Paul's argument, which has its basis in the Jewish symbolic universe, contributed to problems of cultural translation with regard to wisdom concepts.

---

118. Theis 1991: 10–13, 283, 508; Cf. Lamp 2000: 133–34.

119. Baird 1987: 151.

120. Goulder 1991: 516–34; Cf. Tuckett 1994: 201–19.

121. Goulder (2001: 73, 91) concludes that "The opposition in Corinth is substantially the same as that in Galatia, and the issue of the law is as crucial in the Corinthian letters as elsewhere in the Paulines, mutatis mutandis." Schrage (1991: 158–61) understands the emphasis on wisdom to be related in some way to a misunderstanding of Paul's gospel.

122. Lamp 2000: 192.

123. Lamp 2000: 193.

124. Lamp 2000: 193.

125. Munck (1959: 148–49) asserts that "The Greeks for their part sought salvation, as always, through philosophy; they sought wisdom, and the Gentiles who have just been converted in Corinth go on doing the same thing."

Greco-Roman Philosophy as a Contributing Factor

The philosophical context for 1 Corinthians 1–4 was initially considered by Weiss who argued that Stoic philosophy had impacted the Corinthians and thus was a significant concern for Paul when he wrote in 1 Corinthians 1–4.[126] Paige also sees Stoicism or possibly Cynicism in the background of the Corinthian situation.[127] He rightly includes the Roman influences in Corinth that are often minimized when reconstructions of the rhetorical situation are proposed.[128] This reconstruction requires an educated, elite audience in Corinth similar to that envisioned by the "new consensus"[129] while Deming argues for the influence of Stoic-Cynic ideas and their debates concerning political life versus "philosophical" pursuits.[130] Deming is correct concerning the ongoing impact of aspects of traditional Greek life; however this may be extended by a further consideration of the Roman influence on the Pauline community in Corinth.[131]

Downing is not so convinced of the Stoic parallels; rather he sees Cynic influence while Tomlin discerns an Epicurean influence among the Corinthian elite.[132] Tomlin argues that the current tendency to overlook theological reasons for the Corinthian opposition is a reaction against the earlier reconstructions which focused predominantly on doctrinal issues within the community.[133] Thus, he seeks to combine sociological and ideological analysis to better understand the opposition.[134] Tomlin does not try to over-reach in his suggestion and argues for his understanding as a "complement" rather than a competitor to the other "sociological and rhetorical approaches."[135] The Stoic context

126. Weiss 1910: 158–59; cited in Adams and Horrell 2004: 21–23.

127. Paige 1992: 180.

128. Paige 1992: 193.

129. Horrell 2006: 107. The "new consensus" will be discussed on p. 121. Huang (2003: 95–103) provides an excellent discussion of elitism in Corinth.

130. Deming 1995: 61; Yarbrough 1997: 156.

131. Clarke (2000: 11–58) rightly makes a distinction between Greek cities and Roman colonies. The view here is that Corinth was reestablished as a Roman colony.

132. Downing 1998: 85–127; Tomlin 1997: 51–72.

133. Tomlin 1997: 51. Cf. Horrell (1996: 119) who argues that these approaches are not "mutually exclusive" and that "symbolic" and "theological" perspectives "shape" an individual's "action and interaction."

134. Tomlin 1997: 54.

135. Tomlin 1997: 53.

may provide background for some of the difficulties in Corinth in that Roman imperial ideology could draw from Stoic concepts for claims of legitimation.[136]

Paul's Defense of His Apostleship as a Cause of the Conflict

Dahl follows Munck's critique of Baur by rejecting the thesis of the conflict with Jewish-Christians; however, he agrees with Baur that 1 Corinthians 1–4 was a defense of Paul's apostleship.[137] Castelli contends that Paul desired to establish his authority and identity at the center of the Corinthians' communal life.[138] Schüssler Fiorenza and Wanamaker extend Castelli's work and understand Paul as arguing to expand his authority within the community.[139] Schütz also sees a preparatory function in 1 Corinthians 1–4 for the rest of the letter and connects issues relating to Paul's apostleship to this introductory section, as do Holmberg and Given.[140]

Dodd, on the other hand, rightly rejects the idea that Paul is writing to address challenges to his authority in 1 Corinthians 1–4. Rather it

136. Seneca, for example, asserts that kingship/rulership is a natural concept, *Clem.* 1.19. The idea that those in a subordinate position should recognize their superiors provides for a well-ordered society, *Clem.* 1.14–18. The connection between those ruled and those who rule is analogous to the relationship between the immaterial and material parts of the body, *Clem.* 1.3.5—1.4.3. However, this does not argue that Stoics would affirm some of the pretentiousness of the governing officials, *Clem.* 1.19.1; concerning Nero see 1.1.4 and 1.5.7. See Trapp 2007: 179. Reydams-Schils (2005: 84) takes the view that "Cicero and the Roman Stoics were very much preoccupied with the circumstances and manner in which the philosopher should become involved in the state." But see Atherton 1988: 392–427. Cf. Diog. Laert. 7.84–131; Epic. *Diatr* 2.6.6–10.

137. Dahl 1967: 321. Vos (1996: 87–88) sees in the party slogans a challenge to Paul's authority; he contends that „Nach manchen Auslegern betrachtet Paulus die Parolen wesentlich als ein Problem zwischen ihm und der Gemeinde, als ein Problem, bei dem seine apostolische Autorität im Spiel ist."

138. Castelli 1991: 98, 111; Witherington 1995: 145; but see Ehrensperger 2007: 138; Clarke 2000: 224–28; 2008: 173–83.

139. Schüssler Fiorenza 1999: 119; Wanamaker 2003: 137; 2006: 340. Mitchell (1991: 16) rejects this approach and does not see Paul instructing the Corinthians. Wanamaker (2005: 427) claims there is a formational reason for Paul to use "his position of the first to proclaim the gospel to the Corinthians."

140. Schütz 2007: 190; Cf. Holmberg 1980: 45–48, 77–79. Both Schütz and Holmberg follow Max Weber's approach to power, conflict, and authority, which leads them to see conflict as central to the Pauline narrative. For further discussion on Holmberg and his use of power see p. 69. See also Given 2001: 94–95.

is a letter of "admonitions of a spiritual father to his children."[141] From a rhetorical critical standpoint Wuellner dismisses the argument that Paul is defending his apostleship in 1 Corinthians 1–4, specifically in 1:19—3:20, which is where Dahl focuses his argument. Wuellner understands 1:19—3:20 as a digression used to highlight a belief that the community had already accepted in order to re-establish a relationship with the recipients of the letter.[142] While Paul may be addressing the causes for divisions among the community, he concludes his initial argument in 4:14–21 in a manner that would indicate that his apostleship was not in question and that they had previously accepted Paul's teaching and his call to imitate him.[143] Chance rejects Wuellner's argument and furthers Dahl's analysis by arguing that 1 Corinthians 1–4 is forensic rhetoric and thus a defense for Paul's apostleship to the entire community.[144] Chance's critique fails in that he relies on the "listing and labeling" of "rhetorical figures and speech and figures of thought" as conclusive evidence for one's point of view; however, this minimalist approach to rhetorical criticism does not adequately take into account the actual content of the section in view, a charge which, ironically, he levels against Wuellner.[145] Paul was not primarily defending his apostleship in 1 Corinthians 1–4.[146]

Role of Social Status in the Conflicts

The dominant scholarly position regarding the conflicts in Corinth focuses on various issues of social status many of which may be subsumed under the rubric of Roman social identity. Horrell is representative of this approach and concludes that "social groups headed by certain prominent members of the congregation seem to make a good deal of sense as a background to 1 Cor 1–4.[147] Marshall argues more specifically that the difficulties in the ἐκκλησία related to "patronal friendship" that had its basis in the refusal to receive the financial gift offered to Paul. Furthermore, he understands the conflict to have its basis in Paul's

141. Dodd 1999: 44.

142. Wuellner 1979: 186–88.

143. Wuellner 1979: 186.

144. Chance 1982: 155.

145. Wuellner 1987: 450–51; cf. Marchal (2006: 3–16) who provides an excellent summary of the interaction between these two perspectives on rhetorical criticism.

146. This will be addressed on p. 134; cf. 15 n. 75, 248.

147. Horrell 1996: 117.

refusal to accept the Corinthians' financial gift (Phil 4:15). By refusing their money he "shamed and dishonoured them and was held to be responsible for the hostilities which followed."[148] Marshall's strength is that he provides a more comprehensive understanding of the social conventions of friendship, which were designed to obligate recipients to their patrons. His study, however, is somewhat weakened in that he assumes these views were also held outside the elite circles of the empire, which may not necessarily be accurate. Chow follows Marshall closely and understands the focus of the conflict was actually between "the powerful patrons in the church" who had aligned themselves against Paul.[149] Bünker also sees this small group to be the focus of Paul's concern, especially in relation to their interaction with other apostles.[150]

An understanding of the conflicts in Corinth from a social status perspective is also evident in Judge, who argues that "a socially depressed group" was "dominated by a socially pretentious section of the population."[151] Similarly, Theissen contends that the problem emerged because of "internal stratification" with "the majority from the lower classes" who "stand in contrast to a few influential members who come from the upper classes" (1 Cor 1:26–29). For Theissen, the social elites are the "wise," and they are "in opposition to others who do not belong to that group."[152] Meeks understands the household context to be one cause for the factions in 1 Corinthians 1–4 in that it would give rise to "conflicts in the allocation of power and in the understanding of roles in the community." He also follows Dahl in "that the decision to send that delegation may itself have precipitated the factions" and that some, based on 1 Cor 4:18, "doubted the wisdom of asking Paul's advice."[153] These approaches have in common the view that the early Christ-movement contained individuals of both low and high social status. Malherbe reflects this perspective and concludes, "this consensus . . . is quite different from the one represented by Adolf Deissmann . . . more recent scholarship

---

148. Marshall 1987: 177–79.

149. Chow 1992: 100.

150. Bünker 1984: 54–60; Schüssler Fiorenza 1999: 114.

151. Judge 1960: 60.

152. Theissen 1982: 69, 98; 1999: 54; Horrell 1996: 115–16.

153. Meeks 1983a: 51–52, 73, 76 118; Dahl 1967.

has shown that the social status of early Christians may be higher than Deissmann had supposed."[154]

Ancient perceptions of leadership within the context of the patron-client system and their impact on the tensions and expectations between those of high and low status within the community form the basis of Clarke's work. Clarke's study may be strengthened by a detailed analysis of 1:18—2:16 from a theological and epistemic perspective, something this book includes in order to better explain the tensions in leadership.[155] Adams concludes that Paul's "social goal is to build up the boundaries" of the community so as "to engender . . . a clearer sense of its distinctive religious, moral, and social identity."[156] This book builds on Adams' consideration of social identity and moves it to the fore of Paul's identity-forming agenda in 1 Corinthians. Wire sees the conflict focused on status differentials between those experiencing status increases due to their prophetic gifts, and those not gifted in such a manner.[157] Malina and Neyrey understand Paul's approach to be one "that tends to strengthen group cohesion."[158] Their understanding of Paul's approach to group formation is wide of the mark and interprets Paul's rhetoric in the context of Greco-Roman power and domination instead of a Hebrew understanding of family education. Though some of these scholars may need to define social status more clearly so as to make this a more useful label, conflicts based on social status continue to be the dominant interpretive framework for 1 Corinthians.

Some scholars have focused more specifically on social status within the Roman Empire. For example, Williams understands differing social relations within the context of Roman imperial ideology to be the problem within the community and the cause of "fractured relations within the Corinthian church."[159] Elliott sees the social, economic, and political realities of the Roman Empire as the cause of the division

154. Malherbe 1983: 31; Deissmann 1957: 241–43. Here Deissmann's description is very close to that of Malherbe, Judge, Meeks, and Theissen. Cf. Friesen 2004: 326; Longenecker 2009: 270–71.

155. Clarke 1993: 57; see Munzinger 2007: 46.

156. Adams 2000: 102–3.

157. Wire 1990: 1–11, 44–46, 197–201.

158. Malina and Neyrey 1996: 187; cf. Ehrensperger 2007: 117–18; Neyrey 1990: 110–11, 137–40.

159. Williams 2000: 799.

within the community.[160] Robertson also pays close attention to issues of social identity in the Roman Empire. He focuses on the system of relational networks and on Paul's concern that the Christ-movement would begin to function as another option among the social networks within the empire.[161] The interaction of Greek, Roman, and Jewish values in the context of ancient education is central to the work of Dutch who argues that differing social status based on education caused many of the divisions within the community.[162] These four approaches are particularly useful in this study. Williams and Elliott have rightly discerned a critique of the empire in 1 Corinthians 1–4 while Robertson has brought to the fore the importance of social networks, and Dutch has demonstrated the importance of education in the Roman empire and its relevance for understanding the pedagogical discourse in 1 Corinthians 4.

Martin's formulation of the Corinthian context is "that the theological differences" which are evident "all resulted from conflicts between various groups" based on "different ideological constructions of the body."[163] Martin sees a "high-status group" with "a relatively secure economic position and high level of education," while Paul and the majority of the community were "less educated" and "less well-off inhabitants of the Roman Empire."[164] May contests Martin's understanding of the body and instead sees the Corinthian situation as one in which Paul was concerned about the embodiment of social identity and the need for group boundaries, especially in relation to "sexual ethics."[165] Though issues of the body are more evident in 1 Corinthians 5–7, Martin provides evidence to demonstrate the presence of Roman social identity while

160. Elliott 1994: 205.

161. Robertson 2001: 54.

162. Dutch 2005: 3.

163. Martin 1995: xv.

164. Martin (1995: xv–xvi) contends that Paul was of higher status than the low-status group but that his "view of the body is more in harmony with views generally held by lower-status, less-educated members of Greco-Roman society. And the same class lines that divided urban society at large also divided the Corinthian church."

165. May 2004: 4–9, 49–55. Kim's (2008:13–15) argument challenges the general approach of those seeking to understand the problem in Corinth with regard to the body and instead argues for a functional understanding of the metaphorical nature of the body and its relevance for the establishment of difference within the life of the community.

May's theoretical framework serves as a useful heuristic with regard to the utilization of SIT/SCT.

Pickett, who was introduced earlier, argues that aspects of Greco-Roman social identity were continuing to influence the group norms within the ἐκκλησία in Corinth and thus his work is particularly relevant to this book.[166] The role of interpersonal relationships within the community, argues Pickett, and the arrogance of those who aligned themselves with the Apollos party were "responsible for evaluations of Paul and Apollos that divided the community."[167] Pickett's reconstruction is important for two reasons. First, it recognizes that part of the problem in Corinth was related to "misguided views about ministry."[168] Second, in 3:3–4, Paul "underlined the inconsistency between their spiritual identity and their fleshly conduct."[169] Here Pickett approximates the idea of social and theological identity, though his understanding of the social implications of this identity differs from that argued for in this book.

Friesen believes that the category of social status in reconstructions is too imprecise to be of significant value, and he suggests that the social status of the ἐκκλησία in Corinth may not be as stratified as the new consensus suggests.[170] Barclay, on the other hand, notes that 1 Corinthians 1–4 is one of "the fullest discussions of status within the Pauline communities" and "wealth is only *one* factor in determining who 'counted for something' in the churches."[171] In this book, social status will be considered as formative in the situation in Corinth but with the recognition that it is very unlikely that the elites in view would be provincial officials but more likely those of moderate financial means. This approach thus mediates between the two positions.

Barclay adds that the level of social integration that was occurring in Corinth gave rise to the problems in the letter.[172] Barclay's reconstruction is helpful in that social integration appears to be one of the models

166. Pickett's (1997: 32) approach to identity formation was discussed on p. 9.

167. Pickett 1997: 41, 57. Cf. Munck 1959: 143; Horrell 1996: 113; Welborn 2002: 232; Mihaila 2006: 220.

168. Pickett 1997: 41; Thiselton 1978: 513.

169. Pickett 1997: 40–41.

170. Friesen (2004: 333–35) suggests economic status as a more precise model for establishing the demographics of the Pauline communities. Cf. Friesen 2005: 352–70.

171. Barclay 2004: 366 emphasis original.

172. Barclay 1992: 69.

for mission that Paul establishes (1 Cor 9), and it could be that some of the difficulties in Corinth arose from a misunderstanding about the nature of mission as social integration (1 Cor 5:10). Dickson, rightly remarks that this approach is evident in 1 Corinthians, while Barram is correct in noting that moral formation is a vital part of Paul's gentile mission and should not be separated out.[173] Chambers, on the other hand, questions whether Paul actually intended his communities to engage in mission. Schnabel understands Paul's expectations to include a fully-engaged mission by his communities.[174] Chambers' argument rests on the idea that Paul or his co-workers were the only ones involved in proclamation of the gospel;[175] however, this overlooks the equally valid missionary activity of moral formation in which the Christ-following communities were undoubtedly engaged (1 Cor 3:5–15). Barram's idea of mission as moral formation, Paul's teaching on following his example in 1 Cor 10:31—11:1, and Dickson's mission as social integration provide other avenues for mission within the Pauline communities, and combine to weaken Chamber's rather narrow description.[176] One of the reasons that Paul argues for the continuation of previous social identities "in Christ" is that they provide an effective means to extend his mission to the nations (1 Cor 7:17; 9:20–21; 14:23).

Conclusion of the Literature Review for 1 Corinthians 1–4

What may we conclude concerning the opposition and/or the conflicts evident in 1 Corinthians 1–4? The answer to that question also describes the position from which this book is argued. First, Paul's opposition in Corinth was not primarily theological. Second, the opposition was related to the Corinthians' Roman environment and was associated in some way with issues connected to wisdom and teaching. Third, the rhetorical practices that were a point of contention may have related to

173. Dickson (2003: 227-30) describes mission as social integration as "the most basic motif of the (local) missionary stance of Pauline congregations," which emphasizes "the importance of not 'leaving the world'"; Barram 2006: 179. Williams (2001: 226) recognizes that the problem in Corinth was the need for correction concerning "God's plan of salvation" which "is potentially available for all Christians."

174. Chambers 2004: 255; Dickson 2003: 131; Schnabel 2004: 946–48.

175. Chambers 2004: 250–55.

176. Chambers 2004: 346-47; Dickson (2003: 10) defines mission as "the range of activities which members of a religious community desirous of the conversion of outsiders took to promote their religion to non-adherents." Cf. Barram 2006: 69–71.

Roman imperial ideology. Fourth, Jewish concepts of wisdom were not the issue in Corinth, though they may have contributed to issues of cultural translation with regard to Paul's argument. Fifth, the philosophical component of the opposition may have been located in Stoicism, which could function as a legitimating framework for Roman imperial ideology. Sixth, Paul was not primarily concerned with defending his apostleship. Finally, many of the problems in 1 Corinthians 1–4 were related to social status which this book subsumes under the broader rubric of Roman social identity. Clarke had originally concluded that many of these difficulties identified by scholars might be combined in order to offer a full picture of the problems in Corinth.[177] This book extends Clarke's assessment by agreeing that the problems were variegated but then seeks to organize the research through the broader concept of Roman social identity. If Paul was writing to address issues of social identity, then this raises a couple of important introductory questions: how do texts form identity and how may one discern when a text is being deployed for the purposes of identity formation?

WARREN CARTER: TEXTS AND IDENTITY FORMATION

Culture,[178] power,[179] and ideology[180] are vital components of texts that form identity. Texts position the reader within the symbolic universe of the author in an asymmetrical relationship. Texts are thus complicit in narrowing possible meanings while organizing resources so that meaning can form within the context of an interpretive community.[181] Actually, texts and their readers/hearers share in the meaning-making endeavor

---

177. Clarke 1993: 125.

178. Culture is a system of symbols and tools (see Harland 2009: 12). Harland takes the view that culture may "refer to processes of human *meaning-making* embodied in symbols, values, and practices that are shared and passed on by a particular group."

179. Ehrensperger (2007: 179) is helpful here, "the power at work among leaders, between leaders and communities, and among communities oscillates between power-over, power-to and power-with, and frequently some or even all of these aspects are closely intertwined with each other." We understand Paul, in 1 Corinthians, to be employing what may be described as the transformative use of power.

180. In the context of SIT, ideology is defined (Hogg and Abrams 1988: 82) as an "interrelated set of beliefs and propositions whose primary function is explanation." See further discussion of this topic on p. 45.

181. Shkul 2007: 26. Judith Lieu's research addresses the way texts form identity. She will be discussed on p. 75.

but not in an equal manner. Engaging in written discourse requires tools for analysis by both the receptor and the transmitter. Access to knowledge is inherently unequal in a communal setting and requires further clarification concerning the authorial position, narrative position,[182] and identity of the recipients (i.e., gender, ethnicity, education, civic engagement, and status). The way identity forms through texts is an epistemic concern. It is one that Paul addresses in 1 Corinthians 1–4, and this book will draw upon the tools of discourse analysis to understand the way the language of the text functions in forming meaning.[183]

Discourse plays a crucial role in mediating power relationships and thus contributes to the formation of identity. Information does not travel in one direction. It is interacted with, resisted, and redefined by its recipients. The relational function between the encoder and the decoder is of vital epistemic importance. In other words, the community is necessary for understanding to occur. The work of the Spirit, however, is prior to this communal exercise and grounds relational epistemology in Christ-crucified (1 Cor 1:18). The illuminating work of the Spirit, in Paul's estimation, is the epistemic condition necessary to attain wisdom and knowledge (1 Cor 2:14; Rom 8:7). Thus, while texts are certainly vital to forming identity, the corporate experience of being "in Christ" and the ongoing work of the Spirit within the community are the efficient causes of a salient social identity.

The way texts form identity, or more specifically the way the gospels form identity, is a central concern in Warren Carter's *Matthew and the Margins*. Building on the work of Burridge, Carter understands the gospels to form identity as they focus on a central figure, offer instruction, provide a model to follow, and intentionally center on community building.[184] Though Burridge's initial work on βίοι was designed to argue for the genre of the gospels, he correctly points out that the borders between genres were fluid.[185] That is not to argue that 1 Corinthians is to

---

182. These are explained in the discussion of Rom Harré and Luk Van Langenhove on p. 56.

183. Martin and Rose 2003: 15; Van Dijk 2001: 352. See the discursive nature of identity discussion on p. 55.

184. Carter 2000: 7–14.

185. Burridge (1992: 65–69) charts the following "*genera proxima* . . . moral philosophy; religious or philosophical teaching, dialogue and discourse; encomium; story and novel, interest and entertainment; political beliefs, polemic; and history." These genres often are mixed within a single work.

be understood as βίοι, only to note that various genres have overlapping characteristics and concerns.

Carter's four broad characteristics that indicate a text is forming identity are evident in 1 Corinthians.[186] First, it is a letter focused on the central figure of Christ-crucified (1 Cor 2:2, 8). In 1 Cor 2:2, "Jesus Christ and him crucified" was all that Paul claimed "to know." In 1 Cor 2:8, Paul questions the perception of Rome's rulers and declares the one whom they crucified to be "the lord of glory." First Corinthians was written for the recipient's instruction (1 Cor 4:14; 14:37). Paul makes his purpose for writing clear in 1 Cor 4:14, to "instruct" or "form" his "beloved children." In a different way, in 1 Cor 14:37, Paul reminds the Corinthians that his writing is to be understood as "a command of the Lord." First Corinthians provided models to be followed (1 Cor 4:16; 11:1). In 1 Cor 4:16, Paul "encourages" his audience to imitate him. This will be done through the mediation of Timothy who will remind the Corinthians of Paul's "ways in Christ" (1 Cor 4:17). Paul repositions himself as a model to be followed in 1 Cor 11:1 when he instructs the community to "be imitators of me, as I am of Christ." In 1 Cor 16:16, he also suggests that the Corinthians fit into the model set by leaders such as Stephanas. The letter also focuses on building a community (1 Cor 1:9–10). In 1 Cor 1:9, Paul reminds the community that God's faithfulness is responsible for their assembly. Furthermore, God has "called" the people into "fellowship" with "Christ." In 1 Cor 1:10, Paul seeks to build a unified community that will have "the same mind and the same judgment." In 1 Cor 12:12, 27, Paul uses the imagery of the body to describe his community-building program, which was illustrated earlier by a series of metaphors (i.e., 1 Cor 3:9 "God's field" and "God's building," and 1 Cor 3:16 "God's temple"). Carter concludes that Matthew "functions" as "an identity-forming, lifestyle-shaping narrative" and this book argues that 1 Corinthians functions similarly.[187]

Carter also provides a secondary set of characteristics that may indicate identity formation is occurring. Though there is some overlap with the previous grouping, many of these characteristics are central to the argument of 1 Corinthians. First, the group is named. This in-

186. The listing here simply introduces key verses that will be discussed in the exegetical portion of this book.

187. Carter (2000: 8) does not make the connection with Paul's writing to his communities.

cludes both positive and negative ascriptions (e.g., ἐκκλησία, ἀδελφός, νήπιος, φυσιόω).[188] Second, the "central focus" of the group is its "commitment to Jesus" as "the central feature of the community's identity."[189] Third, there are "claims of exclusive revelation" which provide "definitive interpretation of the scriptures" and "as recipients of God's mysteries" the community is to be "separated from all others."[190] Fourth, "rituals and association" are central for communal life: "baptism," "teaching," "worship," and "interacting with other members in appropriate ways: with forgiveness, love, participating in governance, ritual meals, praying its prayer" all "forge identity."[191] Fifth, the community has a "social organization" that "shapes the community's governance" but also argues for continual "interaction with and participat[ion] in its larger society."[192] Sixth, "invective against opponents defines" a "desired way of life 'over against' dominant groups" and resists exercising "power" in a manner similar to those outside groups.[193] Seventh, a worldview described as "apocalyptic eschatology" understands "human experience in a fundamental temporal, cosmic, and social dualism." This understanding includes "the present evil age, which disregards God's purposes, and the future glorious age, when God's purposes will be triumphantly established."[194] The eighth characteristic is "community definition by origin, governance, and practices," which "strengthens shared perceptions of a community's identity."[195] These characteristics are also evident in 1 Corinthians and

---

188. Carter (2000: 9) adds that "these names secure separation from other communities, reinforce group identity, and warn this community not to be like other groups."

189. Carter 2000: 9.

190. Carter 2000: 9.

191. Carter (2000: 9) asserts that "rituals create order, sustain a community in an alternative way of living, and effect transformation."

192. Here Carter (2000: 9–10) argues for an egalitarian impulse that may not be in view in Corinth.

193. Carter 2000: 10.

194. Carter (2000: 10–11) asserts that "this apocalyptic mind-set reinforces their identity as recipients of God's favor, fashions a lifestyle according to God's will, warns of dire consequences for failing to live accordingly, but promises reward and salvation for continued faithfulness."

195. Carter (2000: 11) takes the view that "Dionysius of Halicarnassus (*Rom Ant* 1.9—2.29)" and "Josephus (*Con Ap* 2.145–295)" evidence this pattern, as well.

provide an initial basis for the claim that Paul was seeking to form social identity in this letter.[196]

CONCLUSION

The thesis is put forth that some in Corinth were continuing to identify primarily with key aspects of their Roman social identity rather than their "in Christ" identity and that this confusion over identity positions contributed to the problems within the community. The method utilized is a meditating position between the social history and social theorist approaches to social-scientific criticism. The review of the scholarly approaches determined that a cumulative understanding of scholarly constructions of the conflict in Corinth was appropriate, and the idea was put forth that the difficulties in the ἐκκλησία may have been related to local expressions of the Corinthians' Roman social identity. Warren Carter was found to have developed a framework for determining when a text is seeking to form identity, and it was noted that 1 Corinthians evidences many of those characteristics. But, what do we mean by social identity? This is the concern for the next chapter.

---

196. We will point out the places were these eight characteristics are evident as the specific verses are encountered in exegetical portion of this book. Sawyer (1999: 169) interacts with the important role that those who also preserved texts played in controlling the identity that emerged. Those responsible for preserving Paul's letters were central in the formation of the early Christ-movement's social identity. See Tellbe 2009: 51.

2

The Application of Contemporary Theories
of Social Identity

INTRODUCTION

DAVID HORRELL'S ESSAY, "WHITHER Social-Scientific Approaches to New Testament Interpretation? Reflections on Contested Methodologies and the Future," begins with a survey of Wayne Meeks's methodology, whose approach is described as moderate functionalism, a theoretical framework shared by Gerd Theissen.[1] As a social historian, Meeks draws from the social sciences in an "eclectic" manner while focusing on various issues of social status within the early Christ-movement.[2] This brief summary orients the reader to Meeks's approach and serves as the foundation for Horrell's discussion in the rest of the chapter where he surveys key scholarly developments since the publication of *The First Urban Christians*. First, the field of social-scientific New Testament studies is now widely diverse and has developed into so many differing areas that it is almost impossible to discern a common, overarching methodological approach. Second, most of Meeks's innovative ideas with regard to the social aspects of the Christ-movement are now part of the common field of knowledge in New Testament studies. Third, the work of Bruce Malina and the Context Group is noted as an approach that differs

---

1. Horrell 2009: 7. The significance of this for 1 Corinthians is that in Theissen and Meeks' approach the focus in on what roles were performed in order to restore group unity. Horsley draws from a more conflict-oriented approach which leads him to focus on the roles required to defeat injustice. These differing theoretical perspectives should be kept in mind as one evaluates each (Meeks 1983a: 7; Theissen 1982: 51–53; Horsley 2000: 86; see Horrell 1996: 35–36).

2. Meeks 1983a: 6.

from Meeks's and, as a group, prefers to identify themselves as the proper locus for social-scientific interpretation of biblical texts.

This leads Horrell to ask, "What does count for social-scientific criticism?" Malina contends: (1) Scholars must employ recognized social-scientific models to interpret the text if they want to engage in social-scientific interpretation. (2) There is a distinction between social historians and social theorists. (3) Social science interpreters are rejected if they do not follow the tightly defined disciplinary framework laid out by Malina and some within the Context Group.[3] Horrell raises these issues and then provides a critical analysis of the approach represented by Malina, concluding that a narrow definition of what social-scientific interpretation entails is unwarranted. However, and quite importantly, Horrell does think that "outlining a coherent and explicit theoretical framework at the outset of one's work" is of vital importance. That is what this chapter will do.[4]

Important contemporary approaches to social identity will be described in order to establish the research framework from which the social-scientific and exegetical studies of 1 Corinthians 1–4 will be undertaken. This chapter will not discuss the historical background of social identity studies[5] nor will it focus on social constructionism,[6]

---

3. Horrell 2009: 11–12, 14. See further Tucker 2010b and the earlier discussion on p. 4 in chapter 1.

4. Horrell 2009: 13.

5. James 1890; Cooley 1902; Mead 1934; Blumer 1968; Gouldner 1957; Erikson 1968; Becker 1963; Parsons 1951; Strauss 1969; Goffman 1959. See Tucker (2009b: 55–62) for an overview of the history of social identity studies.

6. The most influential proponents of the social constructionist approach to culture and society are Peter Berger and Thomas Luckmann. They (1966: 116) continue the scholarly debate over the social nature of identity and argue that it is "socially bestowed, socially sustained and socially transformed." Berger and Luckmann (1966: 96) also introduce the concept of the symbolic universe as "the matrix of all socially objectivated and subjectively real meanings; the entire historic society and the entire biography of the individual are seen as events taking place within this universe." Horrell (2001: 151) provides a substantive critique of Berger and Luckmann and notes that their "theory need[s] to be woven into the framework of a more critical social theory, in order to facilitate a critical sociological analysis of the early Christian movement." This book attempts to do just that. Adams (2000: 23–25) points out five limitations in Berger's work, especially as it is employed to analyze specific texts. Luomanen (2007: 208), indebted to Esler, has recently characterized the symbolic universe as "a background technology" within NT studies. Cf. Barth 1969; Douglas 1966, 1973; Geertz 1973; Sollors 1986; Turner 1967; Mauss 1938. See Tucker (2009b: 64–71) for a survey of these.

which is the primary philosophical framework for contemporary identity studies and social-scientific biblical studies.[7] These have been covered sufficiently by other scholars. The specific aim is to determine whether an eclectic use of these theoretical approaches will be useful in organizing the textual material from 1 Corinthians 1–4. First, a rationale for the use of theories from social psychology will be offered. Second, the primary theoretical framework utilized in this book, the twin theories Social Identity Theory and Self-Categorization Theory (SIT/SCT) will be delineated and social identity defined. Third, the way in which SIT/SCT will be further applied in the exegetical portion of this book will be introduced. This includes incorporating the ideas of identity salience, identity hierarchy, and a master identity from the Identity Theory of Sheldon Stryker and Peter Burke.[8]

THE USE OF SOCIAL PSYCHOLOGY ON AN ANCIENT TEXT

A cursory reading of 1 Corinthians 1–4 indicates that Paul was writing to address issues of corporate life, specifically those that had arisen with regard to various group memberships (1 Cor 1:10–12). This study argues that the conflicts between various groups in Corinth were rooted in different degrees of identification with various aspects of Roman social identity, which resulted in a misapplication of the social implications of Paul's gospel. Thus, issues of group construction, belonging, and maintenance are important to uncover in order to ascertain this exigence in 1 Corinthians 1–4. To substantiate the claim that what was occurring

---

7. Horrell 1996; Adams 2000; Elliott 1993; Esler 1994; Börschel 2001.

8. Stryker (1968: 560) defines identity salience "as the probability, for a given person, of a given identity being invoked in a variety of situations." This early definition focused on probability of invocation; however, he and Serpe have nuanced the definition (1994: 17) to "a readiness to act out an identity as a consequence of the identity's properties as a cognitive structure or schema." Identity hierarchy is the way in which these various identities are organized; though one should recognize that more than one identity may occupy an identity nodal point (Stryker and Serpe 1994: 17 n. 1). The master identity, as described by Burke (2004: 10), is when there is "high salience and strong commitment" to a "person identity." It should be noted that discussions of "over-identification" or "different degrees of identification" with key aspects of Roman social identity do not forsake our theoretical framework; rather, as noted by Burke (2004: 10), they bring to the fore the conflict when "two identities are antithetical" or "whenever two identities are activated together," which requires a "compromise position" so that potentially "both can be verified at the same time and the conflict can be removed." In many ways, this describes the way we view Paul's approach to identity formation (see 1 Cor 7:17–24).

in Corinth was an over-identification with key aspects of Roman social identity, we will need to provide a rationale for the use of social psychological theories that takes into consideration social identification and its impact on group formation. Fiske and Taylor note "that normal cognitive processes account for much of how people understand themselves and others," and, building on that insight, much of what one reads in 1 Corinthians may be accounted for by similar means. Thus, while some of the issues in 1 Corinthians may be clarified by reconstructing theological debates, other issues can be plausibly explained through "theories of attribution, psychological control, social schemata, attention, person memory, and social inference."[9] In short, the problems were associated with social identity, self-categorization, and social cognition.[10]

Social psychology, defined as the study of persons in the context of their social relationships and group memberships, provides resources for approaching group-related issues in an ancient text. This raises two questions. First, how may one defend the usefulness of social psychology as a tool for understanding an ancient text? Second, since social psychology offers many different approaches, which theoretical framework is to be preferred and why?

Social psychology as a heuristic device for understanding an ancient text may be supported by three interrelated arguments. First, in this book the purpose for employing social psychology is to gain a better understanding of what Paul was doing in 1 Corinthians 1–4 which evidences significant group related concerns. Paul obviously did not have contemporary social psychological categories in mind as he wrote;

9. Fiske and Taylor 1984: ix; Roitto 2008a: 93–96; 2008b: 142–44. Berger (2003: 26–43) has recently attempted to combine the results of historical psychology and exegesis with intriguing results. Attribution theory looks at the way in which individuals explain the behavior of others. Closely related to attribution theory is psychological control in which personal choices and volition may contribute to a lack of development, growth, and socialization. Fiske and Taylor (1984: 140) describe a schema as "a cognitive structure that represents organized knowledge about a given concept and the relationships among the attributes." Person memory is the knowledge that individuals store about other people. Social inference addresses the processes related to decision-making from the group to the individual or alternatively from the individual to the group. Attention describes the cognitive processes that are active in the selective engagement or rejection of key environmental stimuli. These aspects of cognitive psychology combine to provide a way to describe the processes of reality construction (Fiske and Taylor 1984: 91).

10. Pyysiäinen (2001: 8) concludes that "the contribution of cognitive science to the study of religion is in that it provides a framework for empirical study of how religious concepts are acquired, represented and transmitted."

that would be a grossly anachronistic assertion. This book, however, is engaged in a descriptive enterprise and not a prescriptive one; thus it may utilize the descriptive insights from social psychology as long as it correctly applies the findings of the discipline.[11] The nature of the beginning of the early Christ-movement involved shifting from one group to another for the purposes of social identification.[12] Social psychology can provide insights into what was occurring in the context of those shifting group memberships as well as language to make explicit what was already implicit in the writing event and the phenomena of the text.[13]

Second, if a text is referring to the nature of the human situation, then, even allowing for evolutionary differences, social psychology can reasonably be applied because of the shared human condition.[14] If the discipline of social psychology is universal in scope, then the significance of time is mitigated with regard to understanding aspects of the human condition that are consistent over time.[15] Third, it is legitimate to interpret that which is intrinsic to humankind and to delve into the world associated with the text by means of social psychological categories as long as this is not confused with the actual text. This approach, though often wrongly accused of seeking the "world behind the text," has been employed by social-scientific biblical scholars with convincing results.[16] Thus, the field of social psychology provides language to better explain the exegetical findings for passages that deal with social relationships and group memberships. Having substantiated the usefulness of social psychology in addressing group-related issues in an ancient text, how might social psychological theories assist us in the interpretive process?

---

11. See Clarke for a discussion of the differences here (2000: 103–4, 207; see also Marchal 2006: 84).

12. Meeks (1983a: 215) suggested something quite similar with regard to changing referent groups. Recently, Meeks (2009: 139) reiterated this, "If we think of our identity as formed in large measure by the ways we learn to perform certain roles given us by our society, to act out in our own life stories some culturally common narratives, then our reference groups are those audiences that we imagine approving or disapproving our performances." Meeks (2009: 139) also suggests that there is still significant work to be done with regard to "reference group theory" and "conversion."

13. Shkul 2007: 22 n. 50.

14. Bailey 2004: 49–52.

15. Jenkins 1996: 3.

16. Lieu 2004: 7–11; Bartchy 2003; DeMaris 2008; Elliott 1993, 1996; Esler 1994, 1998, 2003a, 2005; Harland 2005; Kloppenborg 1996; Rohrbaugh 1996; Williams 2006.

THE USE OF SOCIAL IDENTITY THEORY
AND SELF-CATEGORIZATION THEORIES

The analysis within this book is based upon ideas of social identity formation, as described by Henri Tajfel's Social Identity Theory (SIT) and John Turner's Self-Categorization Theory (SCT). A number of New Testament scholars have discussed the applicability of these theories within biblical studies and to 1 Corinthians in particular.[17] Therefore, rather than restating these discussions, we want to explore the ways in which SIT/SCT, with its focus on group membership, provide a means of interpreting 1 Corinthians 1–4 with the help of the evidence provided by the material remains from Corinth. This exploration should bring to light the interaction of the Corinthian Christ-followers with aspects of Roman social identity and imperial ideology.

The various groups to which individuals belong play a significant role in forming their social identity, defined, as mentioned in the introduction, as "that *part* of an individual's self-concept which derives from his [sic] knowledge of his membership of a social group (or groups) together with the value and emotional significance attached to that membership."[18] In this study, group memberships form the basis for much of the interpretation of 1 Corinthians 1–4. First, as members of the Roman colony of Corinth, those living within the colony have a civic identity, understood as a subcomponent of social identity, which forms them into an identifiable group. Second, based on 1 Cor 1:12, evidently many within the ἐκκλησία were socially identifying primarily based on group memberships that were considered deficient by Paul. Third, much of Paul's argument relies on categoric and group memberships for its rhetorical effectiveness (e.g., 1 Cor 1:18, 20, 22, 26). Finally, Paul's solution to the Corinthian Christ-followers' over-identification with various group memberships is to encourage them to reprioritize and recognize that ultimately they "belong to Christ, and Christ belongs to God" (1 Cor 3:23).

17. Esler (1996: 215–40) was the first to employ Social Identity Theory in New Testament studies. May 2004: 22–33; Esler 1998: 29–57, 2003a: 19–39.

18. Tajfel 1978b: 63 emphasis original. This definition functions as the stipulated understanding of social identity for this book (see also Esler 2003a: 20). Building on the fine work of Gleason who researches the development of masculine social identity during the Second Sophistic, a similar understanding of social identity emerges, which may be described as self-definition and public presentation to others with regard to group membership and social categorizations (1995: xvii–xxix). These combined understandings of social identity inform the rest of this book.

In the last thirty-five years Tajfel's SIT and Turner's SCT have become the primary theoretical frameworks from which to study social identity.[19] Social identity develops in relation to others, and the work of Tajfel has proved central to understanding the nature of intergroup relations and their impact on social identity.[20] Social categorization is fundamental to identity salience in Tajfel's work which built on the original thoughts of William James and was formalized in Turner's later work.[21] Social identity forms through social comparisons which allow for distinctions between ingroups and outgroups. These social comparisons result in "depersonalization" in that "the basis of perception is group prototypicality rather than personal idiosyncrasy or interpersonal relationships."[22] Tajfel's work, built on the work of Muzafer Sherif, helps to explain the existence of stereotyping and discrimination between various groups which may appear to have much in common in terms of language, gender, ethnicity, or religion.[23]

Tajfel's research differs from previous research that focused on individualistic understandings of behavior.[24] He recognizes the existence of certain behaviors to be indicative of a specific social identity in the primary position at that given moment.[25] This salient identity, along with the external situation, determines whether or not people will exhibit certain socially acceptable behaviors, which results in a group identity. Central to the research of Tajfel and Turner is their definition of a group

19. Tajfel (1972: 299) initially presented his theory in "La catégorisation sociale" where he concluded, "Partis des processus fondamentaux de la catégorisation sociale, nous sommes intéressés aux valeurs et aux problèmes de l'identité sociale, pour aborder finalement la causalité sociale et par consequent son role dans la pratique sociale."

20. Tajfel 1978a: 27–28.

21. Early research into the self and identity was undertaken by the American pragmatist William James (1890: 291–401). His understanding of identity relates primarily to the moment when individuals come to realize who they really are. This realization is supported through the social resources of both communication and language. His concept of the "social self" is foundational for research on social identity (1890: 294). See Turner 1987: 42.

22. Hogg 2004: 208. Brawley (2005: 20) notes that this "comparison does not ordinarily occur between groups that are radically distinct." This has interpretive significance with regard to the social comparisons that some within the Christ-movement in Corinth were making with their broader civic community.

23. Sherif 1961: 183.

24. Festinger 1954: 117–20.

25. Tajfel 1978a: 44–45.

"as a collection of individuals who perceive themselves to be members of the same social category [and] share some emotional involvement in this common definition of themselves."[26] Tajfel and Turner also extend their understanding of the role of assessment in the life of a group by arguing that a group also "achieve[s] some degree of social consensus about the evaluation of their group and their membership of it."[27]

Richard Jenkins is concerned, however, that approaches to identity not become reified, and thus he argues that one should "distinguish" between "the processes of *group identification* and *social categorization*."[28] Jenkins is correct to point out that the external processes of identity formation are often overlooked in theories of social identity formation. Thus, his corrective with regard to Tajfel and Turner's research on the processes involved in social identity formation will be ameliorated by including his "*internal-external dialectic of identification*" as an added component for the way this study views the formation of social identity.[29]

Tajfel and Turner's work has been advanced and refined by a number of scholars, including Michael Hogg and Dominic Abrams whose work, *Social Identifications,* provides an informative assessment of SIT.

26. Tajfel and Turner 1979: 40. Esler (2005: 4) summarizes Tajfel and Turner's approach by noting that "it focuses on that aspect of an individual's identity that he or she derives from belonging to a particular group (=social identity), especially in relation to out-groups to which he or she does not belong."

27. Tajfel and Turner 1979: 40. The processes involved in this group evaluation are developed further in the work of Daniel Bar-Tal (1990: 39). Brown and Turner (1981: 33–35) argue that this evaluation process occurs at both interpersonal and intergroup levels and is vital to understanding the nature of group behavior.

28. Jenkins (1996: 23 emphasis original) contends that these processes may "feed back upon each other . . . the external or categorical dimensions of identity are not only centrally important but have been underplayed, if not ignored altogether, in most theorizations of identity." Group boundaries is one example of a group performance interpenetration of identification and categorization. Optimal distinctiveness theory, as presented by Brewer (2001: 249), asserts that "distinctiveness . . . is an extremely important characteristic of groups, independent of the status or evaluation attached to group memberships. To secure a loyalty, groups must not only satisfy members' needs for affiliation and belonging *within* the group, they must also maintain clear boundaries that differentiate them from other groups. In other words, groups must maintain distinctiveness in order to survive."

29. Jenkins (1996: 20 emphasis original) describes this framework as an understanding "of the 'self' as an ongoing and, in practice simultaneous, synthesis of (internal) self-definition and the (external) definitions of oneself offered by others." This is important in that Paul alternates between internal and external agency with regard to the formation of identity in Corinth (e.g., 1 Cor 1:26–27; 3:3–4, 18–20).

The theoretical framework for SIT "is that belonging to a group . . . is largely a *psychological* state which is quite distinct from that of being a unique and separate individual, and that it confers *social identity*, or a shared/collective representation of who one is and how one should behave."[30]

SIT focuses on "*intergroup behaviour*" which is "the manner in which individuals relate to one another as members of different groups."[31] One concern of the research is to determine what causes discrimination and intergroup hostilities. This is addressed by building on "the minimal group studies" which found "that social categorization—the discontinuous classification of individuals into two distinct groups—is sufficient to generate intergroup competition."[32] This is because ingroup categorizations serve to reinforce already accepted views of the self. So, from a SIT perspective, "the explanation of social competition rests on two complementary processes: social categorization and social comparison."[33] Thus competition and hostility between groups results from ingroup bias and outgroup stereotyping,[34] which leads to the next aspect of social identification.

One way in which different groups relate is through "*stereotyping*" which focuses "on the way groups are perceived."[35] Stereotypes are a perceptual category in which "generalizations about people" are "based on category membership" in which there is a view "that all members of a particular group have the same qualities," which thus define them as a

---

30. Hogg and Abrams 1988: 3 emphasis original. SIT contributes to this book by providing tools to assess the type of communal life that emerges in 1 Cor 1–4.

31. Hogg and Abrams 1988: 4 emphasis original.

32. Hogg and Abrams 1988: 51.

33. Hogg and Abrams 1988: 53. The concept of a superordinate group will also be important in this book. It is a high-level abstraction that includes "interspecies" social comparisons (e.g. we are members of the human species). This is a group categorization process that goes beyond the ingroup or outgroup context. In Corinth, the ingroup could be those local members of the Pauline movement, while the superordinate group might be the broader members of the Christ-movement, "those who in every place call upon the name of our Lord Jesus Christ" (1 Cor 1:2; see also 4:17). Cf. Tajfel and Turner 1979: 33–47; Jenkins 1996: 105; Hogg and Abrams 2003: 421.

34. Paul emphasizes both distinctiveness from other groups (e.g., 1 Cor 1:18 "those who are perishing"; 1 Cor 2:6, 8 "rulers of this age"; and 1 Cor 2:14 "unspiritual") and similarity within the ἐκκλησία (e.g., 1 Cor 1:18 "those who are being saved"; 1 Cor 2:6 "mature"; and 1 Cor 2:13, 15 "spiritual").

35. Hogg and Abrams 1988: 4 emphasis original.

group.[36] Stereotyping relies on the cognitive resources of social categorization for its effectiveness in organizing social information as well as the impulse from the "judgement of social stimuli."[37] It links belonging to social categorization. Group "attributes" are then internalized and form the basis of outgroup assessment. The individual aspect is referred to as "self-categorization [which] is the cognitive process underlying social identification, group belongingness, [and] psychological group formation."[38] One of the research interests for this study is to understand the ideological basis from which Paul seeks to form the social identity of the Corinthian Christ-followers.[39]

The ideological basis for the construction of social identity, in this study, is understood through a discussion of four interrelated and overlapping concepts which also form the focus of the exegesis of 1 Cor 1:1–9 and 1:10—2:5. First, the foundation for social identity relates to that which provides the symbolic basis through which the formation process moves forward. Roman social identity could draw on Vergil's *Aeneid* for these resources,[40] while Paul argues that it is God's calling in Christ that provides that foundation (1 Cor 7:20). Second, the frame-

---

36. Hogg and Abrams 1988: 65.

37. Hogg and Abrams 1988: 71.

38. Hogg and Abrams 1988: 73–74.

39. Hogg and Abrams' (1988: 82) understanding of ideology was introduced on p. 31. The concern of ideology relates to Paul's understanding of the continuation of previous social identities "in Christ." Furthermore, it considers how Paul's Jewish identity as well as his eschatological expectations inform his mission and strategy. Cf. Kuck 1992: 16; Börschel 2001: 103.

40. This is a foundational concern for Syed (2005: 13–15) who contends that *Aeneid* had a significant "impact on Roman culture." For example, Quint. *Inst.* 1.8.5. "The other aspects of reading require important cautions: above all, these tender minds, which will be deeply affected by whatever is impressed upon them in their untrained ignorance, should learn not only eloquent passages but, even more, passages which are morally improving. The practice of making reading start with Homer and Vergil is therefore excellent." Lines from Vergil were presented by orators, written as graffiti, inscribed on tombstones, taught by grammarians, and, as noted by Syed (2005: 15), "Vergil's works [were] on a par with the Sibylline Books, Homer, and the Bible, all of which were put to similar purposes." Examples of specific passage from *Aeneid* include: 1.263–64 "[They] shall wage a great war in Italy, shall crush proud nations, and for his people shall set up laws and city walls"; 6.851–53 "Remember thou, O Roman, to rule the nations with thy sway—these shall be thine arts—to crown Peace with Law, to spare the humbled, and to tame in war the proud!" The prophetic framework of these sections is supported by the recounting of the foundation of Rome (*Aen.* 1.30–33; see Elliott 2008a: 29–30). This is discussed further on p. 102.

work for the formation of social identity relates to key ordering principles that are shared by a society. Patronage and benefaction, honor and shame, and kinship discourse functioned in this manner in the Roman Empire, as they did within the Christ-movement in the context of God's grace. However, from Paul's perspective, some of the social implications of these ordering principles are to be transformed within the life of the ἐκκλησία.[41] Third, the definition of social identity is focused on group membership and the affective value attached to that membership; however, the values of previous and current groups are quite different. The focus of Roman social identity is on the value of self-presentation and its impact on group membership. For Paul, however, the central value is the cross of Christ and baptism in his name. This should result in an alternative community with a distinct ethos. Finally, the shape of identity relates to the ideological discourse that forms the social identity. The ideological basis in the Roman Empire was Roman imperial ideology with its understanding of wisdom and power. Within the Christ-movement, it is the wisdom and power of the gospel which is to shape and transform social identity (i.e., move it into the salient position in the identity hierarchy). Thus, as Paul Middleton rightly contends, "Christian language and symbols competed for the same ground as Roman Imperial ideology."[42] Paul's main interlocutor in 1 Corinthians is Roman imperial ideology which serves as a parallel narrative for the construction of a worldview; however, he also needed to address social issues within the community of faith, which leads to the next characteristic of Tajfel's work.

SIT also provides insight into the inner workings of the group, its "*intragroup behaviour*."[43] Here the focus is on what is required to maintain group stability and identity. Group unity is sustained by addressing issues related primarily to "self-categorization in terms of a relevant category" and only secondarily to "interpersonal attraction."[44] Issues related to belonging are central to group problems. Groups that lack identity salience also lack a clear sense of communal belonging. In the context of 1 Corinthians, Paul addresses the Christ-followers' difficulties with regard to intragroup behavior in 1 Cor 1:10–12 while addressing issues related to belonging in 1 Cor 3:21–23.

41. These are discussed further on pp. 131, 164.
42. Middleton 2006: 61.
43. Hogg and Abrams 1988: 4 emphasis original.
44. Hogg and Abrams 1988: 105–6.

The study of the importance of a sense of belonging to intragroup behavior in SIT/SCT lacks a component related to intragroup beliefs.[45] This weakness may be ameliorated by the inclusion of Daniel Bar-Tal's research on social identity that focuses on the political implications of shared group beliefs (ideology, norms, values, and goals). His book argues that what defines a group are their shared beliefs, their self-understanding—their social identity. One implication of his theory is that to understand a group one must understand the beliefs which regulate group life in terms of structure and behavior. Bar-Tal refers to the "condition" that is necessary for group existence, which is that the "group members have to believe that they constitute a group and/or that they have something in common that united them."[46] This "condition" provides a corrective to Tajfel and Turner's definition of a group. Two slight criticisms of Bar-Tal's work limit its further usefulness in our study of 1 Corinthians 1–4. First, he does not address the role aberrant shared beliefs would have on communal life (1 Cor 3:1–4; 1 Cor 4:8, 14). Second, he minimizes the role that those outside the group may have on the formation of group identity (1 Cor 2:6–8), though his more recent work includes "the concepts of societal beliefs and ethos."[47]

Social presence is concerned with the processes of self-presentation that lead to behavior changes based on the influence of others within a social setting. From a conceptual point of view, the process may be described as a "negotiation" which relies on the cognitive frameworks of "group identification" and "self-categorization."[48] Social performance is equally important because individuals interact with various groups, and thus social identities constantly shift to address the changing social situation. The most important aspect of social performance is that people "deal with others . . . as *representatives* of some social category, group, or role" and not primarily as individuals.[49] Thus, in the process of social negotiation an identity becomes salient and that results in a specific self-image which leads to actual behaviors based on the group membership within the individual.[50]

45. Esler and Piper 2006: 28–29.
46. Bar-Tal 1990: 39; Esler 2005: 4–5.
47. Bar-Tal 2000: viii–xv.
48. Hogg and Abrams 1988: 128–29.
49. Hogg and Abrams 1988: 129.
50. Hogg and Abrams 1988: 134.

While processes are central in SIT, "*collective behaviour*" focuses on the actual behavior evident in the group.[51] Collective behavior emerges through social identification; however, since "social identity is an aspect of the self-concept," this argues against the idea that "the self becomes obliterated."[52] Salient social identity refers to the recognition by individuals of their membership in a group which results in the "collective enactment of ingroup norms."[53] In the context of Paul's strategy in writing 1 Corinthians, he may be described as seeking to make salient the social implications of the Corinthian Christ-followers' "in Christ" identity.[54]

The concept of "*social influence*," which is the way in which "people affect each others' opinions and behaviours," results in "*conformity* to group norms."[55] In the context of 1 Corinthians, faith may be described as a group norm (i.e., that which is to be embodied by the group), and it results in a commitment to the norms of Christ-movement behavior (1 Cor 2:5; 13:13; 15:14, 17). From a SIT perspective, the focus is on "the influence process associated with groups; that is, how the individual is influenced by the group—*conformity*" and reveals significant information concerning the individual's social identity.[56] Again, the primary means of conformity is through self-categorization, but it is the "cognitive *representation*" of the behavior that produces it. Thus, the actual behavior, likewise, may produce an "image of the normative or stereotypic characteristics of the group," but it is the "dynamic intragroup 'negotiation' of prototypicality or normativeness" that actually has "great power to induce conformity."[57] Paul, then, would be able to influence the

51. Hogg and Abrams 1988: 5 emphasis original.

52. Hogg and Abrams 1988: 152; Campbell 2006a: 88; Berger 2003: 33.

53. Hogg and Abrams 1988: 153.

54. For example, see 1 Cor 13:13, "And now these three remain: faith, hope, and love." This may also be understood as a description of the ideological basis from which Paul seeks to form the Corinthian Christ-followers' social identity. Wolter (1997: 443) argues that the ethos of the early Christ-movement was faith, a viewpoint that has been called into question recently by Horrell (2005: 111). His critique of Wolter is based on the idea that faith is a cognitively laden concept not appropriate for a descriptor of a group's ethos; however, in 1 Corinthians 1–4, wisdom is an ethos-forming concept with behavioral connotations. While faith may be critiqued, on other grounds, as an apt description of a group's ethos, it should not be dismissed simply because it comes from the cognitive domain.

55. Hogg and Abrams 1988: 5 emphasis original.

56. Hogg and Abrams 1988: 158–60.

57. Hogg and Abrams 1988: 173–74.

Corinthian Christ-followers' approach to communal life without being present among them to demonstrate the group norms because "referent informational influence" could "generate conformity via the self-categorization process."[58]

The concept of group prototypicality is an important part of Paul's approach to identity formation. Moreover, Paul often includes a memory component in his discussion of group prototypes (e.g., Timothy 1 Cor 4:17; Paul 1 Cor 11:1–2; and Stephanas 1 Cor 1:16; 16:15–17). Therefore, SIT/SCT should be extended at this point by the inclusion of Maurice Halbwachs' concept of collective memory.[59] Philip Esler describes the way these concepts interact. He contends "that the collective memory of a group is frequently stored in and, at times, manipulated through appeal to, or the creation of, exemplary or prototypical figures."[60] The interaction of these two concepts produces a textual or narrative identity.

The construction of narrative identity is central to the work of Stephanie Lawler. Narratives provide a sense of belonging and create a social context in which identity positions might be negotiated and exchanged as individuals see themselves in the narratives of both ingroup and outgroup prototypical members. Paul uses this discursive practice as a means of social influence in 1 Cor 4:9–13. Identity is always social, and the concept of narrative identity provides a framework by which to understand the way discourse and kinship both contribute to the formation of social identity.[61] Group prototypes, social memory, and narrative identity describe some of Paul's discursive practices in 1 Corinthians 1–4, which leads to the final characteristic of SIT relevant to this book.

The primary means of "social influence is communication," and "*language*" is a central component in forming group identity.[62] Language serves as an effective "large-scale" rhetorical device in intergroup conflicts, reveals "status and power differences," and "dwells mainly upon so-

---

58. Hogg and Abrams 1988: 185. This may be described as a discursive practice of identity formation (see 1 Cor 5:3).

59. Halbwachs 1992: 39–40.

60. Esler and Piper 2006: 37.

61. Lawler 2008: 1–30; Ricoeur 1991: 20–33.

62. Hogg and Abrams 1988: 5 emphasis original.

cial markers of category memberships."[63] Language is the primary vehicle for communicating social comparisons, ingroup bias, and stereotypes.[64]

With this review of Tajfel and Turner's approach complete, what are the areas of concern as we proceed? The nature of our study requires adjustment to SIT/SCT in four areas: the role of situational identity salience,[65] its overreliance on cognitive processes and impersonal agency, its de-emphasis of the discursive nature of identity, and its lack of attention to the existence and impact of multiple identities.[66] These weaknesses, therefore, require the addition of a further group of scholars. First, the Identity Theory of Stryker and Burke with its emphasis on the role of identity salience, the existence of an identity hierarchy, and the presence of a master identity. Second, scholars who also follow Stryker and Burke will address concerns related to an overemphasis on cognitive processes by offering a balanced use of cognition with regard to moral identity and identity change. Third, the corrective with regard to the discursive nature of identity will come from poststructuralist research.[67] Poststructuralist approaches do not form a unified theoretical framework but are a combination of fragmented theories that emerge as

---

63. Hogg and Abrams 1988: 196, 201, 204.

64. This supports the idea that discursive practices in general are sites of identity formation, and in 1 Corinthians, for example, the presence of kinship or ethnic discourse, invective or correction, political or apocalyptic language may all be functioning to create a textual identity that is then embodied within the Christ-movement in Corinth (see Carter 2000: 7–14 and earlier discussion on p. 31 in this book). See Tucker's (2010b) discussion of Meeks's (1983b: 190–91) use of "correlations" between belief structures and the social structures in the early Christ-movement.

65. We are not arguing that Tajfel and Turner do not consider situational identity salience; rather, we contend that a more robust use of the concept of identity salience, identity hierarchy, and master identity provide a way to strengthen Tajfel and Turner's broader theoretical concerns for contextuality (Tajfel 1978a: 44–5; Hogg and Abrams 1988: 153). Henriques (1998: 73), however, contends that a plausible weakness in Tajfel's approach is that he chose to focus foremost on the group rather than the individual. The distinction here is really one of degree rather than the complete abandonment of individual identity salience as a predictor of behavior.

66. See the following scholars for a discussion of these critiques of Tajfel and Turner: Henriques 1998: 61, 75–78; Williams 1992: 144–45; McNamara 1997: 564–66; Hogg, Terry, and White 1995: 262–65. It should be noted that the additions to SIT/SCT are primarily designed to bring to the fore aspects of their theory that are either latent or have been developed more fully by other complementary theoretical approaches.

67. Peirce 1995: 15.

a "reevaluation of mainstream traditions in the social sciences."[68] These scholars will address the role of rhetoric, textual positioning, social force, performance, and discourse.[69] Fourth, Stryker and Burke's approach will account for multiple identities; however, postcolonial scholars and the concept of identity hybridity will provide a more useful way to discuss multiple identities, lacking in SIT/SCT.[70]

Is there a basis for seeking to combine these theories in this manner? Recently Stets and Burke have looked at ways to combine Identity Theory with Social Identity Theory.[71] While there are difficulties in combining the two approaches, Michael Hogg, Deborah Terry, and Katherine White think that building on the "strengths" of these theories may allow us "to actually link society with individual social behavior more effectively."[72] The complexity of processes associated with identity formation requires us to draw from the resources of various social psychological approaches to better understand what is involved in the formation of social identity. Thus, Hogg, Terry, and White conclude that "[i]t may be possible in some way to integrate or articulate identity theory with social identity theory."[73] That is what this book proposes. SIT/SCT is rather widely applied in biblical studies; however the Identity Theory of Stryker and Burke is rarely employed but should be given due consideration within the field.

THE INTEGRATION OF OTHER CONTEMPORARY IDENTITY THEORIES

The Identity Theory of Stryker and Burke

The Identity Theory of Sheldon Stryker and Peter Burke emphasizes the importance that roles play in social identity. If one were to answer the question "Who am I?" it is most likely that responses would center on social roles and would be indicative of a collection of role identities. These identities govern attitudes, behaviors, and relationships and thus are constitutive of one's social identity. Stryker's work was initially cen-

---

68. McNamara 1997: 564.

69. These will be outlined below on p. 55.

70. Cf. Williams 1992: 223; McNamara 1997: 564–65.

71. Stets and Burke 2000: 234.

72. Hogg, Terry, and White 1995: 267.

73. Hogg, Terry, and White 1995: 267.

tral to the development of identity theory, while Burke's work has been in ascendance more recently.

Stryker reasserts the importance of Goffman's role theory in the formation of identity.[74] Instead of focusing on the idiosyncratic interactions of the individual, he studies stable reoccurring interactions and convincingly argues for the principle that society impacts identity which in turn impacts social behavior. Stryker's structural identity approach has been one of the most influential in identity studies for the last thirty years. His work *Symbolic Interactionism* formalized many of his assertions including the idea that "commitment impacts identity salience."[75]

McCall and Simmons' work contributes to identity studies in evaluating the way in which identity performances are the result of interaction with other individuals involved in the social situation. Stryker's work focuses on the normative aspects of identity while McCall and Simmons' work investigates the negotiation that occurs within those various social interactions. The context of these negotiations is the various roles in which individuals engage. McCall and Simmons define a person's role identity as the "imaginative view of himself as he likes to think of himself being and acting as an occupant."[76] They understand ideal identity to be the "prominence" identity that most accurately reflects priorities and behavior patterns. The less important but equally determinative roles are understood within the hierarchy of identity as "salience" identities and are much more context dependent.[77] McCall's work emphasizes the importance of understanding a person's self-disidentifications. Here the focus is on who the individual claims not to be in a given situation. McCall's contribution provides a better understanding of identity within the nexus of what individuals claim as well as what they disclaim.[78]

---

74. Stryker 1968: 558–64; Goffman (1959: 22) emphasizes the importance of social identification and also the importance of role distance. He develops his dramaturgical approach which theorizes that social interactions follow rather predictable scripts, like those of plays. He contends (1959: 22) that this process is established by means of a "front" or "that part of the individual's performance which regularly functions in a general and fixed fashion to define the situation for those who observe the performance." His emphasis on the performative nature of identity underlies the approach of this book.

75. Stryker 1980: 89.

76. McCall and Simmons 1978: 65.

77. McCall and Simmons 1978: 84.

78. McCall 2003: 11–26.

Peter Burke's early work argues that identity and behavior are based on a shared set of meanings.[79] He states that understanding a person's identity assists in assessing the likelihood of certain behaviors. That is, identity precedes behavior. Burke's work developed measurement devices for understanding these meanings. This interest led to the development of identity control theory in which behavior is understood as dependent on both the social structure and internal self-processes. Stets sees this theoretical development as a combination of the work of both Stryker and Burke because the meanings from the social structure and the individual are both incorporated: "The identity standard in the identity control model reflects the meanings of particular groups, roles, or persons to which one is committed."[80] The identity control model relies on the existence of identity hierarchies as the organizing principle for understanding which behaviors are likely to emerge in a given social situation. Burke's recent work characterizes this through the concept of a "master identity" which, he argues, is "higher in the control hierarchy than social or role identities," the implication being that these "role and social identities . . . become consistent with . . . person identities."[81]

Research on identity hierarchies has been undertaken by Peggy Thoits who focuses on the positive benefits of multiple identities, which prior to her work had been primarily understood as damaging to individuals. Thoits' work argues that when an identity is undertaken voluntarily, it is beneficial and provides a guide for behavior and increases a sense of meaning for the person. Imposed identities, however, do not produce the same positive benefits.[82] Her work is indebted to Stryker and Serpe and develops the concept of an ecology of multiple identities and the importance of network-embeddedness in that ecology. Thoits' work has been recently refined by Lynn Smith-Lovin who argues that high-status individuals are more likely to have multiple identities than low-status individuals "because they have networks that extend into more distant reaches of the social system."[83] Smith-Lovin's work offers an ecological model, based on affect control theory, for understanding

79. Burke 1980: 18–29.
80. Stets 2006: 100.
81. Burke 2004: 10.
82. Thoits 1983: 183; Stryker and Serpe 1982: 199–218.
83. Smith-Lovin 2003: 172.

multiple identities and a connectionist model for understanding the way individuals "operate as part of an interconnected cultural system."[84]

Balanced Use of Cognition, Moral Identity, and Identity Change

Following Burke's work on master identities, Stets and Carter argue for the concept of moral identity which serves as a control mechanism for other existing social or role identities. Moral, person identity leads to activation of roles congruent with that identity. The cognitive activation of moral identity may include "care, kindness, and compassion," so this person may choose a role that carries such social meanings, for example "parent, priest, or nurse." These roles are then governed by identifiable groups, for example "a family, a parish, and a hospital."[85] Stets then argues that the concept of moral identity encompasses the three bases of identity: "person, role, and group identities."[86] The concept of moral identity also includes the possibility of identity change, another recent area of research in identity studies, and balances out discussion related to cognition, choice, and morality.

Identity change research focuses on the self as the agent of change or, more recently, on external agents. Jill Kiecolt argues for the role that stress plays. Kiecolt defines "intentional self-change" as "a form of self-affirmation" which "entails intentionally changing some aspect of self-conception, the stable, relatively enduring idea of self."[87] Kielcolt's work is important in that she emphasizes the role cultural images play in the desire to change one's identity; in this way her work follows that of Thoits. Richard Serpe argues for the centrality of cognition and choice in identity change. He connects stability of identity with "the stability of social relationships."[88] Burke's recent work, however, argues for a central role for external mechanisms in identity change. In the context of identity formation, "the mechanisms and processes of identity verification take place within the individual; the content of the identities that are

---

84. Smith-Lovin 2003: 176.

85. Stets and Carter 2006: 293–313.

86. Stets 2006: 103. Brawley (2005: 20) also connects these concepts by arguing that "social identity is interrelated with personal identity inasmuch as membership in groups contributes to the framework that makes sense of life."

87. Kiecolt 1994: 50.

88. Serpe 1987: 44.

being verified is most often provided by the culture."[89] Thus, the tension between cognition, choice, change, and moral identities remains an important area of continued research within identity studies. Identity theory scholars provide a corrective to SIT/SCT in this important area that may be broadly described as the tendency to reinforce the dichotomies between the individual and society.

The Discursive Nature of Identity

Rhetorical strategies are central in forming social identity. Michael Billig suggests that the "intellectual traditions of rhetoric" going back as far as the "sophists of ancient Athens" have much in common with "contemporary social psychology."[90] Billig convincingly argues that issues of "attitude-change" or "persuasive communication," for example, are as important for contemporary social psychology as they were for Aristotle, Cicero, or Quintilian.[91] Rom Harré contends that the nature of humankind is inherently rhetorical and that rhetoric is vital for the maintenance of social identity.[92] Billig discusses the important connection between rhetoric and culture, specifically as it relates to national identity. His work builds on Bar-Tal's research on patriotism and quotes Bar-Tal approvingly—"Patriotism is a functionally positive force, providing stability for the 'ingroup' and a sense of identity for its members."[93] Bar-Tal defines patriotism as "the attachment of society members toward their nation and the country in which they reside."[94] The contribution of both Bar-Tal and Billig is in their emphasis on the importance of national identity in the development of group identity.

89. Burke 2004: 13.

90. Billig 1986: 32.

91. Billig 1986: 32, 81–111. For example, Aristot. *Rh.* 1856b shows a concern for the group rather than the individual: "no art has the particular in view, medicine for instance what is good for Socrates or Callias, but what is good for this or that class of persons." Both Quintilian and Cicero were convinced that the proper ordering of a speech could increase the likelihood of persuasion (cf. Quint. *Inst.* 3.3.1–3; Cic. *Inv. rhet.* 1.5.7). Aristot. *Rh.* 1358b describes the various types of rhetoric that focus on the different persuasive purpose of each setting. Mitchell (1991: 11 n. 38) provides a helpful survey of the way rhetorical studies have been applied to 1 Corinthians.

92. Harré 1980: 205; Billig 1986: 34.

93. Billig 1995: 56.

94. Bar-Tal 2000: 74.

Rom Harré and Luk Van Langenhove collected a series of essays that argue for the centrality of the social negotiation of selfhood and positioning in relations between persons and groups. Harré and Langenhove emphasize the process of identity formation through discursive practices, which they understand as "social acts" that provide positions for individuals within their various group memberships. Sui-Lan Tan and F. M. Moghaddam bring out the importance of "intergroup positioning," which finds resonance with the work of Tajfel and Turner. They further bring to the fore the importance of "linguistic devices" in positioning identity. These devices consist of various "personal stories" and "group myths" that "interact" with both ingroups and outgroups to form identity.[95] In this way, Tan and Moghaddam's work follows the initial work of Goffman as he understands the performative nature of the various social interactions to follow certain socially defined conventions. Harré's work also extends Tajfel and Turner's by removing it from the laboratory environment and repositioning it into the broader culture.[96]

Harré and Moghaddam provide a summary of specific refinements of positioning theory to the broader field of psychology in relation to the self. Central to their work are "positions" that "exist as patterns of beliefs in the members of a relatively coherent speech community."[97] These positions are external in the life of the community and are made visible in the defense of certain beliefs or practices. They are eminently social. In this way, positioning theory, from a linguistic standpoint, is similar to John L. Austin's speech-act theory.[98] Austin's work, and speech-act theory in general, have been thoroughly applied within New Testament studies, and in 1 Corinthians specifically, in the work of Anthony Thiselton who emphasizes that speech-act theory is as much about agency as is it about actual language.[99] Thiselton's solution to the challenge of agency and the performative nature of speech-acts is to "distinguish between *'illocutionary'* speech-acts, which depend for their effectiveness *on a combination of situation and recognition*, and *'perlocutionary'* speech-acts, which depend for their effectiveness on *sheer causal (psychological or rhetorical)*

---

95. Tan and Moghaddam 1998: 183.

96. Moghaddam, Hanley, and Harré 2003: 138.

97. Harré and Moghaddam 2003: 4.

98. Austin 1962: 120.

99. Thiselton 2000: 51–52; 2006b: 69–74.

persuasive power.[100] This language has limited usefulness, and Harré and others rightly argue for "the less technical term 'social force' for the context-dependent act that anyone performs by uttering a certain sequence."[101] The work of positioning theorists is helpful in understanding the way discourse forms identity.

The discursive nature of identity is evident in the work of Mike Baynham who writes within both "cultural studies and ethnomethodology."[102] His writing brings together identity, positioning, and performance theories, and understands social identity as "situated" and "contingent" and "constituted in discourse, set against intrinsic, essentialist notions" of identity.[103] Discourse is the context of identities; however, Baynham's specific contribution is the application of "*speaking position*" as a "linking construct" that captures the way this occurs. Examples of speaking positions include "social roles, ideological stances, and the inter-personal alignments taken up" within the narrative performance.[104]

Social identity as a completely discursive product is too reductionistic. Discourse is an important element among other social processes and practices. Norman Fairclough's book provides a corrective to Foucault's use of discourse, while maintaining the importance of "orders of discourse" to describe the semiotic nature of communication described in these various social practices.[105] Fairclough also resists attempts to reduce discourse to texts, which he understands as vital to the social change process; however, texts are only one element of discourse analysis. Fairclough does, however, see a significant role for written texts in the formation of social identity; he notes, "People make choices about the design and structure of their clauses which amount to choices about how to signify (and construct) social identities, social relationships, and knowledge and belief."[106] He further describes his understanding of the interaction between text and social change by developing his "three-dimensional conception of discourse" that includes "processes of

---

100. Thiselton 2000: 51 emphasis original.
101. Moghaddam, Hanley, and Harré 2003: 141.
102. Baynham 2006: 378.
103. Baynham 2006: 379.
104. Baynham 2006: 380–81 emphasis original.
105. Foucault 1972: 232; Fairclough 1992: 48, 71.
106. Fairclough 1992: 76.

text production, distribution and consumption."[107] The importance of
Fairclough's work here is that it provides a model to understand the way
a text could form the social identity of a group of people. Fairclough's
work has a consistent political undertone to it and describes clearly the
way political discourse exerts hegemonic control over people.[108]

Postcolonial Scholars and Identity Hybridity

The desire to challenge hegemonic control and to uncover the way power
is exerted are central components of the research agenda for postcolonial scholars. These scholars resist attempts to unify discussions on
identity and prefer to speak of identities. This is the approach followed
by Edward Said, Gayatri Spivak, and Homi Bhabha.[109] The foundational
text for postcolonialism is Said's work, *Orientalism*; however, Bhabha's
The Location of Culture has the most to contribute to the study of identity.[110] Bhabha argues for the concept of hybridity, especially as it relates to
the transformation rather than the obliteration of competing identities.
The earlier work of Becker, who argues for the concept of a "master status" identity, is now further refined by the concept of hybridity in which
the competing discourses of various social identities are negotiated and
a transformation of the individual's social identity results.[111] Bourdieu
argues that social "identities are constructed by and within the habitus,
and their constructions are always in flux."[112] This discursive competition occurs in what Pratt defines as a "contact zone," that is "an attempt to
invoke the spatial and temporal copresence of subjects previously sepa-

---

107. Fairclough 1992: 71–2.

108. Fairclough 1992: 67.

109. Said 1978: 259; Spivak 1990: 109; Bhabha 1994: 21.

110. Marchal 2008: 69–84. See further discussion of Marchal on p. 126.

111. Becker (1963: 32–3) studied the role that deviance plays in the formation of
social norms and subculture behavior and found that labeling contributes to the formation of a "master status" to which other identities are subservient (see Jenkins 1996:
154–56). Central to Becker's work is the important role that others' perception of an individual plays in impacting their selfhood and social formation. He correctly argues for
the centrality of society at large and/or various sub-cultures in defining deviance. Thus,
his work points out the way institutions and governments contribute to socialization,
often establishing processes that enculturate boundaries that serve the group in power.

112. Bourdieu 1984: 209 n. 6.

rated by geographic and historical disjunctures, and whose trajectories now intersect."[113]

Bhabha's work, similar to that of Moscovici's, is interested in the negotiation which occurs between the colonizer and the colonized and in the mechanisms deployed to resolve or not resolve identification deviancies.[114] Bhabha's methodological approach is a revised form of Freud's, and he argues that "identity is only ever possible in the *negation* of any sense of originality or plenitude; the process of displacement and differentiation (absence/presence, representation/repetition) renders it a liminal reality."[115] Bhabha's reflection on the role that the colonized plays in the identity formation of the colonizer is a keen insight into the dialectic of identity formation especially evident in the Roman east in the mid-first century CE. Bhabha's concepts of "mimicry" and "hybridity" are key strategies used by colonizing powers to enforce their dominant discourse.[116] Bhabha's work may give too much place to the role of discourse in resistance to colonizing powers; however, discourse is still central to negotiation within that imperial context. The contribution of postcolonialism to identity studies is that it provides an awareness of how deeply engrained political discourse is within the context of the colonizer-colonized situation.

CONCLUSION

By examining research into social identity, this chapter was able to establish a theoretical framework that may be applied to 1 Corinthians 1–4 in order to understand the way Paul sought to form the social identity of those in the ἐκκλησία in Corinth. It also demonstrated that resources from social psychology are useful in uncovering group-related issues in an ancient text.[117] Furthermore, the examination of social identity helped to clarify what is meant by the term social identity, and Tajfel's

113. Pratt 2008: 7; Marchal 2008: 92–5.

114. Moscovici and Zavallini 1969: 129.

115. Bhabha 1994: 51; Moore-Gilbert 2003: 72.

116. Bhabha 1994: 90, 21.

117. My exegetical approach is informed by identifying issues of intergroup behavior, stereotyping and ideology, intragroup behavior, social presence and social performance, collective behavior, conformity and social influence, and language in the text. Thus, as we read 1 Corinthians 1–4, we will take note of particular aspects of Paul's argument that are similar to these findings of SIT/SCT.

understanding of the term was stipulated as the definition which will be utilized in this study. Moreover, SIT/SCT were determined to be the most useful theories for studying social identity; however, it was concluded that an eclectic integration of the work of other scholars would provide the necessary resources to assess the way Paul was seeking to form the social identity of the Corinthian Christ-followers in 1 Corinthians 1–4.[118] Before we address Paul's argument there, we still need to position this book within the ongoing field of research into the way Paul is understood to be forming identity within his addressees.

---

118. The integration of other scholarly perspectives includes the use of the following in my reading of 1 Corinthians 1–4: (1) Jenkins' internal-external dialectic of identification; (2) Bar-Tal's focus on group beliefs; (3) Halbwachs' collective memory; (4) Lawler's narrative identity; (5) Stryker and Burke's identity salience, identity hierarchy, and master identity; (6) Stets and Carter's moral identity and Kiecolt's identity change; (7) discursive approaches to identity formation; and (8) identity hybridity.

3

Paul and the Formation of Social Identity

INTRODUCTION

THIS CHAPTER AIMS TO introduce the particularistic approach to Paul and the formation of Christ-movement identity. It provides a brief overview of William S. Campbell's approach to Paul and identity formation. It will then describe the alternative to Campbell's work, the universalistic approach. Following a brief assessment of the universalistic approach, Paul's goal in the formation of Christ-movement social identity is uncovered. Finally, salient "in Christ" social identity is presented as the chosen theoretical perspective for understanding Paul's rhetorical vision for the formation of social identity in 1 Corinthians 1–4.

THE PARTICULARISTIC APPROACH TO IDENTITY
OF WILLIAM S. CAMPBELL

The introduction to this book mentioned that a particularistic understanding of Christ-movement identity would guide the research for this study. This raises the important question concerning support for this interpretive choice. Furthermore, how may we substantiate William S. Campbell's understanding of Paul's approach to identity formation? Campbell's approach emerges primarily from his research into Romans and Galatians with their focus on the continuation of Jewish identity within the Christ-movement. These two letters have been extensively analyzed by Pauline scholars working in identity studies. This book, however, seeks to expand upon and further substantiate Campbell's approach by applying his work to an extended portion of text outside of Romans and Galatians, i.e., 1 Corinthians 1–4. Moreover, rather than focus on the continuation of Jewish identity in Christ, this study researches its corollary—the continuation of gentile identity in Christ. So, we are not arguing that Paul was seeking to impose his Jewish identity on the predominantly gentile ἐκκλησία, though he does use resources from the Jewish symbolic universe to form the Corinthian community, nor are we arguing that in Corinth the problems were associated with ethnic identity as they were in Romans and Galatians. Rather, Paul was seeking to clarify what the continuing role of gentile social identity is within the ἐκκλησία.

A brief review of Campbell's approach is in order at this point. He interacts with the concept of universalistic Christ-movement identity, concludes that this concept is not sufficiently nuanced, and argues that particularistic identity is more reflective of the realities of the early Christ-movement.[1] The key to understanding Campbell's approach is "the retention of one's particularity in Christ, whether Jew or gentile."[2] He follows aspects of the work of Fredrick Barth and Philip Esler, while at the same time opting for a stronger component for the "primordial aspects of ethnicity" when reconstructing Jewish identity.[3] Campbell understands Paul to be an individual who was not looking to eradicate

---

1. Campbell 2006a: 156.

2. Campbell 2006a: 156. Ehrensperger (2007: 96) follows very closely the particularistic understanding of identity evident in the work of Campbell. In critiquing the work of Sandnes she rightly concludes that "Paul's and his colleagues' perception of the gospel did not bypass or in any way obliterate Israel's identity or future." She (2007: 158–59) also rejects any notion "of Paul as 'stealing' the identity of the Jews as God's people and transferring it to the church." At the same time, she emphasizes the importance of kinship language and connects it with Paul's approach to identity formation in a manner similar to Jewish family education rather than seeing analogs within Roman education approaches (2007: 47–48, 128–31, 134). There are a few scholars who also maintain the continuance of Jewish identity within the Christ-movement who are not discussed in the body of this text but are important for this book. Mark Nanos (1996: 31; 2002a: 89; 2005a: 259; 2002c: 284) argues that the Christ-movement remained part of the synagogue community and that Paul was addressing issues related to confusion of the significance of gentile identity. Nanos contends (1996: 237) Paul did not, however, expect gentile Christ-followers to observe Torah but to "obey the halakhot incumbent upon gentiles who turn to God and associate with his people." Neil Elliott (1994: 66; 2000: 35) argues that the "dejudaization" of Paul results "in the virtual obliteration of his Jewish identity and the Jewish character of his thought." Rather, Elliott asserts (1994: 149–51; 2008a: 21–23) Paul is understood in the context of a Jewish apocalypticism that contains significant elements that were designed to negotiate empire in a subversive manner. See also Gager 2000: 16–19; Segal 1990: xii; Eisenbaum 2004: 695–96; Runesson 2008: 72–74; Brawley 2007: 109.

3. Campbell 2006a: 4–5.

ethnic distinctions nor encourage gentiles to become Jews. His strategy and mission, however, required "a transformation in the symbolic universe of these peoples in the light of the Christ-event."[4]

Campbell sees Paul as establishing community within the context of difference. He questions the scholarly consensus concerning equality and the elimination of difference "in Christ." Building on the work of Iris Young, he calls for an approach that emphasizes "the politics of difference in the contextuality of existence," which ultimately produces "a paradigm very different from historic Paulinism."[5] His aim "is not only to consider historical and social aspects of identity, ethnicity, and difference in the first century but to include, in association with these, Paul's theologizing and the outcome of this in the formation of Christian identity."[6] For Campbell, Paul's agency is vital to the formation of identity within the Christ-movement.

Campbell evaluates Paul's perspective of other missionary movements within the early Christ-movement. He argues for the concept of mutuality between the various leaders and understands Paul's challenges to be related to halakhic interpretative differences rather than theological disputes. Campbell sets out to deconstruct the scholarly image of Paul as a sectarian with regard to Judaism. He concludes, rather, that Paul was a reformer seeking "the renewal of his own people in the new era dawning in Christ."[7] Based on this conclusion, he argues that Paul never confuses Israel and gentile followers of Christ: both groups remain intact. Campbell contends for diversity within the early Christ-movement, recognizes that Peter and Paul were not engaged in competing missions, and that Paul's ultimate opponent was Rome and not Judaism. The Roman imperial context serves as a corrective to the traditional view that the primary focal point of conflict in the early Christ-movement was between the Jews, Jewish-Christians, and Paul's communities. Campbell develops a middle-path between the approach of Horsley and his comprehensive political reading of Paul and the view that Paul's conflict was primarily with the Jewish community.

Transformation and reevaluation of one's previous identity because of newness "in Christ" and not its eradication and removal are central

4. Campbell 2006a: 8.
5. Campbell 2006a: 10.
6. Campbell 2006a: 11.
7. Campbell 2006a: 47.

to Campbell's approach (2 Cor 5:17). From this perspective he develops a model of identity transformation that slightly nuances the traditional model of new creation.[8] Within this model "Paul is the paradigm only for those whose former life was in Judaism rather than for gentile Christ-followers."[9] Campbell builds his case from 1 Corinthians 7 and follows, with a few correctives, the work of Thiselton, agreeing with him concerning the presence of some sort of over-realized eschatology in Corinth. Campbell then shifts his focus to the significance of ethnicity for Paul. He rules out the view that, in Paul, Jewish identity was considered obsolete for those "in Christ."[10] Applying the principles of group formation, he argues for the communal nature of identity formation. Gentile Christ-followers are not to be confused with Israel nor are they the New Israel, or Israel redefined. Instead, God offers an inclusive salvation to "Jews as Jews and gentiles as gentiles."[11] The covenant was given to Israel, and the gentile Christ-followers may share in the blessings of this transformed covenant through Christ; however, it would be incorrect to propose a separate covenant for gentiles.[12]

Although in agreement with Campbell on the issues presented so far, this present study also differs from his approach in some ways. First, Campbell questions whether "the modern concept of 'hybrid' identity offer(s) a solution to the problem of Jew and gentile in Christ."[13] Campbell's concern is that the idea of "fusion" of identities is foreign to Paul's understanding. The use of hybridity in this book relates to the nature of interpenetration of multiple identities in which each does not lose its distinctiveness; it is a "diasporic" activity described by Stuart Hall as the "cultural logic of *translation*."[14] So, in this usage, Paul may be described as working towards the formation of hybrid communities of Christ-followers being socialized into the Jewish symbolic universe, while he engages the ideological resources of Roman imperial ideology and its rhetoric of empire. Paul was not seeking to combine Jew and

---

8. Campbell 1993: 179–83.
9. Campbell 2006a: 89.
10. Campbell 2006a: 93.
11. Campbell 2006a: 127.
12. Campbell 2006a: 137.
13. Campbell 2008a: 158.
14. Hall 2000: 226.

gentile identity into one undifferentiated social identity, which is the overarching concern of Campbell's general approach.[15]

Second, the discursive nature of identity and the role of texts in its formation are not fully developed in Campbell's work. He correctly notes that there is a need for "some reconciliation between the interactive and self-ascriptive" approaches to identity formation "and the continuing importance of primordial dimensions of ethnicity" primarily with regard to Jewish identity.[16] However, later in his book he recognizes that "[i]n one sense we do create ourselves and our identities" but this is still limited.[17] The nature of our study with its focus on Roman identity is much more susceptible to discursive formation. Campbell does not completely reject the role of discourse in identity constructions. However, this study builds on aspects of the work of Warren Carter and components of Judith Lieu's work on textual identity in order to more fully account for the processes that are at work in Paul's technology of letter writing with regard to identity formation.[18]

Third, with regard to Corinth, Campbell sees the difficulty there relating in some way to over-realized eschatology and also understands Apollos to have interfered with Paul's mission in Corinth.[19] This study, however, argues that the problem was with Roman imperial eschatology and that based on Paul's use of μετεσχημάτισα in 1 Cor 4:6a there were no personal problems between Paul and Apollos.

Finally, a question could be raised about the applicability of Campbell's framework, since he focuses on ethnic identity, while this current study focuses on social/civic identity. Two responses are possible. First, ethnic identity is a subcomponent of social identity, as is civic identity. Thus, both ethnic and civic identity may be subsumed under the broader rubric of social identity.

Second, this book argues that Paul, in 1 Corinthians, was concerned with the continuation of gentile identity "in Christ" in a manner consonant with the continuation of Jewish identity "in Christ" in Romans and Galatians. The following aspects of Campbell's approach are evident in 1 Corinthians and inform this present study. They are fully developed in

15. Campbell 2006a: 157.

16. Campbell 2006a: 4–5.

17. Campbell 2006a: 157.

18. See p. 31 for a discussion of Carter and p. 75 for a discussion of Lieu.

19. Campbell 2006a: 86–87, 93.

Campbell's work and only listed here. First, being "in Christ" does not displace previous identities (1 Cor 7:17). Second, the continuance of diversity is a central value in Paul's mission (1 Cor 7:20; 10:23—11:1). Third, circumcision and uncircumcision, significant ethnic identity markers, are reprioritized in the context of lordship (1 Cor 7:18, 22). Fourth, Jews remain Jews "in Christ" while gentiles remain gentiles (1 Cor 12:13). Fifth, the various missions within the Christ-movement were not competing but complementary (1 Cor 4:15; 9:1–2, 5, 19–23). Sixth, Paul's Jewish identity continues to be salient (1 Cor 9:20; Rom 11:1). This, however, may have contributed to problems of cultural translation (1 Cor 11:1; 4:16). Seventh, multiple identities are understood to retain their fundamental significance and are not regarded as irrelevant (1 Cor 1:26; 10:32; Phil 3:5–6). Eighth, the only corporate identity that is evident relates to the use of the phrase "in Christ" and possibly the "body of Christ" (1 Cor 1:4; 4:15; 6:20; 7:17). Ninth, gentiles are closely related to Israel but are not Israel. This aspect is properly discussed in relation to Romans and Galatians, but 1 Cor 10:1 stresses continuity with Israel within this predominantly gentile ἐκκλησία, while 1 Cor 10:18 uses the phrase "Israel according to the flesh" (τὸν Ἰσραὴλ κατὰ σάρκα). Tenth, which relates closely to the previous characteristic and is similarly a concern for Romans and Galatians, God has not rejected Israel (Rom 11:1, 7, 11; but see 1 Cor 9:20). Finally, though Paul continues to socially identify with key aspects of his Jewish identity, he recognizes that Jews and gentiles are eschatological partners together "in Christ" (1 Cor 1:7–8; 7:31). Therefore, it appears that although Campbell's argument has its basis in Romans and Galatians in relation to the continuance of Jewish identity, significant aspects of it are evident enough in 1 Corinthians to substantiate its usefulness in assessing the continuing role of gentile identity in the ἐκκλησία in Corinth. However, before we can uncover Paul's goal in forming the social identity of the Christ-followers of Corinth, we should briefly review other scholarly approaches to Paul and identity formation. Since the scholarship in this area is vast, we will limit our assessment to approaches that directly relate to the argument put forth in this book.

THE UNIVERSALISTIC APPROACH TO "CHRISTIAN" IDENTITY

Campbell's approach challenges the accepted scholarly view concerning the nature of Christian identity. The dominant view is described as the universalistic approach to Christ-movement identity. What follows is a brief discussion of six key scholars who are representative of this view.[20] The purpose of this summary is not a full critique of the universalistic approach; that is beyond the scope of this book. It is, however, designed to orient the reader to six important scholars in this ongoing debate.

Philip Esler: Transcending Identity

Social identity as an interpretative grid for understanding Paul's writings is central to the research and writing of Philip Esler who defines social identity as "that part of a person's self-concept (admittedly from a much larger whole) that derives from his or her membership in a group."[21] His works on Galatians and Romans argue, with varying degrees of application, that inter-group conflicts within the early Christ-movement principally related to ethnic identity. The presence of Greeks and Jews together led to competing visions for life within the community of Christ-followers. His work primarily builds on that of Tajfel, Turner, Barth, and Bar-Tal.[22] Paul's rhetoric, in Esler's reconstruction, is understood as re-aligning Christ-followers' multiple identities under the rubric of one unified identity "in Christ," an identity that transcends other social identities.[23] This one identity, however, does not obliterate Christ-followers' ethnic identity: "They are incorporated within one new

---

20. This is the largest group of scholars because this is the most widely held view, and thus some rather important scholars are left out of the larger discussion but are mentioned here for thoroughness and for their tangential relevance to this book. Richard Hays (1997: 17, 38–39, 123–24; 2005: 5) argues for a universalistic understanding of "Christian identity" but maintains a vital role for Israel's scriptures. Giorgio Jossa (2006: 12, 45, 101) argues for an early emergence of "Christian identity" (i.e., pre-70 CE) based on Jesus' teaching and doubts that Christianity was ever part of the synagogue community. Francis Watson (2007: 54, 56, 83) contends for a distinct "Christian identity" defined against Judaism based on Christian teaching concerning "the nullity of circumcision." Likewise, N. T. Wright (2003: 220) sees no continuing relevance for Jewish identity within Christianity. John M. G. Barclay (1996: 385, 387–93; 2007: 112; see also Gruen 2002: 105) understands "ethnic identity" to be "irrelevant" for Paul's mission. Beverly Gaventa (2007: 72) argues that "in Christ" social identities are obliterated; "those who are 'in Christ' cannot also be in the identity business of being first of all female and male." See Tucker (2009b: 87–124) for a further assessment and review of this approach.

21. Esler 2003a: 20.

22. Esler 1998: 40–57; 2003a: 53; 2005: 4–5; Esler and Piper 2006: 23–44.

23. Esler 2007a: 106.

identity but not at the price of losing their subgroup identities."[24] Esler's approach, however, ultimately folds into a universalistic understanding of identity because the transcendent aspect of the "in Christ" identity eventually overshadows other identities which then lose their fundamental significance.

Central to Esler's work is the contention that Mediterranean culture in antiquity was group oriented.[25] Esler follows Malina's concept of "collectivism" in which "first-century Mediterranean [p]ersons always considered themselves in terms of the group(s) in which they experienced themselves as inextricably embedded."[26] While it is true that Paul's statements are aimed at forming social identity, the individual dimension of social identity still impacts its formation.[27] Esler should not be understood as completely denying the individual element. For example, he explains, "To employ social-scientific research, moreover, does not entail neglect of the individual"; he believes that one simply does not "have access" to those individuals through our surviving texts.[28]

Ethnic differentiation is another key element in Esler's reconstruction of the early Christ-movement. Ethnic conflict in Rome is an important component of his work on that letter.[29] It is unclear to what extent the social identity of the earliest Christ-followers was differentiated in relation to Judaism (Gal 6:16). While there is no doubt that issues of Greek and Jewish identity were part of the later history of the Christ-movement, it may be that Esler overstates the level of conflict based primarily on ethnicity within the earliest Christ-movement whose symbolic universe was thoroughly embedded within Judaism. Esler is, however, correct to point out the challenges related to living together in community within the earliest Christ-movement. For example in relation to Corinth, where Esler follows Mitchell's claim that Paul's rhetorical purpose was to call the Corinthians to unity (1 Cor 1:10), he asserts, "Most of the problems Paul addresses are either variations of this theme of division and factionalism or, if not, can only be solved by the unity

24. Esler 2003a: 307; Campbell 2006a: 149–51.

25. Esler 1994: 29–30. Cf. Adams 2000: 24–25; Wolter 1997: 443; 2006: 202; Van der Watt 2006: v–vii.

26. Cf. Malina 2001: 62; Ehrensperger 2007: 58; Campbell 2006a: 153.

27. Lieu 2004: 130.

28. Esler 1998: 13.

29. Esler 2003a: 74.

the Corinthian believers should manifest in Christ."[30] Ethnicity, though an important component of identity, is only one aspect of the constellation of difficulties related to learning to live with one another within the earliest Christ-movement.

Bengt Holmberg: Conflict Oriented Identity

Christian identity emerges within the conflicts between Jewish and gentile Christ-followers, argues Holmberg.[31] He rejects ethnic identity as a concern for Paul and suggests that "the fundamental identity, common to Jews and Gentiles in the church, is neither Jewish nor Gentile, but simply Christian."[32] While we agree that the pre-eminent identity is that shared "in Christ," Holmberg too quickly dismisses the role that difference plays in the development of Christian unity. He argues, concerning Antioch, that when "Jewish identity conflicts with Christian identity, the former must be abandoned."[33] Holmberg relies on social-scientific theories to understand the text, and here the sociological model, informed by conflict orientation, guides his understanding of the way the emerging identity was formed. He asserts "that (external and internal) conflicts are vital for the shaping of identity."[34] While undoubtedly there were conflicts within the early Christ-movement, all too often the number and intensity of these conflicts are over-emphasized. If this fledgling movement was in a constant state of high conflict, it would not have survived. Also, a commitment to Weber's understanding of power leads Holmberg to an unnecessarily binary conclusion concerning the formation of identity at this early stage within the Christ-movement.[35]

Theological considerations are not excluded from the formation of social identity within the work of Holmberg, which sometimes occurs

---

30. Esler 2005: 150; Mitchell 1991: 199–200.

31. Holmberg (2008b: 15) notes that the focus on conflict "can be overdone."

32. Holmberg 1998: 415; 2008a: 176–77. His assessment of the essays presented in his 2008 edited work shows little movement from his 1998 article.

33. Holmberg 1998: 416.

34. Holmberg 1998: 421.

35. Cf. Holmberg 1998: 398; Ehrensperger 2007: 2–3, 17, 20. The specific concern here is Weber's view of power as domination and power-over. Weber's (1947: 152) classic definition of power is "the probability that one actor within a social relationship will be in a position to carry out his own will despite resistance, regardless of the basis on which this probability rests."

within social-scientific approaches to the New Testament.[36] Holmberg writes, "The Holy Spirit creates the identity of the church and shows it to her, and the church's role in this process is to become aware of and obedient to these experience-based insights."[37] This theological reality led the early Christians to shift away from ethnic categories of identity in a process Holmberg describes as *"reciprocal identity displacement."*[38] The tension between Jewish and Christian identity, in Holmberg's approach, is resolved through redefining the point of the conflict. He suggests that the conflict is actually "between Christian identity and Jewish-Christian self-definition."[39] Even though Holmberg is trying to resolve the tension inherent in the position he holds, redefining the categories shifts the problem from identity to self-definition.

Holmberg understands identity and self-understanding to be a "group phenomenon." He further defines the Jewish identity markers (e.g., circumcision, Sabbath keeping, and food laws) as "outward dimensions of Jewish identity," while at the same time recognizing that "there are other dimensions as well."[40] Specifically, he has in mind the internal dimensions of identity. His work is indebted to that of Ben F. Meyer especially in relation to the central role of the resurrection of Jesus in the formation of Christian identity and the distinction between identity and self-definition.[41] However, the use of identity and self-definition in

36. Meeks 2005: 167–68.

37. Holmberg 1998: 421.

38. Holmberg 1998: 422 emphasis original.

39. Holmberg 1998: 424.

40. Holmberg 1998: 417.

41. Meyer (1986: 19; Holmberg 2008b: 24–27) argues for the centrality of "Easter" in the formation of the Christ-movement and for "'identity' as a principle of unity and 'self-definition' as a principle of diversity." In relation to Corinth, Meyer notes that "the distinctive problems that arose in the Christian community in Corinth go back to pagan Hellenistic culture." While this may overstate the case, he rightly understands their "practices" as "self-shaping" and sees that much within 1 Corinthians relates to "mistaken ideas and practices" of "standard Hellenistic horizons and self-understanding." Specifically with regard to 1 Corinthians 1–4 he (1992: 163) sees the problem as "the transposition of Jewish religious ideas to Greek and Hellenistic 'wisdom' (1 Cor 1–4) and the impact of popular philosophy on 'some.'" Meyer's (1989: 190–91; see 1987: 258–59) understanding of Paul's mission is that Paul sought to "put the gospel ahead of all other self-definition" and thus "the gospel transcended Jew and Greek, slave and freeman, male and female." We are in agreement with Meyer's first assertion, although it does not follow that Paul sought to obliterate social distinctions in the manner in which Meyer conceives. Paul actually employs the particularistic language of kinship

the Holmberg-Meyer construct is problematic from the perspective of social psychology. Tajfel and Turner understand self-definition as an integral and inseparable part of the ongoing processes of social categorization which contributes to the formation of identity.[42] Furthermore, the separation of identity and self-definition is difficult if not impossible to maintain in practice.[43]

James D. G. Dunn: Paul's Jewish Identity

The focus on Paul's role in the formation of early Christ-movement identity and the way his Jewish identity impacted his gentile mission are central to the research of James Dunn. The theoretical framework for his discussion of identity resonates with the current discourse in identity studies. He understands identity "at least" to "some degree" to be "a social construct" and argues "that identity should not be understood as something fixed or single."[44] These two components are evident in his reconstruction of Paul's self-identity. Dunn does not primarily focus on social identity; however, he notes concerning the distinction between social identity and self identity that "there is no clear line of distinction between these two."[45] In this way, Dunn unintentionally contributes to the lack of precision within New Testament studies when addressing issues related to identity. The enfolding of personal and social identity categories is seen in his discussion of the transitional nature of Paul's identity, "which mirrors precisely the emerging identity of Christianity."[46] One would like to see more reflection on the dynamic interplay between the individual and the corporate aspects of identity. This would provide more clarity as to the aspects that Dunn understands as similar.

The concept of markers of Jewish identity is often associated with Dunn's work; these markers include circumcision, food laws, and Sabbath keeping.[47] This, however, is too reductionistic an understanding of identity. While these are important components of Jewish identity during this

and ethnicity to define Christ-movement identity. Cf. Johnson Hodge 2007: 152; contra Meyer 1987: 262.

42. Turner 1999: 11.
43. Cf. Holmberg 2008b: 25, 29; Campbell 2006a: 151.
44. Dunn 1999: 176.
45. Dunn 1999: 176 n. 10.
46. Dunn 1999: 193.
47. Dunn 1990: 191–92.

period, they are not to be confused with Jewish identity proper which was far more complicated and not reducible to these few but important markers.[48] This rather narrow definition of Jewish identity results from Dunn's understanding of the nature of Paul's rhetorical constructs, especially in Galatians in which these markers are evident. It must be remembered, however, that these texts are fragmentary[49] and that a broader contextual framework is necessary for a more complete understanding of Jewish identity in relation to the early Christ-movement (e.g., Roman imperial ideology).

Dunn's approach ultimately unfolds into a universalistic understanding of Christ-movement identity, one in which Jewish identity does not retain its significance. He notes in this regard, "faith in Jesus as Christ becomes the primary identity marker which renders the other superfluous."[50] While we are in agreement with the first part of this statement, it is not clear that Paul viewed Jewish identity as superfluous— Paul was no sectarian.[51] Campbell concludes, "Paul's *theology* does not provide a rationale for separation but on the contrary seeks a resolution of the separation in the coming eschatological triumph of God."[52] The Antioch event is central to Dunn's explanation of the emergence of an identity that is separate from a Jewish one. He conceives of Paul as one who "*made a parting of the ways inevitable*" between Judaism and early Christianity by undermining the law and thus undermining Jewish identity.[53]

Daniel Boyarin: Universalistic Hellenized Identity

Daniel Boyarin understands Paul as a non-apocalyptic, Hellenistic, Jew whose identity forming program was universalistic in orientation.[54]

48. Wolter's construction of the centrality of ethos for a complete understanding of identity nuances Dunn's concept of Jewish identity markers (2006: 201).

49. Ehrensperger 2007: 3.

50. Dunn 1990: 196.

51. Campbell 2006a: 46.

52. Campbell 1991: 130 emphasis original.

53. Dunn 1991: 139 emphasis original; Frey (2007: 321), though maintaining that Paul never left Judaism, provides some correctives to Dunn, concluding that "even though Paul relentlessly worked for the unity of Jewish and Gentile Christians, it may well be the case that he actually contributed more to the later split between the increasingly Gentile church and Jewish Christianity."

54. Judge, Clarke, Winter, and Nguyen were discussed in the introduction. Thus they are not assessed here; however, their approach coheres most closely with the group of

While "the Parousia is for Paul" important, his apocalyptic mindset is subservient to "the unification of humanity."[55] Boyarin prefers "allegory" to apocalyptic and concludes that it is "a serious hermeneutic error to make one's interpretation of Paul depend on the apocalyptic expectation." He does acknowledge that "in the strictest sense of" apocalyptic "the Christ event is precisely apocalyptic," that is "revelation."[56] Boyarin may be straining here in order to eliminate apocalyptic from a category while at the same time defining it in a narrow sense that then allows his critique to stand. While debates about the level of apocalypticism in Paul occurred recently between Martyn and Engberg-Pederson, it seems that to dismiss apocalyptic as formative in Paul's rhetoric is special pleading.[57] A nuanced understanding of apocalyptic that allows for historical continuity is the preferred middle ground.

While Paul is to be understood as a Hellenistic Jew, often the Hellenistic aspect almost completely excludes Paul's Jewishness. For Boyarin the two are combined.[58] Dale Martin notes concerning Boyarin that he "rejects any firm separation between Hellenistic Judaism on the one hand and Palestinian or Rabbinic Judaism on the other. Admitting that all Judaism was Hellenized to some extent, he also retains the du-

---

scholars who emphasize the Hellenistic context. Troels Engberg-Pedersen also researches within this conceptual framework. He sees several correlations between Paul's approach and Stoicism (2000: 288) and understands conversion to be an identity forming experience with communal implications (2000: 34–36, 53–54). Halvor Moxnes (2005: 266–67; 2003: 3–29) argues that early Christ-movement identity emerged within the nexus of Judaism and the broader Roman world. He focuses primarily on "the cultural stuff" of the earliest Christ-movement. Moxnes (2005: 267–68; 2008: 168) understands "ethnicity and the formation of boundaries" as "integral" to "the cultural assumptions" of "early Christian writers," as well as "family and kinship relations." This implies that passages traditionally understood to contain significant abstract doctrinal content are to be reinterpreted as focusing on the concrete dimensions of "identity formation." Moxnes may be over-reaching here. There is a tendency to "downplay" the theological content of the New Testament writings in favor of other preferred readings; however, the concept of theologizing provides a better corrective than the almost complete dismissal of theological content. See Campbell 2006a: 159.

55. Boyarin 1994: 36.

56. Boyarin 1994: 35.

57. Martyn 2002: 61–102; Engberg-Pedersen 2002: 103–14. Hanson (1975: 157–58) takes the view that "tying together the old epoch and the new in one historical continuum was the one historical entity Israel." Boyarin (1994: 59–68) downplays this aspect of Paul's argument. Paul used dualism and division to draw attention to the profound significance of the events taking place in history, cf. Isa 65:16c–25.

58. Boyarin 1994: 17.

alism as important for his understanding of Paul."[59] He understands
Paul's approach to identity formation to be one of universalistic identity, though Boyarin's preference is for the concept of particularistic
identity.[60] The tension between universalistic and particularistic identity is seen in that Paul was willing to allow Jews to "continue observing
such commandments if they chose to, *until such observance conflicted
with the fundamental meaning and message of the gospel as Paul understood it*, namely the constitution of all of the Peoples of the world as
the new Israel."[61]

First, it is not clear that Paul understood all people "as the new Israel."
Second, the oppositional thinking inherent in Boyarin's reconstruction
of Paul's rhetoric establishes Paul as one seeking to discard aspects of
Jewish identity that are not consistent with the apostle's arguments
elsewhere.[62] Boyarin argues that identity is formed in opposition, which
resonates with the work of Dunn.[63] Both Jewish and Christian texts do
this through the use of legends, historical allegory, and reconceptualizing
heresy. While Boyarin's further work deals with a later period, it is clear
that the foundation for "the parting of the ways," in Boyarin's estimation,
is partly traceable back to Paul's writings. Campbell understands another
series of events to lead to the parting, "when social and political forces
such as the Jewish Roman War, the *fiscus Judaicus*, and the Bar Kochba
revolt combined with the advent of the dissolution of the boundaries of
Israel by gentile 'Christianity' defining itself as 'New Israel.'"[64] The difficulty here relates to understanding Paul as one who lays the foundation
for Christ-movement identity while not implicating him in the actual
identity that developed later in the first through early third centuries of
our era. Third, tension is also seen in the identity-forming potential of
baptism. Galatians 3:28 is central to Boyarin's understanding of Paul's
identity forming strategy. He associates a social "function for baptism,
namely, the creation of a new humanity in which indeed all differences
would be effaced in the new creation in Christ."[65] The function of ritual

59. Martin 2001: 55.

60. Boyarin 1994: 155, 226.

61. Boyarin 1994: 112 emphasis original.

62. Cf. Rom. 9–11; Campbell 1991: 43–53.

63. Cf. Dunn 1990: 197–200; Boyarin 2004: 65–73; 1994: 53–55.

64. Campbell 2006a: 52–55.

65. Boyarin 1994: 187.

in forming social identity is a welcome contribution by Boyarin to identity studies. He also rightly notes "that this new creation could" not "be entirely achieved on the social level *yet*."[66] While we are in agreement with Boyarin's statement, it actually contravenes his broader thesis that Paul argued for an undifferentiated universalistic identity. Boyarin draws together the complexities involved in the emergence of Jewish identity; however, the lack of significant mention of Roman imperial ideology is an important omission.[67]

Judith Lieu: Textual Identity

The role that texts play in the creation of social identity is central to the work of Judith Lieu. She argues that there was no prior, essential, social identity for the early Christ-movement but that one was created rhetorically as these texts were read and "embodied."[68] This textual identity, however, should not to be confused with an "essentialized Christian" social identity.[69] The difficulty with this view is that as these texts were read, a social identity was being formed as those texts negotiated existing social identity positions. Thus, understanding social identity evident in a text should be anchored in the historical situation of the recipients even if locating that situation and those people "behind the text" proves to be a difficult task.[70]

Lieu's work also emphasizes the way in which texts are interpreted and re-interpreted to create social identity, for example in Paul's rhetorical strategy of "a radical retelling" of Israel's history.[71] In other words, it is clear Paul is employing the symbolic resources of Israel's story in forming the identity of the early Christ-movement (e.g., 1 Cor 1:19, 31; 2:9, 16a; 3:19b–20). Lieu's discussion of boundaries resonates with much of the research mentioned previously concerning their fluidity and social constructedness, and she argues for permeable, negotiated boundaries within Judaism during the first century CE.[72] Paul, as one thoroughly

---

66. Boyarin 1994: 188 emphasis original.

67. Elliott 2004a: 67.

68. Lieu 2004: 61. For further discussion on this issue, see Tucker 2009a: 71–77.

69. Lieu 2004: 23.

70. Holmberg 2008b: 7.

71. Lieu 2004: 79; 2002b: 6.

72. Cohen (1999: 6) remarks, "boundary is an expression of Jewish identity, not synonymous with it."

embedded in Judaism, argues in a similar fashion and allows "considerable ambiguity and instability in" the "construction of the boundaries"
which likely created some of the misunderstanding between Paul and
the Corinthians.[73] While we are in agreement with Lieu's argument,
Jewish identity had proven to be remarkably fixed during the Hellenistic
period, and Lieu may be overstating its fluid nature.[74]

A further difficulty with Lieu's work is that, as she seeks to uncover
the way Christian identity emerged within the nexus of Judaism and the
Roman world, it is unclear what, if any, aspects the early Christ-movement
contributed to the emergence of a unique identity. She alludes to the con-

73. Lieu 2004: 130–31.

74. The embodiment of Jewish identity is a concern in both 3 Maccabees and the
Letter of Aristeas. The book of 3 Maccabees, written in a style similar to the Greek
novels, describes the challenges of Jews with regard to enculturation into Greek society
(3 Macc 3:3–7, 15–24). The Jewish confidence in God is revealed in 6:15 which declares, "Not even when they were in the land of their enemies did I neglect them." This
text presents one option for the embodiment of identity; however Aristeas presents an
option that seeks to integrate Jewish identity within the broader Hellenistic culture,
while still maintaining a just and righteous standard within society (*Let. Aris.* 168–99).
Formational wisdom characterizes the teaching of Ben Sira, a "scribe" (γραμματεύς;
Sir 38:24; 50:27; 1 Cor 1:20), whose teaching (51:23) contains significant intertextures
from Proverbs concerning ethical formation (cf. Sir 1:27; Prov 1:7; Horsley 2007:
131–33). The rise of Hellenism in Judea with its emphasis on *paideia* became for Ben
Sira an approach to the world that could be cautiously embraced and redeployed in a
manner that reflected the glory and wisdom of Torah (see 45:5, 17; 49:4; DeSilva 2002:
158). Judea was under the control of the Seleucid Empire, and Horsley (2007: 149)
insightfully remarks that "Sira and the others of the Judean cultural elite" may have
been memorializing "the glories of their great prophets, kings, and priests of old" in a
manner similar to the Greeks during the "Second Sophistic." The autochthony of Jewish
identity served to maintain communal cohesion in the context of the empire (Jos. *AJ*
13.293–98; *Ap.* 2.145–296; Philo *Spec.* 4.149–50). Both Josephus and Philo were writing
to outsiders concerning Jewish social identity and in this case both emphasized the role
that unwritten regulations and traditions played in its maintenance (Saddington 2007:
235; Goodman 2007: 34). Josephus' awareness of group identity in 13.297–98 includes
differing ingroup/outgroup definitions and unwritten customs. He writes that these
unwritten customs were "rejected by the Sadducean group (τῶν Σαδδουκαίων γένος
ἐκβάλλει)." Philo recognizes the importance of "customs" and "unwritten laws" (ἔθη
ἄγραφοι νόμοι) for continuity and stability within a community (*Spec.* 4.149–50). Past
"customs" (ἔθος) and "traditions" (παράδοσις) and the public process by which they
are passed down are sites of contestation and power (Acts 25:16). Mandel (2007: 26)
argues that what was central to both Josephus and Philo was "public instruction" which
led to "widespread familiarity." The use of rhetoric for self-presentation and continual
community-formation is also evident in the writings of both Josephus (Runnalls 1997:
754) and Philo (Conley 1997: 696–97, 713). Cf. Sanders 1999: 2; Campbell 2006a: 5;
Cohen 1999: 27.

cept of kinship as practiced within the Christ-movement; however, this concept has analogs in both Jewish and Roman settings yet Lieu attempts to differentiate this fictive kinship within the Christ-movement and the broader culture.[75] Lieu's work here could be extended through a clearer connection with the concepts of kinship found in Israel's scriptures.

Denise Kimber Buell: Ethnic Reasoning

Ethnic reasoning and the dynamic interaction between fixity and fluidity are central elements of the identity forming program of the early "church." Denise Kimber Buell, while writing primarily about the later first through early third centuries, argues that early Christian texts used ethnic categories in forming identity.[76] It should be noted that most of the texts studied by Buell are from an era later than 1 Corinthians; however, from a methodological standpoint much of her framework may be applied to the earliest Pauline communities throughout the Roman Empire, as long as one does not read back into Paul's writings the ethnic argumentation of later writers.[77] Ethnic reasoning is a discursive strategy within early texts which defines "ethnicity through religious practices, viewing ethnicity as mutable even if 'real,' universalizing ethnicity and religion, and using ethnic ideas as polemic."[78] Buell understands these later authors to be arguing for a universalistic "Christian" identity. In her earlier writing, she contends that "being in Christ" does not "eliminate the other various measures of identity—Judean, Greek, slave, free, male, and female."[79] While this appears to argue for the existence of particu-

---

75. Cf. Lieu 2004: 166; Aasgaard 2004: 297–98; Ehrensperger 2007: 58.

76. Lopez (2008: 22–24) sees the centrality of the Roman Empire and its domination of defeated people groups to be the context of Paul's mission, which operates from a Jewish symbolic universe. She (2008: 117–18, 157, 162) also recognizes the gendered nature of Paul's rhetoric which often echoes that of Roman propaganda. Diana Swancutt (2001: 255; 2006: 8; 2003: 127) argues that Paul's pedagogical approach employs the resources of Israel's scriptures to counteract an over-identification with "*Romanitas*" and refers to his approach "as a rhetoric of identity."

77. Buell and Hodge (2004: 243–50) do interact in significant ways with Paul's writings and they provide a glimpse into the way to apply Buell's earlier framework to the Pauline discourse. Campbell (2006a: 5 n. 19) raises a similar caution.

78. Buell 2005: 33.

79. Buell and Hodge 2004: 248.

laristic identity, later she concludes "that Paul does" not "envision a new people, distinct from Israel."[80]

Buell's concept of identity formation occurring on the borders of fluidity and fixity is both a help and a hindrance. She argues that certain boundaries are fixed but that these boundaries may be ritually redrawn or discursively rendered culturally insignificant.[81] In this way she has rightly considered the complex interrelationship between the essentialist and constructionist positions of identity formation. There are some questions to be asked of this approach. First, it is not clear what mechanisms trigger the border crossing between fixity and fluidity and what distinguishes identity from other culturally defined categories, such as religion.[82] Second, this framework assumes a type of strategic essentialism[83] while rejecting the possibility of hybrid identity as a viable option to the fluidity and fixity framework.[84]

Buell's approach seeks to problematize identity concepts based primarily on ethnicity; in this, her work diverges from that of Campbell in two ways. First, she questions the validity of essentialist readings[85] whereas Campbell argues for "the continuing importance of primordial dimensions of ethnicity."[86] Second, she argues "that interpretive frameworks that implicitly or explicitly make race or ethnicity a primary site of difference between Jewishness and Christianness in the ancient world will continue to produce a harmful paradox."[87] One could, however, simply argue for a particularistic understanding of early Christ-movement identity in which ethnicity is not obliterated but transformed. Early Christ-movement identity does not need Judaism as a foil. Ehrensperger notes, "the interpretation of Scriptures is a crucial issue that we must

80. Buell and Hodge 2004: 249.

81. Buell 2005: 7–10.

82. Buell (2005: 10) acknowledges this weakness but encourages the reader to withhold judgment *a priori*.

83. Buell (2005: 15) desires to "show how Christians conceptualized themselves not only as a group formed out of members of other peoples, but also as a people themselves."

84. What is often unclear in Buell's work is whether she is affirming particularistic or universalistic identity in a given context. This lack of definition is also seen in her (Buell and Hodge 2004: 249) desire not to limit ethnicity by defining it.

85. Buell 2005: 12.

86. Campbell 2006a: 4.

87. Buell 2005: 12.

address in the process of reformulating Christian identity without anti-Judaism."[88] This is exactly what Campbell seeks to accomplish; in other words, the recognition of an ethnic component in the formation of early Christ-movement identity does not necessarily have to lead to an ethnoracial universalism such as Buell reconstructs but simply implies that Jews relate to God as Jews while gentiles relate to God as gentiles.[89]

Analysis and Approach

The preceding critical review of key scholars provides a framework from which to organize research into the way Paul sought to form social identity in 1 Corinthians 1–4. Paul's goal in writing to the Corinthian Christ-followers was to persuade them to make adjustments in their current social identity hierarchy so that what resulted would be a salient "in Christ" social identity. This would reprioritize the Corinthians' various group memberships so that their primary identity position would be the realization that they belong to Christ and not to this present age (1 Cor 3:23; 2:6–8). Thus, we will draw insights from Esler who focuses on the significance of the group context and the use of SIT/SCT. Holmberg and Dunn, with their emphasis on the "Christian" context bring to the fore the primary importance of being "in Christ." Campbell's emphasis on the Jewish context provides a particularistic understanding of identity that allows for the continuance and relevance of previous social identities in the Christ-movement. Boyarin's stress on the importance of the Hellenistic context assists us in demonstrating the significance of the Roman cultural setting in Corinth. Finally, Lieu and Buell, with their awareness of the role of texts, ethnicity, and kinship discourse in the formation of identity, bring out the discursive nature of Christ-movement social identity. It is recognized that a cumulative or aggregate approach does have its dangers; however, the preceding analysis of these various approaches did not intend to overlook the problems associated with those scholarly viewpoints; rather it was designed to position our approach within the current studies on the formation of early Christ-movement identity.

88. Ehrensperger 2004: 18.
89. Campbell 2006a: 127.

PAUL'S GOAL IN SOCIAL IDENTITY FORMATION

How are we to understand what Paul sought to form in the Corinthian Christ-followers in Corinth? Our approach to answering that question builds on two concepts. First, we utilize Stryker's concept of an identity hierarchy. This expands the conceptual framework of SIT/SCT to include a significant role for identity positions.[90] Second, the identity hierarchy is organized through the concept of identity salience which is present but not emphasized in SIT/SCT.[91] Stryker and Serpe define identity salience "as a readiness to act out an identity as a consequence of the identity's properties as a cognitive structure or schema."[92] The goal for Paul is to see the transformation of gentile Christ-follower identity, which means that the "in Christ" social identity has the salient position in the identity hierarchy, which increases the likelihood that it will be invoked in a given social situation.

The concept of an identity hierarchy is crucial in understanding Paul's mission and strategy with regard to the continued relevance of social, ethnic, and cultural identity. Identity hierarchy relates to identity salience, i.e., which identity is turned on in a given social situation. One's ethnic, cultural, and social identity are key indicators for social categorization and serve as indispensable aspects of communal life. Four examples of identity hierarchies will demonstrate Paul's concern with social identity formation in 1 Corinthians.

First, 1 Cor 1:22–24 may be seen as Paul's instruction with regard to behaviors associated with ethnic groups functioning too high in the identity hierarchy. Paul presents his case in the context of ethnic differentiation. He suggests to the Corinthian Christ-followers that these characteristics of one's ethnic identity are to be reevaluated in Christ who has become the power and wisdom of God. Read this way, Paul is not disparaging Greek pursuits of wisdom nor Jewish longing for power; he is only recategorizing these in the context of being called by God (1 Cor 1:24). Calling functions as a means of social cognition and serves as the foundation of the "in Christ" social identity.[93]

---

90. Stryker 1980: 60. Paul describes something close to an identity hierarchy in Phil 3:5–8; 2 Cor 11:22–23; Rom 11:1; Acts 23:6; 26:5.

91. Turner 1985: 78.

92. Stryker and Serpe 1994: 17.

93. This will be argued on p. 131.

Second, in 1 Cor 7:18–20, calling continues to serve as that which re-orients social life. Ethnic identity is not opposed with reference to circumcision and uncircumcision, but it is reprioritized. This occurs as Paul teaches the community to stay in the social situation they were in when they began to follow Christ. He does not call the community to discontinue practices associated with their ethnic identity; he simply reminds them that what is foremost is "keeping the commandments of God" (1 Cor 7:19; Gal 5:6, 6:15). Winter insightfully remarks that "[e]thnicity and social identity were the results of the providential over-sight of God (7:18, 21, 23)."[94]

Third, in 1 Cor 10:32, Paul argues that ethnic differentiation is relevant, and those communal behavior choices should be made with social identity in view. He encourages the community not to offend Jews or Greeks, that is those who are not "in Christ," by associating exclusively within their ethnic identity. He also tells the Corinthians not to offend those within God's community. This verse could be understood as referring to those outside the Christ-movement with regard to the first two and to those within with regard to the final group. Or, more likely one could understand καί assensively, rendering the verse, "Jews and Greeks, even those belonging to the ἐκκλησία." In that case, Paul is describing those within the ἐκκλησία in the context of their continuing ethnic identities.

Finally, in 1 Cor 12:13, Paul argues for the unity of the body in the context of ethnic definition. This verse should not be read as doing away with social categories but as realigning them in the context of one's baptismal identity. As mentioned above, Paul's goal in writing was to persuade those "in Christ" to adjust their current social identity hierarchy. An example of an identity hierarchy would be the *pater familias*, a man who is a husband, father, a slave-owner, and a part of the ἐκκλησία; this transformation results in a salient identity position that has its basis in the understanding that the community belongs to Christ. That is what Paul was seeking to form. What is a salient "in Christ" social identity? That is what we shall address next.

SALIENT "IN CHRIST" SOCIAL IDENTITY

Paul's use of ἐν Χριστῷ is contextually determined and addresses key aspects of both theological and social life within the community of

---

94. Winter 2001: 239.

Christ-followers. Dunn recognizes three ways in which Paul uses the term ἐν Χριστῷ. First, he uses it in an "objective" manner which refers "to the redemptive act which has happened 'in Christ' or depends on what Christ is yet to do."[95] In this category, one may place concepts related to the gospel message (e.g., justification, grace, and calling). Second, Paul also uses it in a subjective way to describe Christ-followers.[96] In this category one may place discussions concerning the social implications of the gospel (i.e., the outworking of the objective aspects of Christ's redemption). Third, he uses it to refer to his own ministry and mission.[97] Here one may place references that address Paul's social identity which includes his Jewishness, apostleship, and ongoing relations with members of the Christ-movement. Thus, Paul's use of ἐν Χριστῷ is differentiated and requires exegetical attention to discern which aspect is being emphasized in a particular epistolary discourse.

Paul employs all three nuances of ἐν Χριστῷ in 1 Corinthians 1–4. The "objective" aspect of God's grace given "in Christ" is evident in 1 Cor 1:4; chapter five of this book argues that this was the framework for Christ-movement social identity. What was lacking within the Corinthian ἐκκλησία was a proper understanding of the way being "in Christ" defined and shaped existing social identities; this is the concern of chapter six. Thus, Paul uses ἐν Χριστῷ in the subjective sense in order to teach the Corinthians concerning their ongoing sanctification and life "in Christ" (1 Cor 1:2 and 1:30) while also employing this language to provide correction (1 Cor 3:1 and 4:10). So, Paul actually also uses ἐν Χριστῷ as an ingroup-outgroup label in the shaping of the Corinthians' social identity. This is evident in Paul's final categoric use of ἐν Χριστῷ in the context of his mission. In 1 Cor 4:15 it functions as an implicit critique of Roman educational (i.e., pedagogues) and imperial ideology (i.e., father), while in 1 Cor 4:17 it is used in a manner that follows the contours of Jewish teaching and learning discourse, Paul's preferred method of teaching. For Paul, ἐν Χριστῷ is a key corporate ordering principle that integrates objective, subjective, and ongoing ministry components in relation to social identity formation.

---

95. Dunn 1998: 397. This "objective" component is still described using kinship discourse (Johnson 2007: 19). Furthermore, Brawley (2007: 108) anticipates this connection and notes that "the relationship of being justified is closely allied to identity."

96. Dunn 1998: 398.

97. Dunn 1998: 398.

As an ongoing ordering principle, ἐν Χριστῷ is inherently social and focuses on building a community. Dunn explains, "Likewise we can hardly avoid speaking of the community, a community which understood itself not only from the gospel which had called it into existence, but also from the shared experience of Christ, which bonded them as one."[98] Here he comes close to the idea of a salient "in Christ" social identity, the concept that is employed in this book to explain Paul's desired overarching social identity position in 1 Corinthians 1–4. Dunn points out the centrality of both calling and the gospel in the formation of the community. It is plausible that a misunderstanding about the nature of both of these had contributed to the instability of the ἐκκλησία in Corinth. For example, 1 Cor 7:20 and 24 indicate a misunderstanding about the nature of calling and by extension a misunderstanding about the nature of the continuation of social identity in the context of that calling (1 Cor 7:17–24). Also, 1 Cor 15:1–2 reveals that the Corinthian Christ-followers still did not understand the basic structure and content of the gospel. Thus, Paul restates the basic framework as well as a number of the social implications that follow from accepting the gospel message (1 Cor 15:3–11). The concepts of the gospel and calling are vital to Paul's understanding of social identity formation ἐν Χριστῷ.

Dunn also suggests that the ἐν Χριστῷ experience connects the Corinthians corporately and socially. This does not mean that there is not an individual component to being ἐν Χριστῷ. W. D. Davies' remarks are worth repeating here: "The formula which Paul most frequently used to describe the nature of the Christian man [sic] was that he was 'in Christ . . . In short ἐν Χριστῷ is a social concept, to be ἐν Χριστῷ is to have discovered true community."[99] Thus, being "in Christ" was a way for Paul to describe the unity of those within the ἐκκλησία, but for some reason, in Corinth it was not functioning in such a manner, and the result was that the community had become destabilized (1 Cor 1:10–12). It is possible to describe ἐν Χριστῷ as Paul's preferred overarching social identity position, a position that does not obliterate previous identities but reprioritizes them. Paul is an example of this in that his Jewish identity remains salient as he continues his mission among the gentiles (1 Cor 9:19–23).[100]

98. Dunn 1998: 401.

99. Davies 1980: 86.

100. Tomson (1990: 276) thinks Paul developed "flexibility" and a "moderate view"

Identity salience is one way to describe the interpenetration of the objective and subjective aspects of ἐν Χριστῷ. Identity salience relates to the way in which various identities interact based on changing social circumstances. A salient identity is one that is turned on in a given situation. It has emerged from its previous location lower down in an identity hierarchy and has begun to impact social categorizations as a master identity. The concept of a master identity also works in connection with hybridity in that each identity position remains discrete within the hierarchy and is not blended into irrelevance. Campbell rightly contends that Paul does not seek to blend Jewish and gentile identity into one "undifferentiated" Christian identity.[101] If Paul's rhetorical strategy is to see salient "in Christ" social identity form in his auditors, then he desires to see the community living out the social implications of the gospel. Davies contends, "There is a social aspect to the Pauline concept of being 'in Christ'; union with Christ however personal had meant incorporation into a community that could be described as one body."[102] Thus, being "in Christ" is an objective experience that is also lived out subjectively in the life of a community of Christ-followers who are furthermore part of God's mission in the world, a mission in Corinth that functioned primarily by means of, as recently described by Dickson, "social integration."[103] Thus, it may be asserted that Paul's goal in the transformation of gentile social identity means that the Corinthians' "in Christ" social identity is functioning in the salient position within their identity hierarchy. The Corinthians' previous identities are not obliterated but continue "in Christ" in a fundamental and significant manner.

David Horrell: "In Christ" Identity

David Horrell, however, would question this conclusion. He focuses on the importance of being "in Christ" for the formation of a universal-

---

within "his tradition" concerning the "idolatrous intention[s]" of gentiles. Bockmuehl (2000: 171) likewise concludes, "Paul has come to follow a lenient halakhah" with regard to the gentiles.

101. Campbell 2006a: 102.

102. Davies 1980: 90. If this is the case, other Pauline expressions of social identity may plausibly be subsumed under this descriptor (e.g., holy ones, body of Christ, kinship terms [e.g., brothers], and ἐκκλησία). These terms, however, continue to have a theological and social significance that should not be ignored.

103. Dickson 2003: 228–61. This concept was described on p. 30.

istic understanding of Christ-movement identity. Thus, his work deserves specific attention at this point. Horrell thinks that Paul's letters contributed significantly "in the construction of Christian, as distinct from Jewish, identity."[104] He argues that Paul believed "that the people of God—the 'true' Israel, as he sees it—find their identity in Christ alone," and his debate "with his Jewish-Christian opponents, concerns a fundamental question of boundaries and *identity*."[105] While one could quibble with Horrell's assertion here and his belief in the rapid emergence of the presence of oppositional thinking as a rhetorical strategy, he is correct that from Paul's perspective, the Corinthians' social identity has its basis "in Christ" alone.[106]

This becomes for Paul, according to Horrell, the new ingroup: "*The distinction to be drawn in terms of moral obligation and social interaction is not between Jew and Gentile but between those who are in Christ and those who are not.*"[107] Here Horrell minimizes the ethnic differences within the early Christ-movement and concludes that "Paul's understanding of (Christian!) identity and ethical responsibility remains profoundly Jewish . . . reconfigured and recentred around Christ."[108] However, Horrell does not go far enough. Paul's symbolic universe was thoroughly Jewish; the Scriptures used in the Pauline communities belonged to Israel, and their messiah was a Jew who lived and taught within a Jewish ethos; these gentile communities throughout the Roman Empire were also immersed in a Jewish symbolic universe. Horrell rightly notes that Paul's writings are "community-shaping . . . documents" with fluid boundaries between "ethical and theological" content.[109] That is to say, theological and ethical content both "serve to structure the identity and interaction of the Christian community."[110] In Horrell's view, theology is seen to precede identity formation. This is a distinction between his work and that of Campbell who understands identity to be a precursor to theology.[111] It may be argued, however, that there is a contrapuntal interaction between

104. Horrell 2002b: 278.

105. Horrell 2002b: 274 emphasis original.

106. Horrell 2002a: 321–22.

107. Horrell 2002a: 343 emphasis original.

108. Horrell 2002a: 343–44.

109. Horrell 2001: 147.

110. Horrell 2001: 148.

111. Campbell 2006a: 52.

identity and theology and that such a fine distinction may be unhelpful. We follow Horrell's work at key points but his universalistic understanding of "in Christ" identity requires correction in that Paul uses ethnic and kinship discourse to form the identity of the Christ-movement. Thus, these categories of identity retain their fundamental significance "in Christ" and are not obliterated. They may, however, be reprioritized if they are not consistent with the social implications of the gospel.

Caroline Johnson Hodge: Gentile Kinship "In Christ"

The framework of multiple identities serves as the interpretive grid for Caroline Johnson Hodge. She resists the universalism and particularity binaries when discussing identity and maintains "that Paul uses embodiedness to construct universalizing arguments, arguments that revolve around an embodied Israel and assume its continued election."[112] Central to Hodge's approach is challenging "the traditionally popular notion that Paul advocates the melding of differences into one 'Christian' identity."[113] She remarks, "although *Ioudaioi* and gentiles now share a common ancestor, Paul does not collapse them into one group (of 'Christian,' for example). Gentiles-in-Christ and Jews are separate but related lineages of Abraham."[114] For Hodge, ethnicity and kinship language are central for Paul's rhetorical constructs.[115]

Consideration of the transitional nature of Paul's identity and the fact that he never left Judaism are important tenets to her understanding of the way Paul sought to form gentile "in Christ" identity. Hodge remarks that "as an 'entrepreneur of identity,' Paul manages both the multiple facts of his own identity as a teacher of gentiles and the new possibilities of aggregate identity for gentiles-in-Christ."[116] She rightly understands Paul as one who never broke from Judaism but incorporated the concept of "adaptability" into his teaching.[117] While Paul's ministry shows evidence of adaptation to his audience, the example provided by Hodge (i.e., Philodemus) would have been more convinc-

112. Johnson Hodge 2007: 127–28.

113. Johnson Hodge 2007: 127.

114. Johnson Hodge 2007: 5.

115. Johnson Hodge 2007: 4. In this way, her work resonates with the concept of ethnic reasoning of Buell (2005: 7–12).

116. Johnson Hodge 2007: 120.

117. Johnson Hodge 2007: 121–25; 1 Cor 9:19–22.

ing if it were found within the Hebrew Scriptures. Her understanding of identity hierarchies is instructive and her kinship reading of being "in Christ" is insightful, though it could be extended by also understanding being "in Christ" as a social identity.[118] She comes close to this with regard to Gal 3:28 where she takes the view that "Paul calls for a unity of those in Christ, but not an erasure of other identities. We might imagine this 'in-Christness' superimposed over other facets of identity, like being called in the 1 Corinthians passage above."[119] For Hodge, gentiles are now "within the larger network of Israel." Paul does not tell the gentiles "to become *Ioudaioi* or cease to be Greeks, but he expects gentiles-in-Christ to make radical adjustments to their identities."[120] In this way, Hodge's work extends that of both Campbell and Buell, though some of her exegetical decisions may limit the usefulness of her approach when applied to 1 Corinthians.[121] The most significant problem with her approach, however, is that she over-estimates the fluid nature of identity.

CONCLUSION

This chapter found that social identity within Pauline studies is a robust field of research and one in which contours may be observed. Certain scholars have applied with rather convincing results many of the theories surveyed in chapter two and thus have contributed to the development of an interpretative grid for this book. Among these, the work of Esler stands out. Moreover, scholars have researched the role that texts play in forming identity, and the work of Lieu is substantial in this regard. Some, however, tend to emphasize the newness of "Christian" identity over that of Jewish identity. In contrast, the continued relevance of Jewish identity is a hallmark of the work of Campbell. Boyarin adds the importance of Roman identity in the development of Paul's rhetoric. Ethnicity and kin-

118. Johnson Hodge 2007: 131–32.

119. Johnson Hodge 2007: 126.

120. Johnson Hodge (2007: 131) continues, "they must give up their gods and religious practices in order to proclaim loyalty to the God of Israel; they must accept Israel's messiah, scriptures, stories of origin, ethical standards, and even ancestry."

121. While we are in agreement with the statement on p. 131 that "Christ is the link for gentiles to the linage of Abraham," the way this works in 1 Corinthians is unclear (Johnson Hodge 2007: 132, 5). Also, her discussion of Pauline studies on p. 9, while helpful, may actually mask significant soteriological and anthropological differences especially in relation to the "radical" interpreters. The moniker "beyond the new perspective on Paul" more accurately reflects the work of Campbell and Ehrensperger.

ship are stressed by scholars who understand Paul's discourse to be focused on the maintenance of particular aspects of social identity. Finally, salient "in Christ" social identity was presented as the understanding taken by this book with regard to Paul's identity-forming strategy. A social-scientific and exegetical study of 1 Corinthians 1–4 remains. This will utilize the method described in the introduction and resonate with the understanding of social identity uncovered in chapter two, an eclectic combination of insights from Pauline scholarship organized around the concept of salient "in Christ" social identity. However, before that can be done, the historical and cultural context of Roman Corinth must be established in order to substantiate the claim that social identity, specifically its civic component, contributed to the divisions in Corinth; this will be the focus of the next chapter.

4

The Impact of Civic Identity in Roman Corinth

INTRODUCTION

JAMES WALTERS ARGUES THAT the increased internal conflict in Corinth was, in part, because of a lack of external conflict, which has its basis in the evolving civic identity in Roman Corinth during the mid-first century.[1] This chapter takes this idea as its point of departure and seeks to extend it by surveying the material and textual record for evidence of the transitional nature of civic identity in Corinth. The role that the Roman character of Corinth played in its civic identity, Walters argues, contributed to the socio-economic diversity of the community of Christ-followers; here he follows the contours of Theissen's work, which has been challenged by Friesen.[2] Walters does not provide sufficient evidence for such a cross-section of social status within the Corinthian ἐκκλησία and is thus open to some of the criticisms leveled against Theissen and Meeks, who hold similar positions.[3] Walters is most effective in describing the way civic identity functioned at both the personal and social levels while also making an initial case for the way identity issues impacted Paul's mission, though this chapter will extend his work in this regard. Walters suggests that weak group identity and the boundary issues associated with it impact the factionalism inherent in the Corinthian correspondence.[4] Following Mitchell, he makes a case for this factionalism being the reason for Paul's rhetorical approach in the letter. One question that arises from this line of reasoning: Why does

1. Walters 2005: 397–417.

2. Theissen 1982: 102. This will be discussed further on p.121.

3. Cf. Walters 2005: 415; Friesen 2005: 365; Theissen 1982: 69; Meeks 1983a: 79; Meggitt 1998: 128.

4. Walters 2005: 413; Mitchell 1991: 182, 301; Adams 2000: 99.

the lack of external pressure produce more internal pressure? He offers several reasons (e.g., varying social strata, levels of commitment, and allegiances); however, these conflicts would be present with or without external pressure. Despite his convincing case concerning the role of civic identity within the Corinthian ἐκκλησία, Walters does not fully consider the broader implications of this situation for the formation of local social identities within the Christ-movement in Corinth.

This chapter argues that Corinthian civic identity, understood as a component of social identity, was in transition during the first century CE, and this may explain the lack of difficulties of the Christ-movement with the Corinthian civic Roman officials while at the same time it contributed to their internal divisions. The aim of this chapter is to demonstrate the way aspects of civic-religious life are relevant for the social-scientific reading that will occur in this book. First, it will establish an understanding of Roman imperial ideology in the Corinthian context. Second, it will assemble archaeological, literary, numismatic, and epigraphic evidence to support the assertion that Corinth's culture was generally Roman though its civic and social identity was in transition. Third, it will suggest that specific status-oriented Mediterranean ordering principles combined with the urban environment, allegiance to the emperor, and Roman religion to construct Roman social identity. Finally, evidence of the potential involvement of the Christ-followers in Corinthian civic life will be presented to support the contention that some within the ἐκκλησία were continuing to identify primarily with key aspects of their Roman identity.[5]

CORINTHIAN CIVIC IDENTITY AND ROMAN IMPERIAL IDEOLOGY

Civic-religious identity[6] functions at both a personal and a social level and serves as a "linking device whereby individuals more or less con-

5. It is hoped that this book is able to fill a gap between the group of scholars who stress "remaining in the calling" in relation to Jewish identity and those who stress a universal Hellenistic Christian identity. We are seeking to apply the stance of the former group in the context of Roman identity in the first century CE. In other words, the focus of the former group has been on the continuing relevance of Jewish identity "in Christ"; this books looks at the corollary of this viewpoint, the continuing relevance of Roman social identity "in Christ."

6. The contemporary category distinctions of identity are sometimes difficult to separate in antiquity. Civic or civic-religious identity would not have been distinguish-

sciously align themselves, or allow themselves to be aligned, with particular groups."[7] The primary model for religious identity was the civic model which linked an individual to a particular city or colony. Woolf refers to this as "*polis*-religion" and describes it as an "ordering principle."[8] Consequently, it was the *sacra publica* (i.e., *polis*-religion) that embodied and defined religious identity in antiquity. Moreover, because the provincial elites maintained and oversaw any modifications, they played a decisive role in shaping the collective religious norm in a city or colony.[9] This chapter seeks to understand the way issues related to civic-religious identity impacted the formation of social identity in Corinth.[10]

In the early empire, the basis for Corinthian civic identity[11] was Roman imperial ideology, which included the various discursive practices designed to reinforce the power of the senate, the emperor, the provincial ruling elites, and to maintain those aspects of Roman social identity that provided social cohesion.[12] It relied on honor and shame

---

able from social identity. Also, the definition of social identity for this book incorporates civic identity because of its focus on group memberships; see p. 3.

7. Rives 1995: 4.

8. Woolf 2003: 40. Woolf (2003:44) notes that other models or "ordering principles" for religious identity include the use of "votive objects, inscriptions, curse tablets, [and] magical papyri." He (2003: 41, 47) also recognizes that though the following could be employed in various ways, "myth, ordering of religion by place, [and] oracles" would contribute to ancient religious identities as would alternative religions such as "Bacchic, Judaism, Mithraism, and Christianity."

9. Woolf (2003: 51) describes this process by noting that "the creation of Roman *coloniae* . . . entailed the establishment of a Roman version of *polis*-religion, complete with euergetistic priesthoods, control of the cults by the magistrates and decurions, and public festivals at central sanctuaries."

10. Rives (1995: 13) developed a similar approach to Roman Carthage and noted the role Roman imperial ideology played in developing "a collective religious identity." See also Walters 2005: 397–417 and Pickett 2005: 125.

11. Civic identity is defined by Damon (2001: 127) as "an allegiance to a systematic set of moral and political beliefs, a personal ideology of sorts, to which a . . . person forges a commitment. The emotional and moral concomitants to the beliefs are a devotion to one's community and a sense of responsibility to the society at large."

12. De Ste. Croix (1981: 44) remarks "*Imperialism* involve[s] some kind of economic and/or political subjection to a power outside the community." Brunt (1990: 291) notes that what was unique about Roman imperialism was the "belief that it was universal and willed by the gods." Zanker (1988: 4) rightly notes that "through visual imagery a new mythology of Rome and, for the emperor, a new ritual of power were created." Elliott (2008a: 29) points out that "the Roman ideological system" was "remarkably adaptive." Ando (2000: 19) concludes that Roman imperial ideology functioned "to define those who belonged and to exclude those who did not."

discourse, the patronage and benefaction system, and kinship language to establish control throughout the empire.[13] Allegiance to the emperor was compulsory, while the Roman myths of origin and various markers of Roman social identity combined to provide a complement of social practices infused with an ideology of ingroup belonging. Roman imperial ideology relied on a threat of force and the population's acceptance of an eschatological vision in which their betters were destined to rule them as ordained by the gods. Evidence to substantiate these assertions is provided in what follows in this chapter.

Roman imperial ideology also relied on the communicative resources of oratory and rhetoric for its persuasiveness. The elites throughout the empire were prepared to rule through education in which oratory was central. Greek moral philosophy, combined with the Roman value of preparation for empire-building, formed the core of their educational focus.

Evidence for Roman imperial ideology in Corinth, which will be presented in this chapter, may be seen in the urban environment, especially in the continual presence of the emperor and his family on statues, coins, buildings, and monumental inscriptions. The imperial cult was the primary means for ideological reinforcement while public, religious feasts and the Isthmian games celebrated the agonistic culture that supported the continued domination by the senate, the emperor, and the provincial elites. Roman imperial ideology forcefully imposed was the basis from which social identification emerged and functioned as a set of status-oriented discursive practices that proved to be transformative in various provincial political situations. Total allegiance to the emperor was the one consistent component throughout the empire and served as a key ordering principle for Roman social identity. These four factors: the urban environment, imperial religion, status-oriented discourse, and allegiance to the emperor combined to produce local expressions of Roman social identity.[14]

For Paul, this ideological basis required a reconfiguration in the corporate life of the Christ-movement. The Corinthian Christ-followers' transformed identity "in Christ" could mimic components of imperial ideology except in those places where it contradicted the social implica-

13. Theissen 1999: 34–37.
14. Revell 2009: 1–39.

tions of the gospel.[15] This is the focus of Paul's rhetoric in 1 Corinthians 1–4. The continuation of key aspects of social identity within the community of Christ-followers had resulted in the development of an ideological basis that misunderstood the social implications of the gospel and the proper alignment within the identity hierarchy of various components of their social identities, which were to be reprioritized but not opposed "in Christ."

THE ROMAN CHARACTER OF CORINTH
IN THE FIRST CENTURY CE

Archaeologists and classicists have increasingly emphasized the Roman character of Corinth from the mid-first century BCE onwards.[16] New Testament scholars have begun debating this issue, as well. For example, concerning language use in Corinth, Meeks supposes that Latin was only spoken among the elites.[17] Winter, on the other hand, argues that Corinth was a thoroughly Roman colony in language and culture, distinct from all its neighbors in the province of Achaia.[18] Chow concludes that "the official language in Corinth, especially in the early days, was probably Latin."[19]

Corinth had flourished from the 8th to the 5th centuries BCE and had served as a leader in the Achaean League, a position which ultimately led to its demise.[20] During an uprising against the Romans,

15. Bhabha 1994: 122–23; Walters 2005: 397–417.

16. E.g., Broneer 1941: 388–90; Wiseman 1979: 438–548; Bookidis 1987; Williams 1987: 26–37; Engels 1990; Alcock 1993; Gill 1993b: 259–64; Gregory 1994; Walbank 1997: 95–130; and the ongoing excavation reports from ASCSA entitled, *Corinth*.

17. Meeks 1983a: 63, 79; Tucker 2008: 72–91.

18. Winter 2001: 11. Adams (2003a: xix) remarks that "in the east . . . the Romans behaved as if vernacular languages did not exist, but here by contrast they were prepared to use Greek as a lingua franca, and consequently Latin did not cause language death, since it remained very much in the background." Latin still could function as an identifier of Roman identity in the law courts, military and other civic settings.

19. Chow (1992: 40 n. 3) rightly points out Kent's conclusion concerning the official status of Latin within Corinth (see also Nguyen 2008a: 122). Kent (1966: 19) concludes "that of the 104 texts that are prior to the reign of Hadrian 101 are in Latin and only three are Greek, a virtual monopoly for the Latin language." Kent relies on numismatic evidence to conclude that Latin was the official language. He (1966: 18) writes, "the coins of the duoviri show that Latin was the official language as late as AD 69."

20. Polyb. 38.3–11; 39.7–17.

consul Lucius Mummius burned and destroyed the city in 146 BCE.[21] All that remains of the Greek city are sections of the *agora*, pillars of a central temple, and a fountain.[22] Julius Caesar rebuilt Corinth in 44 BCE as a Roman *colonia* (πολίτευμα) and named it *Colonia Laus Iulia Corinthiensis*.[23] Initially, the majority of the population was Roman with a large number of military veterans, as well as freedpersons, and the urban poor from Rome.[24] The Roman character of the city is also reflected in the many Latin names associated with it in the New Testament and the Argive petition.[25]

The Argive petition comes from a letter also known as Pseudo-Julian, Letters 198, which Spawforth has convincingly argued should be dated to the mid-first century CE.[26] This letter presents Corinth as a thoroughly Roman colony in the first century. For example, the anonymous letter writer from Argos describes Corinth as a "foreign . . . country" in comparison to its Greek neighbors (409b). Furthermore, Corinth is described as having rejected "the laws and customs of ancient Greece" and replaced them with the laws "from the sovereign city [Rome]" (409c). Moreover, Corinth is said to have received great "advantages since they received the colony from Rome" (409d). The Corinthian expression of *Romanitas* may have extended to "hunting shows" in "their

21. Paus. *Descr.* 2.1.2; Diod. Sic. 27.1; 32.4.5.

22. Cic. *Tusc.* 3.22. Walbank (1997: 95) provides a survey of the destruction layer. Schnabel (2004: 1182) remarks, "the territory of the city was given in part to the city of Sikyon; for the most part it was Roman *ager publicus*." See Arafat (1996: 89–97) for a discussion of Mummius and ancient views of the destruction of Corinth.

23. Str. *Geogr.* 8.6.23. There has been some disagreement over exactly when the city was re-founded and who was responsible. It is clear that Julius Caesar had planned to re-found it as a colony, but its actual foundation did not occur until shortly after his death. Though Octavian is often credited with carrying out the foundation, Walbank has shown that it must have been Marc Antony, administrator of Caesar's will, who actually did it. After Actium, Antony's name was erased from memory and his achievements credited to Augustus. See Walbank 1997: 98–99.

24. Plut. *Vit. Caes.* 57.5; App. *B Civ.* 136.4–6. The number of inhabitants from Greece is part of a continuing debate; see Walbank 1997: 95–96, 103–7. A component of the difficulty is that Pausanias does not report the ongoing inhabitation of Greeks in Corinth; see *Descr.* 2.1.2. For a further discussion of the literary evidence concerning the Greek population in Corinth, see Gebhard and Dickie 2003: 262–65; and see Spawforth (1996: 174) for evidence concerning the Roman population.

25. Winter 2001: 19–22; Meeks 1983a: 55–63. Orr and Walther (1976: 42) note, for example, Aquila, Priscilla, Crispus, Lucius, Gaius, Tertius, Erastus, Quartus, Fortunatus, and Achaicus.

26. Spawforth 1994: 212–16; Murphy-O'Connor 2002: 96; Winter 2001: 5.

theatres" and the imposition of taxes in order to "purchase the pleasure of indulging their temperaments" (409a). Corinth had embraced key aspects of Roman life; however, as Murphy-O'Connor rightly notes Pliny the Younger recognized "the Province of Achaia [as] pure and genuine Greece."[27] Previous and current Greek and Roman identities interpenetrated one another to produce a localized expression of Roman social identity in the mid-first century CE.

Corinth became the capital of the Roman province of Achaia in 27 BCE.[28] In Roman Corinth, the urban environment was renewed; old temples were restored and enlarged (e.g., Apollo and Asclepius).[29] Lang notes that the Asklepios temple was originally a shrine for Apollo and describes an inscription which reads, "I belong to Apollo" ('Aπέλ[λ]ονός ἰμι).[30] Furthermore, new shops, baths,[31] and markets were built (e.g., the South Stoa),[32] new water supplies developed and old ones restored (e.g., fountains of Glauke and Peirene),[33] and many public buildings were added (e.g., civic buildings and a theatre seating close to 15,000), all with distinctively Roman architectural elements. For example, the Lechaion Basilica, which dates to the first century BCE, and the Julian Basilica, though dated to the second century by Weinberg, served civic functions, as did the large South Basilica which was built in the mid first-century

27. Murphy-O'Connor 2002: 98; Plin. *Ep.* 8.26.

28. Str. *Geogr.* 17.3.25; Cass. Dio 53.12–13.

29. Stillwell concludes, concerning the temple of Apollo, that it "underwent extensive repairs under the Roman occupation, and we know that it was re-roofed" (Fowler and Stillwell 1932: 115–34, here 124). See Paus. *Descr.* 2.4.6; Pfaff 2003: 112–15, 125–27; Roebuck 1951: 1, 22–26; Wiseman 1979: 467–68; Rothaus reinterprets some of the findings of DeWaele and Stillwell and also suggests that Temple E was used for the "Imperial cult" (2000: 42–45, on the imperial cult see 41); see also Gooch 1993: 15–17.

30. Lang 1977: 3.

31. The Roman Baths North of the Peribolos of Apollo, the so-called "Baths of Eurykles" (Biers 2003: 317) and "The Fountain of The Lamps" are two that can be dated to the mid-first century CE (Wiseman 1979: 512).

32. Broneer 1954: 91–99; 107–11, 132–45. Fotopoulos provides a discussion of the Roman administrative reconstruction of the South Stoa and a rejection of the existence of a shrine of Sarapis in shop XX (2003: 118–20). Broneer's description of the athletic mosaic (107–11, see also plates 30 and 31) from the South Stoa is employed by Dutch as evidence for the continued connection with the Greek past in Roman Corinth (2005: 52–53). See Wiseman 1979: 513–21 for discussions on the remodeling of the Stoa.

33. Hill discusses the relevant Roman periods for Peirene and Glauke (1964: 2, 64–90, 225–27; see also Engels 1990: 179–81; Str. *Geogr.* 8.6.21; Paus. *Descr.* 2.5.1; Cic. *Leg. agr.* 1.2.5).

CE.[34] Furthermore, Romano has recently published a fragmentary inscription that supports the idea that "some manifestation of the imperial cult" is possible "in the Julian Basilica."[35] The restored text reads, "This is a dedication to the Caesares Augusti and the colony of Corinth" (CAE[SA]RIBVS · AVGVSTIS // [E]T · COL [·LA]VD · IV[L·C---]).[36] In the first century, Corinth's *forum/agora* was larger than any in Greece. The grid layout followed the plan of Roman "centuriation"; however, many of the buildings in the forum were not aligned with that Roman orientation but maintained their previous Greek alignment.[37] The *colonia* had begun to reestablish itself as an important political and cultural center in the eastern part of the Roman Empire, but its Greek past would continue to interpenetrate its Roman present.[38]

As a newly founded Roman *colonia*, Corinth would have been susceptible to the transition in "*polis*-religion" that was occurring throughout the empire.[39] The Roman *sacra publica* in general were experiencing transition and redefinition during the late republic, the principate, and the early empire.[40] Woolf argues further that "*polis*-religion" was losing its control over people throughout the empire.[41] Local social and cul-

---

34. Weinberg 1960: 58–77, 109; Stillwell 1952: 135–31, 211; Engels 1990: 47; Welborn 2005: 7–8.

35. Romano 2005a: 100.

36. Romano 2005a: 97.

37. Oakes 2008: 9.

38. Paus. *Descr.* 2.6—3.1; Romano 2006: 62–85; Engels 1990: 13–14; Fowler and Stillwell 1932: 170; Murphy-O'Connor 2002: 24–28.

39. Woolf 2003: 41. The significance of these transitional circumstances includes the following: the Corinthian Christ-followers could integrate into civic-religious life without much difficulty; this could also account for the lack of conflict with the Roman civic authorities, and could provide a plausible scenario in which the Pauline mission might be extended (Ebel 2004; Thiselton 2006a; Thrall 2002).

40. *Res Gestae* 20; Suet. *Aug.* 31.4. Beard and Crawford (1985: 28) prefer to describe it as "in decline—either neglected or merely manipulated as a useful weapon in the political battles of the governing elite." They also note that the "Roman state cult was the crucial defining element of the religious system as a whole. Here was to be found the 'Romanness' of Roman religion; here was the centre around which other elements took a secondary place" (1985: 29; see also Woolf 2003: 41).

41. Woolf 2003: 48–50. Some of the reasons for this transition within the *sacra publica* were related to immigration and increased mobility throughout the empire as well as the lack of integration of "lower status worshippers" (Woolf 2003: 48). In the east, public cults were not understood as secondary in the same manner as they were in Rome. Finally, different experiences with Roman imperialism contributed to uneven acceptance of these public expressions of political and religious unity (49–50).

tural identities were constantly intersecting with an emerging sense of Roman social identity. On the broader scale, the senate still made the final decisions concerning transformations in the *sacra publica* and had a significant impact on the civic-religious identity of those within the empire. They also enforced a level of suppression if religious cults caused civil unrest or disruption.[42] The Romans saw clear connections between religious identity and socio-political authority.[43] They supported and maintained "*polis*-religion" among their subjects although Corinth would have sustained some control over its own *sacra publica*.[44]

Civic Identity in Transition

Three lines of evidence buttress the contention that the civic identity of those living in Corinth was in transition during the early empire: (1) the emergence of the imperial cult; (2) the affirmation, removal, and reinstatement of Corinth as a senatorial province; (3) the influence of the Greek past of Corinth on the current Roman colony.

Evidence for the imperial cult[45] in Corinth comes from Pausanias and the remains of Temple E, identified either as the Temple of Octavia, the Temple of Jupiter Capitolinus, or "the Capitolium."[46] Also, coins

42. E.g., the Bacchic cult in 186 BCE; *ILLRP*, 511; Livy 39.8.1–8; Cic. *Att.* 1.13.3.

43. Cic. *Dom.*1–3; *Att.* 1.16.6; 1.18.5; 4.3.3–4; *Phil.* 1.10.25. Beard and Crawford (1985: 38) describe Roman religion as "embedded within the political system." Fay (2008: 78) concludes that "the Imperial Cult was a form of politics and had nothing to do with next-world orientation."

44. Økland 2007: 72; Walbank 1996: 211. Rives (2007: 116) remarks, "If civic cults played a crucial role in establishing civic identity and were consequently integral to civic organization, we must keep in mind that they were at the same time semi-autonomous." Finney understands the importance to mission of this fact, "[i]n creating local assemblies within and alongside the peoples of cities of the Mediterranean, Paul was building a multi-ethnic *ekklesia* which would stand as an alternative society to the Roman imperial order" (2005: 27; but see Woolf 2003: 49). Cf. Økland 2004: 104–7; Paus. *Descr.* 2.2.8.

45. Økland rightly remarks, concerning the imperial cult, that it "worshipped deified members of the imperial family as well as personified abstracta like the *genii*. In Corinth, the cult of the *genius* of the colony was mingled with the imperial cult because of its close identification with the *gens Iuliae*" (2004: 101 emphasis original; Coutsoumpos 2008: 173–77).

46. Paus. *Descr.* 2.3.1, Fowler and Stillwell 1932: 85 n. 1; Paus. *Descr.* 2.4.5, Stillwell, Scranton, and Freeman 1941: 234–36; Walbank 1996: 204; Økland 2004: 102. Fowler and Stillwell suggest that this temple is to be identified as "a temple of the *Gens Julia*, perhaps containing a statue of the sister of Augustus with the attributes of Venus, the legendary

cataloged by Edwards contain the "head of Tiberius" on the obverse and on the reverse a "hexastyle temple inscribed *GEN IULI*."[47] Although this does not establish that Temple E is the Temple of Octavia identified by Pausanias, it does support the presence of the imperial cult in Corinth.[48]

Williams concludes that the imperial cult in Roman Corinth centered on Temple E.[49] A monumental inscription uncovered in the Theatre reads, "[Sacred] to the deified Julius Caesar" (DIVO IVL[io] CAESARI [sacrum]) and suggests the presence of the emperor cult quite early in the history of Corinth.[50] Walbank dates this inscription based on "the letter forms" which "indicate a date either in the late Republic or in the very early Empire." Moreover, she remarks on this find that "[c]olonies were always centres of Roman influence, especially in matters of religion, and it is not surprising to find a cult of Divus Iulius at Corinth."[51]

Julius Caesar is claimed to have refounded Corinth, and significant identification with him follows from that fact. Edwards cataloged a coin which reads, "The praise of Julius Corinth" (LAVS IVLI CORN) and shows the "head of Julius Caesar" wearing a "laureate."[52] Walbank considers it plausible that Antony "initiated the establishment of a cult of Divus Iulius at Corinth."[53] Augustus in turn linked his position with the deified Julius Caesar on a coin whose obverse shows Augustus while the reverse pictures Julius Caesar.[54] Walbank dates this coin to "between 27 and 26 B.C." It carries images of "the new *princeps* and the deified founder of Corinth, with the implication [being] that Augustus as *divi filius* shared in his adoptive father's divine status."[55] These remains provide evidence for a continued expression of the imperial cult in Corinth; if Williams' dating for Temple E during the reign of Tiberius is accepted then it would

---

ancestress of the family" (1932: 85 n. 1). Williams provides an updated discussion on the first temple (Williams and Zervos 1990: 326–31). Fotopoulos gives a substantial critique of Walbank's suggestion (2003: 137–38). Walbank also considers the possibility of "Zeus Capitolinus" (1989: 369, 371–79, 381–82).

47. Edwards 1933: 19.

48. Stillwell, Scranton, and Freeman 1941: 233–34.

49. Williams 1989: 156–63; Fotopoulos 2003: 138.

50. Kent 1966: 31.

51. Walbank 1996: 201.

52. Edwards 1933: 16, no. 16.

53. Walbank 1989: 201–2.

54. Edwards 1933: 18, no. 34.

55. Walbank 1989: 202.

reveal an "increased importance of the imperial cult" there.[56] Likewise, an inscription found near the Acrocorinth describes "Spartiaticus" (SPARTIATI[co]) as a "priest of the divine Julius" (FLAM DIVI IVLI).[57] West dates "the inscription . . . before the disgrace of Agrippina in 55 A.D., very soon after the death of Claudius."[58] Moreover, Walbank notes that this inscription is "an indication that the cult of Divus Iulius was of lasting importance in Corinth."[59] The Spartiaticus inscription shows that there was a recognized priesthood of the imperial cult in the province of Achaia during the mid-first century CE.

Fotopoulos rightly suggests that "the presence of a *flamens* necessitates an altar or a temple for the sacrificial rites of the cult."[60] The altar in the forum near Temple E, however, predates its earliest structure but appears to be similar to the *Ara Pacis,* and it is plausible that it functioned in the context of the imperial cult during the mid-first century CE.[61] Celebrations in honor of the emperor would have been attended by the entire *colonia* and the sacrifices offered in public view.[62] The imperial cult served as a means of reinforcing allegiance to the emperor and acknowledging his *imperium*.[63] Walbank concludes, concerning Corinth in the mid-first century CE, that there was "a sense . . . that the whole colony was under the informal patronage of the emperor and his family."[64]

The political upheaval following the assassination of Caesar and the ensuing civil war made it difficult for Corinth to thrive. It did, however, experience significant growth under the reign of Augustus who established it as the provincial capital in 27 BCE, repairing the roads

56. Fotopoulos 2003: 138; see also concerning Tiberius, Val. Max. 1.1.

57. West 1931: 50, no. 68.

58. West 1931: 52; but see Fotopolous (2003: 138) who dates it "from the time of Nero's reign", as does Walbank (1989: 202, 211–12). Cf. Pseudo-Julian 408ff (Winter 2001: 274).

59. Walbank 1989: 202, 211–12.

60. Fotopoulos 2003: 138. *Flamines* were priests in the local expressions of Roman religion (Beard, North, and Price 1998: 208; Witherington 1995: 296).

61. Økland 2004: 103–4; Scranton 1951: 140–41; cited in Chow 1992: 40.

62. Fotopolous (2003: 139) remarks that "the imperial cult does seem like a probable source of sacrificial food sold in the city's *macellum*, a source that would have created added pressure and motivation for Christians in this Roman colony to buy and eat whatever was for sale."

63. *OLD* 844; Spawforth 1995: 151–68; Winter 2001: 19, 274.

64. Walbank 1996: 209.

and public buildings, and re-establishing Corinthian control over the Isthmian Games which were initially celebrated in Corinth and then later at the Isthmus near the temple of Poseidon.[65] Pausanias recounts how at one point the games were given to Sicyon, but Gebhard concludes that "the Corinthians were in control of the games by the time of their celebration in 40 B.C."[66] She also points out that when this control was returned, the games were held in Corinth, and "the festival did not come to be held regularly at the Isthmian sanctuary until A.D. 50–60."[67] In support of this chronology, Broneer dates the reconstruction of the Temple of Poseidon to "about the middle of the first century after Christ."[68] Furthermore, Romano notes the presence of a circus in Corinth and likewise concludes that the games may have been held "within the *limites* of the Roman city of Corinth."[69] Kent catalogs two inscriptions that are relevant to this discussion: first, "Sextus Olius Secundus" who served as the "president of the games." Second, "L. Castricius Regulus" whose "public career probably extended from about 10 B.C. to A.D. 23," while the inscription dates to "approximately A.D. 25." Kent notes, "The Tiberea Caesarea Sebastea were additional games instituted shortly after the accession of Tiberius." He dates this to around "A.D. 23; Tact. *Ann.* 4.7–9."[70] The Isthmian Games and the religious and political structures associated with them were in transition during the first century CE but were also important components of the unique formulation of Roman social identity in Corinth.

In 44 CE, under the reign of Claudius, Corinth was reaffirmed as a senatorial province and the capital of Achaia, an honor it had lost under Tiberius in 15 CE. This provided the necessary support for Corinth to once again emerge as a key center of trade and commerce.[71] This civic transition continued past the time of Paul's original visit to Corinth. First, Nero had declared all of Greece to be free, including the province of Achaia, but this freedom was revoked by Vespasian because "the

---

65. Str. *Geogr.* 8.6.22.
66. Paus. *Descr.* 2.2.2; Gebhard 1994: 82.
67. Gebhard 1994: 94.
68. Broneer 1971: 101.
69. Romano 2005b: 609.
70. Kent 1966: 69, no. 152; 72, no. 153; 73.
71. Tac. *Ann.* 1.76.4; 1.80.1; Suet. *Claud.* 25.3; Str. *Geogr.* 8.6.20.

Greeks had forgotten how to be free."[72] Second, as a result of Vespasian's reversal, Corinth was again declared a senatorial province, but its name was changed to *Colonia Iulia Flavia Augusta Corinthiensis* to reflect the Corinthians' relationship with Vespasian. It was, however, changed back to *Colonia Laus Iulia Corinthiensis* "after the death of Domitian."[73] Kent catalogs an inscription which reads, "col·iul·FLAV·AVG·corinthiensis"; he remarks that "[f]rom the coins of Corinth we know that under the Flavians the official name of the colony was changed to *Colonia Iulia Flavia Augusta Corinthiensis*."[74] Furthermore, West catalogs a coin whose obverse reads "Emperor Caesar Domitian Augustus Germanicus" (IMP CAES DOMIT AVG GERM) and whose reverse reads "Colony of Julius Augustus Corinth" (COL IVL AVG COR). This coin provides evidence for the change back to the city's founding name.[75] During the first century CE, Corinth's civic identity in general was in transition in various ways, and this undoubtedly impacted the social identity of those living within the colony, including those within the Corinthian ἐκκλησία.[76]

It was during the reign of Claudius that Paul's mission to Corinth emerged. Corinth was a colony whose unique history and culture provided a vital opportunity for the Pauline mission. The history of classical Corinth still impacted the civic identity of the newly founded Roman colony.[77] Favorinus chastised the inhabitants of Corinth by saying that they were Romans acting like Greeks,[78] while Philostratus notes that after "Nero had set Greece free . . . the cities went back to their Doric and Attic ways."[79] The Romans in Corinth and throughout the empire,

72. Plin. *HN* 4.6.22; Paus. *Descr.* 7.17.4; Philostr. *V A* 5.41.

73. Romano 2003: 298, n. 89.

74. Kent 1966: 42, no. 82; Edwards 1933: 26, nos. 91–93; West 1931: 18–19, no. 20.

75. West 1931: 28, no. 106; Engels 1990: 17–20; Amandry 1988: 101–2.

76. It would be difficult to demonstrate that Paul was aware of this in a specific way, and the argument here is based on a cumulative case approach rather than noting a specific awareness of this cultural shift by Paul in the letter to the Corinthians. Paul may be seen as a leader of small groups of Christ-followers who is responding to the effects of the transition in civic identity, rather than as one seeking to analyze its cause in an explicit manner. This is quite similar to the way leaders of faith communities engage in their task today.

77. Piérart 1998: 86–87; Bookidis 2005: 151–64.

78. Koenig 2001: 141–44; White 2005: 101. Winter compares the defense of Favorinus with Paul but also concludes that "*Romanitas* was the dominant force in the Roman colony" (2003b: 303 emphasis original).

79. Philostr. *V A* 5.41; Dio Chrys. *Or.* 37.25–27; White 2005: 61–110. It is recognized that Nero gave this freedom after Paul's initial visit in Corinth; however, the time period

as the process of Romanization continued, adopted various components of Greek culture and provided it with a new Roman context.[80] Romans adapted and appropriated the mythological stories of ancient Corinth for their civic purposes (e.g., Bellerophon, Aphrodite, Poseidon and Helios).[81] The transitional nature of Corinthian civic identity led to a unique set of problems and resulted in an approach to mission in which Paul addressed issues related to social identity and the social implications of the gospel. The various local social identities in Corinth[82] had combined with the broader concept of Roman social identity supported by foundation myths, communal markers, and key status-oriented ordering principles to provide a sense of what it meant to be Roman in the principate and the early empire.

There were two broad ethnographical approaches with regard to the myth of Roman origins within the late republic, the principate, and the early empire. The first approach connected Roman identity with non-Greek roots, primarily focused on Trojan ancestry as evidenced by the writings of Vergil and Livy.[83] The second approach emphasized continuity with classical Greece and is exemplified by the writing of Dionysius

---

is close enough to consider it plausible that aspects of this cultural interpenetration were occurring in the mid-50s CE.

80. Hor. *Epist.* 2.1.156–57; cited in Whitmarsh 2001: 9–10. Woolf argues that the Romans enculturated values traditionally associated with the Greeks through a "mixture of adoption, adaptation, imitation, rejection, and prohibition" (1994: 120 and cited in Whitmarsh 2001: 11). The Greek approach to education and the cultural concept of *paideia* are areas in which the Romans relied on the existing cognitive-cultural resources of the Greeks.

81. Fotopoulos 2003: 148–50, Engels 1990: 99–100. For Bellerophon see Str. *Geogr.* 8.6.20, Paus. *Descr.* 2.2.4, 2.4.1, Hom. *Il.* 6.144–221. Robinson (2005: 113) remarks, concerning fountains "Peirene and Glauke," that they were vital "in the formation of" Corinthian "collective identity." For Poseidon and Helios, see Paus. *Descr.* 2.1.6, 2.4.6, 2.5.1–3. Melikertes-Palaimon was also honored in conjunction with the Isthmian games (Gebhard 1994: 94).

82. These social identities could include various family, business, and social identifications; while Corinth was a Roman colony its Greek past continued to influence aspects of civic-religious life. For example, the grid layout followed the plan of Roman "centuriation"; however, many of the buildings in the forum were not aligned with that Roman orientation; rather they maintained their previous Greek alignment (Oakes 2008: 9; Adams and Horrell 2004: 6; Romano 2003: 279–301).

83. Verg. *Aen.* 1.286–88; Livy 1.1; 1.2.6; Ov. *Met.* 13.623–14; Ennius, Cato, and Varro emphasized the Trojan connection as well (*OCD* 1996: 23); cf. Paus. *Descr.* 1.12.2.

of Halicarnassus.[84] Dench rightly notes that the "Romans loved to tell themselves stories in which they viewed themselves, or aspects of themselves, as an 'other people.'"[85] They incorporated and transformed the various people groups they conquered, and their identity functioned based on a socially constructed history that provided legitimation for their position as an imperial power.[86]

Roman social identity, when compared to the "other," was understood to be civilized. Romulus' Asylum as a story of Rome's origins is described by Dionysius of Halicarnassus as a place where those who are "fleeing from their calamities" will find "daily instances of . . . sociability and kindness."[87] Dench remarks, concerning Dionysius' description, that "early Rome is more generally a distinctly civilized place in keeping with the city's truly Greek ancestry."[88] Aeneas serves as a prototype of the one who was the king of a civilized land, defined in contrast to a "barbarous" land.[89]

Markers of Roman Social Identity

The abstract concept of civilization was made concrete through various status-oriented markers of Roman social identity. These include but are not limited to: the toga, citizenship, Latin, and the law. For example, on the *Ara Pacis*, Aeneas is shown with his toga pulled over his head in the posture of a priest, while Jupiter declares that the wearers of the toga are destined to be the rulers of the world.[90] During the Augustan age, "togas" were "an emphatic symbol of . . . Roman identity" even though they were not worn daily.[91] By the time of Claudius, *Suetonius* records a court case in which the disagreement was over whether or not a non-citizen

84. Dion. Hal. *Ant. Rom.* 1.89.1.

85. Dench 2005: 62.

86. Whitmarsh 2001: 12.

87. Dion. Hal. *Ant. Rom.* 2.15.4.

88. Dench 2005: 102. Livy, on the other hand, has no problem describing the early Romans as "rude and uncivilised" (1.8) and Romulus' reign as that of a tyrant (1.16.4). Miles (1995: 153) argues that Livy's narrative resonates with the life of Julius Caesar.

89. Verg. *Aen.* 1.520–60; here 539.

90. Verg. *Aen.* 1.280–84; Suet. *Aug.* 40.5; *gens togata*.

91. Dench 2005: 276–77.

could wear the Roman *toga* or be required to wear the Greek *pallium*.[92] Clothing could serve as a marker of Roman civic and social identity.[93]

Roman citizenship also served as a marker of identity, though it might be difficult to ascertain in certain situations. During the time of Augustus, Suetonius recounts that citizenship was withheld from foreigners so that Roman blood would remain pure.[94] At this stage, citizenship functioned as a marker of identity. In time, however, Claudius would seek to extend citizenship to those throughout the empire, a practice lampooned by Seneca. He wrote, "[Claudius] made up his mind ... to see the whole world in the toga, Greeks, Gauls, Spaniards, Britons, and all."[95]

Language in general was a primary means of determining ingroup and outgroup status. Suetonius describes one encounter with a Roman citizen where Claudius not only chastised "a man of high birth, a leading citizen of the province of Greece, because he did not know Latin; but even deprived him of the rights of citizenship."[96] Cicero argued that the Latin language held the citizenry together even though he acknowledged the existence of Roman citizenship simultaneous with a previous citizenship based on geographic location.[97] If one desired to communicate with a broader audience, however, Greek was preferred since it was still the *lingua franca* throughout the Mediterranean basin.[98]

Roman law provided the resources to legitimate the position of the Romans as the destined rulers of the world.[99] The dynamic construction of law also supports the creation and transformation of social identity. In addition, Roman law and civic administration were a means by which different ethnic and social groups could exist within the empire.[100]

---

92. Suet. *Claud.* 15.2.

93. Nguyen 2008a: 103–4, who cites Epic. *Diatr.* 1.29.42–43.

94. Suet. *Aug.* 40.3–5.

95. Sen. *Apocol.* 3. As the pride and privileges associated with citizenship began to diminish, class emerged as a key indicator of Roman social identity in certain provinces (Heater 2004: 19). The emperor Caracalla issued the *Constitutio Antoniniana* in 212 CE, which provided citizenship to all free inhabitants of the Roman empire (see Dench 2005: 93–151).

96. Suet. *Claud.* 16.2.

97. Cic. *Leg.* 2.2.5; Cic. *Verr.* 5.167; Cic. *Brut.* 140 originally cited in Adams 2003b: 185.

98. Dench 2005: 314.

99. Verg. *Aen.* 1.286–96.

100. Pomp. *Dig.* 49.15.5; *Res Gestae* 6.

Dionysius of Halicarnassus makes it clear that Romulus established a system of just laws at the foundation of the city.[101] The practice of using law as an expression of Roman social identity relates to the way in which jurists appropriated legal precedents within the context of new and changing social environments.[102] Roman law provided a measure of consistency during the expansion of the empire and allowed for the inclusion of various provincial elites and social groups who brought with them social, religious, and cultural practices that may not have cohered with the *mos maiorum*.[103] Roman law combined with Roman myths of origins, social practices (e.g., clothing, citizenship, and language), and with the power of Roman imperialism, which resulted in local expressions of Roman civic and social identity.[104] These markers existed within the broader status-oriented cultural ethos of the Mediterranean basin, an ethos expressed by means of honor and shame expectations, and patron-client relationships, and communicated through kinship language.

THE ORDERING PRINCIPLES FOR ROMAN SOCIAL IDENTITY

Roman social identity formed within the cultural context of honor and shame discourse, relied on the structure of the patron-client system and was made concrete in relationships through the use of kinship language. What follows is not a thorough analysis of these three aspects of identity formation but a discussion of the components of these topics which will have direct relevance for the exegesis of 1 Corinthians 1–4 in this book. These three topics have been the focus of much scholarly attention within New Testament studies and are central to a proper understanding of the cultural framework in which the Pauline communities existed and the Christ-movement emerged.[105]

101. Dion. Hal. *Ant. Rom.* 2.9.1–2. Suetonius reports that Caesar came to understand "his word as law" (*Iul.* 77.1) and that Caligula represented a total disregard for Roman law (*Calig.* 14.1; 29.1). The application of this principle of law was somewhat uneven throughout Roman history.

102. Ulp. *Dig.* 1.1.10.1.

103. Cic. *Top.* 5.28; Cic. *Caecin.* 65–78; Aristid. *Or.* 60, 102; *OCD* 824; Borkowski and du Plessis 2005: 27–8. Huskinson (2000: 7) notes, concerning the *mos maiorum*, that "'ancestral custom' . . . was much quoted in the early empire as a benchmark of social practice, harking back to a supposedly noble past."

104. Balsdon 1979: x; Winter 2002b: 67–99; 1995: 178.

105. The following list includes those New Testament scholars who research honor and shame, patronage, and kinship discourse, and are also referenced in this book:

Honor

Honor functioned as a key status-oriented ordering principle in Roman society. Cicero declared, "By nature we yearn and hunger for honor."[106] Honor is defined by deSilva as "respect for being the kind of person and doing the kinds of things the group values."[107] Moxnes provides the social identity context by noting that "since the group is so important for the identity of a Mediterranean person, it is critical to recognize that honor status comes primarily from *group* recognition."[108] The result of aggregate group evaluation provides the standard by which honor or dishonor is culturally defined.[109] Seneca is often quoted in this regard: "The one firm conviction from which we move to the proof of other points is this: that which is honorable is held dear for no other reason than because it is honorable."[110] Honor provided a system of symbols by which group belonging could be determined and social cohesion maintained.

Since honor was socially constructed, it could be granted in a number of ways. Birth was one significant way in which honor was ascribed,[111] though honor could also be recognized through adoption as it was with Augustus.[112] Also, honor could be earned through grants of citizenship, by entrance into public office, by a display of wealth, through "embody-

---

Moxnes 1996: 19–40; DeSilva 1995, 2000; Malina 2001: 27–57; Jewett 2003: 551–74; Moxnes 1991: 241–68; Elliott 1996: 144–56; Hanson 1996: 62–79; Lampe 2003: 488–523; Esler 1994: 19–36; Hanson and Oakman 1998: 19–97; Malina and Pilch 2006: 331–409; Pilch 2001; Osiek, MacDonald, and Tulloch 2006: 6–12, 194–219; Neyrey 1998: 14–34; Osiek and Balch 1997: 36–87; Johnson Hodge 2007.

106. Cic. *Tusc.* 2.24.58. Hellerman (2005: 35) rightly recognizes the complexity of Roman culture and notes, "it would be overly simplistic, of course, to suggest that honor served as the sole force energizing social relations in the ancient world. Human societies are much too complex to support such reductionism, for other dynamics often come into play." Malina adds the importance of "the symbols of authority, gender status, and respect" that are necessary for a proper understanding of honor (2001: 30; cf. Osiek and Balch 1997: 38–40). Pitt-Rivers (1977: 20) notes the gendered nature of honor. Osiek, Macdonald, and Tulloch (2006: 7–8) conclude that "the honor/shame code was actualized with significant variations [and] by the first century depended on the degree of Roman influence."

107. deSilva 2000: 25; cf. Pitt-Rivers 1977: 1.

108. Moxnes 1996: 20 emphasis original; Dio Chrys. *Or.* 31.20.

109. Dio Chrys. *Or.* 31.17; 1 Cor 4:3.

110. Sen. *Ben.* 4.16.2.

111. Malina and Pilch 2006: 68; Sir. 3.11; Herodas *Mime* 2.32; 1 Cor 1:26.

112. Suet. *Aug.* 1–8; Gal 4:5.

ing virtues prized by the group," or by successfully responding to a public "challenge" in a culture that was highly "agonistic."[113] In a general way, one's name, language, clothing, and treatment by the courts would also have been ongoing indicators of honor.[114]

Shame provides a contrasting framework for understanding honor. Shame is defined in two ways: first it is "being seen as less than valuable because one has behaved in ways that run contrary to the values of the group."[115] Second, it may be understood in a more "positive" manner as "sensitivity to the opinion of the group such that one avoids those actions that bring disgrace."[116] Økland rightly notes that shame affects women and members of the socially lower classes in a way that honor does not.[117] Honor and shame provided the ideological basis for the evaluation of group norms, the establishment of boundaries, and collective behaviors while reinforcing socially accepted presence, performance, and conformity within the various expressions of Roman culture. The concepts of

113. Plin. *Ep.* 10.5–7, 10; deSilva 1995: 228; Phil 3:20; Horsley 2000: 80; Cic. *Cat.* 3.25; deSilva 2000: 28–29. Jewett (2003: 558) remarks that "the new age brought by Christ crucified grants honor to the lowly and brings shame to the boastful, eliminating the social system of 'challenge and response' in the competition for honor." While we are in agreement with Jewett's general approach to the use of honor and shame in Paul, it is not clear that this social structure has been eliminated but rather reprioritized. Paul is capable of redeploying the resources of shame for his broader rhetorical purposes (see 1 Cor 4:14).

114. deSilva 2000: 32. This is evident in the Roman convention of taking the name of one's former master (Clarke 1993: 27–28). With regard to language, it may be the presence of an accent, code-switching, or the refusal to speak the expected language in a given setting (Adams 2003a: 17–19). Clothing relates to the use of the toga by Roman citizens, as well as the width of the purple stripe that was permitted to be worn by certain elites (Kim 2004: 92–95). As for the courts, citizens had access to the courts in ways non-citizens did not and elites were treated more favorably in those same courts as compared to the *humilores* (Stegemann and Stegemann 1999: 63–65).

115. Arist. *Rh.* 2.6.1–3. Neyrey provides a helpful discussion of Aristotle's understanding of shame (1998: 31).

116. Arist. *Rh.* 2.6.14–18; deSilva 2000: 25.

117. Suet. *Aug.* 34–40.5; 1 Cor 14:33b–37. For a further discussion of women see Økland 2004: 201–3, and for the socially lower class see Theissen 2007: 221 and Kim 2008: 59–60, 117. Neyrey (1998: 32) describes this as "the social expectations encoded in the gender stereotype," though it has also been noted that the border between the private and the public was often transgressed in Roman society, and thus it may be too stark to argue for a primarily gendered understanding of shame. Cf. Osiek, Macdonald, and Tulloch 2006: 8–9; Winter 2003a: 40–58.

honor and shame were supported by the status-oriented structures of the Roman patron-client system, discussed next.

Patronage

The Roman patron-client system reinforced social identities throughout the empire. It is defined by Saller as "an exchange relationship between men [sic] of unequal social status."[118] Seneca argues that it was "the practice that constitutes the chief bond of human society."[119] Those involved in this relationship are described as the *patronus* and the *cliens* but other terminology could be used as well.[120] Dionysius of Halicarnassus traces patronage back to Romulus and describes it as an improvement on that "ancient Greek custom" which was defined exclusively in asymmetrical terms. Romulus' patronage system, by contrast, was seen as a "relationship" which supported "a bond of kindness befitting fellow citizens."[121] Dionysius delineates the responsibilities of the patron as well as the duties of the client and concludes that this system is a "superior . . . manner of life."[122] Cicero, on the other hand, connects the honor framework and the patronage system by suggesting that those "who consider themselves wealthy, honoured, the favourites of fortune, do not wish even to be put under obligations by our kind of services."[123] He reflects an elite perspective on the stratified nature of Roman society and then concludes, "It is bitter as death to them to have accepted a patron or to be called clients."[124] The patron-client system functioned as a means of defining intergroup behavior while distributing political power among the emperor and the elites throughout the empire.[125] As with the honor and shame discussion,

---

118. Saller 1982: 8. Chow (1997: 104–25) provides a thorough overview of evidence for patronage in Roman Corinth. Clarke (1993: 135–57) lists the numismatic and epigraphic artifacts for the various Roman leaders during successive eras throughout Corinth and the province of Achaia.

119. Sen. *De Ben*.1.4.2; originally cited in deSilva 1995: 226.

120. Saller (1982: 7–8) warns against assuming that when "the words *patronus* and *cliens*" are employed it follows that patronage is in view. He lists other key terms to notice when studying patronage such as "*amicus . . . officium, beneficium, meritum,* and *gratia*."

121. Dion. Hal. *Ant. Rom.* 2.9.1–3.

122. Dion. Hal. *Ant. Rom.* 2.10.1–4.

123. Cic. *Off.* 2.69.

124. Cic. *Off.* 2.69.

125. Dio Chrys. *Or.* 3.86–90. Moxnes (1991: 245–46, 249–50) provides a useful summary of Dio's thoughts on political patronage employing the language of friendship.

it should be noted that the surviving literary and epigraphic evidence for patronage primarily reflects an elite understanding of the system which functioned as one of the key ordering principles in the maintenance of Roman social identity.[126]

Evidence for patronage in Roman Corinth comes from numismatic, epigraphic, and literary artifacts.[127] Chow has done much work in this area and concludes "that patronage provided *one* of the ways through which relationships in Corinth would have been organized."[128] Patronage may be understood as an ordering principle in the ongoing construction of Roman social identity.[129] Patronage was often expressed through public benefaction (e.g., Gaius Julius Spartiaticus, Junia Theodora, Erastus, and Babbius Philinus). In the Spartiaticus inscription, the patron is identified as "the deified Claudius," and the monument is dedicated "to their patron" by "the tribesmen of the tribe of Calpurnia."[130] Concerning Junia, Winter remarks, "To date, the only official Greek inscription found in first-century Corinth is to a high-class woman who was a Roman citizen residing there (*c.* A.D. 43 or 57)."[131] Erastus served as an *aedilis* in Corinth and paid for the pavement connected to the theater.[132] Babbius appears on "four architectural fragments," and West thinks "that his benefactions were an important factor in the beautification of the colony. In return for his generous gifts, the colony made him *pontifex* and *duumvir*."[133] The political-social structure throughout the empire mirrored a patron-client relationship, with the emperor being the ultimate patron, while his clients functioned as brokers who in turn had clients of their own throughout the population of the empire.[134] This

126. Saller 1982: 10; Fischer 1970: 230–32; Wallace-Hadrill 1989: 63–88.

127. Meritt 1931; West 1931; Edwards 1933; Kent 1966; Amandry 1988.

128. Chow 1992: 124 emphasis original.

129. Lampe 2003: 488.

130. West 1931: 50–53 n. 68; Witherington 1995: 414–15.

131. Winter 2003a: 183, 205–10. These inscriptions describe the various benefactions which Junia provided to those connected with both Lycia and Corinth.

132. Kent 1966: 99–100 n. 232; cf. Gill 1989: 293–300; Meggitt 2004: 219–25.

133. West 1931: 108 n. 132; see Scranton 1951: 21–22; Kent 1966: 73 n. 155.

134. Mart. 2.18. Saller's (1982: 42 ns. 6–8) discussion provides good evidence of the emperor's *beneficia* and his agency in political appointments within the Roman Empire. Specific and helpful examples include: "Magistracies, Governships, and Priesthoods, Sene. *De Ben.* 1.5.1; Citizenship, Pliny *Ep.* 10.5.1; Sene. *De. Ben.* 3.9.2; Freedman status, *Dig.* 48.19.8.12." Each of these examples is listed because of its potential relevance, in a general way, to those living in Corinth.

hierarchical social structure gave access to political power, honor, and influence while providing a means by which the population within the empire could receive resources in the context of "limited good."[135]

The social identity of the patron could be enhanced and expressed by the number of clients loyal to the patron; the size of the morning greetings, the *salutatio*; or the presence of clients at the dinner parties thrown by the patron.[136] These expressions of the patron-client relationship were all designed to increase the honor of the patron rather than the status of the client.[137] However, patronage contributed to the formation of the social identity of the client, as well. It gave the client access to resources that would otherwise be unavailable within the Roman political and economic system (e.g., legal assistance, food, clothing, and money).[138] If clients were involved in a literary patronage relationship such as that of Maecenas with Horace and Propertius, this would allow them to have a measure of control over their literary output while recognizing, as Horace did, that "gifts rarely come with no strings attached."[139] A client could advance both socially and politically through strategic patronage relationships, even entering the ranks of a *novus homo* as did Cicero.[140] Even though friendship language was employed when referring to patronage, Marchal rightly remarks that "these arrangements were also

135. Foster 1965: 296. Foster further describes this as a "cognitive orientation" (1965: 294). Limited good is a way of understanding the way "peasants view their social, economic, and natural universes...as one in which all of the desired things in life such as land, wealth, health, friendship and love, manliness and honor, respect and status, power and influence, security and safety, *exist in finite quantity* and *are always in short supply...* [and] *there is no way directly within peasant power to increase the available quantities*" (1965: 296; see Malina 2001: 89–106; Witherington connects limited good with honor and shame, 1995: 155 n. 12).

136. Mart. 11.24.10–12; Mart. 4.8.1; Tac. *Ann.* 3.55; Suet. *Vesp.* 21. These are all examples of performative aspects of identity.

137. Hellerman 2005: 38.

138. Jones (1935: 357–58) provides evidence for these gifts in the writings of Martial. He cites Mart. 2.32; 12.34; 10.57; 1.20 as evidence of benefactions received from a patron.

139. Hor. *Epist.* 1.7.22–23, 44; cited in Gold 1987: 112, 220 n. 4.

140. Harrison 2003: 202–3. This term is employed here in the broad sense "to designate a variety of political newcomers, including men who were the first in their families to enter the senate, equestrians who reached the consulate, and, perhaps, those of senatorial rank who were the first in their families to becomes consuls" (Dugan 2005: 3). Gleason (1995: xxvi–xxvii) has rightly noted the importance of rhetoric in the formation of the social identity of a new man.

exploitative in nature to the majority of women and men in the lower classes."[141]

Patronage functioned through a set of generally accepted social principles except in the case of freedpersons who had legal requirements associated with their continuing relationship with their former master.[142] Like regular patronage, these requirements also increased the honor of the patron while increasing the status of the client/freedperson by association with the more powerful patron. This is one of the reasons that freedpersons would take the name of their former master and even have it engraved on their gravestones.[143] Furthermore, Kent and West describe Corinthian gravestones which provide evidence of freedmen and their civic involvement, as well as references designed to provide continuing identification with the imperial family.[144]

Corinth was initially populated with freedpersons from Rome who were able to fill positions in the civic government, which would have contributed to their social mobility (e.g., Erastus, Babbius Philinus, Titus Flavius Antio[chus], and Tiberius Claudius Primigenius).[145] Wiseman notes, "The office of *duovir* at Corinth was open to freedmen."[146] Evidence for Erastus and Babbius was mentioned above while Kent catalogs an inscription in which Antio[chus] and Primigenius were described as "outstanding members of the club" (COLLEGIANIs PRIMI<s>). This monument is dated by Kent to around "A.D. 120." Furthermore, he identifies them as a "freedman" and "the son of a freedman" respectively.[147] This unique political situation contributed to the local configuration of Roman social identity in Corinth.

Patronage also functioned within elite circles in which "political allies or personal intimates" would seek to reinforce already existing structures to ensure the continued political success of those involved in

---

141. Marchal 2006: 44.

142. Suet. *Claud.* 25.1–2; cited in Chow 1997: 121.

143. Martin 1990: 48; Chow 1997: 120. Engels (1990: 71–72) provides a brief discussion of the tombstones in Corinth and their relation to changing conceptions of identity.

144. Kent 1966: 113–19; West 1931: 60–61 no. 76 and no. 77; cf. Meritt 1931: 86–91.

145. Str. *Geogr.* 8.6.23.

146. Wiseman 1979: 498; Clarke 1993: 10; Chow 1997: 114–15.

147. Kent 1966: 34–35 no. 62; originally cited in Martin 1990: 30–33.

this "friendship."[148] Plutarch describes this in relation to contrived political discourse, detailing the way *amici* should comport themselves so as to gain a rhetorical advantage while reinforcing the previously agreed-upon course of action.[149] This use of patronage for political benefit flows from the ideological concept of the emperor as the primary patron of the empire so that all within the empire serve as his clients.[150] Chow has noted the lack of "explicit references in Corinth to the early Roman emperors as patrons"; however, the concept of patronage is inherent in naming the colony *Colonia Laus Iulia Corinthiensis*, as well as naming their voting tribes after those associated with the imperial family (e.g., Agrippa and Calpurnia).[151] West remarks that "the tribes of Corinth ordinarily took their names from the *nomina* of relatives or friends of Augustus."[152] The previously mentioned Spartiaticus inscription mentions the tribe of "Calpurnia" which West observes "took its name from Caesar's wife."[153] This inscription also describes Spartiaticus as the patron of the Calpurnia tribe, and Walbank likewise notes that his priesthood would have been by imperial appointment.[154]

Numismatic evidence from Corinth also supports the centrality of the emperor in the patron-client system. By the time of Tiberius severe penalties were associated with the misuse of coins which contained imperial images.[155] By the mid-first century CE, Corinth was functioning as a faithful client of the emperor in Rome.[156] Further, the inner-workings of provincial politics in the Roman Empire were made concrete through

148. Gold 1987: 134; Garnsey and Saller 1987: 149.

149. Plut. *Mor.* 813B; cited in Clarke 1993: 35.

150. Garnsey and Saller 1987: 149–50.

151. Chow also notes both of these 1992: 43–44, no. 1 and no. 2; as does Clarke 1993: 11.

152. West 1931: 91 no. 110.

153. West 1931: 50–53 no. 68, here 53.

154. Walbank 1996: 211–12.

155. Suet. *Tib.* 58. For example, Edwards (1933: 18) catalogs a coin, no. 28, that shows the head of Augustus on the obverse and both Gaius and Lucius on the reverse. Also, no. 40 shows Tiberius on the obverse with the hexastyle temple of *gens Julia* on the reverse (19). Caligula is on no. 45 whilst Claudius is on no. 50. See Chow 1992: 44 n. 3 for further examples. Though the presence of imperial images on coins does not imply emperor worship, it did reinforce imperial ideology and thus was "a useful medium through which to advertise the legitimacy and viability of their governments" (Ando 2000: 215, Suet. reference above originally cited at 221).

156. Walbank 1996: 209.

the use of kinship language. This provided ideological legitimation to those who were being ruled by the *imperium* of Rome.

Kinship

Kinship language was also status-oriented and was employed throughout the empire to reinforce various aspects of Roman social identity.[157] It was designed to create a sense of belonging while providing a nurturing environment in which group norms could be enculturated.[158] Paul uses kinship language in the Corinthian correspondence to form the Christ-followers' social identity as a group who belong to Christ and are thus part of the family of the God of Israel. How does kinship language form identity? It provides a rhetorically constructed family that supplies autochthony, belonging, behavioral norms, and a future orientation and inheritance.

Autochthony may be constructed through a myth of origins, as was seen in the writing of Vergil and Dionysius of Halicarnassus. Johnson Hodge rightly notes that "patrilineal descent [was] the prevailing kinship structure of the ancient world" and that this connection with the past provides legitimation for the identity claim, which she refers to as identity "authenticity."[159] This past was often socially constructed and combined the resources of consent and descent discourse with social memory. Ando provides examples of this in Aelius Aristides, Plutarch, and Tacitus and concludes, "At one level such metaphors arose from the Greek tendency to divide the world into Greeks and barbarians, and on that level their usage must reflect the Greeks' desire to lump themselves together with Romans as common participants in a single ethnic and political reality."[160] Kinship language was employed to provide a socially

157. The concept of fraternal *pietas* is one way in which kinship language formed Roman social identity. See Cic. *Orat.* 1.4. where his devotion for Quintus has social implications for their political activities (see Bannon 1997: 107; see Elliott 2008a: 125–28 for the *pietas* of Aeneas).

158. Hdt. 8.144.2; Stackhouse 1995: 90. Davies (1999: 50) remarks concerning the Herodotus reference that "identity was forged out of the normal processes of human interaction and exchange arising from an agelong awareness of sharing in the same ethnic character, in the same religious tradition, and in the same language."

159. Johnson Hodge 2007: 19, 22; Suet. *Iul.* 6.1.

160. Ando 2000: 69. Esler (2007a: 106) recently argued that the gospel of John presents a similar vision: "John formulates his vision of the identity of Christ-believers, namely, as a decisive movement away from the Judean ethnic identity into which Jesus

constructed past that served as a status-oriented ordering principle throughout the Roman Empire.

Kinship discourse provided a sense of belonging in the context of both intergroup and intragroup interactions which often occurred within the *familia* or the *domus*.[161] Birge describes the family or household as those who "extended backwards in time to include ancestors and forward into the present to include . . . those connected by blood and marriage, slaves, freed persons connected by legal bonds, and clients."[162] This more inclusive understanding of who belonged to the *domus*, according to Garnsey and Saller, was caused by "the rapid turnover of membership in the Roman aristocracy under the emperors" who lacked "an agnatic lineage . . . that would be recognized by their peers from other regions of the empire."[163] Kinship discourse served political purposes, but it was also employed within voluntary associations, argues Harland, as "expression[s] of identity and belonging."[164]

Kinship discourse functioned as a means of social presence and performance while reinforcing collective behavior and conformity to group norms.[165] Augustus employed kinship language in order to effect his moral reforms,[166] invoking the ways of the ancestors as social presence in *Res Gestae* 8: "By new laws passed on my proposal I brought back into use many exemplary practices of our ancestors which were disappearing in our time, and in many ways I myself transmitted exemplary practices to posterity for their imitation." Augustus was described

---

was born to an identity that transcends ethnicity." See p. 67 for a further discussion of Esler's understanding of identity. See Preston (2006: 115–19) for a discussion of the interpenetration of Roman and Greek identity in Plutarch.

161. Ulp. *Dig.* 50.16.195.1–4; Cic. *Q Fr.* 1.3.3. See p. 44 for a discussion of these terms in Tajfel and Turner. Adams 2009: 67–68.

162. Birge 2002: 2.

163. Garnsey and Saller 1987: 129.

164. Harland 2005: 512–13. Harland also cites Plut. *Mor.* 480C; 479C–D; 491B. Aasgaard (2004: 106) provides a helpful discussion on these and other portions of *De frat. amor.* and concludes that it reflects "widespread attitudes towards family life: the need for harmony, the importance of family honour, and the perception of a decline in the quality of family relations." In 1 Corinthians Paul employs this term in 1 Cor 1:10, 11, 26; 2:1; 3:1; 4:6; 7:24, 29; 10:1; 11:33; 12:1; 14:6, 20; 15:1, 31, 50, 58; 16:15.

165. See p. 47 for a discussion of these terms. West (2002: 7–9) supplies an excellent discussion of Augustus and provided the citations of Suetonius that follow in this section.

166. Suet. *Aug.* 34.

as one who was prudent with regard to his clothing, economical in his eating habits, faithful in his childrearing, and respectful in the death of family members.[167] These descriptions were designed to reinforce collective behavior throughout the empire, something Augustus felt was his responsibility. He employed the resources of kinship language because of its rhetorical impact.[168]

The empire was understood as an extended *familia* or *domus* with the emperor as *pater patriae* "the father of the fatherland,"[169] possessing *patria potestas* "power of the father." The kinship structures of the Roman family, argues Severy, "were used by Augustus to consolidate and legitimize his hold on power. He drew on the cultural icon of the Roman father to articulate his relationship to the state, and he came to administer that state through family slaves and freedpersons."[170] In the context of the Roman Empire, kinship discourse was transformed from "domestic patriarchy" into "imperial patriarchy" and contributed to the formation of Roman social identity by establishing behavioral norms throughout the empire.[171]

Kinship language functioned to support claims of imperial success and an *imperium sine fine* "empire without end," a time in which peace and prosperity had come to all under the power of Rome.[172] Augustus is described as a son of a god in the context of a prophecy, "Behold, at last, that man, for this is he, so oft unto thy listening ears foretold, Augustus Caesar, kindred unto Jove. He brings a golden age; he shall restore old Saturn's sceptre to our Latin land."[173] Koester, building on the work of Georgi, remarks, "The Roman world was dominated by prophetic eschatology."[174] Koester lists the following characteristics of Roman imperial eschatology:

> (1) The new age is the fulfillment of prophecy, and it corresponds to the promises given in the primordial age. (2) The new age includes this earth as well as the world of the heavens: Apollo as

167. Suet. *Aug.* 73; 76; 64; 65.

168. Suet. *Aug.* 27.

169. *Res Gestae* 35.1; Suet. *Aug.* 58.

170. Severy 2003: 21.

171. Carter 2001: 197 n. 80.

172. Verg. *Aen.* 1.276–79; Hor. *Carm.* 4.5, 15; West 1997: 185–86, 191–92.

173. Verg. *Aen.* 6.791.

174. Koester 1992: 11; Verg. *Ecl.* 4.

Helios is the god of the new age; the zodiac sign of the month of Augustus's birth appears on the shields of the soldiers. (3) The new age is universal; it includes all nations: the new solar calendar is introduced by the vote of the people of the cities all over the empire. (4) There is an enactment of the new age through the official celebrations of the empire, like the secular festivities of the year 17 BCE, mirrored by the subsequent introduction of Caesarean games in many places. (5) The new age has a savior figure, the greatest benefactor of all times, the *divi filius*, usually translated into Greek as υἱὸς τοῦ θεοῦ—"Son of God"—the victorious Augustus.[175]

Lanci concludes, "Roman imperial eschatology was more than political propaganda. It was a significant part of the matrix of first-century CE Greco-Roman religions."[176] The use of kinship language in the context of imperial eschatology is expressed clearly by Ovid, who connects Augustus, upon his "assumption of the office of *pontifex maximus*," with Aeneas, Julius Caesar, Vesta, and Rome's continued success.[177] The *Ara Pacis Augustae* was a monument in which kinship images functioned as a semiotic discourse of public familial control over Rome by the private family of Augustus. Severy describes this saying, "By 9 BCE Augustus' special responsibility for Rome's relationship with the gods was being presented on the analogy of the father's spiritual responsibility for his family."[178] The discourse of kinship provided the ideological basis for the imperial cult as it developed throughout the early empire and as it came to be practiced in colonies such as Roman Corinth. Kinship language functioned rhetorically to form the social identity of those within the Roman Empire by providing a myth of origins, a socially constructed sense of belonging, a set of communal norms, and an ideological basis for ordering knowledge. It provided the discursive framework for the practice of patronage and reinforced the broader conceptual field of honor and shame throughout the empire. These three status-oriented cultural phenomena (honor, patronage, and kinship) combined with the urban environment, Roman religion, and allegiance to the emperor to support the local construction of Roman social identity and the extension of its empire throughout the Mediterranean basin. The practical

---

175. Koester 1992: 12.

176. Lanci 1992: 6.

177. Ovid *Fast.* 3.419–28; cited in Severy 2003: 102–3.

178. Severy 2003: 113.

wisdom needed to maintain the empire was often the focus of Roman philosophical and educational pursuits.

ROMAN WISDOM

Wisdom within the Roman Empire was focused on the practicalities of life and of ruling an empire.[179] The resources of Greek philosophical ideas were often co-opted and redeployed in the service of imperial ideology, though Ando rightly notes that these Greek ideas were "thoroughly for contemporaries so identified with what they considered Roman that they considered such ideas Roman in origin."[180] "Wisdom" is the English gloss primarily for two Latin words: *sapientia* and *prudentia*.[181] Cicero, in the oft quoted passage from *Inv. rhet.*, discusses the general concept of virtue[182] and concludes, "wisdom (*prudentia*) is the knowledge of what is good, what is bad and what is neither good nor bad."[183] In his description of the way in which wisdom functions, he concludes that "wisdom (*sapientia*) exercises its influence by knowledge (*scientia*) alone."[184] The social framework for wisdom is both private and public; Cicero continues, "the virtue of prudence when displayed in a man's private affairs is usually termed personal sagacity and when in public affairs political wisdom."[185] Stoic concepts of wisdom provided the cognitive resources necessary for the formation of some local expressions of Roman social identity.

Epictetus understood "wisdom" (γνώμης) in the context of "piety" (εὐσεβείας), the way in which one viewed the role of god in the affairs of life.[186] This approach to life was highly deterministic and characteristic of the Stoic understanding of reality.[187] One of the reasons for the acceptance of all that occurred was that it was willed by "God [who] is one and the same with Reason, Fate, and Zeus; he is also called by many

179. Cic. *Part. or.* 22.77–78; see Colish 1985: 83–89.

180. Ando 2000: 47.

181. *OLD* 1509–10, 1690.

182. Cicero defines virtue as "a habit of mind in harmony with reason and the order of nature" (*Inv. rhet.* 2.53.159). Virtue consists of: "wisdom, justice, courage, temperance" (*Inv. rhet.* 2.53.159).

183. Cic. *Inv. rhet.* 2.53.160.

184. Cic. *Part. or.* 22.76.

185. Cic. *Part. or.* 22.76.

186. Epic. *Ench.* 31.

187. Epic. *Diatr.* 1.17.27.

other names."[188] Also, there was a fundamental distrust of the ability of humans to properly judge the appropriateness of a situation; Epictetus records, "It is not the things themselves that disturb men, but their judgments about these things."[189]

Seneca conceived of wisdom as the highest pursuit for humanity. He writes, "Cast away everything of that sort, if you are wise; nay, rather that you may be wise; strive toward a sound mind at top speed and with your whole strength."[190] The pursuit of wisdom was to have practical impact and moral development in those who pursued it and not simply be "the study of words."[191] Seneca's understanding of one who is sagacious is one who "will not upset the customs of the people, nor will he invite the attention of the populace by any novel ways of living."[192] He describes the communal aspect of this wisdom using the concept of the "two commonwealths" (res publicae) to which all humanity belongs, which results in tension between the universal and the local citizenship.[193] For Seneca, wisdom was a political concept that relied on the resources of education for its effectiveness.[194]

Wisdom functioned as a virtue in Stoic thought.[195] The development of wisdom, moral progress, and self-mastery were understood to occur through human agency.[196] Wisdom was thought necessary to enlarge and maintain the empire, an aggregate wisdom to rule that had its basis in the mos maiorum.[197]

---

188. Diog. Laert. 7.135.

189. Epic. Ench. 5, see also 20.

190. Sen. Ep. 17.1.

191. Sen. Ep. 108.23.

192. Sen. Ep. 14.14.

193. Sen. De Otio 4.1–2.

194. Sen. Ep. 88. Stoic wisdom to rule and live well culminates in the emperor Marcus Aurelius. Though his reign is significantly later than the time of Paul's writings, many of the Stoic principles of wisdom evident in Paul's day are also evident in Marcus Aurelius.

195. Diog. Laert. 7.121–28; Cic. Tusc. 5.82.

196. Epic. Diatr. 3.2.1–5; Stowers 2003: 529–31.

197. Rhee 2005: 13; Nguyen 2008a: 74–76.

CORINTHIAN CHRIST-FOLLOWERS
AND CIVIC COMMUNITY

First Corinthians provides evidence for considerable contact with those outside the Christ-movement; however, there is also a lack of evidence for significant conflict with those same outsiders.[198] The letter contains insight into the relations that the Christ-followers had with the broader civic community in Corinth. Their interaction with those outside their community offered opportunities for extending the Pauline mission; however, this connection also created a number of the problems within the ἐκκλησία. Paul ultimately presents this contact as helpful but provides guidelines for the way these relationships should proceed (1 Cor 9:19–23).[199] Paul's writing may be seen as a continuation of his mission which included initial evangelism, community formation, and ongoing nurture (1 Cor 3:1–2; 4:15).[200]

Textual Examples

In 1 Cor 4:8–13, Paul describes the experience of the Christ-followers in Corinth as lacking many of the difficulties that Paul and others within the Christ-movement had experienced. In Corinth, a person's wealth and status were highly valued.[201] This was similar to other cities in the Roman east; however, the demographic makeup of the colony, including the freedpersons and retired military, may have contributed to this community value (1 Cor 4:8; 2 Cor 8:4).[202]

The Corinthian Christ-followers were also confident in the court system. In 1 Cor 6:1–11, Paul argues that they were putting too much confidence in this human institution, which Saunders notes was also "an extension of the imperial powers [and] the Imperial Cult."[203] The courts were not accessible to the majority of individuals in the Roman Empire so the fact that they were engaged in litigious activity suggests

---

198. One piece of evidence for this claim is Paul's expression of judgment within the community against the law courts (1 Cor 6). Also, Paul's collection in 1 Cor 16:1–2 may be seen as an alternative to the established localized version of patron/client benefactions. See further Walters 2005: 397–417.

199. Butarbutar 2007: 167–92.

200. Barram 2006: 10.

201. Williams 1994: 33; Donahoe 2008: xviii–xix.

202. Murphy-O'Connor 1996: 268–73; Thiselton 2006a: 324–25.

203. Saunders 2005: 234.

that at least some within the ἐκκλησία possessed significant financial resources.[204] Paul chastised the Christ-followers for allowing those on the
outside to adjudicate their disputes when their confidence should have
been in the community and its ability to rule on problems, or, even more
appropriately, they should have been willing to be wronged because of
the transformation of their identity "in Christ" (1 Cor 6:7).[205]

The community of Christ-followers' good social relations are also
evident in their willingness to participate in the cultic meals in the various temples in Corinth (1 Cor 8:7–13). The civic identity of the colony
was indistinguishable from its religious identity. This may be the reason
that many of the Corinthians did not see a problem with continuing the
practices mentioned in 1 Corinthians 8. The differences in economic and
social status among the Christ-followers in Corinth may have reinforced
this behavior. Paul, however, understands that this conduct could have
broader implications for his mission and thus encourages liberty in the
context of God's glory.[206]

To extend the previous argument, note that the Christ-followers in
Corinth also dined with outsiders in their homes and in other communal settings (1 Cor 10:27—11:1). If they were not involved in the civic
life of the community, one would not expect this to be a significant issue.
Further, the members of the Christ-movement did not sense the need
to change their approach to their civic life once they had accepted the
gospel.[207] Paul ultimately argues that they might continue their behavior;
however, their social ethics should seek the benefit of others.[208]

Paul also notes that outsiders were visiting the houses that were
being used for community gatherings (1 Cor 14:1–25). This fact appears
to be important in terms of the Corinthians' openness to those who
did not follow Paul's gospel. Who would these outsiders include? They
could be non-adherents, spouses, or guests; in any case, Paul addresses
the community's sense of social-standing and suggests that they present

204. Cf. Friesen 2004: 323–61; Longenecker 2009: 243–78.

205. Cf. Campbell 2005: 307; May 2004: 81–91; Horrell 2000a: 343; Finney 2006:
24–56.

206. Cf. Økland 2004: 160; Fotopoulos 2003: 263; Gooch 1993: 127.

207. Schnabel (2005: 195) provides a good summary of the mission strategy of Paul
in Corinth. He notes specifically, "Instruction concerning moral behavior was imperative for Gentile Christians who had to learn the ethics of the revealed will of God in
theory and in practice."

208. Cf. Winter 2001: 301 n. 58; Fotopoulos 2003: 251; Gooch 1993: 104–8.

themselves in an orderly way, so that the outsiders might not think they were "mad" (μαίνεσθε).[209]

Problems: Social Integration, Wealth, Patronage

Paul presents the relationships that the Corinthian Christ-followers had with outsiders, on the whole, as good and provides guidance on the way to interact with those groups. He sees in this an opportunity and encourages certain behaviors that will further his mission.[210] So how did this type of relationship occur in Corinth? The transitional nature of the Corinthian civic identity was one reason for openness among these Christ-followers, especially in comparison to those in Thessalonica where such openness did not exist.[211] Social integration within the community of Christ-followers did support the broader Pauline mission, but it also contributed to some of the difficulties that are evident in 1 Corinthians.

Wealth was the significant indicator of status in the pre-industrial, agrarian society of the Roman Empire and may have contributed to the internal problems in Corinth. Through the grid of social status, Theissen and Meeks describe the Pauline community at Corinth as a cross-section of rich and poor.[212] Wealth, however, serves as a more effective measure. Friesen argues for an economic model based on seven graduated cat-

209. Winter 2001: 135; Horrell 1996: 183. The apparent interaction with ἄπιστοι and ἰδιώτης is more acutely seen in the Corinthian assembly's gatherings. Paul anticipates a scenario in which these "outsiders" would visit their meetings, which further supports the contention that there was an openness and accessibility to these individuals within the broader civic community. Again, concern for the outgroup predicates on proper behavior within the ingroup. Gehring (2004: 157–66) addresses the issue of the meeting locations, i.e., meeting in homes separately or in one location.

210. Gill 1993a: 337.

211. Barclay 1993: 514. Tellbe (2001: 135) anticipates how certain interpreters of Paul come to understand Paul's negotiation of identity: "Paul draws new boundaries between Christians and non-Christian Jews as well as between Christian and non-Christian gentiles that would ultimately have legitimated a separation from the local Jewish community." Paul should not, however, be held responsible for the way his writing was misunderstood. Oakes argues for methodological sophistication when researching the complex relations the individual communities had with the Roman Empire. In Philippi and Thessalonica he sees conflict with Rome in the life of the communities; however, Oakes (2005: 321) concludes, "He is not writing anti-Roman polemic. Neither is he aiming specifically at preventing participation in the imperial cult." Paul's approach to Roman imperial ideology is particular to each community to which he writes. See also Börschel 2001: 142.

212. Theissen 1982: 94–96; Meeks 1983a: 72–73.

egories of wealth and poverty in the imperial economy and concludes that the majority, if not all of the Pauline community, lived around the poverty line, more clearly defined as subsistence living.[213] Longenecker provides a significant improvement to Friesen's poverty scale and suggests that there is evidence for a larger number of people in the "middling groups" than Friesen allows. Longenecker increases the number of this group to "17% [ES4]."[214] Though Clarke considers the possibility that some within the ἐκκλησία were from the provincial elites,[215] it is also possible that they might have come from this "middling" group rather than from ES1–ES3 which includes the "imperial elites, regional or provincial elites, [and] municipal elites."[216]

Chloe[217] (1 Cor 1:11) and Phoebe[218] (Rom 16:1–2) are candidates for the expanded ES4 category, while the economic location of Erastus (Rom 16:23) is at least ES4.[219] The Pauline community at Corinth closely

213. Friesen 2004: 348; 2005: 352–70. Barclay provides a substantive corrective to Friesen's work and this book follows closely the understanding of Barclay on this issue. He concludes, "perhaps we can say no more than that most of Paul's converts (and Paul himself most of the time) lived at or near subsistence level, though we suspect there were some with more economic means (but we cannot tell precisely who or how much 'more')" (2004: 365–66; cf. Meggitt 1998: 4–5, 50, 73, 179). Friesen's work is similar to Meggitt's without the extensive use of binary categories. Horrell (2004: 358) notes that "Meggitt has downplayed the extent and significance of socio-economic diversity among the so-called non-elite and thus among the early Christians at Corinth." Horrell's article critiques Murphy-O'Connor's conception of house-churches meeting in a Roman villa, and Horrell, for his part suggests the possibility of meeting in one of the upper rooms "on the East Theater Street" (368; cf. Murphy-O'Connor 2002: 178–85). Jewett's (1993: 23–43) suggestion for the existence of tenement churches in Rome and Thessalonica may also be considered for Corinth. Horrell notes Jewett's work as well. Jongkind (2001: 147–48) points out the evidence for tenement housing in Corinth.

214. Longenecker 2009: 262–64, 70. Friesen's chart (2005: 365) included the following levels on the "'Poverty Scale' (PS) PS1 *Imperial Elite*; PS2 *Regional or Provincial Elites*; PS3 *Municipal Elites*; PS4 *Moderate Surplus Resources*; PS5 *Near Subsistence Level*; PS6 *At Subsistence Level*; PS7 *Below Subsistence Level*." Longenecker revised Friesen's "Poverty Scale" and renamed it the "economic scale" [ES] and thus utilizes ES1, ES2, etc. rather than PS1, PS2, etc.; however, Longenecker maintains the same seven category descriptions but adjusts the percentages in those categories (Longenecker 2009: 249–50).

215. Clarke 1993: 57.

216. Longenecker 2009: 245.

217. Chloe (Χλόη) appears to be from ES4, see Friesen 2005: 365–66. Gaius and Stephanas could be included in this group as well (Rom 16:23; 1 Cor 16:17–18).

218. Pheobe (Φοίβη) appears to be a helper/leader (προστάτις) in Cenchraea, who may safely be placed at least on the same level as Chloe, see Meggitt 1998: 148.

219. Rom 16:23 describes Erastus as ὁ οἰκονόμος τῆς πόλεως "city treasurer" and a Christ-follower in Corinth. Kent concluded that the phrase Paul used to describe

mirrored the economic structure within the broader civic community, and Longenecker's argument for an expansion of the "middling" group is a welcome advance in the scholarship.[220]

Some in the Christ-movement in Corinth were undoubtedly poor, and Paul, while at Corinth, received financial support from the Macedonians (2 Cor 11:8–10; see also 1 Cor 7:17–24; 11:22). The ἐκκλησία may have been made up primarily of the group that contained "small farm families, labourers (skilled and unskilled), artisans (especially those employed by others), wage earners, most merchants and traders, [and] small shop/tavern owners" which is categorized by Friesen as PS5 [ES5]. However, they may also plausibly be placed in ES4 and their economic status could then be assessed higher.[221] The shift up in the economic scale would increase the economic disparity within the ἐκκλησία and, correspondingly, the likelihood of difficulties related to Roman social identity (1 Cor 1:26).[222]

A secondary possibility that is often suggested for the internal difficulties relates to confusion over the practice of patronage within the ἐκκλησία.[223] The Corinthian Christ-followers found themselves in a social system that provided social cohesion. The Pauline community was populated by some living at the ES4 and ES5 levels. This situation may have led to a struggle for spiritual prestige and influence and a vying for positions of prominence within the Christ-following community (1 Cor 1:12) similar to that occurring within the broader Corinthian community.

This approach to Paul and his perspective on the civic community brings up an important interpretive distinction of this book. Paul is not seen as a politically subversive figure though Roman imperial ideology is his primary interlocutor, nor is Paul understood as one who seeks to dominate the Christ-followers in Corinth, thereby re-inscribing the imperial practices of the empire. Rather, he is seen as one who seeks

---

Erastus was one that would have been appropriate to someone performing the tasks of an *aedile* in Corinth (1966: 99–100; Clarke 1991: 146–51; 1993: 46–56; Theissen 1982: 75–83; Gill 1989: 298–99; Witherington 1995: 187–88; Meggitt 1998: 140–41; 2004: 225; Friesen 2005: 369).

220. Cf. Stegeman and Stegeman 1999: 291–96; Hanson and Oakman 1998: 112–13, 128; Longenecker 2009: 270–71.

221. Cf. Friesen 2005: 365; Longenecker 2009: 245, 256.

222. Clarke 1993: 45.

223. Chow 1992; Clarke 1993: 85–88.

to form an alternative community with a distinct ethos (i.e., a culturally relevant and specific group identity). We need to briefly address two
scholars whose work differs slightly from the approach presented here.[224]
Thus, we will summarize only the points that are relevant to this study
and then offer a brief analysis of Paul and his civic engagements.

Richard Horsley: Politically Subversive Paul

Richard A. Horsley argues that Paul sought to form "an alternative society" which was in direct "opposition to Roman imperial society."[225] This
alternative ἐκκλησία was necessary because Paul understood himself to
be in an apocalyptic struggle with the powers of darkness (1 Cor 1:20;
2:6–8; 3:12–15; 7:31; 10:11). Thus, the "rulers of this age" are enemies of
God's empire, and for God's mission to be successful in the world the
Roman Empire has to be destroyed.[226] Moreover, Paul's alternative communities are not to conform to the world's expectations with regard to
justice and economic exploitation but are to "maintain their solidarity as
an exclusive community that stands against the larger society."[227]

This book seeks to temper Horsley's approach. First, Paul continues
to use significant aspects of Roman imperial ideology in the formation
of his communities. He relies on the accepted Roman household structure and organizes his communities in a manner that is quite similar to
the hierarchical framework of the larger Roman society.[228] Second, Paul's

---

224. Two other scholars that could be discussed here are Neil Elliott and Peter
Oakes. Elliott's (2008a) approach is quite similar to Horsley's with regard to the high
degree of political subversion in Paul's writing. Oakes (2009: 101–26), on the other
hand, argues that Paul seeks to undermine key aspects of the Roman political system
(e.g., honor, household, hierarchy, patronage, and power). The approach taken in this
book understands Paul as less subversive than Horsley, Elliott, and Oakes because he
still functions effectively within the Roman political and religious landscape; however,
it does not follow that we view Paul as completely overtaken by the Roman political
structure the way Marchal (2008: 96) does.

225. Horsley 1997: 242.

226. Horsley 1997: 244; 1 Cor 15:24–28.

227. Horsley 1997: 252.

228. In 1 Cor 3:23, Paul's argument relies on a hierarchically ordered subordinate
function (see Garland 2003: 125). Elliott (2008a: 143) contends that "Roman imperial
ideology promulgated just such a hierarchy, with the descendants of Aeneas at the top
and unworthy peoples—including the Judeans—beneath them." In 1 Cor 1:16, Paul
draws on the existing household structure in his baptism of Stephanas' "houseful."
Adams (2009: 66–68) suggests using the concept of "houseful" in which "coresidence"

rhetoric often appears rather binary in its formulation; however, that may be a function of his apocalyptic worldview rather than a complete rejection of the world's political system. For example, in 1 Corinthians 1–2 it may appear that Paul sees no continued usefulness for the world's wisdom, but his concern is specifically with wisdom when it is used for salvific purposes. Thus, he is not against wisdom in general. The same may be said for the use of rhetoric. Third, Horsley's conception of Paul's approach to communal formation sees the ἐκκλησία as a sect. However, Paul's expectation for mission as social integration in Corinth argues against the primarily sectarian nature of community in Corinth (1 Cor 5:9–10; 10:31—11:1). Thus, rather than an "alternative society" opposed to the empire this book argues for an alternative community with a distinct ethos.[229] The ἐκκλησία in Corinth then is more differentiated with regard to the empire. It is resistant to it at certain points while being consonant with it at others.

Paul was politically subversive in Horsley's reconstruction but not in a straight-forward manner. The gospel opposed the empire most acutely with regard to "the whole system of hierarchical values, power relations, and ideology of 'peace and security' generated by the 'wealthy, powerful, and nobly born' and dominated by 'the rulers of this age,' at the apex of which stood the imperial savior."[230] Overall, Horsley's work is a welcome corrective with regard to understanding Paul's interlocutor as the Roman Empire rather than Judaism, but the egalitarian impulse that Horsley sees in Paul is not evident in his letters. Paul's approach focused on the continued relevance of previous social identities which included gender (1 Cor 7:17–24; 12:13). Furthermore, Paul is quite comfortable using many of the same power relations that were evident within Roman society (1 Cor 4:17; 16:16). So, it may be better to argue that Paul rejects the pretentious use of power. Finally, Horsley is quite correct in asserting that the ideological bases from which the Roman Empire and the Christ-movement function are in opposition. In many ways, the battle between

---

could occur without the extension of "family ties." Furthermore, 1 Cor 7:17–24 may be understood in the context of existing cultural household structures.

229. In a sense, it was alternative to the existing identity forming ordering principles within the Roman Empire. However, it does not follow that Paul was seeking the overthrow of the empire through his mission to the nations.

230. Horsley 2004: 3.

these two movements was an ideological battle; in this Horsley's work is quite helpful.

Joseph Marchal: Paul as a Defender of the Status Quo

Joseph Marchal argues that Paul uses the ideological resources of the Roman Empire and that he provides a rationale for maintaining the status quo within the imperial context. Thus, he is far from a critic of the empire and is not politically subversive but participates in the continuation of patriarchal structures on which the empire was founded. Marchal's work has been in Philippians, but it is relevant here in that he questions Horsley's view that Paul was aligned against the Roman Empire. Marchal's study of the rhetorics of the text of Philippians focuses on Phil 3:18–21 and 2:6–11 as examples of existing malestream interpretations which present Paul as anti-imperial, but it overlooks significant discourses of power evident in the text. Musa Dube's four questions guide Marchal's research, which uncovers rhetorics of imperialism that call into question the accepted view that Paul was anti-imperialistic.[231] Instead, he is seen one who "reinscribes and mimics the imperialism of his time."[232] For Marchal, Paul uses power for domination in a manner quite similar to the leaders within the empire. The rhetorics of imitation and the resources of the postcolonial concept of mimicry are critiqued and redeployed by Marchal. Mimicry is found to be a less than useful concept when it does not fully take into account issues relating to "gender, as well as ethnicity, sexuality, and empire."[233] Marchal's solution is to replace Bhabha's understanding of mimicry with a more complex heuristic framework that builds on the work of Rey Chow, Anne McClintock, and Meyda Yeğenoğlu.[234] Ultimately, Paul's rhetorics

231. Marchal (2008: 23) notes that "Dube list four questions that can be used to evaluate ancient texts on their literary-rhetorical grounds: 1. Does this text have a clear stance against the political imperialism of its time? 2. Does this text encourage travel to distant and inhabited lands, and how does it justify itself? 3. How does this text construct difference: is there dialogue and liberating interdependence or condemnation of all that is foreign? 4. Does this text employ gender and divine representations to construct relationships of subordination and domination?"

232. Marchal 2008: 55.

233. Marchal 2008: 88.

234. Marchal (2008: 74–5; 84–6) does this by incorporating Chow's three levels of mimeticism and McClintock and Yeğenoğlu's work on the intersection of gender and colonial mimicry. These combine into "multiple intersecting categories of analysis" so

of imitation are described as "a version of coercive mimeticism" and a continuation of the power discourse of Roman imperial ideology.[235]

While Marchal provides a corrective to the reading of Horsley, we remain unconvinced with regard to the following. First, Marchal's understanding of Paul's discourse as "power-over" is too limited and requires further qualification. Kathy Ehrensperger has argued persuasively that Paul also uses power for transformation: "power-to" or "power-with."[236] Moreover, Marchal's conclusion that Paul's imitation discourse is a form of "coercive mimeticism" fails to account fully for the presence of educational discourse. Ehrensperger also argues that Paul's teaching on imitation "actually demands . . . creativity and self-responsibility . . . in the formation of their lives in Christ."[237] Marchal is correct to see in Paul's rhetoric discourses of imperialism; however, his approach to Paul and imperialism over-corrects in the areas of hierarchy and household. It may be suggested that for Paul, it was Christ *and* Caesar except in those areas in which ideological positions conflicted, and in those areas it was Christ whose lordship was adhered to because the community belonged to God through Christ.

When we argue that Paul's primary interlocutor was Roman imperial ideology, it would be easy to assume this follows the approach of Richard Horsley. However, we will argue that Paul is against Caesar in a differentiated manner. This approach might lead one to conclude that we follow Joseph Marchal in arguing that Paul was thoroughly immersed in an ideology cognizant with an imperial worldview. However, we wish to maintain a middle path between the work of these two fine scholars. It will be evident that at key places in his discourse Paul is offering a critique of the epistemic resources of the world and its power, which for Paul was the Roman Empire (i.e., rejection of the world's wisdom and power). On the other hand, there are significant places in which Paul is seen to be arguing in a manner that is quite similar to that of those in power within the Roman Empire (i.e., acceptance of household and hierarchy).

----

that "the letter to the Philippians can also be read as a cross-gendered, cross-ethnic argument for imitation within an imperially militarized zone."

235. Marchal 2008: 78, 88.

236. Ehrensperger 2007: 133.

237. Ehrensperger 2007: 154.

CONCLUSION

This chapter found that there is evidence that the civic identity in Corinth was in transition during the first century CE and that this may shed light on the rhetorical situation to which Paul was responding. We established a definition of Roman imperial ideology and then demonstrated the Roman character of Corinth. It was then discovered that the Greek past of Corinth continued to influence civic life within the Roman colony. The foundation and key markers of Roman social identity were examined (i.e., urbanism, religion, and the emperor), and the role of Mediterranean status-oriented ordering principles were found to be culturally significant in the local maintenance of that identity. Finally, it was revealed that the Christ-followers in Corinth showed no evidence of having difficulties with the civic authorities, and 1 Corinthians actually suggests that some had integrated into the civic and social life of the community. This chapter furthers the argument of this book by concluding that it is probable that the group divisions within the ἐκκλησία in Corinth were based on varying levels of civic and social identifications with key aspects of Roman social identity. Thus, with these details established, we can turn to a Social Identity Theory reading of 1 Corinthians 1–4 to test the hypothesis that issues related to group belonging and Roman social identity were Paul's concern in 1 Corinthians 1–4.

5

The Foundation and Framework for Salient "in Christ" Social Identity

INTRODUCTION

T HE PURPOSE OF THIS chapter is to read 1 Corinthians 1:1–9, which serves as the letter opening and thanksgiving, in order to determine the way Paul lays the foundation and describes the framework for social identity formation in 1 Corinthians 1–4. The foundation[1] is understood as God's calling in Christ and supports staying in the social situation in which one received his or her calling (1 Cor 7:20). Furthermore, the framework[2] is described as God's grace, understood as the concrete processes related to God's gifts and the reciprocal responses to those gifts.[3]

---

1. The centrality of group beliefs in the formation of social identity is fundamental to the work of Bar-Tal (1990: 36) who defines group beliefs "as convictions that group members (a) are aware that they share and (b) consider as defining their groupness." The lack of "in Christ" identity salience in Corinth is related to a misunderstanding of some of these group beliefs, which had occurred since Paul had left the community (Winter 2001: 4). Paul writes 1 Corinthians, in part, to correct the way the Corinthians understand and interpret core convictions that from Paul's perspective, should be defining the group and providing it with internal cohesion (Bar-Tal 2000: 35). This foundation of social identity is expressed by Paul through the use of calling language.

2. The framework for identity, as understood in this context, is a partial and contingent description of the broader, complex process of identity formation. The framework in view here is one that focuses on the way Paul's discourse contributes to key components of this process, accessible to the reader through the text of 1 Corinthians. The framework of God's grace is revealed in 1:4–9 and contains verbal, cognitive, and behavioral components, all of which are central to Tajfel and Turner's SIT/SCT approach to social identity formation (1979: 33–47).

3. Crook (2008: 25–38) convincingly argues that χάρις is "grounded in the ancient system of patronage and benefaction."

THE FOUNDATION FOR SALIENT "IN CHRIST" SOCIAL IDENTITY: GOD'S CALL (1:1–3)

The beginning of ancient Greek letters normally followed a rather programmatic pattern.[4] Paul adheres to the general contours of accepted epistolary practice; however, in his longer letters the salutation and the thanksgiving sections may indicate the topics that are to be addressed.[5] First Corinthians is such a document, and the opening of the letter serves an important teaching function for those who hear the letter read.[6] It functions as the "surrogate" presence of the author who is absent from the addressees (1 Cor 5:3–5).[7] It creates rhetorical spaces that "carry the residue of history upon them, but also, perhaps, something else: a physical representation of relationships and ideas."[8] Paul, in writing this letter

---

4. Porter (1997: 569) summarizes some of these issues, "the epistolary opening has a number of formal features, such as the greeting and thanksgiving . . . which are part of performing certain functions in the letter, such as establishing and maintaining contact between the sender and recipients and clarifying their respective statuses and relationships." Cf. Mitchell 1991: 22; Witherington 1995: 47. Both Mitchell and Witherington rely on the resources of rhetorical criticism to understand Paul's structure in 1 Corinthians.

5. Horsley 1998: 39; Cousar (1996: 28) argues that the opening of 1 Corinthians "telegraphs important themes in the body" of the letter. Cousar only includes 1:4–7 in his analysis. However, 1:1–9 contains similar themes, which are explicated throughout the letter. Klauck (2006: 306) sees an "elaboration of the recipients in 1:2, and an extended thanksgiving that serves as the proem in 1:4–9." Richards (2004: 132) asserts that, because Paul uses it in a specific way, "he places his thanksgiving at the beginning of the letter (right after the 'sender to recipient'), which was a less common location for a thanksgiving." This provides a rationale for including 1:1–9 in this book when the discourse unit proper is 1:10—4:21. Thus, we follow Schnabel's (2006: 82) contention that „Die semantische Kohärenz von 1,10—4,21 wird im allgemeinen nicht bestritten, aber unterschiedlich beschrieben." But cf. Jewett 1978: 389–444; Ciampa and Rosner 2006: 212–13.

6. Harvey (1998: 156–57) identifies the oral patterning in 1 Corinthians. Partridge (2007: 76) connects individual identity with communal existence in relation to performance. Porter (1997: 540) recognizes the fact that these letters were read publicly but is convinced that "the way in which this would have been done" is beyond reconstruction.

7. Dormeyer (1998: 205–7) notes the significant parallels with "friendship letters" exemplified by Pseudo-Demetrius *Typ. Epist.* 1.

8. Mountford 2001: 42. Code (1995: 7) thinks that the discussion on rhetorical space relates closely to issues of power, in that rhetorical spaces "produce uneven possibilities of establishing credibility and being heard."

to the Corinthian Christ-followers, provides these discursive[9] representations where the negotiation of social identity may occur (1 Cor 3:16).

God's calling is the foundation of a salient "in Christ" social identity. This statement raises the question: what is the significance of the circumstances of one's call? The argument put forth here is that Paul's use of calling language in 1 Corinthians indicates that existing social identities are of fundamental significance and not obliterated[10] "in Christ." They continue albeit in a transformed manner. In 1 Corinthians, calling language is focused primarily in chapters 1 and 7. The noun κλητός occurs in 1 Cor 1:1, 2, 24 while the verbs ἐπικαλέω occurs in 1:24, and καλέω occurs in 1:9; 7:15, 17, 18, 20, 21, 22, 24.[11] The adjective κλῆσις occurs in 1 Cor 1:26 and 7:20.

Paul's discourse of calling is a foundational ordering principle in the formation of a salient "in Christ" social identity. In 1 Cor 1:1, Paul uses calling as an indicator of a key identity position in his mission; he is "called by the will of God to be an apostle of Christ Jesus." Furthermore, one of Paul's first corporate descriptors of God's ἐκκλησία in 1 Cor 1:2 is that they are "called to be holy." The Corinthians' primary social identification, their public displays of devotion and their ritual expressions of faith (i.e., group norms) are founded in God's call. In 1 Cor 1:9, the Corinthians' call is further given a focal point; they are "called into the fellowship of his Son." Finally, in 1 Cor 1:1, Paul's call "to the nations" has its basis in Israel's scriptures, as does the Corinthians' corporate call as gentiles "in Christ" (Jer 1:5; Isa 42:6).

God's call does not obliterate ethnic identities; rather, in 1 Cor 1:24, they continue to be part of Paul's social categorization of those who understand the salvific importance of Christ: "but to those who are called, both Jews and Greeks, Christ the power of God and the wisdom of God." In 1 Cor 7:20, Paul writes, "In the call (κλήσει) in which each was called (ἐκλήθη), in this remain (μενέτω)." Often the call is restricted only to the

9. Baynham 2006: 378–81; Gumperz and Cook-Gumperz 1982: 7.

10. This does not mean that key aspects of a person's social identity remain unchanged. It is clear from 1 Cor 6:9–11; 10:7, 8, 14, 20–21 that some transformation is required. First Corinthians 7:17–24 addresses the way certain identities continue "in Christ." This principle may be applied, by extension, to other social identities except in those places where they violate the social implications of the gospel.

11. In 1 Cor 10:27, "calling" relates to being invited to eat with an unbeliever, while in 1 Cor 15:9 it refers to Paul's unworthiness to be called an apostle. These two uses are irrelevant for the present discussion.

call to be a Christ-follower. However, is this limited interpretation warranted? First, in 1 Cor 1:26, Paul uses κλῆσις in the context of existing social identities. He writes, "for consider your calling (κλῆσιν)." Fitzmyer rightly contends that the use of κλῆσις is broad and includes ethnic and social identities in which the call to faith is received.[12] The circumstances related to one's call continue to be relevant within the Christ-movement (1 Cor 1:26; 7:20). Thus, in the context of Corinth we must inquire into the relevance of Roman social identity.

In 1:1, Paul's theologizing concerning "calling" (κλητός)[13] forms his identity and also the identity of the community in Corinth and serves as the first of two vital concepts in Paul's identity-forming strategy. God's call and will (θελήματος) establish a position for Paul within the community from which to encourage the Corinthians to live in a specific manner. Sosthenes is also mentioned as Paul's co-writer. He thus, by extension, has received a call similar to that of Paul.[14] Paul was in an asymmetrical relationship with the Corinthians; however, it does not follow that this was a relationship in which he was the only communal authority figure.[15] Sosthenes, who may have been another authority figure, is identified with the kinship term "brother" (ἀδελφός).[16]

Paul's Jewish identity interpreted through the Christ-event establishes the position from which he argues in 1 Corinthians.[17] As one thor-

---

12. Fitzmyer 2008: 308.

13. Harrison (2003: 274) notes parallels with Epictetus and his "Cynic mission" (Epict. *Diatr.* 1.29.47). Paul employs κλητός twice, ἐπικαλέω, and καλέω in 1 Cor 1:1–9. 1 Corinthians 7:20 is key to understanding a particularistic approach to social identity in Paul, and it also contains καλέω. BDAG 549, 373, 502–4; M&M 318, 348.

14. Murphy-O'Connor 1993: 562–79. For simplicity Paul will be referred to as the writer of the letter. Keener (2005: 20) avers that "Sosthenes may have been Paul's rhetorically proficient scribe (cf. Rom 16:22), helping with multiple devices that counter criticism of his speech." Aasgaard (2004: 297) sees in the use of the article with the kinship language an extension of "authority" to Sosthenes both among "the addressees" and Paul.

15. Ehrensperger 2007: 35–36; Richards (2004: 119–20), in reflecting on the nature of Paul working among other leaders in the Christ-movement, suggests "the authorial voice of 'Paul' was a 'we.'"

16. Aasgaard 2004: 2, 48, 124; See p. 113 for a discussion of kinship.

17. Harré and Van Langenhove (1998a: 9) argue that this position is constantly shifting, reflecting "the meaning of speech-acts and other forms of behaviour itself as it occurs within the confines of a mutually agreed upon context which can [be] called the narrative convention." So, this narrative positioning is one way in which texts can form identity.

oughly embedded in Judaism, Paul argues in a manner similar to Israel's prophets, and thus analogs to his arguments are to be found primarily in the Hebrew Bible. This view, however, is contested by Malherbe who remarks, on the contrary, that when Paul argues he relies on "hellenistic elements," and when Paul engages in "pastoral care" he appropriates this tradition more "than most of his pagan contemporaries."[18] However, while Paul was influenced by a combination of elements, a methodological reason to first look for analogs from moral philosophers whose worldview would have been so different from Paul's is unclear. Malherbe's approach is also related to the fact that, for him, Paul's "self-understanding and theology" are "at once Hellenistic and Christian" so that he overlooks the important fact that Paul never left Judaism.[19] Moreover, Wilk's work provides another way forward by offering the two categories of Paul's self-understanding (Selbstverständnis) and the impact of the Christ-event (Christusbotschaft). These two important organizing rubrics provide a framework for understanding Paul's apprehension of the prophetic tradition of Israel.[20] However, this is not to say that the Roman identity of the Corinthian Christ-followers did not impact the way they heard Paul's arguments; it undoubtedly did. Nor does this viewpoint argue for a binary relationship between Judaism and Hellenism. There was, to a certain extent, mutual interaction and redefinition between both symbolic universes.[21]

The "call" (κλητός) of God establishes the foundation of the community, as well as the exercise of leadership among its teachers. Calling language is central to the discourse of 1:1–9, and it assures the community that their origin is from God, in opposition to that of other voluntary associations.[22] In 1:1, Paul reminds the Corinthians of his

18. Malherbe 1989: 76–77.

19. Campbell (2006a: 51) dates the parting of the ways to "around 160 C.E." See below the discussion of 1 Cor 9:20–21 on n. 51 p. 139. Dunn (1999: 179), though he would not agree with the implications of the argument being made here, does acknowledge that Paul did not "convert from one religion ('Judaism') to another ('Christianity'), since the term 'Christianity' did not yet exist, and the Nazarene movement was still within the matrix of Second Temple Judaism."

20. Wilk 1998: 340–80, 401–8. See Sandnes (1991: 218) on the use of the prophetic tradition.

21. Meeks 2001: 136.

22. Ascough (2002: 3; 2003: 47–70) interacts with the ways in which both groups were similar and dissimilar. Schrage (1991: 102) contrasts this with the Corinthians' position

calling and re-positions himself as one who has some level of temporal authority within the ἐκκλησία. Harré and Van Langenhove note three ways the "discursive practices of positioning" express identity: "by stressing one's agency in claiming responsibility for some action; by indexing one's statements with the point of view one has on its relevant world; or by presenting a description/evaluation of some past event or episode as a contribution to one's biography."[23] Paul's discursive strategy in 1 Corinthians includes all three of these. This calling and his role in the foundation of the community re-establish his position so as to allow him to effect the formation of the Corinthians' social identity. The calling of God thereby positions Paul within the community and in 1:2 provides the impetus for holy living. God's call works equally to establish identity both for Paul and for the Corinthian Christ-followers.

Paul re-establishes a transformative asymmetrical power relationship with the community by reminding them that he is an "apostle from Christ Jesus" (ἀπόστολος Χριστοῦ Ἰησοῦ). His identity as an apostle is central to his identity-forming agenda.[24] Horsley understands Paul to be "responding to the challenge to his authority."[25] However, he too quickly reads conflict into the relationship. The use of ἀπόστολος does not require the challenging of this term among the community. Moreover, apostleship has its basis in the Hebrew Bible's concept of one who is God's messenger (cf. Isa 18:2; Jer 49:14). One of the reasons for Paul's concern for the formation of identity within the community is that he was seeking their stability since he would not always be with

---

as an eschatological community: „Sie sind Gemeinde der Endzeit, von Gott gerufen und ihm zugehörig, nicht irgendein Mysterienverein oder eine Kultgenossenschaft." Aasgaard (2004: 116) recognizes the similarities in relation to kinship language that "it served to strengthen the common identity and sense of belonging of the members of these groups [voluntary associations] which had many features in common with the Christian communities."

23. Harré and Van Langenhove 1998b: 62. Hays (1997: 15 emphasis original) takes the view that "God's *call* . . . both authorizes and motivates his mission. It is God, not Paul, who ultimately initiates and drives the proclamation." Schütz (2007: 134) notes that Paul's call is central to his self-understanding.

24. Taylor (2005: 99) recognizes "that apostleship of Christ was a defining aspect of Paul's self-identity." He also goes on to say that this "is widely recognized in scholarship." While this is true, the social identity of Paul's apostleship is the focus of this current study, and this aspect, though not completely disconnected from his self-understanding, is somewhat under-researched, due in part to the way in which identity is used as a heuristic device within New Testament studies.

25. Horsley 1998: 39.

them. Ehrensperger describes this as planned obsolescence, and it is central to Paul's discourse.[26] Though he was in a hierarchical relationship with the community, he did not exercise power in a dominating manner. Mutuality and the recognition of difference are key components in Paul's apostolic practice.[27]

The needed transformation within the Corinthian community will not be accomplished by Paul alone. The agency of other leaders is vital to the process. Sosthenes is an example of one of those leaders, and later Timothy (1 Cor 4:17) will serve as a prototypical member of the ingroup conceived of by Paul.[28] There is no way to determine whether this is the same Sosthenes mentioned in Acts 18:17.[29] What is important in this reference to Sosthenes is the reminder that Paul was not a solitary authority figure proclaiming the gospel around the Mediterranean basin but one who worked within a group of teachers strengthening communities of Christ-followers throughout the Roman Empire (1 Cor 16:19–20).[30]

Sosthenes is referred to as "the brother" (ὁ ἀδελφός). The use of the definite article indicates he was already known within the Corinthian community; furthermore, based on 1 Cor 16:15–16, he also may be described as a group prototype.[31] Identity as an important category of Christ-movement discourse is supported by the centrality of kinship and ethnic language in the soteriological and anthropological discourse within Paul's letters. Johnson Hodge concludes that Paul "teaches the gospel using ethnic and kinship language to articulate God's plan for salvation *in terms* of these identities."[32] Moreover, Nanos argues that this kinship language extends to fellow Jews, as well as to members of the Christ-movement.[33] Finally, Hays thinks that Paul's understanding of kinship and thus a "new self-understanding might have been difficult

---

26. Ehrensperger 2007: 126; Hays (1997: 16) describes Paul as one who wrote with "considerable political tact."

27. Ehrensperger 2004: 194; Odell-Scott 2003: 15–30.

28. Thiselton 2000: 69; Esler and Piper 2006: 35. The relationship with Apollos as a co-worker will be discussed on p. 213.

29. Garland 2003: 26.

30. Furnish 1961: 369.

31. Esler and Piper (2006: 18) apply this concept to Mary, Martha, and Lazarus.

32. Johnson Hodge 2007: 9 emphasis original.

33. Nanos 1996: 110–13.

for newly formed Christian communities . . . to grasp and internalize."[34] While kinship and ethnic categories may not appear in contemporary definitions of Christian identity, it does not follow that they were not central to the theologizing of Paul within his communities.

Identity is supported through the act of naming in 1:2. Carter asserts, concerning Matthew's community, that "names secure separation from other communities, reinforce group identity, and warn this community not to be like other groups."[35] Paul and Sosthenes name this group in ways that lay the foundation for their social identity. First, they are "God's *ekklēsia* in Corinth" (τῇ ἐκκλησίᾳ τοῦ Θεοῦ τῇ οὔσῃ ἐν Κορίνθῳ) and thus are not to be like other civic groups because they belong to God. Second, they are "sanctified by means of Christ Jesus" (ἡγιασμένοις ἐν Χριστῷ Ἰησοῦ), and so the Corinthian Christ-follower's lifestyle is to be distinct from those not "in Christ." Third, the Corinthians have a calling (κλητοῖς ἁγίοις) which underlines the purpose and unique plan for their community. Fourth, the Corinthians are part of a larger group of Christ-followers, "together with all those who in every place call upon the name of our Lord Jesus Christ, both their Lord and ours." This strengthens the Corinthians' ingroup identity and provides the appropriate superordinate group with which to relate.[36] The Christ-followers' social identity expressed in Corinth is also a reflection of the social identity of the other Pauline communities throughout the Mediterranean basin as evidenced by the Corinthians' commitment to assist those in Jerusalem (Gal 2:9–10; Rom 15:25–27; 1 Cor 16:1–4; 2 Cor 8–9).[37] In 1:2, Paul begins to negotiate the social identity of the Corinthian Christ-followers through naming them in a manner that reflects the call of God. Then in 1:3, Paul introduces aspects of the distinct ethos which should characterize them.

Paul names the group "the *ekklēsia* of God," which furthers his focus on the corporate nature of identity in this letter. Schrage contends, "Despite of all the problems and confusions, Paul holds on to the eschatological quality of the addressees."[38] Paul's conception of ἐκκλησία

34. Hays 1997: 19.

35. Carter 2000: 9. Brawley (2005: 22) contends that "the absence of a name for this group in Acts complicates social identity from the beginning."

36. Jenkins 1996: 105.

37. Harrison 2003: 309–13.

38. Schrage 1991: 102 author's translation.

finds its analog within the alternative community envisioned by Israel's prophets.

Walter Brueggemann compares formation in the prophets to community formation as it seeks to "nurture, nourish, and evoke a consciousness and perception alternative to the consciousness and perception of the dominant culture around us."[39] Horsley, on the other hand, understands the ἐκκλησία as "basically political" and a group which "constituted an alternative to the established assembly of the city of Corinth."[40] While we are in agreement with Horsley in terms of the "alternative" nature of the group, there was more continuity with the existing political structures than Horsley allows. Paul's alternative communities were both contiguous and dis-contiguous with Rome.

Scholars debate the source of Paul's use of ἐκκλησία. For example, Fee connects Paul's usage with the LXX references "to Israel as a gathered people (Deut. 4.10)."[41] Horsley not surprisingly sees Paul "utilizing the standard deliberative forms and the standard terms of Greco-Roman political rhetoric to argue for the unity and concord . . . of the body politic."[42] Finney concludes, "Writing to a predominantly Gentile audience, Paul may well have employed *ekklesia* not only to represent a 'cultic community' as such, but more pertinently to represent the assembly of those who are 'in Christ,' in pointed juxtaposition and 'competition' with the official city assembly."[43] This may be a place in which issues of cultural translation created communication difficulties within the Christ-movement. However, it seems slightly more plausible that Paul's use of ἐκκλησία most closely approximates the meaning of this term within the prophets (Joel 2:16). This community belongs to the God of Israel.[44]

Paul's rhetoric at this point geographically limits God's ἐκκλησία to the one "in Corinth." As the previous chapter argues, Corinthian civic/social identity was in transition during the first century CE, which may

39. Brueggemann 2001: 3.

40. Horsley 1998: 40.

41. Fee 1987: 32.

42. Horsley 2000: 74.

43. Finney 2005: 27; cf. Aristot. *Pol.* 45; Thuc. 1.87; Xen. *Hell.* 1.7.9; Joseph. *AJ* 12.164; 19.332.

44. Fee (1987: 31) contends that Paul's description of the community emphasizes the fact that "the church belongs to God (cf. 3:9), not to them or to Paul (or Apollos), and by this slight change in address Paul disallows at the outset one of their tendencies—to think too highly of themselves."

provide general background for the way Paul argues in 1 Corinthians. Some in the Corinthian civic community relished their past glory as a famous Greek city while positioning themselves to be more influential within the political environment in the Roman east.[45] The Romans, for their part, desired the autochthony inherent in Greek culture while the Greeks desired a share of power within the empire, at least on the local level.[46] Spawforth argues for the mutual political benefit for local governing elites as well as Roman officials who were enamored with the Greek athletic contests.[47] The resulting hybridity of Roman and Corinthian social identity may also have been occurring within the Christ-following community as they sought to live their life together in light of the coming of Israel's messiah.[48]

Paul's desire for holiness within his communities has its basis in the Corinthians' participation with Christ.[49] He argues that they "have been sanctified by means of Christ Jesus." The implications of this union with Christ include a sense of consecration, which leads to a reorientation of the Corinthians' moral framework (1 Cor 1:18—2:5), a resocialization of their social structures (1 Cor 3:1–4), and a reconfiguration of their cognitive outlook (1 Cor 2:14–16). All of these are evident in 1 Corinthians 1–4 and combine to strengthen the Corinthians' identity "in Christ." So being "in Christ," while having specific soteriological implications, is to be understood within the framework of an emerging social identity. Social-scientific approaches to New Testament interpretation

45. Str. *Geogr.* 8.6.20–23; Paus. *Descr.* 2.1.1—5.5; Cic. *Rep.* 2.7–9.

46. Whitmarsh (2001: 175–78) discusses the way the exile trope was used for purposes of identity formation by Greek speakers in the Roman Empire. Cf. Dio *Or.* 37.25–28; Whitmarsh 2004: 176; see Dion. Hal. *Ant. Rom.* 14.6.6.

47. Spawforth (2007: 389) asserts that "Acceptance by subject-Greek elites of the Roman estimation of Greek culture was a form of political obeisance to Roman power, an expression of subject loyalty no less than its more instantly recognizable manifestations such as the imperial cult, declarations of *pistis* on Greek local coins, pursuit of Roman office, and so on." Cf. DeMaris 2008: 46–50.

48. Prabhu (2007: 12) understands hybridity as "linked to the question of resistance to homogenization or assimilation and it thus implies an engagement with what we might broadly call subaltern agency." The domination by the Romans towards marginalized groups, both Jew and gentile, rendered them in a type of subaltern state. Paul's gospel and thus the agency of God could provide an alternative existence within the empire.

49. Martin (1995: 132) rightly concludes that "identity is established through participation in a larger entity" (1 Cor 15:12–24; see Sanders 1977: 452–63).

do not need to preclude theological questions. This book seeks to bridge the social-scientific research on the group dynamics of the early Christ-movement while considering the way these dynamics gave rise to the theological issues related to Jewish and gentile Christ-follower identity.[50]

Paul's understanding of calling informs the way he believes God's work through Christ impacts communal life. He names the Corinthians "those called to live in a holy manner" (κλητοῖς ἁγίοις). This calling provides a resocialization of the Corinthians' environment (1 Cor 7:17–24) in that the values of the broader culture may not always align with the values of those "in Christ." Paul himself remains Torah-observant,[51] but for the Corinthian Christ-followers of whom he does not require Torah observance, God's demand for holiness does not diminish (Lev 19:1–2 LXX).[52] Communal holiness is still necessary for gentiles "in Christ" who now belong to God.[53]

---

50. Meeks' (2007: xvi–xvii) introduction to the new edition of Schütz provides important contextual information concerning this issue.

51. Nanos (2002a: 3), writing about Galatians, takes the position that "Paul who writes this letter is a Torah observant Jew, known as such by his addressees when he had lived among them." This same assumption applies to the Corinthian correspondence; however, we should briefly address 1 Cor 9:20–21 with regard to Paul's continued Torah-observance. First, does the ὡς in 1 Cor 9:20a (καὶ ἐγενόμην τοῖς Ἰουδαίοις ὡς Ἰουδαῖς) "to the Jews I became as a Jew," suggest that Paul considered himself a former Jew? In 9:20, Paul does not say, "To the Jews I became as a Jew," "(*though I myself am not a Jew*)", because, based on Phil 3:5–8 Paul's Jewish identity continues to be salient. Second, the presence of ὡς may be a reminder of "the diversity that existed in the worldwide community of 'Jews'" (Acts 6:1; see Rudolph 2006: 182 n. 21, 198). In this understanding, "To the Jews I became as a Jew," may be Paul's statement of his principle of social identity adaptation. Third, does the phrase οὐ ὑπὸ νόμον "not under the Law," indicate that Paul no longer observes Torah? Bockmuehl (2000: 171) suggests that ὑπὸ νόμον may refer to those holding to a more "strict interpretation of the law" or more specifically to the "Pharisees." In this reading, Paul no longer holds to Pharisaic Halakhah, but this does not preclude his continued Torah-observance. See Rudolph (2006: 153–55) for a further discussion of this topic.

52. Bockmuehl (2000: 171) explains, regarding the Torah's authority, "The apostle himself in 1 Corinthians 7.17–20 makes clear that his 'rule for all the churches' is for Jews to keep the Torah . . . and for Gentiles to keep what pertains to them—and only that. In either case, what matters are the applicable commandments of God."

53. Campbell 2006a: 93; Hays (1997: 16) notes the requirement for holiness from the gentiles in Corinth; however, he surprisingly interprets this as gentiles now being "members of the covenant people of God, Israel." Schrage (1991: 102) expresses some uncertainty, "ist ungewiß," concerning the relationship between the ἐκκλησία and historic Israel.

For Paul, Jesus Christ and him crucified is the identity-organizing reality within his communities. The experience of being "in Christ," however, is a shared reality of all the Pauline communities throughout the Roman Empire. The lack of "in Christ" identity salience within the Corinthian Christ-followers also had a cognitive element that was in need of reconfiguration—they did not clearly understand themselves as part of the larger group of Christ-followers (1 Cor 7:17; 14:33; 2 Cor 8:1). SIT/SCT note that identity is formed through ongoing comparison with others and the perceived relationship to the superordinate group. Hogg and Abrams conclude that this ongoing comparison and its resulting recategorization may produce "a shared superordinate identity."[54] This comparison establishes difference and defines an outgroup, while reinforcing social identity by more clearly defining the ingroup.[55] For the Corinthian Christ-followers, this could indicate that they were categorizing themselves with those from the civic community in Corinth instead of with those from other Christ-movement communities throughout the Mediterranean basin.[56]

So Paul, in 1:2, reminds the Corinthians that they are part of a broader group of Christ-followers "together with all those who call on the name of our Lord Jesus Christ." Paul highlights themes that become central to his rhetorical strategy. The Corinthians are "together with all" (σὺν πᾶσιν), that is, they are not alone in their mission. The substantival use of the participle defines the Corinthians' involvement in Paul's theology of "calling" (τοῖς ἐπικαλουμένοις). God called the Corinthians, and likewise they have called upon Christ. The community-organizing identity is limited to and reinforced as those who call "on the name of

54. Hogg and Abrams 2003: 421. Superordinate identity was introduced on p. 44 n. 33.

55. Tajfel 1981: 145; Turner 1985: 78. The ingroup/outgroup debate in Corinth related in some way to differing epistemological frameworks which gave rise to differing group categorizations. This is the classic understanding of SIT/SCT.

56. De Vos 1999: 214. The superordinate group is the larger movement of Christ-followers, to which the Jerusalem ἐκκλησία may point (1 Cor 16:1–4; 2 Cor 8:4, 9:13). Elliott (2004b: 100) sees this as a survival strategy; "[c]ontributing to the needs of the Jerusalem church establishes a mutual relationship that could be reversed, should the precarious balance of food security shift and the Corinthians find themselves in need." This provides an economic program for the early Christ-following communities, one that was an alternative to the Roman economic system. The Jerusalem Christ-followers are seen as part of this larger superordinate group of all those communities who follow Christ throughout the Roman Empire.

our Lord Jesus Christ." Paul thus names what he sees as the salient in-group identity, those who align themselves and thus identify primarily with Christ.

This does not obliterate difference; the Romans in Corinth continue to relate to God as Romans, and the same applies to Greeks, Egyptians, and Jews.[57] Difference and the continuation of diversity within unity are seen as Paul reinforces the importance of interconnectedness with members of the wider Christ-movement by noting in 1:2 that the same is true for those "in every place." Those in other regions of the empire are related to the Corinthians because of the work of Christ; however, they still remain within their ethnic and kinship groups. What unifies these disparate groups is the lordship of Jesus Christ. In verse 2, Paul compounds the importance of this by stating "both their lord and ours." Identity salience forms through proper assessment of superordinate groups, ingroups, and outgroups. For Paul, the superordinate group is the larger Christ-movement, while the ingroup consists of those "in Christ" and the outgroup refers to "the rulers of this age" (1 Cor 1:2; 2:6).

In 1:3, the ethos of God's community in Corinth is to be one of "grace" (χάρις) and "peace" (εἰρήνη). Paul, in a rather programmatic fashion, desires characteristics such as these to be emblematic of the Corinthian community (cf. 2 Macc 1:1; 4 Macc 1:1). These hallmarks of communal life are not generated through human effort but, as a distinct ethos, have their basis in "God our Father" and "Jesus Christ our lord."[58] The source of this communal ethos is God; however, this ethos is also an implicit critique of human governments,[59] specifically Roman imperial ideology.[60]

57. Cf. Campbell 2006a: 127; Brawley 2007: 109; Yeo 2008: 81–82. Cf. Rom 14:5, 10, 13; 1 Cor 7:17–24; Acts 21:20.

58. Keener (2005: 21) notes "Paul's divergence from the usual pattern." He "invoked not only 'God our Father' for a blessing . . . but also 'our Lord Jesus Christ' (1:3)." Wolter (1997: 443) argues for "faith" as the group ethos. Geertz' (1973: 127) understanding of ethos as an "underlying attitude towards themselves and their world that life reflects" is helpful in considering the role of "grace" and "peace" within Paul's communities.

59. Bryan (2005: 90) explains "that much of the vocabulary of imperial rhetoric also resonated with the language of the Septuagint . . . the religious language of Hellenism." So, one should expect to see religious/political language in Paul because of his familiarity with LXX vocabulary. It does not follow, however, that he was not concerned with Roman imperialism.

60. Beard, North, and Price (1998: 348 emphasis original) take the view that one should not envision a monolithic understanding of Roman imperial cult: "that is, there

Caesar may have wished to have himself proclaimed the "father of the fatherland" (*Pater Patriae*), but the reality is that the God of Israel is the father of the Christ-movement and of the "world" (κόσμος). Paul's use of κύριος, while having broad resonance with the monarchic language of the ancient Near East, at least alludes to the fact that all competitors to the Lordship of Jesus Christ are pretenders. Horsley rightly understands the title, Lord Jesus, to refer "to Christ's political role as the exalted universal Lord."[61] Also, it is clear to Paul that "peace" comes not from any human government or empire but only flows from the God of Israel and God's messiah, Jesus.[62] Paul, in 1:1–3, begins to lay the foundation for the social identity of the community of God in Corinth.[63] He then continues by establishing the framework for that identity.

THE FRAMEWORK FOR SALIENT "IN CHRIST" SOCIAL IDENTITY: GOD'S GRACE (1:4–9)

The process of building a community of Christ-followers is grounded in God's grace. So Paul, in 1:4, expresses sincere thanks to God for the Corinthian Christ-followers "on the basis of God's grace" (ἐπὶ τῇ χάριτι τοῦ Θεοῦ). The identity-forming potential of God's grace is clarified in that it was not of the Corinthians' own creation but "was given" (τῇ δοθείσῃ) to them "through Christ Jesus" (ἐν Χριστῷ Ἰησοῦ). O'Brien recognizes this connection with regard to this letter: "In no other introductory thanksgiving is the grace of God found to be the basis or ground for the giving of thanks."[64]

The grace of God mentioned as the source of the Corinthians' identity is now extended into the framework of group formation. Paul's discourse points back to a specific point when this grace "was given" (τῇ δοθείσῃ), that is to say the Corinthians' conversion or more precisely a point in time when a new identity emerged (2 Cor 5:17). Depending on the Corinthians' previous religious identification, shifting from one

---

is no such thing as '*the* imperial cult.'" The expressions within the provinces in the Greek east differed widely and any discussion of Roman imperial ideology in this book reflects the tenuous relationship between surviving texts and the actual practice of the imperial cult in Corinth.

61. Horsley 1998: 40; Verg. *Aen.* 6.791–95.

62. Cf. *Res Gestae Divi Augusti* 13, 26; Verg. *Ecl.* 4.4–10; Elliott 1994: 184–89.

63. Hays 1997: 17.

64. O'Brien 1977: 111.

religious movement to another may not be in view here.[65] The Pauline communities were still within Judaism and did not separate in any significant fashion from the synagogue. Esler is helpful; he questions the continued use of the term "conversion." He asks whether conversion does not "simply entail an intensification of" the Corinthians' or Paul's "devotion to the God of Abraham."[66]

The use of the passive voice here as well as the definite article (τῇ δοθείσῃ) indicate that Paul does not have in mind simply a vague past experience of God's grace but one shared by the whole community.[67] Communal rituals play a significant part in the process of identity formation, and it is likely that Paul has in mind entrance into the community through baptism. Dunn, however, understands here a primary focus on the work of the Spirit. He does note that "baptism is such a transaction [change of ownership], where the baptisand formally gives himself into the hands of a new Master."[68] However, while the work of the Spirit is primary, the identity-forming communal activity of baptism should not be too quickly disregarded. This communal experience should have contributed to a stable social identity. Instead it was destabilizing community life (1 Cor 1:12–17). This verse (1:4) not only points the Corinthian Christ-followers back to their entrance into the community, it also establishes a process of social remembering that is vital to salient social identity. Castelli is quite helpful here; she views "ancient Christian sources as themselves the creators and purveyors of collective memory."[69] In this way, Paul is seen as contributing to the role of social memory within the early Christ-following communities.

In 1:5, the result of the Corinthians' entrance into the community of Christ-followers is that they "have been enriched" (ἐπλουτίσθητε), that is to say the framework from which they are to live has been made complete "in him" (ἐν αὐτῷ). The use of "make rich" (πλουτίζω) may be an indicator that Paul understands a preoccupation with wealth to be a key

---

65. Davies 1978: 11. This would be the case for Jewish Christ-followers; if the Corinthians were part of a local expression of Roman religion, then there would be some sort of referent group transition.

66. Esler 2007b: 134.

67. Thiselton (2000: 89–90) understands the passive δοθείσῃ as a "Semitic use, which underlines God's agency."

68. Dunn 1970: 117–18.

69. Castelli 2007: 24.

component of the Corinthians' current understanding of their identity (1 Cor 1:26; 4:8).[70] Paul attempts to transform this understanding by applying the resources of communal memory to remind the Corinthians that all they have received has its source in God through Christ.[71] The Pauline community in Corinth also elevated other important markers of Roman identity: "speech" (λόγος) and "knowledge" (γνῶσις). So Paul begins to remind the Corinthian Christ-followers, as a group, that these important aspects of their identity (i.e., riches, speech, and knowledge) find their proper place as a result of their "in Christ" experience not in their current categorization of the importance of Roman identity within the community.[72]

The Corinthians' confusion concerning the appropriate role of persuasive "speech" (λόγος) has its basis in a general way in their over-identification with the role of rhetoric in the Roman Empire. Scholars often reference the impact of the sophists in Corinth,[73] but although their impact in Corinth is significant, it does not follow that Paul was equally influenced or that he argued in a manner similar to the sophists. The analogs for Paul's discourse are clearly within the prophetic tradition of Israel (e.g., Jer 9:22–23; 31:31–34),[74] and his contention that convincing

70. O'Brien (1977: 117 emphasis original) supports this contention by noting that "the *wealth of the Christian life* was often expressed by the word πλοῦτος and its cognates. The recurrence of this theme in the Corinthian correspondence suggests that the Corinthians themselves had informed Paul, either by letter (cf. 1 Cor. 7:1) or verbally by messengers (16:7), about their riches."

71. Guijarro (2007: 90) contends that "collective memory is an important factor in the process of group identity formation. This approach can be especially useful to explain the construction of new collective identities that defined the groups of Jesus' disciples after his death."

72. Welborn (2005: 115), noting the rhetorical impact of Paul's critique, concludes that "rhetorical skill and sophistical knowledge are the attainments which are most valued by those who participate in Hellenistic culture."

73. Litfin 1994: 137–40, 186; Winter 2001: 31–43; Winter 2002a: 183–85.

74. O'Day (1990: 267) concludes that "Jeremiah's critique of wisdom, power, and wealth as false sources of identity that violate the covenant are re-imaged by Paul as a critique of wisdom, power, and wealth that impede God's saving acts in Jesus Christ." Baker (2008: 5.9) takes the view that in Jer 31:31–34 the "prophet [is seeking] to develop a new common in-group identity that would better serve the post-exilic community." Paul may be understood to be doing something quite similar in 1 Corinthians 1–4. Furthermore, evidence for seeing Paul within the prophetic tradition of Israel comes from 1 Cor 9:16–18 where Paul is unable to resist the call to be the messenger of God. He is one who has had this "necessity" laid upon him (9:17; cf. Exod 4:10–17). Moreover, Paul's revelatory language in 1 Cor 9:1 and 15:5–9 coheres quite closely to Jer 1:5.

speech has its basis in God's gift argues for his primary reliance on God for effective communication and not on rhetorical brilliance.

According to Paul, the over-emphasis on knowledge as a marker of social identity requires adjustment. Though knowledge is important, the Corinthians' insight does not originate in their own ability but has its basis in God's gracious gifts, which provide them with the communal resources to live life with skill. Paul's understanding closely aligns with the Proverbs (Prov 1:7; 3:5–7; 9:10; 15:33; 22:4).[75] In a later correspondence with the Corinthians, in 2 Cor 5:11, Paul relies on this wisdom literature tradition and argues that "the fear of the Lord" (τὸν φόβον τοῦ κυρίου) is a vital motivator for a mission-centered approach to life. This is important because the confusion over the appropriate identity hierarchy within the community impacted the Corinthians' ability to extend Paul's mission in Corinth (1 Cor 5:9–10).

The basis in 1:6 for the Corinthians' ongoing social identity is "Christ's testimony" (τὸ μαρτύριον τοῦ Χριστοῦ), taken as an objective genitive.[76] The richness of the Corinthians' communal experience in both speech and knowledge is to be a reminder of what "has been confirmed" (ἐβεβαιώθη) within the community. These indicators and the value-system which frames their use in Corinth are not to be the primary markers of identity. That is reserved for the gracious gift of God's grace through Christ. Paul, in this verse, re-constructs a past for the Corinthians which readjusts their current engagement with their own collective memory, something he does more explicitly in 1 Cor 11:23–26.[77] Paul begins to construct a narrative for the Corinthians' social identity that has its basis in their previous corporate experiences in which "Christ's testimony was confirmed" by means of the gifts they had received from God.[78] This testimony is now in danger of being used in

75. Perdue 2008: 91, 180.

76. Garland (2003: 34) construes it as an objective genitive. Cf. Fitzmyer 2008: 132; Thiselton (2000: 94) contends that "on grammatical and contextual grounds alone it is difficult to decide whether Χριστοῦ represents a subjective genitive (of Christ in the sense that Christ does the witnessing) or an objective genitive (in the sense that Christ is the object of the witness, i.e., the gospel and the Holy Spirit witness to Christ or about Christ)."

77. Peterson 2007: 138–39.

78. Kirk (2005: 5 emphasis original) supports the importance of this by asserting that "a community *marks* certain elements of its past as being of constitutive significance. Both identity and continuity, in fact the very survival of a community, depend upon its constant revitalization of these memories."

a manner that would actually hinder the ongoing witness of the gospel (1 Cor 14:24). Paul is strengthening this community of Christ-followers by reminding them of their shared calling and past experience which brought this community into existence, provided them with gifts of grace, and will also sustain them to the "end" (τέλος).

The framework for identity is extended to include apocalyptic eschatology[79] in 1:7. The clause is introduced by "so that" (ὥστε), which indicates that the actual result of the Corinthians' call is that the community "does not lack any gift of grace (χαρίσματι)." The "gift of grace" is not to be limited to the "spiritual gifts" discussed in 1 Corinthians 12–14. They are the practical resources provided to the community by which they learn what it means to live together as a community of Christ-followers, being resocialized within the Jewish symbolic universe.[80]

Paul's description of the Corinthians as "those who wait eagerly (ἀπεκδεχομένους) for the revelation (ἀποκάλυψιν) of our Lord Jesus Christ" is a clear indicator of his understanding of their social identity. O'Brien comes close to this when he describes this clause as "almost another definition of a Christian."[81] This is Paul engaging in apocalyptic identity formation in which the present identity of those within the Christ-movement is to be transformed on the basis of the revelation (ἀποκάλυψιν) of Jesus Christ (1 Cor 15:20–28) that is to come in the future. The Pauline framework of social identity involves a proper assessment of the group within God's broader work in the world and the Corinthians' relation to that work (1 Cor 4:8). Moreover, Elliott thinks Paul was "informed by the covenantal and apocalyptic traditions of Israel, and by the *apokalypsis* of Jesus Christ (Gal. 1.15–16), Paul understands his *parousia* to actualize an invasive power that is at odds—indeed, at war!—with the imperial power of 'rulers of this age' (1 Cor 2:8)."[82]

---

79. Kuck 1992: 166–68; Carter (2000: 10) defines "apocalyptic eschatology" as "a way of understanding the world. It views human experience in a fundamental temporal, cosmic, and social dualism. There are two ages: the present evil age, which disregards God's purposes, and the future glorious age, when God's purposes will be triumphantly established."

80. Coutsoumpos (2006: 2) rightly recognizes the process of resocialization that was occurring but overstates the distinction between the early Christ-movement and Judaism. Pickett (1997: 98) refers to this as "secondary socialization."

81. O'Brien 1977: 125.

82. Elliott 2004a: 68. Vollenweider (2002: 56) asserts that Paul's apocalyptic perspective integrates wisdom motifs. He writes, "In religionsgeschichtlicher Perspektive steht

Paul now connects his previous communal memory building, from 1:6, with a future ideology that assures the community of continued existence in 1:8. This creates resources for forming the Corinthians' identity so that their past recollections are able to inform their current behaviors in light of their future hope "in Christ" (3:11–13). God's work within the community continues since he "will confirm" (βεβαιώσει) the community "in the day" (ἐν τῇ ἡμέρᾳ). Earlier in the discourse, "Christ's testimony had been confirmed," but now the identity of the Corinthian Christ-followers is that which "will be confirmed" (βεβαιώσει).[83] In this current context, Paul reminds the Corinthians that this confirmation will be sure "to the end" (τέλους). The use of τέλος by Paul may be an indication that identity formation is occurring in a text. It describes the goal that Paul has in mind for his community-building strategy (cf. 1 Cor 10:11; 15:24; Rom 6:22; 10:4).

The present experience of this predominantly gentile community continues to have its basis in the ongoing history of ethnic Israel, and in this case Paul draws upon apocalyptic imagery from the Hebrew Bible (cf. Amos 5:18–20; Ezek 30:1–4; Joel 2:1–2; Zeph 1:14–18) to inform the Corinthians' thinking concerning the revelation of Jesus Christ that is to come "in that day." Paul's communities continued to relate closely to the synagogue communities throughout the Mediterranean basin, and thus allusions, echoes, or explicit references to Israel's Scriptures would not have gone unnoticed (1 Cor 7:19).[84] Paul's vision was one in which Jew and gentile lived together in mutuality and diversity, each relating, in their own way, to the God of Israel (1 Cor 1:24; 10:1),[85] Jews as Jews and gentiles as gentiles.[86] Thus, Paul ends his long sentence of thanks-

die paulinische Argumentation im Horizont einer apokalyptischen Theologie, in der sapientiale Motive und Themen eschatologisch umgebrochen werden."

83. O'Brien 1977: 127. This dual "confirmation" serves a boundary-marking function (Bar-Tal 2000: 36) within the community as the Corinthians await Christ's return.

84. Ehrensperger (2008a: 301; see 2008b: 13) questions the significance a "set of texts" would have had "within the newly formed, predominantly Gentile groups of Christ-followers."

85. Nanos (2005b: 61; 1996: 23) understands the Pauline communities to be subgroups of the broader synagogue community, and thus Paul's discourse would have been intelligible to the gentiles. Even if Nanos is too precise in claiming this, previous and ongoing links are still plausible.

86. Normally, in discussions of Christ-movement identity, Abraham is referenced because of the number of times he is mentioned in Romans and Galatians. In the Corinthian correspondence, however, Abraham does not play a role except in 2 Cor

giving with a restatement of the way the Corinthians' relationship to God and their participation with Jesus Christ impacts their life in the community.

The thanksgiving section of the letter ends in 1:9 with a non-pro-grammatic reminder that "God is faithful" (πιστὸς ὁ Θεός).[87] While conforming to the broad contours of the thanksgiving section of ancient letters, Paul is already forming the identity of the addressees by laying the foundation and making clear the framework by which stable com-munal life may occur. He then draws again from communal memory, re-minding the Corinthians that God "had called" (ἐκλήθητε) them. Paul's understanding of calling provides the necessary resources by which to identify this community—they have been called by God.

The second vital concept in Paul's identity-forming strategy is fellowship. Hays thinks that the Corinthians' "calling is not just to per-form a mission or to obey certain norms; rather, the community is fi-nally called into a relationship of intimate mutuality with one another in Christ."[88] The intended result of God's calling "in Christ Jesus" is a "shared-communal-life-together."[89] This is the continued vision of God's community in Corinth, and thus Paul argues that they were "called into a shared-communal-life-together" (ἐκλήθητε εἰς κοινωνίαν). This expansive understanding of κοινωνία follows Garland's translation, "common-union," although he takes the genitive as objective and con-strues the phrase as "their sharing in Christ."[90] While Garland's choice

---

11:22. Thus, Paul can discuss the relationship of gentiles to the God of Israel without reference to Abraham. See Campbell 2006a: 127.

87. O'Brien (1977: 131) convincingly argues that "this benediction or confirming climax . . . is not stereotyped." Schubert (1939: 183) takes the view that the combination of the thanksgiving and the salutation produce insights into the purpose of the letter and the specific issues Paul will address. Cf. Lim 2007: 49–51.

88. Hays 1997: 19. Hainz (EDNT 304), on the other hand, argues that "participation" is in view here and thus "fellowship/participation (with someone) through (common) participation (in something)." See 1 Cor 10:16–18. L&N 446 define it as "an association involving close mutual relations and involvement."

89. BDAG 553 places this verse under "participation, sharing." Cf. Wis 8:17–18 which sounds very similar to the experience the Corinthians were having with wisdom but not with each other. For Paul, sharing in wisdom is useless without sharing in life together. Cf. Joseph. Ap I.35. LSJ 969 emphasize the communal connection "by common origin or kinship especially of brothers or sisters." While helpful, the examples they provide appear to be of "real" kinship and not fictive kinship.

90. Garland (2003: 35) concludes that "Common-union with Christ creates com-mon-union with other Christians and precludes common-union with idols (10:14–22)."

of an objective genitive is possible, a genitive of source is more likely in that the resulting state is dependent on a prior agent. Also, Paul uses the genitive of source in 2 Cor 3:3, referring to the Corinthians as "letter[s] from Christ," and the present usage is somewhat analogous to that.[91] This emphasis on social-life-together is not simply for public comportment but for furthering Paul's mission among the nations (1 Cor 3:13–15; 9:20–21). If the Corinthian Christ-followers had properly discerned the mission significance of their "fellowship" or "shared-communal-life-together" then the various group-oriented problems within the community would have been less of a distraction from their broader purpose of extending the Pauline mission in Corinth. O'Brien prefers instead to argue that "had the Corinthians been aware of this high calling they might not have permitted groups within the community."[92] What O'Brien overlooks is that group formation is a normal aspect of social identity and that the groups that had formed were a result of normal life together. What needed to occur, from Paul's perspective, was for the groups in the Corinthian ἐκκλησία to recategorize their identity by redefining the ingroup and the outgroup. This would allow for a more stable community and strengthen the mission among the nations.

The foundation and framework for salient "in Christ" social identity evident in 1:1–9 is centered on God through the Lord Jesus Christ. The Christological foundation and framework in the opening portion of this letter is more central to Paul's rhetorical purposes than in the other undisputed Pauline letters.[93] O'Brien discounts the liturgical background for this language and argues that "their use here is explained by the immediate context. Paul had stressed the divine initiative at almost every point in the passage"; however, he also argued "that God's

---

Thiselton (2000: 104) defines it as "communal participation." Hauck (*TDNT* 3.798) references Epict. *Diatr.* 2.20.6 in the context of "a two-sided relationship . . . emphasis may be on either the giving or the receiving" and may be rendered "participation, impartation, fellowship." M&M 351 note that the Epictetus reference relates to "fellowship with Zeus." Cf. Philo *Spec.* I.221, I.131. This usage is foreign to the Hebrew Bible but in some ways approximates Paul's use in 1 Cor 10:16; see BDAG 553.

91. Wallace 1996: 110.

92. O'Brien 1977: 132.

93. Thiselton (2000: 90 emphasis original) asserts that "*there are ten references to Christ in the first ten verses. Only overfamiliarity with biblical texts can obscure the remarkable repetition.*"

gracious activity was intimately bound up with His Son."[94] While Christ is central in the formation of identity, the outgroup that needed to be addressed for the community to be stabilized was the Roman Empire. The Christological references can be understood as a polemic against the propaganda of Rome concerning the divinity of the Emperor. This component is not addressed in O'Brien's otherwise fine exegesis of this passage.

Jesus is referred to as God's son in 1:9 and 15:28. While the first reference comes as the climax of a series, the reference in 15:28 may be an anti-imperial polemic. At the revelation of Jesus Christ, all things will be subjected to him, but unlike the Roman emperors, Jesus then willingly relinquishes all the empires of the world so that God "may be all in all." Jesus as the "Son of God" is an implicit critique of the pretensions of the Roman Empire. This recognition of the status of Jesus as God's son serves as a reminder to those Christ-followers within the Corinthian community that Rome's power is passing away (1 Cor 2:6–8). The Corinthian ἐκκλησία is a community that has been called to a "shared-communal-life-together," and the Corinthians should consider their connection with other Christ-followers as their primary superordinate group. The Corinthians should cease seeking identity salience with their local governing authorities or the transient and illusionary power of Rome. Both were key components of Roman identity which was competing for the position of master identity in the Corinthian community of Christ-followers.[95]

---

94. O'Brien 1977: 133.

95. Bryan (2005: 91) is not as convinced concerning the anti-Imperial polemic in relation to "Octavius Caesar 'divi filius' (son of god) . . . as a direct comparison with call[ing] Jesus 'son of God' because he believed him to have been 'sent' . . . by the God of Israel." Oakes (2005: 322) builds on the work of Simon Price and notes that "the Roman imperial cult in the Greek east" was "an expression of the place that Greeks gave to Roman power in their universe: a great translocal, divine force on a par with that of the Hellenistic monarchs. Paul rearranges this universe." To Oakes and Price, one could also add that he rearranges this universe as a Jewish symbolic universe. Also, the problem in Corinth was not persecution from the governing authorities but a general sense of acceptance and co-existence with them (1 Cor 6:1–11; 1 Cor 7:12; 1 Cor 8–10; 1 Cor 14:24).

CONCLUSION

It was discovered that 1:1–9 functions as a traditional letter opening and thanksgiving but was non-programmatic in its content to the point that Paul had already begun to address what he understood as the core issues related to life in the community, that is the need to re-establish a salient "in Christ" social identity. In sum, the foundation for social identity is the Corinthians' calling "in Christ," while the framework for this identity is God's grace. Paul establishes these important identity-forming concepts in 1:1–9. In the next chapter, we will turn to 1:10–25 to understand the way Paul deals with the problem of a lack of salient "in Christ" social identity within the life of the ἐκκλησία.

6

The Lack of Salient "in Christ" Social Identity in Corinth

INTRODUCTION

THE PURPOSE OF THIS chapter is to uncover the way Paul begins to address issues related to the lack of salient "in Christ" social identity in Corinth. First, the problem will be described in the context of Tajfel's cognitive, evaluative, and emotional components of a group. Second, the way Paul's words transform the understanding of social identity and thus group memberships will be analyzed. Third, God's calling and choice will serve as a way to understand the continuing significance of previous social identities. Finally, Paul's proclamation among the community will be seen to reinforce previously agreed-to group norms.

PROBLEMS WITH SOCIAL IDENTITY (1:10)

Tajfel, in defining a group, recognizes three features: "cognitive—the sense of the knowledge that one belongs to a group; evaluative—the sense that the notion of the group . . . may have a positive or negative value; [and] emotional—the sense that the cognitive and evaluative aspects . . . may be accompanied by emotions."[1] Within the Christ-movement in Corinth these three components are functioning inadequately. So, Paul writes 1:10–17 to begin the process of reconstituting and redefining Corinthian Christ-movement social identity by pointing out this inadequacy within the community. This is evidenced as Paul notes the instability within the ἐκκλησία and introduces a way forward through a correct understanding of the cross of Christ and baptism in his name.

---

1. Tajfel 1978a: 28.

A variety of proposals are put forth by scholars about Paul's introduction in 1:10 to the problem he will address in 1:10—4:21. None, however, consider the lack of a salient "in Christ" social identity. For example, Mitchell sees political factions in Corinth and believes that Paul is writing in 1:10 to restore unity (i.e., concord) within the community.[2] Witherington views Paul as declaring "*schismata* ('cracks, dissensions') [as] a major problem . . . within the still somewhat unified congregation in Corinth (cf. 11:18)."[3] Fitzmyer contends that Paul is addressing preferences for "preachers who have evangelized them or somehow influenced their lives."[4] These three scholars, like many others, focus on the behavioral issues evident in the text to discern the problem Paul addresses in 1 Cor 1:10—4:21. I would suggest that in 1 Cor 1:10, Paul is concerned with the Corinthian Christ-followers' understanding and definition of groups within the Christ-movement.

Paul begins to define the problem, which was a lack of salient[5] "in Christ" social identity, by addressing the way the community ought to think about one another. Thus, 1 Cor 1:10–17 reveals that problems associated with social identity were adversely impacting communal life. This is evident in 1:10–11 where Paul calls for divisions and quarrels to cease. In 1:12, the presence of differing group memberships again indicates a problem with social identity in that social identity is associated with groups. Furthermore, in 1:13–16 group leaders and ritual associations reinforce the idea that social identity was a concern. Finally, in 1:17, issues related to wisdom and the cross of Christ may indicate ingroup and outgroup comparisons, which are central to the formation of social identity. Thus, it may be plausible to understand one of the problems in Corinth to be the way the Corinthian Christ-followers understood their existing group memberships and by extension the way their local expressions of Roman social identity influenced corporate life within the ἐκκλησία. The reading that follows seeks to substantiate this claim.

Paul seeks to adjust the dominant identity within the Corinthian Christ-followers' identity hierarchy as he writes, "And I encourage

2. Mitchell 1991: 198–99.

3. Witherington 1995: 95.

4. Fitzmyer 2008: 137.

5. Salient social identity describes a social situation in which an identity is switched on, is in the dominant position in the identity hierarchy, and thus represents that component of identity that is most likely to impact behavior.

(παρακαλῶ) you, brothers and sisters (ἀδελφοί)." Fitzmyer sees in Paul's use of παρακαλῶ "an urgent appeal."[6] While Fitzmyer is representative of the dominant view, is this the best way to understand the term? Bjerkelund argues that Paul's use here does not require an emphasis on correction, dominance, or urgency.[7] It is rather, a relational term, argues Ehrensperger, which provides guidance and direction even when the relationship exists in the context of hierarchy.[8] Which view is to be preferred? First, based on the presence of παρακαλῶ in 1:10 and 4:16, its primary function is that of a discourse marker. Second, the diplomatic letters referenced by Bjerkelund provide evidence for the way asymmetrical relationships can function without the sense of threat or domination. Third, the presence of sibling language indicates Paul's understanding of his relationship with the Corinthian Christ-followers. Fourth, Paul's use of παρακαλῶ in 1 Thess 4:1, with its focus on formation discourse, makes sense without the imposition of the ideas of urgency and warning. Though the Corinthian Christ-followers are in an asymmetrical relationship with Paul, it does not follow that he is commanding them. Thus, the use of παρακαλῶ functions to indicate Paul's first concern of the letter as he seeks to encourage the formation of salient "in Christ" social identity within the ἐκκλησία (Gal 4:19).

The target for his encouragement is the "brothers and sisters." The term ἀδελφός is a key group identifier in 1 Corinthians. With regard to 1 Corinthians 1–4, it occurs in 1:1, 10, 11, 26; 2:1; 3:1; and 4:6. Here it is part of a stereotypical Pauline structure designed to indicate his understanding of the relationship between him and the recipients of his letters.[9] What is the basis for translating ἀδελφοί as "brothers and sisters"? First, the letter addresses women as well as men; thus the inclusive understanding is possible. Second, the numerous examples given in BDAG indicate that the inclusive use is probably in view. Moreover, Paul's usage of this term has its basis in Israel's scriptures, though Artz-Grabner

---

6. Fitzmyer 2008: 140.

7. Bjerkelund 1967: 141–47.

8. Ehrensperger 2007: 175.

9. Aasgaard (2004: 278) contends that "The almost obligatory address in these formulas serves to create confidence, to impart a sense of closeness, and to convey a feeling of a common knowledge, which is hidden from outsiders: as siblings they share a secret landscape together (1 Thess. 4.13)."

notes the possibility of the influence of Roman voluntary associations.[10] Ehrensperger further defines ἀδελφοί as "an identity designation with an emphasis on the way those who are part of this group of siblings should relate to each other in everyday life."[11]

The Roman civic use of *frater* with its political rhetoric and claims of fraternal *pietas*[12] combined with Paul's understanding of ἀδελφός as indicating group solidarity and mutual concern[13] may be described as a contact zone of "cultural translation" with regard to the social implications of living in the "idealized *consortium*"[14] as compared to an ἐκκλησία of fellow-siblings. Cultural translation is an important topic because of the possibility for misunderstanding that arises from cross-cultural communication. It is possible that this led to some of the difficulties in Corinth (1 Cor 5:9–11).

That Paul uses ἀδελφός as a designation for social identity is supported by his claim that it is founded on identification with Christ. The prepositional phrase "through the name of our Lord Jesus Christ" is one of the places where Paul employs a genitive after διά, which stresses intermediate agency (Gal 4:7). For Paul, the agency of Jesus Christ, discursively established here through the invocation of his name, is central to social identity and unity; it reminds his auditors to whom they belong (1 Cor 1:13, 30; 3:23). This early statement concerning the name of Jesus Christ will also appear in Paul's later argument concerning the level of diversity that is to exist within the community (1 Cor 12:12).

10. Artz-Grabner 2006: 64–65. Cf. Paul's use in Rom 9:3; 10:1; 11:25.

11. Ehrensperger 2007: 60; see Deut 3:18; 15:3; Prov 17:17; Jer 22:18.

12. Bannon (1997: 93) explains that "Fraternal *pietas* most often manifested itself in two kinds of political activity: cultivating networks of friends and clients, and co-ordinated efforts to advance each other's careers or to secure their common interest in family prestige." Cf. Cic. *Ac.* 2.1; Cic. *Off.* 2.49–50; Plut. *Luc.* 1.1–2. The role of political brotherhood as an identity-forming discourse is evidenced in the foundational myths of Romulus and Remus as well as Aeneas in the *Aeneid* 1.257–96; 6.761–79. Cf. Bannon 1997: 168. See also p. 102 on the Roman foundation myth in the formation of Roman social identity in this book.

13. Ringgren (Botterweck, Ringgren, and Fabry 2006: 192) concludes that "with the extension of the idea of brotherhood to all fellow tribesmen and fellow countrymen came also the increased demand for solidarity. Since all Israelites are brothers, one should help everyone who becomes poor (Lev. 25:35f.). Deuteronomy especially emphasizes this duty (15:7, 9, 11f.)."

14. Bannon (1997: 7) thinks that "the concept of *consortium*" came "to represent an idealized form of fraternal *pietas* through which brothers resolved conflict through cooperation."

The lack of this diversity produced communal instability grounded in a misapprehension of the particularistic nature of identity and the unity which shall result (1 Cor 12:24). Paul's rhetorical vision for the community continues with regard to their speech patterns which appear to have been a significant cause of disunity (1 Cor 1:12, 15; 3:4). He writes, "that (ἵνα) you would speak (λέγητε) the same thing." The ἵνα clause is functioning as the second direct object of παρακαλῶ and contains the specific content of Paul's teaching which addresses the Corinthians' communal speech practices.[15] Robertson and Plummer argue that this is Paul's way of appealing for peace.[16] Similar usage is seen in Xenophon who writes, "Agreement is deemed the greatest blessing for cities . . . everywhere in Greece there is a law that the citizens shall promise under oath to agree."[17] The implication in Xenophon is that all the citizens agree to follow the previously agreed-upon law. In the same way, Paul wishes the Corinthian Christ-followers to return to that which they had previously agreed to follow, which will contribute to the return of harmonious speech patterns.

Paul's topic is now clear; he is concerned with the purported divisions within the community. His desire is "that there might not be divisions (σχίσματα) among you." The Corinthians are separating themselves into sub-groups, which is contributing to a lack of community concord.[18] Here the implications of ingroup and outgroup stereotyping and legitimation begin to emerge.[19]

Paul now restates his rhetorical vision for unity in more positive terms. He desires "that you might be made complete (κατηρτισμένοι)." He employs a perfect passive participle intimating the continued restoration of a previous condition, as for example in the mending of torn

---

15. Cf. the use of the subjunctive λέγητε in this verse with the indicative λέγει in 1 Cor 1:12.

16. Robertson and Plummer 1911: 10. Wanamaker (2005: 420; Welborn 1997: 1–42) references the political topos but argues that "the metaphoric and moral character of the language 1:10 . . . has not been discussed."

17. Xen. *Mem.* 4.4.16; cited in Mitchell 1991: 63.

18. Josephus relates the dying charge of Mattathias to his sons, writing, "But most of all I urge you to be of one mind" (*AJ* 12.283). In 1 Macc 2:49, as Mattathias prepares to die, he declares, "Arrogance and strife have become strong" (cf. 1 Cor 4:4, 18, 19; 5:2; 8:1; 13:4, φυσιόω). An ethos of arrogance had produced "divisions" among the community which further destabilized the ἐκκλησία in Corinth (1 Cor 1:13).

19. Ashforth and Mael 1989: 32–33.

nets (Matt 4:21; Mark 1:19). From an identity formation standpoint 1 Corinthians 1–4 is urging a return to the Corinthians' original calling (1 Cor 1:1–9; 7:17–24).[20] Paul's teaching on unity is necessary because of the lack of "in Christ" identity salience within the community.

The unity that Paul seeks centers on the continuing reality of Jesus Christ among the Christ-following community, a unity that does not obliterate difference. However, the language of 1 Cor 1:10 seems to argue for unswerving uniformity. Thus, is there warrant in claiming that difference continues within Paul's understanding of unity? There are three interrelated reasons for asserting that the unity that Paul calls for here does not obliterate difference. First, his "rule in all the churches" is that individuals are to remain in the social situation in which they were called (1 Cor 7:17). This rule would result in the continuation of diverse ethnic and social identities within the Christ-movement. Second, Paul expects a person's conscience (συνείδησις) to guide the ordering of diverse expressions of social life (1 Cor 10:25, 27–29); however, proper consideration for other members is required (1 Cor 8:7, 10, 12). Third, the continuation of diversity is a key social implication of Paul's body metaphor (1 Cor 12:4–6, 12–31). The nature of the metaphor requires attention to difference and diversity. These three pieces of textual evidence support the contention that Paul's view of unity does not call for, in Horrell's language, "unvaried conformity" but rather an appreciation of diversity amid unity.[21]

The next phrase anticipates Paul's broader discussion of the cognitive, evaluative, and emotional elements of social identity in 1:18—2:5. He continues with parallel prepositional phrases, "in the same way of thinking (νοΐ) and in a unity of mindedness (γνώμη)." The use of νοΐ and γνώμη point to the cognitive and affective components of social

---

20. Dionysius of Halicarnassus recounts the expected troubles that a city will encounter in the context of competing identities and concludes, "all will agree that order (καταρτίζω) ought to rule over confusion … and you will do wrong in demanding the reverse" (*Ant. Rom.* 3.10.6). In Phld. 8:1, Ignatius writes, "I therefore did what belonged to me, as a man devoted to unity (κατηρτισμένος)." The concern of Ignatius in this way is somewhat similar to Paul's, except for the application of ecclesial authority in 8.1c.; originally cited in Mitchell 1991: 75. Cf. LSJ 910; Epict. *Diatr.* 3.20.10; Gal 6:1; HRCS 743; M&M 332, P Oxy VIII. 1153[16]; *TDNT* 3: 475–76. The use of καταρτίζω in this verse emphasizes the proper condition that should exist within the community, a condition that existed in the Corinthians' calling.

21. Horrell 2005: 119.

identity formation.[22] In 2:16, the νοῦς becomes the integrative metaphor for the community, while in 1 Cor 14:14–15, 19, it becomes the
distinguishing marker of effective communication. The evaluative and
emotional elements of γνώμη are brought together in Paul's opinion
concerning some of the matters that have caused division within the
community (1 Cor 7:25, 40; 2 Cor 8:10), issues in which Paul allows
for differences and thus continues a particularistic understanding of
identity. Paul's conception of unity incorporates aspects of diversity
(1 Cor 12:4–6). Early in Paul's argument, he makes it clear that there is an
epistemic condition with regard to the formation of salient "in Christ"
social identity; this idea accords well with the findings of Jenkins in relation to social identity in general.[23]

Group-Based Problems within the Community (1:11–12)

Baptism in the early Christ-movement was on the way to becoming
a social identity experience. Paul, however, argues that in Corinth it
had become inconsistent with his vision for the community and their
continued involvement in the Pauline mission. Paul begins in 1:11 by affirming the Corinthian Christ-followers' position as his fellow-siblings,
"my brothers and sisters (ἀδελφοί),"[24] but lays out the evidence for
his previous assertions. The explanatory γάρ reinforces the idea that
Paul's understanding of the situation is legitimate, which is necessary
for the social construction of identity.[25] Paul continues, "it has been
made known (ἐδηλώθη) to me concerning you." This information about
the community came "from Chloe's people" which further modifies
ἐδηλώθη. The content of the information from Chloe's people is still unclear but the implied subject of ἐδηλώθη, "it," is now further described
with the ὅτι clause functioning as the subject of the aorist passive
ἐδηλώθη, "that (ὅτι) there are quarrels (ἔριδες) among you." That is to
say, the ἔριδες among the Corinthians result in σχίσματα (1:10). SIT
provides insight into the inner workings of the group, its "intragroup
behaviour." Here the focus is on "negotiation" and "self-presentation,"

---

22. BDAG 202, 680; Esler 2003b: 51–63; Esler 2004: 106–24.
23. Jenkins 2000: 22–23.
24. P[46] omits the μου.
25. Cf. Berger and Luckmann 1966: 79; Horrell 1993: 103.

described as "social presence and social performance."[26] It is clear from 1:11 that the problem relates to intragroup interaction. What is not clear is the actual cause of the division, which Paul begins to define in 1:12.

The divisions within the community are presented in 1:12 as Paul focuses on leaders within the Christ-movement and employs the Corinthians' own words for the purposes of ideological legitimation.[27] He begins with "now I mean this," which links this evidence with the information that was communicated from Chloe's people. Paul generalizes and addresses the community as a whole when he writes "that everyone (ἕκαστος) of you says (λέγει)." His use of λέγει contrasts with his desire for the Corinthians' speech in 1:10, and his use of ἕκαστος is undoubtedly rhetorical. The Corinthian Christ-followers' division is over which prototypical figure they are to follow, between those whose primary social identification is with Paul, Apollos, or Cephas.[28] Christ was added by Paul for rhetorical effect; however, this claim about the Christ group requires some attention.

In the literature review for this book, we briefly surveyed the scholarly debates with regard to the rhetorical exigence in 1 Corinthians 1–4. One of the main areas of scholarly interest relates to the parties or factions described in 1 Cor 1:12; 3:4, 22. In 1:12, Paul declares, "Now I mean this: that every one of you says, 'I belong to Paul' (Ἐγὼ εἰμι Παύλου), or 'I belong to Apollos' (Ἐγὼ δὲ Ἀπολλῶ), or 'I belong to Cephas' (Ἐγὼ δὲ Κηφᾶ), or 'I belong to Christ' (Ἐγὼ δὲ Χριστοῦ)."[29]

---

26. Hogg and Abrams 1988: 4–5.

27. Clarke's (1993: 97) helpful study connects the Corinthians' group preference to their boasting and taking pride in certain individuals; "[t]he other major instance of boasting may be seen in Paul's discussion in 1 Corinthians 1.10–12 of the personality-centred parties." Diodorus Siculus notes that when the "betrayal" of "the generals Hippocrates and Demosthenes" was clear, then "the multitude were divided according to party" (Diod. Sic. 12.66.2, cited in BDAG 981; Mitchell 1991: 72). Dionysius of Halicarnassus applies this same concept to "the supporters of Marcius" in the context of a political dispute (*Ant. Rom.* 7.59.7–10).

28. Pogoloff (1992: 175 emphasis original) describes the level of commitment prevalent among followers of certain teachers: "[s]uch competition in *sophoi logoi* sometimes became quite divisive . . . One philosopher and another or one rhetor and another were often strenuous competitors. The group following a particular teacher could be so strong that they could be described as a *secta*, a 'sect' or 'party.' This is the word Seneca the Elder uses to describe the followers of Apollodorus versus Theodorus, rival rhetoricians in Roma in the first century B.C.E." Cf. Sen. *Controv.* 10.15; deSilva 1999: 119.

29. Birge (2002: 14 n. 41) provides a rationale for these translations by noting that "[t]he word belong is a dynamic equivalent for the verb 'to be' accompanied by a noun

In 3:4, he restates this a little differently, "For when one says, 'I belong to Paul,' or 'I belong to Apollos,' are you not merely human?" In 3:21–22, he concludes by saying, "So then let no one boast in humankind, for all are yours, whether Paul or Apollos or Cephas." The purpose here is not to solve all the scholarly problems associated with Paul's rhetoric with regard to the divisions. Rather it is to provide an argument for the reason we think there were three parties who were associated, in Paul's mind, with leaders in the early Christ-movement. Furthermore, because of its relevance for identity studies, we will address David Odell-Scott's recent view that the Christ party was a specific group within the ἐκκλησία. The other scholarly issues related to these verses were addressed in the literature review and will not detain us here.[30]

Four interrelated points, three of which build on the work of Betz and Mitchell, support the argument that the Christ group was a rhetorical creation by Paul and functioned as his desired social identity position for the ἐκκλησία in Corinth.[31] First, the Christ group mentioned in 1:12 is not mentioned in 3:4 and 3:22 where Paul addresses specific issues of social identification and boasting. The absence of this group identifier is significant. Second, building on the general approach of this book, the Christ group is the one in which all are to socially identify, as seen for example in 3:23, "You belong to Christ." Furthermore, in 2 Cor 10:17 Paul actually encourages boasting but only "in the Lord" (cf. 1:2, 13). Third, a logical extension of the understanding of the Christ party argued for here would be that it is functioning metonymously as a descriptor of "the body of Christ" in the rest of the letter (1 Cor 1:4–9, 30; 6:15; 10:16–17; 11:3, 27, 29; 12:12–27). Fourth, Paul's rhetorical creation, "I belong to Christ," sounds quite similar to his focus on the formation of a salient "in Christ" social identity in 1 Corinthians 1–4, which thus supports the argument of this book. Here is where we part from Betz and Mitchell in that they suggest that this Pauline creation was "an ironic addition by the apostle as he describes the noisy sloganeering" evident in Corinth.[32] There is nothing in the context of 1:10–17 that indicates that this is an

---

in the genitive case, e.g., ἐγὼ μέν εἰμι Παύλου, 'I belong to Paul' (3:4) (LSJ, s.v. εἰμί c.II.d. 'to express that a thing belongs to another')."

30. See Thiselton 2000: 129–33; Schnabel 2006: 90–96; Artz-Grabner 2006: 69–70; Fitzmyer 2008: 142–45; Keener 2005: 24–25.

31. Betz and Mitchell 1992: 1141–42.

32. Betz and Mitchell 1992: 1141.

ironic statement, and furthermore it would limit the persuasive impact of 3:23 if Paul was not convinced that the Corinthians' identity had its basis in their belonging to Christ.

Recently, Odell-Scott has questioned this understanding of the Christ group and argues rather that this is the group with which Paul was most concerned.[33] He suggests that those from this group were seeking to establish a theocracy based on their human relationship with Jesus. Particularly, Odell-Scott points to "James the brother of the Lord and Peter" as exemplars of this group.[34] First, Odell-Scott's approach is somewhat similar to F. C. Baur's reconstruction of the conflict within the early Christ-movement and is thus open to critiques similar to those applied to Baur. He over-emphasizes conflict within the Christ-movement and imports the Antioch experience into his interpretation of the Corinthian correspondence. Second, Odell-Scott argues that belonging to Christ cannot be understood as a positive group label because that would result in the restriction of difference and the continuation of existing identities within the Christ-movement.[35] However, unity, which for Odell-Scott comes from a "critique of theocratic privilege," does not imply uniformity, and 1:10 may be read as a call for transformed cognitive processes that allow diversity to continue within the ἐκκλησία (7:17, 20, 24; 8:4–6; 10:31–33).[36] Third, Odell-Scott is unable to account for the parallel expressions in 3:4 and 3:22, which weakens his overall argument (see 1 Clement 47:3). Finally, the household context as argued by Birge, along with her discourse analysis of the "I belong to so-and-so statements" which are framed by "I urge you" in 1:10 and 4:16, is more persuasive than Odell-Scott's reinterpretation of "I belong to Christ."[37]

Paul's concern for the ἐκκλησία in Corinth relates to the fact that the Corinthians were identifying with certain sub-groups for the purpose of self-enhancement, which is one of the key findings of SIT especially as it relates to threats to ingroup identity.[38] Those from Chloe reported to Paul concerning the quarrels among these various sub-groups (1 Cor 1:11), and Paul expresses his desire for the Corinthians to be of the same

33. Odell-Scott 2003: 59, 62.

34. Odell-Scott 2003: 52.

35. Odell-Scott 2003: 151, 165.

36. Odell-Scott 2003: 163.

37. Cf. Birge 2002: 8–9; Odell-Scott 2003: 53, 152.

38. Tajfel and Turner 1986: 16.

mind and same purpose (1 Cor 1:10). He then shifts his attention to the important reasons for the community to be united: their current communal practice is contrary to the gospel, misunderstands the nature of baptism, adversely impacts the Pauline mission and results in an inappropriate definition of their social identity.

Baptism and Roman Social Identity (1:13–17)

In 1:13, Paul contends that Christ as the head of the body cannot be divided into parts. He writes, "Has Christ been divided (μεμέρισται)?" The idea expressed by μεμέρισται is that each sub-group within the ἐκκλησία was claiming its own portion of Christ, an idea that is completely inappropriate according to Paul who rather viewed the community as belonging to Christ (1 Cor 3:23).[39] Christ is to be understood as the head of one body (1 Cor 12:12), a body in which there is a type of unity that at the same time allows for diversity (1 Cor 12:13, 25, 27).[40] He then asks two more rhetorical questions which, based on the presence of μή, require a negative answer: "Was Paul crucified (ἐσταυρώθη) on your behalf?" and "Were you baptized (ἐβαπτίσθητε) into the name of Paul?"[41] The community-defining message of the cross and the identity-

39. This term is from μερίζω meaning "to divide," BDAG 632. LSJ 1103 note that its use in the passive construction, as here, can mean to be split into parties or factions. HRCS 910–11 remark that the LXX usage focuses on the division of an inheritance; see BDB 323: חלק ל in the passive is to be apportioned out. M&M 397 see similar usage to the others but with slightly more emphasis on assigning material possessions. TDNT 4: 594 μέρος may be used as a political *topos* meaning a party or with a juridical sense of a portion (cf. 1 Cor 11:18; 12:27). Paul also uses μερίζω in 1 Cor 7:4, 17 (Rom 12:3; 2 Cor 10:13). Cf. Matt 12:25–26; Mark 3:24–26 which both emphasize that something that is divided cannot continue. Also, the presence of the perfect tense should be noted. The previous apportioning out continues to impact the present situation from the point of view of the author; in this case, the previous allotment results in present factions. Finally, there is a textual variant in relation to μεμέρισται; P[46vid] contains μη before μεμέρισται but should not be considered original in that it appears to have arisen as a harmonization with the rest of the verse and in this case the shorter and harder reading is preferred. Also, the negative particle is unnecessary in that the question clearly requires a negative answer. Contra Hansen 2007: 191–98.

40. Kim 2008: 97–102. Weiss 1910: 16; Schrage (1991: 152) asserts that both 1 Cor 1:13 and 12:12 have the relatively rare ὁ χριστός. See Thiselton (2000: 136–7) who also notes this use of the article. 1 Cor 12:27 contains μέρος which resonates with the diversity in the context of unity from 1 Cor 1:13.

41. Joseph. *AJ* 13.6; cited in Thiselton 2000: 137. See 1 Cor 11:24–26 and the centrality of the ongoing identification and proclamation of the Lord's death. Cf. Peterson 2007: 135–38; Koester 1998: 344.

forming experience of baptism are employed by Paul as evidence that the Corinthians have fundamentally misunderstood the social implications of the Pauline mission, especially as it relates to their identification with group leaders or prototypes.[42]

The community misunderstood the identity-defining significance of baptism. In 1:14–15, Paul is thankful that his involvement with baptisms within the community was minimal. He begins, "I thank (εὐχαριστῶ) God."[43] Earlier Paul had thanked God for the grace the Corinthians had received (1 Cor 1:4), but now he writes, "I thank God that I did not baptize (ἐβάπτισα) any of you" because that would have inadvertently contributed to the division within the community. He then remembers that he baptized Crispus, possibly "the synagogue leader" from Acts 18:8, as well as Gaius, a Roman who evidently was able to have "the whole assembly" within his house (Rom 16:23).[44] The reason that he was thankful for this was "that someone (τις) could not say (εἴπῃ)" (the use of the subjunctive εἴπῃ and the indefinite pronoun τις as the subject suggest that he does not have a specific group in mind at this point) "that you were baptized (ἐβάπτισα) into my [Paul's] name." Paul, in a general fashion, addresses the issue of naming and thus a primary means of social identification within the community. The person involved in one's baptism should be relativized. Tajfel and Turner argue for the centrality of language as the means of communicating social influence and that "the mere perception of belonging to two distinct groups . . . is sufficient to trigger intergroup discrimination favoring the in-group."[45] The divisions that were occurring do not require theological issues or opponents but can simply arise from the normal categorization process. Baptism should define social identity in relation to Christ and not in relation to the person who performed the baptism.

In 1:16, Paul recalls, "Now I also baptized (ἐβάπτισα) the household (οἶκον) of Stephanas" and then brings the matter to a close by

42. Stommel (1959: 6–8) suggested that Roman bathing practices were integral in the development of some local Christ-movement baptismal practices. DeMaris (2008: 50) recently suggested that baptism in Corinth was a ritually-subversive act against Roman hegemony; however, it is equally likely that a significant number within the ἐκκλησία were treating baptism in a manner consonant with Roman patronage and water practices which functioned as status-ordering principles. See further Tucker 2010a.

43. Some mss do not include τῷ Θεῷ but see Schnabel 2006: 85.

44. Bock 2007: 579. But see Jewett 2007: 980–81.

45. Tajfel and Turner 1986: 13.

saying "I do not remember, beyond these, if I baptized (ἐβάπτισα) any others." The previous two examples were individuals; however, "the household of Stephanas" was baptized, not just Stephanas. This allows for a plausible scenario in which social identity, intragroup behavior, and group belonging could become issues. If Stephanas and his household identified with Paul and others did not, then one could conceive of a way in which the person involved in the baptism became for that household a group prototype. For Paul this could serve as a means by which commitment and conformity to expected group norms might be furthered (1 Cor 16:15–17). May understands the issue of group norms and the "interaction on the basis of group membership . . . as symbols of distinction" to be two of the reasons "social identity theory" serves as a useful heuristic for understanding "the ways in which Paul seeks to regulate intergroup activity."[46] It should be noted that the same applies to the intragroup activity as well. In 1 Cor 16:16, Paul clearly thinks that "the congregation should 'fit into' the order provided by the 'first converts of the household of Stephanas.'"[47] Moreover, this is an example of the way Paul understands Roman social identity to continue to be relevant within the Christ-movement.

This problem would have been acute in the Roman Empire in that the οἶκος/*familia* "household," with its reliance on kinship discourse, provided a key ordering principle for defining social identity. So, when Paul identifies "the household of Stephanas," he is addressing a central component of Roman social structure. Here οἶκος refers to those who are under the authority and influence of Stephanas. A similar use of οἶκος occurs in Gen 7:1 in relation to Noah's household, while Isaeus 10.4 employs οἶκος in the context of a dispute over the estate of Aristarchus which includes family members as well as all of the possessions within the estate. It is plausible that one of the difficulties within the Pauline community was a misunderstanding of the continued role of the οἶκος/*familia* within the ἐκκλησία.[48] Had its significance been obliterated, transformed, or reprioritized "in Christ" (1 Cor 11:34; 14:35; 16:19; Rom 16:5)? The centrality of the οἶκος/*familia* within the civic life and the boundary crossing event of baptism combine to produce a contact zone

46. May 2004: 22.
47. Ehrensperger 2007: 173.
48. Økland 2004: 131–67.

of identity formation.[49] Before we move on to 1:17 we should briefly discuss the social implications of baptism and social identity in 1 Cor 12:13.

Clarke understands the discussion on baptism to be related to identification with political figures which were central to civic life in the empire.[50] If Clarke is correct, this would be evidence for a misunderstanding of the ongoing role of social identification within the community (1 Cor 6:1–11). While the misplaced focus on leaders is likely, a misunderstanding about the nature of the transformation of identity that has occurred "in Christ" through baptism appears as a focus in this passage.[51]

In 1 Cor 12:13, Paul writes, "In one Spirit (πνεύματι) we were all baptized (ἐβαπτίσθημεν) into one body (σῶμα)." The importance of baptism for Paul is that it transfers one into the body of Christ and is the embodiment of a transformed identity (2 Cor 5:17). This transformed identity does not remove one's previous identity. The next phrase in 12:13 asserts, "whether Jews or Greeks, slaves or free." Ethnic and social identity are extraneous salvifically; however, those identities continue to be important "in Christ" in a reprioritized manner (1 Cor 7:17–24). The misunderstanding of the Corinthian Christ-followers related to the way their previous identity was to function within the Christ-following community (1 Cor 3:3–4). For Paul, the Corinthians' previous identity was not to be opposed but transformed.

In 1:17, Paul summarizes his argument concerning the Corinthians' lack of understanding of their "in Christ" social identity and transitions into his next topic of discussion concerning Christ as the wisdom and power of God. He begins with γάρ which is repeated in 1:18 "to introduce several arguments for the same assertion," in this case that Christ is the wisdom and power of God.[52] For Paul, this is to be the content of the primary identity-forming discourse within the community. He takes the view that "Christ did not send (ἀπέστειλέν) me to baptize (βαπτίζειν) but to preach the gospel (εὐαγγελίζεσθαι)."

Since baptism has become the focus of social presentation and communal behavior, Paul asserts social influence to remind them that

---

49. Adams 2000: 93.

50. Clarke 1993: 92.

51. Dunn 1970: 117–18; Horrell 1996: 82–84.

52. BDAG 189.

his primary purpose is to "preach the gospel" not "to baptize."[53] He also recognizes that there is a problem with regard to the use of language as a means of social influence, so he reminds them, by the use of a descriptive genitive, that his preaching was "not with wisdom of speech (σοφία λόγου)." He is not disparaging baptism or the importance of communicating clearly but pointing out that either of these activities has the potential to redefine social identity, as evidenced in 1:12. His purpose in preaching the gospel in the manner he does is to avoid the possibility "that the cross of Christ might not be effective (κενωθῇ)." Paul takes the position that anything that obscures "the cross of Christ" (ὁ σταυρὸς τοῦ Χριστοῦ) within the community must be de-emphasized, and this includes the elevation of certain aspects of the Corinthians' Roman identity, personal preferences for leaders, or desire for social status within the civic community.

Paul is arguing that an improper reliance on old categories of power and identity could limit the ethos-transforming power of the cross of Christ. This transformation may be described as a process of judging all aspects of Christ-followers' identity that are not congruent with the "in Christ" identity. This understands identity as a social and theological category that includes both participation in the death of and belonging to Christ. Thus, being "in Christ" provides the cognitive resources (e.g., narratives, memories, norms, or social schemata) to understand and apply the social implications of the gospel. Paul's solution for this dilemma (i.e., those still relying on old power structures) begins in 1:18 where he makes this contrast between power and identity more explicit by describing a social identity shaped by the gospel.

PAUL'S SOCIAL CATEGORIZATION: INGROUP AND OUTGROUP (1:18-25)

In 1:10-17, Paul points out the lack of salient "in Christ" social identity in the Corinthians ἐκκλησία and contends that a transformed understanding of the cross of Christ and baptism in his name is the way to address this problem. Next, Paul describes for the Christ-followers in Corinth what an identity shaped by the wisdom and power of God looks like. He does this by means of "the word connected with the cross," a

---

53. Understanding both βαπτίζειν and εὐαγγελίζεσθαι as epexegetical infinitives of purpose.

metonymous way to refer to the gospel. He thus clarifies the essence of the gospel while employing ethnic and cultural discourse, a way to form social identity, to help the Corinthians to understand the social implications of belonging to Christ and accepting his gospel.

Tajfel describes social categorization "as the ordering of [the] social environment in terms of groupings of persons in a manner which makes sense to the individual."[54] Paul argues within a similar framework by adjusting the community's perception of the outgroup and by offering a redefinition of the ingroup. Jenkins notes that categorization is an epistemological concern, and "categoric identity" is employed in order to "orient behavior"; categorization then functions at "the conjunction between power and knowledge," a contact zone of categorization.[55] Paul's social categorization in 1:18–21 is one way he attempts to change the social identity of his hearers from an identity primarily shaped by the world's view of wisdom to one shaped by the gospel accurately applied in the life of the community.

In 1:18, Paul's rhetoric categorizes people into two social groups, one positive and the other negative.[56] The γάρ connects this argument with 1:17; thus Paul supports his assertion with a reference to Christ being the wisdom and power of God, and his mission is to proclaim that message (Isa 61:1 LXX).[57] The shaping of the social environment in Paul's discourse centers on the descriptive genitive "the word connected with the cross" (ὁ λόγος ὁ τοῦ σταυροῦ).[58] This rhetorically constructed environment is populated with two cognitive entities but further distinguished as an antithesis with regard to the Corinthians' view of the message. Antithesis is an identity-forming discursive strategy for Paul.[59]

54. Tajfel 1978b: 61.

55. Jenkins 2000: 7–10, 19.

56. The contrastive μέν δέ is used to distinguish strongly the two groups.

57. Wilk (2005: 135) rightly understands an "allusion" to the Isaiah passage in this section. Cf. Dickson 2003: 174–76.

58. The second article ὁ in this phrase is employed for specification. P[46], B, and 1739 do not include this second article. Brown (1995: 159) notes that the cross calls the Corinthians' identity into question. Litfin (1994: 219) remarks, "Paul has asserted that it was his commission from Christ simply to proclaim the Gospel, not to use σοφία λόγου (1:17). The Apostle's point is that both the form (straight-forward proclamation) and the content (the crucified Christ) were for him divinely ordained." Käsemann (1971: 50) asserts that "the cross helps no one who does not hear the word of the cross and ground his [sic] faith on that." Cf. Stuhlmacher 1987: 328.

59. Watson (2007: 218, 229–34) understands Paul's antithesis to be that which creates "ideological space" and serves as a means of constructing "communal identity." Watson's

Those within the outgroup, "those who are perishing," understand the message as "foolishness." The ingroup, on the other hand, is categorized as "we who are being saved." Notice that Paul includes himself in this group (2 Cor 2:15), those for whom the message is "the power of God," taken as a genitive of source. It is power that has its source in God. Paul's argument in 1:18 is designed to realign the Corinthians' social categorization in hopes of adjusting current levels of intergroup discrimination; they are embracing local aspects of their Roman social identity that are in need of reprioritization within the ἐκκλησία in light of "the word connected with the cross."

Paul, in 1:19, continues to support his previous assertion concerning Christ by another use of γάρ and more specifically by a quotation from Isa 29:14 LXX that is introduced by "for it is written" (γέγραπται).[60] The reference further categorizes the two groups by defining more clearly God's action in relation "to those who are perishing" (1 Cor 1:18). Paul is further establishing a "system of orientation which helps to create and define the individual's place" within the Pauline community.[61]

In the present argument, this orientation relates to both wisdom and power. In the original Isaianic oracle, the worship of the people of God is described as pretentious (Isa 29:13) with incongruence between the outward and inward spiritual shape of the community involved in worship. This orientation resulted in a lack of understanding of God's actual work among them. In a similar fashion, Paul employs this reference in order to teach the Corinthian Christ-followers that the wisdom on which they are relying, God will "frustrate" (ἀθετήσω).[62] Paul, pos-

---

(2007: 54, 56, 83) view of identity falls short because of his use of Jewish identity as a negative foil for "Christian" identity. However, his recognition of the identity-forming power of antithesis is most important. Wilk (2005: 136) does not see a complete antithesis here; however, he is relying on a definition of antithesis that is too limited. Paul is capable of comparing aspects of binary categories while not engaging in a complete antithetical argument (see Watson 2006: 100). Watson's approach seeks to redefine aspects of what is understood as a Pauline discourse of antithesis. Adams (2000: 108) is undoubtedly right when he sees the "central antithesis" as "the contrariety between the wisdom of the world and the wisdom of God."

60. We follow Wilk's (2005: 134) approach that argues that a quotation refers to "a reference marked with a quotation formula," whether the Corinthians would have understood it as such or not. Stanley (1992: 37) argues for the citation introduction formula, "clear interpretive gloss," and "demonstrable syntactical tension."

61. Tajfel 1978b: 63.

62. Davis 1984: 71.

sibly under the influence of Ps 32:10 LXX, changes the final word in the LXX quotation from "hidden" (κρύψω), which accurately translates the hithpael הִתְהַלֵּל from the MT, to "frustrate" (ἀθετήσω) in order to make it clear that he is not speaking of an esoteric form of wisdom but one that should be plain to everyone. Paul's categorization focuses on the idea that none of these other systems of wisdom ultimately leads to salvation, a point he makes more forcefully in the next verse.[63]

Categorization serves as a guide for social structuring based on cognitive assessments "often related to value differentials" designed "to enhance the subjective differences on certain dimensions between categories and the subjective similarities within categories."[64] What results is an ingroup-outgroup approach to social structuring. In 1:20, Paul engages in a similar process of "social stereotyping" as he rhetorically positions three groups outside the ingroup, based on external differences in relation to the Corinthians' search for wisdom, as compared to Paul's (1 Cor 1:20a–c), and internal similarities with regard to the Corinthians' actual approach to wisdom, which differs from Paul's (1 Cor 1:20d).

If social identity is shaped by group memberships, then the following rhetorical questions are designed by Paul to make it clear that not all group memberships are equally beneficial with regard to the values associated with them. He begins in 1:20[65] by asking: "Where is the wise? Where is the scribe? Where is the debater of this age?"[66] These three are understood as "rhetorical" outgroups, and Paul provides a reinterpretation of the social significance of these groups within the Pauline communities. They serve metonymically for any attempt to secure salvation by means of wisdom. They do not require a derisive attitude towards, for example, Jewish scribes, as in Wilk who understands Paul to be rewriting Isa 33:18b "as indicating the incompetence of Jewish sages to know the

---

63. Stanley 1992: 186; 2004: 79–83; Ciampa and Rosner 2007: 698. Stanley (2004: 82) also notes that this language could refer to the "Greco-Roman myths about gods who bring down humans possessed by hubris or who destroy people and places without cause."

64. Tajfel 1978b: 62.

65. Williams 2001: 50; Wilk (2005: 137–39) also finds allusions to Isa 33:18b; 19:11–12; 44:25b in 1 Cor 1:20.

66. Adams (2000: 106) considers the importance of apocalyptic in Paul's argumentation: "history is divided into two ages, though Paul only speaks of 'this age' (ὁ αἰὼν οὗτος, 1:20; 2:6–8; 3:18), not of the coming age."

wisdom of God as revealed in Christ."[67] There is no indication in this passage that Paul is making an accusation concerning the incompetence of Jewish scribes. These groups are "cognitive entit[ies]" used for rhetorical purposes by Paul to further his argument against any attempt to understand salvation as wisdom, not as an argument to eliminate the social significance of wisdom in general. Watson resists the idea that the issue is with wisdom but instead asserts that this passage "is covertly directed against the followers of Apollos, who believe that wisdom and the gospel are compatible."[68] While the connection with Apollos is not fully convincing, notice that Watson does not draw the negative inference concerning Jewish scribes in this context. The sum total of the knowledge of these three stereotypical groups of wisdom-seekers is rendered foolish by God: "Has God not made the wisdom of this world[69] foolishness?" (1 Cor 2:6–8, 16; 3:18). This recategorization is designed to resocialize the ἐκκλησία in relation to the broader Roman society with regard to its general outlook concerning wisdom and salvation,[70] as Adams explains, in order to overcome the Corinthians' "overvaluation of culturally defined wisdom."[71]

Paul's social categorization has its basis in the work of God, who, according to 1:20, made the world's wisdom unfruitful salvifically. According to 1:21, God decided to save those who believed in what the world understood as foolishness. Tajfel notes that categorization brings together "social objects" and "system(s) of belief."[72] Paul's use of Isa 29:14 is clear; the world's conception of wisdom is incompatible with "the word connected with the cross."[73] Paul grounds his assertion in 1:21 by writing,

67. Wilk 2005: 138.

68. Watson 2007: 154. Paul's relationship with Apollos is addressed on p. 213.

69. Adams (2000: 105) notes the "high frequency" of the use of κόσμος as an indicator of its importance in 1 Corinthians. Also, it is "consistently used in a negative way," and from a sociological perspective it is used to "contrast the κόσμος and the church." For Adams, Paul employs κόσμος as just mentioned in order to address "the issue of weak group boundaries in Corinth."

70. See Paus. *Descr.* 2.4.1 and the reference to Athena Chalinitis in Corinth. Keener (2005: 28) notes the Jewish critique of wisdom with regard to salvation: *Jub.* 36:5; *Sib. Or.* 3:229, 584–90; *Let. Aris.* 137.

71. Adams 2000: 108.

72. Tajfel 1978b: 62.

73. Adams (2000: 111–13), however, may push the binary relationship between the world and those who believe too far. Paul realizes the Corinthian Christ-followers are in a new age; however, they still have to exist within the Roman Empire. So, while there is

"the world, in the wisdom of God, through wisdom, did not know God."
The epistemic condition is that God is not revealed salvifically through
wisdom. Rather "God was pleased to save (σῶσαι) those who believed
(τοὺς πιστεύοντας) through the foolishness of preaching." The social
categorization is now apparent; there are two "categoric" identities being
constructed: one which is "perishing" and is associated with the world,
and the other which includes "those who are being saved."[74] Paul's argument in 1:18–21 orients the Corinthian Christ-followers' behavior and
creates ideological space for them to adjust their over-identification with
their current social environment with regard to wisdom.[75] Paul's categorization functions to create this ideological space in which a gospel-
shaped social identity may be formed.

Social categorization is required because of the existence of more
than one referent group.[76] The existence of multiple groups and the resulting intragroup interaction are subject to the process of social comparison in which the distinctions between the various sub-groups are
discerned, and ingroup and outgroup membership may be clarified. A
similar process appears in Paul's discourse in 1:22–24 with regard to his
shaping of social identity within the Corinthian ἐκκλησία.

Paul relies on a social comparison that has its basis in a particularistic understanding of ethnic identity described in 1:22–24 as two
different approaches to wisdom and power. Buell refers to this as ethnic
reasoning which is a discursive strategy within early texts which defines
"ethnicity through religious practices, viewing ethnicity as mutable even
if 'real,' universalizing ethnicity and religion, and using ethnic ideas as
polemic."[77] In a stereotypical fashion in 1:22 he notes, "Jews ('Ιουδαῖοι)
ask for signs" and "Greeks (῞Ελληνες) search for wisdom." In 1:23
the message of "Christ-crucified" is described as a "stumbling block
(σκάνδαλον) to Jews" and "foolishness to the gentiles (ἔθνεσιν)." Notice
that Paul has shifted from ῞Ελληνες in 1:22 to ἔθνεσιν[78] in 1:23 but returns

---

a disjunction between the two approaches to social existence, to argue that "there is no
continuity between them" may be too strong. Paul is not against wisdom in general, only
the reliance on wisdom for salvific purposes (Ciampa and Rosner 2007: 698).

74. Jenkins 2000: 7–10.

75. Jenkins 2000: 19.

76. Meeks 2009: 139–40.

77. Buell 2005: 33. See p. 77 for a discussion of Buell.

78. BDAG 276; LSJ 480; *TDNT* 2.11, 367; Lopez (2008: 7) proposes reading Paul "as
the apostle to the defeated nations."

again to Ἕλλησιν in 1:24. For Paul, Greek identity and gentile identity are interchangeable; however, the same does not apply to Ἰουδαῖοι; it is more rhetorically stable in 1:22–24.[79] Paul's argument here relies on an already existing social comparison for its effectiveness. He is redeploying relevant ethnic categories for his broader rhetorical purpose which is to emphasize the importance of transformed cognitive processes in understanding as plausible that which was previously rejected as foolish, "Christ crucified" (Χριστὸν ἐσταυρωμένον).

In 1:24, Paul returns to what he had argued was the foundation for the Corinthians' identity, their "calling" (1 Cor 1:1–2, 9), which is further defined in the context of an ethnic comparison and classification, "both Jew and Greek (Ἕλλησιν)." He then reorients the community to the centrality of Christ and argues that Christ is both "God's power (δύναμιν)" and "God's wisdom (σοφίαν)." Both wisdom and power are key components in the identity-shaping process: wisdom as a cognitive resource that creates congruence between internal belief and external behavior, and power as that which assures that this congruence occurs. Power, however, may be exercised in a dominating or an empowering manner in the formation of identity.[80] Paul employs it in an empowering way so that the community's "in Christ" identity may be transformed and their perception of power redefined in the context of "the weakness of God" which then is understood as "stronger than human power." The cognitive dimensions of identity formation which are evident here in social categorization and social comparison result in social identification. This is a process of ascription distinct from the first two but still part of the larger process of shaping social identity.[81]

---

79. This could be an indication of Paul's reflection on the nature of ethnic identities. Johnson Hodge (2007: 5, 131) alleges that "although *Ioudaioi* and gentiles now share a common ancestor, Paul does not collapse them into one group (of 'Christian,' for example). Gentiles-in-Christ and Jews are separate but related lineages of Abraham." While we are in agreement with the statement on p. 131 that "Christ is the link for gentiles to the linage of Abraham," the way that works in 1 Corinthians is unclear in that Abraham is not referenced (1 Cor 10:1).

80. Ehrensperger 2007: 34, 132.

81. Jenkins 1996: 23.

CALLING AND THE ROLE OF PREVIOUS ROMAN
SOCIAL IDENTITIES (1:26–31)

Social identification provides the "cognitive mapping"[82] necessary to understand similarity and difference and to navigate the historic references, metaphors, and analogies used to ascribe identity. Here Jenkins' model "of the *internal-external dialectic of identification* as the process whereby all identities—individual and collective—are constituted" is important in that Paul addresses specific aspects of communal identification in 1:26–27.[83] Identities are not simply asserted but negotiated within the context of communal life, which describes accurately Paul's efforts in communication with the Corinthian Christ-followers.[84]

Paul relies on a concept similar to social identification in 1:26 as he focuses on calling and previous social identities within the community. Specifically, he begins by employing the resources of social memory, asking the community "to remember" their social identification at the time of their "call" (κλῆσιν).[85] This past social identification is reinforced by the use of kinship language designed to support ingroup classification by referring to them as "brothers and sisters" (ἀδελφοί). In Corinth, the divisions within the Christ-movement revolved around issues of social identification. These divisions had created relational barriers within the ἐκκλησία which, Robertson argues, had become one among a number of potential relational networks within the Corinthians' broader social environment with which they could identify.[86] Paul, drawing from Jer 9:22–23, reminds the Corinthian Christ-followers of the circumstances of their call, thus shaping identity within the community.[87] He writes, "not

---

82. Kitchin and Freundschuh 2000: 2. The use of this term relates primarily to the structuring of the cognitive processes in general; however, in relationship to some of the Pauline metaphors in chapter 3, the spatial elements will emerge, see p. 226.

83. This concept from Jenkins was introduced in chapter 2; see p. 43.

84. Jenkins (1996: 20–21, 113) explains that identity "is never unilateral" but emerges from the interaction between the way one views oneself and the way one is viewed within one's community.

85. Esler 2005: 10–12. The verb βλέπετε is construed as an imperative, and its cognitive function is in view rather than its physical function. Paul desires to focus the Corinthians' attention on the event that was central to forming the community, their "call."

86. Robertson 2001: 31.

87. Robertson and Plummer 1911: 25.

many were,"[88] which is repeated two more times: "wise according to the flesh (σάρκα)," "powerful (δυνατοί)," or "of a noble birth (εὐγενεῖς)."[89] Paul is pointing out that the Corinthians' previous social identity was lacking in status and recognition within the broader cultural framework. They were not wise, influential, or well-born, so in some ways, when they were called, they embodied the despised nature of "the word connected with the cross" in 1:18–25, a point Paul will make more evident in 1:27–28.

A social identity shaped by "the word connected with the cross" embraces what the world often despises. The ἀλλά in 1:27 emphasizes a strong contrast from 1:26 with regard to the Corinthians' current social identification. When God picked those who would make up his people, he did not choose them from the elite classes. Rather God chose[90] those whom the elites within the empire would have rejected as acceptable candidates for anything except the most demeaning and inhumane stations in life.[91] Paul continues, "God chose the foolish things of the world," and God's purpose for this choosing is clear in the next clause, "in order that (ἵνα) God might shame (καταισχύνῃ) the wise."[92] The association of wisdom with the Roman apprehension of Greek educational identity is now called into question.[93] The Corinthians' reliance on any school of philosophy with regard to salvation will ultimately be displayed publicly as an unacceptable means of righteousness, holiness, or redemption (1 Cor 1:30).

The next antithesis addresses an over-reliance on power for security, an allusion to Roman identity and Rome's pretentious claims with regard to its empire. Paul writes, "God chose the weak things of the

88. In other words, some were. Horrell (1996: 134) provides an important warning concerning this passage: "the rhetorical nature of Paul's declaration should certainly make us wary of reading 1.26 simply as a piece of sociological information."

89. Similar aspects of Roman identity were uncovered in chapter 4; see pp. 91, 107, 117. Cf. Herodas Mime 2.32 "those who may vaunt their birth (τῇ γενῇ φυσῶντες) with better cause" (Cf. Sharpley 1906: 11; M&M 679; Welborn 2005: 87–88).

90. Paul employs the aorist middle form of ἐκλέγω three times in these two verses, emphasizing the electing work of God.

91. Still 2006: 783.

92. Honor and shame terminology is evident throughout the letter (1 Cor 1:27; 11:4, 5, 22 καταισχύνω; 1 Cor 4:14 ἐντρέπων; 1 Cor 4:10 ἄτιμος; 1 Cor 6:20; 7:23; 12:23, 24 τιμή. Cf. Neyrey 1998: 13–34; Finney 2005: 20). See the earlier discussion on p. 106 dealing with honor as an ordering principle of Roman social identity.

93. This will be discussed when dealing with 1 Cor 4:15 on p. 259.

world." That which Rome would view with derision is what God chose. God's purpose is likewise, "in order that he might shame (καταισχύνῃ) the strong." Those who are relying on the political power of Rome will soon find out that God has chosen another approach to power (1 Cor 2:6–8).

Paul continues to shape the Corinthian Christ-followers' social identity by arguing that God's choice of that which the world despises brings into relief the cross of Christ which then leaves no room for boasting by humanity. He has just illustrated this in 1:26 by a social comparison related to the Corinthian Christ-followers and introduced the idea in 1:27 that God's choice puts to shame those who socially identify themselves as wise and powerful. In 1:28–29 he continues by pointing out that God's purpose in choosing those who are despised is to put an end to those who are wise and powerful, and to deconstruct any residual grounds for boasting within the community. In 1:30–31 the implications of following Christ are made obvious as Paul reconstructs the ingroup: Christ is the wisdom of God but not only that. He is also righteousness, holiness, and redemption. The identity-forming antithesis introduced in 1:26 is now complete: those who are not wise, powerful, and well-born have become righteous, holy, and redeemed.[94] This describes a gospel-shaped social identity.

In 1:28, God's choice further shapes social identity. Paul includes his third successive use of the clause "God chose" (ἐξελέξατο ὁ Θεός) but this time the verb has two direct objects. "The base things of the world" (τὰ ἀγενῆ τοῦ κόσμου) are further described as "even the despised things" (καὶ τὰ ἐξουθενημένα), that is to say, appositionally, "the things being nothing" (τὰ μὴ ὄντα). The combination of clauses fully describes those whom God chose: the base, despised, nothings of humanity; the antithesis could not be starker.[95] The purpose clause that follows explains why God chose the way he did, "for the purpose (ἵνα) of making powerless the things that are powerful."

In 1:29, Paul summarizes 1:26–28 by making clear God's purpose in choosing as God did. The conjunction ὅπως encompasses the three previous ἵνα clauses. The focus of this summary includes God's election in relation to "all humankind" (πᾶσα σάρξ) and brings into relief the centrality of the Roman honor-shame culture. In 1:27, Paul

---

94. Winter 2002a: 193.

95. Thiselton 2000: 185.

uses the present active subjunctive καταισχύνῃ "might shame," and in
1:29 he employs the aorist middle subjunctive, μὴ καυχήσηται "might
not boast in themselves"; both of these terms directly address issues of
social identity. Thiselton recognizes this and understands Paul to be al-
luding broadly to issues related to "dishonoured reputation, loss of face,
and public humiliation which deprives the self of its social identity."[96]
Thiselton has discerned the social identity context of 1:26–31; the focus of the honor-shame framework was the maintenance of a culturally
defined, acceptable, public presentation and identity. The next phrase,
"before God," with its allusion to Jer 9:23–24, correlates with the Jewish
tradition of having failed God and reflects the acumen with which
Paul weaves Roman honor-shame references with Jewish concerns for
faithfulness to the requirements of God. God's purpose in choosing the
despised was to put an end to the wise and the powerful while decon-
structing any further grounds for boasting before God. The focus on the
wise appears to be related to Greek philosophy, while the concern for
power has Roman imperial ideology as its focus. The boasting would
include both but also addresses those within the community to some
degree. It should be noted, as well, that if the Corinthians' involvement in
the civic functions of Roman Corinth is accepted, this provides a more
plausible scenario for Paul's arguments being focused primarily within
the community.

In 1:30, Paul begins his contrasting perspective with the prepositional phrase "from him" (ἐξ αὐτοῦ), which reinforces the electing work
of God that has constituted the Corinthian community, thus increasing
their cognitive awareness of their social identity and group membership.
His primary indicator of the sphere of a transformed identity is now
clear: "You are in Christ" redefines the Corinthians' assessment of their
group membership. He also redeploys the emotional resources of the
group by further describing Christ in relation to that which had created
much of their initial emotional upheaval and division: "who became
wisdom (σοφία) to us from God." If wisdom is to be found within the
community, it is found "in Christ" through "the word connected with the
cross," the message that Paul proclaims which has the power to shape
identity (1 Cor 1:18). He then completes the identity-forming antithesis
by further describing who Christ has become for the community: "but

---

96. Thiselton 2000: 187.

also righteousness and holiness and redemption" (δικαιοσύνη τε καὶ ἁγιασμὸς καὶ ἀπολύτρωσις).

In 1:31, Paul continues to shape identity as he employs the citation formula καθὼς γέγραπται and subsequently loosely cites Jer 9:22–23 and possibly 1 Sam 2:10, "Let the one who boasts, boast in the Lord." Paul wants the Corinthians to understand that there is an acceptable ground for boasting, and that is in the work of the Lord and identification with him, not in social categories such as wisdom which will not result in salvation, or power which will not result in security. With this antithesis complete, Paul now shifts his argument to the way "the word connected with the cross" establishes the shape of identity through proclamation.

THE SOCIAL IDENTITY FORMING PROCLAMATION OF PAUL (2:1–5)

Group leaders shape the social identity of group members by embodying ingroup values and proclaiming those values within the group. They are expected to reflect the prototypical position of the group itself and are selected because they reinforce the previously agreed-upon group position on a particular issue. Paul, as the founder of the ἐκκλησία in Corinth, was the original leader; however, he had moved on, and his position was no longer that of primary group leader. In Paul's absence he expected those such as Stephanas (1 Cor 16:15–17), Timothy (1 Cor 4:17; 16:10), possibly Apollos (1 Cor 3:4–6, 22; 4:6; 16:12), or others within the Pauline network to serve as group prototypes; however, it is not altogether clear from the text that Paul's rhetorical vision for the community was the salient one. Thus, Paul writes to remind the Corinthians of his approach to communication when he was among them in the hope that it would contribute to conformity to a renewed set of group norms. Paul describes these under the rubric of faith in 2:5 in terms of behavior (1 Cor 7:17; 11:15; 14:33–34; 16:1, 19).

In 2:1, Paul employs himself as a group prototype who did not rely on the resources of human wisdom when proclaiming the gospel. He reminds the Corinthians that "when I came to you, brothers and sisters (ἀδελφοί), I came (ἦλθον) not with superior speech or wisdom." This last phrase is designed to negate the influence of Roman identity in relation to speech, whether Greek philosophy or Roman imperial ideology.[97]

---

97. Pogoloff 1992: 10; Winter 2002a: 147–48; Finney 2005: 29.

Paul continues, "as I proclaimed (καταγγέλλων) to you," the adverbial participle of manner indicating the way he came to them. What he taught them was "the testimony dependent on God" (τὸ μαρτύριον τοῦ Θεοῦ), taking the genitive as source.[98] The testimony had its basis only in God and not in anyone else. Paul employs the resources of social memory to construct the community in a way that reaffirms his original rhetorical vision for the straightforward proclamation of the gospel.

In 2:2, Paul begins with γάρ and provides a reason for his previous approach to teaching. He writes, "For I determined (ἔκρινα) not to know anything among you." The aorist ἔκρινα connects back to ἦλθον in 2:1 for its temporal background and to 1:23 for its ideological context. So, at the time of his coming to Corinth, Paul had decided to know nothing "except Jesus Christ and him crucified (ἐσταυρωμένον)." For Paul this would overcome the two social pressures in Corinth: Greek philosophy and Roman imperial ideology. Jesus would be seen as the wisdom and power of God.

In 2:3, Paul's description of his demeanor in general also functions as a piece of evidence in his argument to reconstruct his preferred group prototype in Corinth. His emotional state of mind was "in weakness (ἀσθενείᾳ) and in fear (φόβῳ) and in much trembling (τρόμῳ)," a stark contrast to one who relies on the resources of philosophical wisdom or political power (Acts 18:9). Paul's self-presentation in the intragroup settings amounted to a social performance which is now being relived rhetorically. It is a form of negotiation and a way to reconnect his social presence with the community of Christ-followers in Corinth. For Paul, it is clear that God had already legitimated his message, and thus he reminds the Corinthians of that in the next verse.

Paul returns to the content of his proclamation in 2:4. He writes, "my message and my preaching" which best describes all of the verbal proclamation activities in which he engaged while among the Corinthians. Paul

---

98. NA[27] reads μυστήριον and is attested quite early (e.g., P[46vid?], ℵ*, A, and C) but may have made it into the mss because of the use of the same word in 1 Cor 2:7. However, the same may be said for the reading preferred here, μαρτύριον, which is attested in e.g., ℵ[c], B, D, and G. This latter reading may be explained by a connection with the same word used in 1 Cor 1:6; however, the external witness slightly favors the latter reading. Furthermore, the testimony that had its basis in God fits the context better than a discussion about the mystery of God that is more relevant to Paul's argument in 1 Cor 2:7 (cf. Garland 2003:88; Fee 1987: 88; Schnabel 2006: 153; Weiss 1910: 46; Gladd 2008: 123–26).

then casts another identity-forming antithesis concerning his proclamation which "was not with persuasive words of wisdom" (οὐκ ἐν πειθοῖς σοφίας λόγοις). Paul did not employ an approach to communication that relied on rhetorical brilliance while in Corinth. The use of πειθοῖς describes a generally negative picture of attempting to influence someone to engage in improper behavior (Matt 27:20). Strüder is convincing in noting that Paul's approach to proclamation rather relied on the agency and power of the Spirit to shape identity.[99] Paul declares that his proclamation was not validated through rhetorical brilliance "but (ἀλλ')" in proof produced by the Spirit (πνεύματος) and power (δυνάμεως)."[100] In this move Paul's language acutely becomes a means of social influence. He is specifically seeking to affect the Corinthian Christ-followers' opinions and behaviors related to public teaching.

Paul's purpose becomes clear in 2:5; he wants to be assured that the Corinthians' faith, that is their commitment to the norms of behavior within the community, is centered on God's power and not anything else. This is vital to Paul's strategy of shaping identity later in the letter (1 Cor 13:13; 15:14, 17; 16:14). He concludes this aspect of his argument, "so that your faith (πίστις) might not rest in human wisdom." His purpose in 2:4 is that the Corinthians would not rely on the identity-forming potential inherent in human wisdom, whether it was Greek philosophy or Roman imperial ideology. Paul's rhetorical vision for the community, on the other hand, is that their faith would rest "in the power of God." The Corinthians are not ultimately to rely on any other power than God's power, nor any other wisdom than God's wisdom, to shape their social identity. Issues of wisdom, power, and identity are central to the discursive strategy Paul undertakes in 1:18—2:5; at the center of this strategy is the argument that "the word connected with the cross" has the power to shape and thus transform identity.

---

99. Strüder 2005: 3. Brawley (2005: 23) recognizes the important role the "coming of the Spirit" had with regard to "the group identity" of the early Christ-movement.

100. The strong contrastive ἀλλά is used to point out that Paul's proclamation contained ἀποδείξει "proof," construing the genitives πνεύματος καὶ δυνάμεως as subjectives, in that this demonstration is shaped by the Spirit not by rhetorical brilliance. There is a hendiadys in this clause in that the two words are both describing the Spirit. The use of power is made obvious because of its connection with important aspects of Roman civic identity and Roman imperial ideology.

CONCLUSION

This chapter uncovered Paul's strategy in 1:10—2:5 in addressing the Corinthian Christ-follower's lack of salient "in Christ" social identity. First, it was discovered that there was a misunderstanding concerning the fundamental significance of the Corinthians' "in Christ" social identity. Second, Paul's solution for this problem was to recast his rhetorical vision for communal life by means of the wisdom and power of the gospel message. Third, he pointed out the way God's calling and God's choice invert many of the social values of the world. Finally, Paul reminded the Corinthians of the way he modeled Christ-movement ingroup values while proclaiming the gospel among them, and therefore they should likewise rely on God's power within the ἐκκλησία. What was the major hindrance with regard to a salient "in Christ" social identity? That is the topic for the next chapter.

7

Hindrances and Solutions for a Salient
"in Christ" Social Identity

INTRODUCTION

THIS CHAPTER DESCRIBES WHAT Paul understands as a hindrance to salient "in Christ" social identity: an over-reliance on the world's wisdom and power (i.e., Roman imperial ideology). Then it uncovers Paul's solution for overcoming this: the agency of the Spirit and the mind of Christ (i.e., transformed cognitive processes). Finally, it provides a second example of an over-reliance on the world's wisdom and power: divisions based on loyalty to prototypical group leaders.

HINDRANCE: OVER-RELIANCE ON THE WORLD'S
WISDOM AND POWER (2:6–9)

In 2:6, Paul addresses the Corinthian Christ-followers' misunderstanding in relation to their social categorization of power and their over-confidence in the political acumen of Rome, which had become a hindrance for the development of a salient "in Christ" social identity.[1] Paul begins "And we speak wisdom to the mature" (σοφίαν δὲ λαλοῦμεν ἐν τοῖς τελείοις). Welborn argues that the presence of δέ sets up a contrast, an "antithetical moment" with 2:1–5.[2] However, the presence of δέ does not require an adversative sense; rather, as indicated by Schnabel, it may be understood as copulative.[3] Thus, the δέ connects Paul's argument with

---

1. We understand this to be an extension of the Corinthians' social identification with Rome, which relied on political patronage with provincial governors to secure its empire.

2. Welborn 2005: 187.

3. Schnabel 2006: 164 n. 398.

his previous assertion in 2:5 that the Corinthians' faith is to be in God's power and not in the wisdom of this world. The dual identity-forming factors of wisdom and power are what Paul and others speak among the mature.

Paul employs the plural "we speak" (λαλοῦμεν) when describing the approach to proclamation taken among the ἐκκλησία. Welborn detects in the use of λαλοῦμεν an indication that Paul is being ironic. He argues that Paul does not use his normal verbs of proclamation but rather a term which generally has "a negative connotation."[4] If one already accepts, as do Horsley and Welborn, that Paul is using sarcasm or irony in 1 Cor 2:6–16, then pointing to its further use in 2:6, 7, 13 provides strong evidence for that view. However, Paul often uses λαλοῦμεν in a manner that is demonstrably not ironic or negative. In fact, in Paul sometimes connects this verb with the qualifier "in Christ" (2 Cor 2:17; 12:19). Furthermore, in 1 Thess 2:4 Paul uses λαλοῦμεν to describe his proclamation of the gospel. Welborn's suggestion that Paul's use of λαλοῦμεν in 2:6 indicates the presence of irony fails to convince.

The use of the first person plural of λαλέω is sometimes taken to indicate that 2:6–16 is either a digression or an interpolation.[5] First, we have already seen that Paul employs this same verb elsewhere in similar contexts. Second, Collins makes a case that the use of "we" which is seen in 2:6 and 2:16 forms a conceptual *inclusio* around Paul's reflection on his ministry in 2:1–5 and 3:1–9. Furthermore, Collins broadens this "we" to include the entire community.[6] Ehrensperger is more persuasive,

---

4. Welborn 2005: 189.

5. Weiss 1910: 52; Widmann 1979: 50.

6. Collins 1999: 123. All are not convinced of this. Does λαλοῦμεν in 2:6 include Paul, his co-workers, or the broader Corinthian ἐκκλησία? In 2:4, Paul refers to his message and preaching using the first person singular verb, while in 2:5 he describes the "faith" of the community using a second person pronoun. These verses indicate that Paul's preaching affected the faith of the recipients of his ministry. Should this same community be understood to be active participants in proclamation by Paul's use of λαλοῦμεν in 2:6? Fee (1987: 101 n. 13; Garland 2003: 91) contends that Paul's teaching is in view. Schrage (1991: 1.248), on the other hand, contends that "Without doubt ἡμῶν in v. 7b and *we* in v. 12 signify *all* Christians." The debate also hinges on the construal of δέ. Thiselton (2000:230) takes the view that "Paul and his fellow believers do indeed, however (contrastive δέ), communicate a wisdom." He is able to conclude that a more expansive understanding of those speaking is compatible with a contrastive, rather than copulative understanding of δέ (Welborn 2005: 187). Though there appears to be some distinction between 2:4–5 and 2:6, if Paul is understood as presenting a separate message of wisdom for an elite group of Christ-followers, that would work against his rhetorical aims in 1:18—2:5 (but see Soards 1999: 58).

however, in suggesting that Paul uses λαλοῦμεν to point out that he is but one among a group of co-workers who are responsible for verbal proclamation.[7] This is a subtle way of reminding the Corinthian Christ-followers that this message is not only that of Paul but of others within the Christ-movement. Ehrensperger's view does not negate Collins'. Thus, "we speak" would include the entire community as well as co-workers, such as Apollos. This will be important with regard to Paul's critique of Roman imperial ideology. However, what is the content that this group speaks?

Paul actually begins 2:6 with "wisdom" (σοφίαν) which is employed in 1 Corinthians with greater frequency than in any other of the Pauline letters. The immediate question that arises is this: does Paul view wisdom here as Christ-crucified or is he addressing the practical aspects of wisdom for life in a manner similar to the book of Proverbs? Thiselton connects it with the wisdom tradition within Israel and concludes that it "denotes *habits of judgment applicable to life. It concerns the formation of a Christian mind, which issues in a right action.*"[8] Schnabel understands significant continuity here with wisdom previously mentioned in 1:24, 30 and contends, "The keyword 'wisdom' is to be understood in connection with God's saving revelation in Jesus' death on the cross—this is the message Paul proclaims."[9] Horsley argues that the word order in the Greek emphasizes that "the content or means of salvation" in Paul's understanding of wisdom differs from that just described in 1:17, 21.[10] Fitzmyer considers the possibility that Paul is drawing from the language of some in Corinth; however, he connects the use of wisdom here with "the message of the cross" from 1:18.[11]

We may discern Paul's view of wisdom by recognizing the following: first, Paul's use of the term is differentiated in 1 Cor 1–3, and thus to argue that wisdom only refers to Christ or the gospel does not give full weight to Paul's discourse. Second, Paul was dealing with the practical aspects of communal life within the Christ-movement rather than abstract doctrinal concepts. Third, σοφία normally is used by the LXX to translate חָכְמָה, and that context should be given consideration when

---

7. Ehrensperger 2007: 46.

8. Thiselton 2000: 230 emphasis original.

9. Schnabel 2006: 164–65 author's translation.

10. Horsley 1998: 58.

11. Fitzmyer 2008: 175.

deciding Paul's meaning. A contextually sensitive reading of σοφία might conclude that both the gospel and the social implications that flow from that message are in view in Paul's use of σοφία.[12] Thus, we would suggest that in 2:6, Paul has in view the functional aspects of knowledge and insight with regard to practical living in community that has its basis in the gospel of Christ-crucified.[13] The latter part of our understanding takes into consideration the insights of Schnabel, Horsley, and Fitzmyer, while the former part builds on the understanding of Thiselton.

While Paul's conception of wisdom included both the gospel and its social implications, it does not follow that Paul understood this wisdom to be the possession of only an elite few. Hunt notes this and writes: "This cross-centered σοφία is the distinctive possession of believers"; furthermore it "distinguishes them from this world and defines their very community."[14] So, the entire community has been given this wisdom by the agency of the Spirit. The challenge for Paul was to find a way to encourage the ἐκκλησία to make that identity salient.

The wisdom that God gives through his Spirit is "to those who are mature" (ἐν τοῖς τελείοις). Scholars have asked whether Paul is speaking to only a segment of the ἐκκλησία or the whole community. Thiselton argues that Paul is only addressing a segment, i.e., those who are "spiritual adults," otherwise the contrast in 1 Cor 3:1 loses some of its rhetorical force.[15] Barrett also suggests that Paul has determined that a

12. Support for this interpretive choice comes from a brief survey of the use of σοφία. Classical usage provides the context of practical living (*Il.* 15.414; *Eth. Nic.* 6.7.1–7; Hdt. 1.30). The religious context is developed in the LXX (Isa 33:6; Jer 51.15; Ps 104:24, Prov 1:7; Sir. 1:1; 4 Macc 1:15–18). It is also related to the Spirit in several places (Isa. 11:2; Wis. 7:7; cf. outside the LXX, Eph. 1:17).

13. BDAG 934; HRCS 1278–9; *TDNT* 7.465–526; 7.519–22, Wilckens discusses the current passage extensively; however his earlier approach to 1 Corinthians 1–4 is most evident in this section. In the MT חכם carries the idea of skill in handiwork (Exod 28:3), but the religious-ethical component is often brought out in the Hebrew Bible. The phrase חכם לב in Prov 10:8 and 16:21 emphasizes the cognitive dimension of wisdom; BDB 315; *HALOT* 314–15. Roman writers use *sapientia* to translate σοφία. Juv. in *Sat.* 13.19 writes, "Great indeed is Philosophy (*sapientia*), conqueror of Fortune, and sacred are the precepts of her book."

14. Hunt 1996: 87.

15. Thiselton 2000: 231. Paul writes to the entire ἐκκλησία as a singularity (1:2); however, the nature of his epistolary discourse (e.g., περὶ δέ in 7:1, 25; 8:1; 12:1; 16:1, 12), the presence of various house-churches (e.g., Stephanas 1:16; 16:16–18; Gaius 1:14; Rom 16:23; possibly Chloe 1:11; Priscilla and Aquila Acts 18:2–3), and differing experiences with Roman imperialism undoubtedly bring to the fore various sub-groups within the ἐκκλησία. Cf. Fitzmyer 2008: 81, 277; Clarke 2008: 133–37.

segment within the ἐκκλησία have shown themselves unable to receive God's wisdom because of their poor behavior.[16] The problem with this view is that Paul could then be accused of doing what he had already criticized others for—categorizing Christ-followers into groups who have wisdom and thus behave in a certain manner, and those who have yet to attain such knowledge.

Horsley argues that Paul uses τοῖς τελείοις because some in Corinth were already employing this term with regard to their "self-understanding" as the spiritually elite.[17] Wilckens follows a similar approach but adds an emphasis on a Gnostic background; Reitzenstein connects it with the mystery religions, and Conzelmann with the philosophical tradition.[18] The problem with these scholarly views is that they require the concepts of "the heavenly"/"perfect man of wisdom" and an "initiate"/"initiation" context that is foreign to 1 Corinthians. Parallel usage is important, but the present context is too dissimilar for these studies to be of much use with regard to determining Paul's audience.

There are two further reasons for understanding τοῖς τελείοις as referring to the whole group. First, based on 2 Cor 5:21, the entire people of God are already considered perfect. Thus, Willis rightly concludes, "The designation *teleioi* is not a convincing proof that Paul accepts two strata of Christians—pass/fail and honors."[19] Second, Paul has already made it clear in 1 Cor 1:30 that the wisdom being spoken of in this passage is the gospel of Christ and not an esoteric wisdom reserved only for the initiated.[20] The contrast here is between those who follow Christ—they are capable of receiving God's wisdom—and the "rulers of this world" who are not.[21] It is not between two different levels of Christ-followers.

A better understanding of Paul's use of τελείοις may emerge by considering it in the context of identity formation. Thus, we propose

16. Barrett 1968: 69.

17. Horsley 1998: 57.

18. Wilckens 1959: 52–54; Reitzenstein 1978: 431–36; Conzelmann 1975: 60.

19. Willis 1989: 113.

20. See BDAG 994–95 on the use of τέλειος within the mystery religions. For a recent re-consideration of this viewpoint see Sibilio (2005: 22), especially chapter 3. He rightly points out the significance of Demeter, Isis, and Melikertes in Corinth. Thrall (2002: 60) suggests "that this religiosity" contributed to "the preliminary success of the Pauline mission."

21. Hunt 1996: 83; Gal 4:1–3.

that Paul's use of τέλειος in this letter serves as an identity marker and approximates that which may be described as salient "in Christ" social identity (1 Cor 2:6; 14:20).[22] Aristotle argues in *Eth. Nic.* 7.13.2 that "happiness is essentially perfect" (εὐδαιμονία τῶν τελείων), but with regard to persons, Plato employs τέλειος with the idea of being accomplished (*Cra.* 403e).[23] The LXX translates תָּמִים with τέλειος, as for example in Gen 6:9 where Noah is understood as "blameless" before the community. In Deut 18:13 there is a striking parallel with reference to a group of people and not just to an individual: "You shall be blameless (τέλειος/ תָּמִים) before the Lord your God."[24] The NT employs τέλειος nineteen times, with Rom 12:2 and Matt 5:48 serving as two intriguing parallels, the former for its similarity in terms of its cognitive emphasis and transformation of the mind, and the latter as a allusion to the Jesus tradition or possibly the Pauline tradition influencing the development of the Gospel of Matthew.[25] Nolland points out that the use of τέλειος relates to the requirement to resist "pagan practices."[26] In the case of the Corinthian Christ-followers, it was the power of Rome and its ideology that was drawing them away from wholehearted devotion to God. This makes Paul's teaching in 1 Cor 14:20 much more clear: "but in your thinking be mature (τέλειοι)." Paul's use of τέλειος is a corporate discursive strategy designed to recategorize the ingroup (i.e., the entire ἐκκλησία) away from divisions based on the Corinthians' various social identifications towards a transformed way of thinking concerning those same identifications.

The wisdom that Paul and his co-workers speak is "not a wisdom of this age" (σοφίαν δὲ οὐ τοῦ αἰῶνος τούτου). The apocalyptic elements

---

22. LSJ 1769; BDAG 995 considers this word as "being mature" but leaves open the possibility of "a cult initiate." M&M 629 reference P. Oxy II. 237[vii. 15] with regard to a group who have "attained maturity." This would serve as one example in which τέλειος is used to refer to a group of people.

23. Wright (2003: 48) contends that "M. Aur. *Med.* 3.7 holds 'the same view' as that of Plato."

24. HRCS 1342; *HALOT* 1748–50; 2 Sam 22:31 הָאֵל תָּמִים דַּרְכּוֹ "As for God, his way is blameless." The idea here is that God's manner is faithful. Nolland (2005: 271) cites the Deut 18:13 reference. Tigay (1996: 173–74) rightly notes the implicit critique of "pagan techniques" which detract "from a wholehearted loyalty to God." See Josh 24:14.

25. Ehrensperger 2010; Gruenwald 2008: 416.

26. Nolland 2005: 271.

introduced in 1:20 are now reinforced.[27] The world's wisdom is flawed in that it cannot produce salvation, no matter how much it is presented as such (*Aen.* 1.270–95; 6.791–95, 851–54).[28] Paul further clarifies those associated with this form of "wisdom" by writing, "the rulers of this age, the ones who are being made powerless" (τῶν ἀρχόντων τοῦ αἰῶνος τούτου τῶν καταργουμένων). Scholars have debated whether the phrase "the rulers of this age" refers to cosmic authorities or human rulers. Is it possible that some combination is in view?

Cosmic rulers are in view according to Barrett. He argues that this coheres with the cosmology of the ancient world where these "supernatural beings controlled the destiny of men."[29] Schlatter connects these with cosmic powers mentioned in Dan 10:13.[30] Likewise, Schrage argues that "the rulers of this age are the powers and dominions that are enemies of God."[31] A sometimes closely associated view is a combination approach which understands these cosmic authorities to be working through human political and religious figures. Collins believes that the context indicates that Paul has these rulers in mind.[32] Thiselton argues that the reason for this viewpoint is that humanity is more than a collection of individuals and that Paul understood the crucifixion to have cosmological significance beyond just the murder of a political prisoner by Rome.[33] Similarly, Theissen understands an actual reference to human leaders and a symbolic reference to cosmic ones.[34] A third view is that this phrase refers to human rulers. Sandnes argues for the "Jewish Sanhedrin," though most contemporary scholars rightly focus on Roman political figures rather than the Jewish leaders in Israel.[35] Horsley makes a connection with the Roman Empire in general and specifically with

27. Adams 2000: 16.

28. M&M 621; Roman emperors and the Ptolemies referred to themselves as saviors; Moulton and Milligan specifically point out inscriptional and papyrological evidence for this by Julius Caesar and Nero (cf. Koester 1990: 667; Finney 2005: 21; Borg and Crossan 2007: 165–67).

29. Barrett 1968: 70.

30. Schlatter 1969 [1934]: 111.

31. Schrage 1991: 250 author's translation.

32. Collins 1999: 129. Contra Berger 2003: 256 n. 22.

33. Thiselton 2000: 238.

34. Theissen 1987: 378.

35. Sandnes 1991: 81.

those responsible for Christ's crucifixion in 2:8.[36] Fitzmyer thinks that "human rulers" are likely.[37] Schnabel agrees, "The usage 'ruler of this world' does not refer to supernatural, God-opposing demonic powers, rather to earthly rulers."[38]

Which view of "the rulers of this age" is to be preferred? There are three related reasons for seeing τῶν ἀρχόντων τοῦ αἰῶνος in 1 Cor 2:6, 8 as earthly rulers, the Roman authorities in the first century CE. First, understanding τῶν ἀρχόντων τοῦ αἰῶνος as earthly rulers makes the most sense in the context of the discourse on earthly wisdom and God's wisdom in 1 Cor 2:6—3:4. Second, Paul uses ἄρχων in a way that refers to earthly rulers in Rom 13:3. Third, Paul argues that there was an epistemic deficiency[39] with regard to the crucifixion of Christ in 1 Cor 2:8, and that condition is only meaningful in the context of human rulers as compared to cosmic rulers (see Mark 1:24). Seyoon Kim has recently argued that Paul's understanding of "the rulers of this age" should be expanded to include cosmic forces along with the emperor and other Roman officials. His argument relies on 1 Cor 15:24 which appears to include cosmic forces. This is based on the presence of πᾶς in 1 Cor 15:24 which, for Kim, indicates a "comprehensive designation" that "includes the Roman emperor and his officials along with other forces as instruments of the Satanic reign."[40] However, ἄρχων is not used in 1 Cor 15:24; rather Paul uses ἀρχή which normally refers to cosmic forces (see Rom 8:38). Thus, Kim's argument, while plausible, fails to convince. Therefore, it seems better to view τῶν ἀρχόντων τοῦ αἰῶνος in 1 Cor 2:6, 8 as the Roman authorities in the first century CE.[41]

---

36. Horsley 1998: 58.

37. Fitzmyer 2008: 175.

38. Schnabel 2006: 166 author's translation.

39. Epistemic deficiency is concerned with the reasons these rulers failed to recognize who Jesus was and what was the purpose of his mission of redemption. From one point of view Pilate and Herod Antipas would be representative of this group (see Acts 4:27; Luke 23:1–24; 7–15); however, as Clarke (1993: 114 n. 26) contends, citing Godet, they are "representatives of human intelligence and politics." Three reasons these rulers failed to recognize the significance of Jesus: (1) Paul has already argued, in 1:20, that God has made the wisdom of the world foolishness; (2) God's wisdom may only be known by revelation (2:10); (3) God may have chosen to withhold that knowledge from these rulers (2:7).

40. Kim 2008: 24.

41. Orr and Walther 1976: 153–54; Horsley 1997: 244; Morris 1987: 53–54.

The outgroup in the case of Paul and the Corinthians, then, is the Roman Empire. Paul, in the previous clause, has critiqued the Corinthians' reliance on the world's wisdom, and in the present clause, through the substantival use of the passive participle τῶν καταργουμένων, he reinforces the fact that these rulers are "being made powerless" by God.[42] Thus, within the ἐκκλησία, the primary reliance and identification should not be on philosophical wisdom and political power, both of which are identity-forming components that depend on rhetoric for their persuasiveness.[43] For Paul, the Corinthians' over-reliance on the power and wisdom of this world will continue to result in divisions within the ἐκκλησία because it will always diffuse the salience of their "in Christ" social identity.

In 2:7, Paul now expands the category of wisdom that "we speak" among the ἐκκλησία and argues that the political ideology of those who crucified Christ ultimately results in a lack of wisdom and understanding. The proclamation of the gospel is "God's wisdom" (Θεοῦ σοφίαν) that is spoken "in a mystery" (ἐν μυστηρίῳ).[44] The perfect participle, τὴν ἀποκεκρυμμένην "was kept hidden," indicates something in the past that is continuing to have an impact on the various epistemic approaches of humankind with regard to salvific wisdom. It is unknowable without the revealing agency of the Spirit.[45]

Vergil (*Aen.* 6.777–807) presents *Augustus Caesar, Divi genus* "Augustus Caesar, son of a God," as the predetermined ruler of Latium who would bring security, wisdom, and peace to the world.[46] Paul, however, recognizes that "God" actually had another "predetermined (προώρισεν) plan for the ages" which was not for the glory of Rome

---

42. Fitzmyer 2008: 176.

43. Ando 2000: xii. This approach actually reveals one of the weaknesses of Pogoloff's (1992: 66) approach in that he does not fully consider the interconnectedness of philosophy, wisdom, power, ideology, and rhetoric. His otherwise brilliant work is too stark with regards to its binary approach.

44. Reitzenstein (1978: 358) associates this with the mystery religions in that τέλειος and μυστήριον are both found in 1 Cor 2:6–7 and are part of formulae within "Oriental religions" as well as "Gnosticism" (see Hunt 1996: 5–6).

45. Munzinger 2007: 14; Scott 2006: 43.

46. *Aeneid* may have been translated by Polybius into Greek by the 40–50s CE and distributed to key cities in the Greek east, including Corinth. Evidence for this comes from Seneca, *Cons. Polyb.* 8.2; 11.5–6. Cf. Elliott 2008a: 28–30. See the earlier discussion on p. 45 n. 40 for the importance of *Aeneid* to Roman imperial ideology.

or Augustus but "for our glory (δόξαν)."[47] Paul is making an implicit attack on imperial ideology and those who are still elevating their civic identity within the community of Christ-followers.[48] The predetermined wisdom of God is more powerful than the pretentious claims to power by Rome, typified, for example, in the *Ara Pacis Augustae* "altar of peace of Augustus" reliefs.[49] Paul's apocalyptic thinking emerges in contradistinction to these claims and, as Thiselton remarks, "*guarantees the security of those who are marked as the Lord's own*."[50] Whereas Rome reinforced unity and social identification throughout the empire through coins (in Corinth specifically through a combination of Roman and Greek figures),[51] Paul reinforces unity and social identification through confidence in God's predetermined plan of wisdom for the glory of those who follow Christ.

God's wisdom had to have been hidden from the political authorities or they would not have crucified Christ. Paul continues to discuss σοφίαν in 2:8 with the relative pronoun ἥν pointing back to 2:6 and the content of the proclamation. The wisdom of God hindered the perceptions of the Romans so that "none of the rulers of this world (τῶν ἀρχόντων τοῦ αἰῶνος) comprehended" what God was actually doing among them. He then explains why this was necessary: "for if they had

47. The relative pronoun ἥν has σοφίαν as its antecedent, indicating that God had predetermined wisdom from before the ages, for our glory.

48. The various expressions of imperial ideology within the provinces must be kept in mind, as there was no one agreed-upon expression of the way the honors due the emperor would be offered. Beard, North, and Price (1998: 209) explain that "it is impossible now to reconstruct exactly how any individual emperor negotiated the delicate boundary between (god-like) humanity and outright divinity." The role of civic identity was discussed on p. 89.

49. See Moretti (1948: 8) and Rossini (2007: 2–6) for a discussion of the way these reliefs make power claims. Elliott (2008a: 125) describes the way in which Augustus and Aeneas are placed side by side, offering sacrifices to Rome's gods, both "with their togas pulled over their heads in prayer" intimating "their relationship as ancestor and descendant." The presence of the imperial family on the reliefs further conveys the sacred power of Augustus' family.

50. Thiselton 2000: 242 emphasis original.

51. Amandry 1988: 36–38; Edwards 1933: 4–9, 76. For example, *RIC* 219, Augustus; *RIC* 22, Tiberius; *RIC* 38, Caligula; *RIC* 64, 74, Claudius; *RIC* 85, Germanicus. Walbank (2003: 338) asserts that the coins minted between 44 BCE and 68/9 CE often carried "the names of the annually elected duovirs." They had other local emphases as well, but also "assiduous attention paid to the imperial family." This reinforced the close ties and social identification between Corinth and Rome.

known, they would not have crucified the Lord of glory (τὸν κύριον τῆς δόξης)."[52] In other words, if this wisdom had not been hidden in a mystery then they would not have crucified Christ.[53] The attributive genitive τὸν κύριον τῆς δόξης echoes Ps 23:10 LXX (Acts 7:2). By using this construction Paul specifies the glory and identity of Christ while emphasizing that Rome, with its claim to glory (*Aen.* 6.851), failed to recognize true glory in its midst. Those whom God predetermined have that wisdom and glory.[54] So, why substitute God's glory for the fading power of a pretentious empire? That is Paul's question to the Corinthian Christ-followers.

The political leaders of the world could not discern God's wisdom. In 2:9, which begins with the strong adversative ἀλλά,[55] Paul makes it clear that those within the ingroup (i.e., those who love God) have access to this wisdom. To further substantiate his identity-forming antithesis, he employs a quotation introduced by a citation formula: καθὼς γέγραπται "just as it is written." The source of the quotation, however, is an ongoing matter of scholarly debate. Ciampa and Rosner argue for "a loose quotation of Isa 64:4 (64:3 LXX)."[56] Collins states that this "is not a quotation of the Jewish Scriptures."[57] Wilk is unsure about the quotation of Isaiah in this passage,[58] while Berger connects it with various apocalyptic sources focused on God revealing secrets that had been previously hidden.[59] Hiel summarizes the various possibilities including Isa 64:4 (64:3 LXX), Isa 53:15 (52:15 LXX), Ezek 40:4 LXX, 44:5,

52. He employs a second class conditional construction here which assumes the impossible for the purposes of the argument.

53. Tac. *Ann.* 15.44; Joseph. *AJ* 17.10.10. For a discussion of the role of crucifixion as a means of imperial control see Hengel 1977: 39; Fears 1981: 910–23; Finney 2005: 30–33.

54. Horsley (1998: 59) summarizes the Roman state of affairs: "the imperial rulers have been undone precisely by their own repressive terrorizing of subject peoples." There were, however, some within the empire who also questioned Rome's approach to power, glory, and domination, for example: Lucr. *De Re. Nat.* 3.61; cited in Hardwick (2000: 357). Also, Ov. *Met.* 15.75–95, 565–621, 745–870; Galinsky (1967: 191) argues Ovid at least expresses "indifference to Augustan ideals."

55. Frid (1985: 606) points out that this construction is "an elliptical mode of expression."

56. Ciampa and Rosner 2007: 701.

57. Collins 1999: 131.

58. Wilk 1998: 9.

59. Berger 1978: 271.

Sir 1:10, and concludes that Paul is not referring to one passage but to several "brought together" thus increasing "the persuasive authority and rhetorical force not of any particular OT text or context but of the OT scriptures as a whole and in general."[60] Fitzmyer provides a helpful outline of the evidence, including Pseudo-Philo 26.13, which, while not being the source of Paul's quotation, may indicate that "perhaps both Paul and Pseudo-Philo have derived it from a common Jewish source known in the first Christian century."[61] Ehrensperger, after considering the various choices, contends that this citation provides an example of the fluid nature of textual traditions and the significance of authorial shaping.[62]

The purpose of Paul's shaping of this textual tradition is to reveal the content of God's wisdom that is hidden in a mystery (2:7). This is wisdom that the "rulers of this age" are unable to understand (2:6), but it is wisdom available to the mature (2:6). The quotation reads, "The things that no eye has seen, or ear heard, or heart[63] conceived, are the things God has prepared for those who love him." The clause begins with the relative pronoun ἅ, which along with ἥν from 2:7, points back to σοφίαν in 2:6.[64] The contrast that Paul sets up is that none of the "rulers of this age," with their claims of power and wisdom, compare with "the things" that God has in store for those who love him. Paul's "authorial shaping" is quite similar to that of Jeremiah 5:21, a context that is often ignored when discerning the shaping of Paul's source(s). It reads: "Hear this, you foolish and senseless people, who have eyes, but do not see, who have ears, but do not hear." Jeremiah's addressees and their rulers were relying on their own political and military power (Jer 5:14–17) and thus were unable to hear God's wisdom. The "rulers of this age" in 2:6 are in a similar situation, so why would the Corinthian Christ-followers continue to identify with an ideological system that God will bring to nothing, when

---

60. Hiel 2005: 66.

61. Fitzmyer 2008: 179.

62. Ehrensperger 2008b: 22–23.

63. The genitive phrase καρδίαν ἀνθρώπου "the heart of humankind" is similar in meaning to Paul's use of νοῦς in 2:16 (cf. 1 Cor 1:10) and reflects a Hebrew idiom with regard to bl. See Jer 3:16; 51:50 (28:50 LXX). Cf. Garland 2003: 97; König and Whitmarsh 2007: 5; *HALOT* 513–15; HRCS 719–23.

64. The antecedent is not grammatical but logical. Frid (1985) points out the elliptical nature of this section. See further Fitzmyer 2008: 177.

God has prepared "things" for those who love him that are beyond human imagination?[65]

Paul's quotation makes it clear that the empire does not control the future.[66] This future orientation is in contrast to Roman imperial eschatology, its claim to *Pax et Securitas*, and its coinage declaring *Spes Augusta*.[67] Sutherland rightly concludes, "For the Romans it [coinage] was also a shrewd and adroit means to another end, namely, the formation of public opinion on matters of Imperial policy."[68] The Romans were prone to think that their power and rule were never-ending. Some within the ἐκκλησία are likewise relying on Rome's power (1 Cor 6:1–11) without the full realization of "the things" which God has prepared for "those who love him." For Paul, the acceptable way for the ἐκκλησία to relate to God and thus gain true insight is through an ethos of love and not by substituting this love for the world's rhetoric, wisdom, or power, which ultimately results in not-knowing.[69] As Lémonon writes, "Love and community construction are to guide discernment."[70] The hindrance of Roman imperial ideology can only be overcome through the agency of the Spirit, and Paul addresses that issue next.

---

65. Garland 2003: 97–98. Tajfel (1978a: 28) describes similar categories in his understanding of social categorization (i.e., cognitive, emotional, and evaluative). Smith (2005: 2, 58) describes the way that *Aeneid* draws on visual imagery. Likewise, the visual was the primary means of communication in the *Ara Pacis Augustae*. Torelli (2001: 54) describes the way Pausanias ignored aspects of imperial monuments in his description of Corinth. Cf. Elsner 2007: 100.

66. Fitzmyer (2008: 179) discusses scholars who reject the futuristic understanding here and suggests that "the eschatological blessings of salvation" are in view in Paul's quotation.

67. *Aen.* 6.792–98; 1 Thess 5:3–6; Elliott 1994: 189–90; *RIC Claudius* 115; Hardin 2008: 28–32. Witherington (1995: 295–8) argues, "Roman imperial eschatology was part of the larger enterprise of imperial propaganda meant to aid in binding the empire together."

68. Sutherland 1940: 76.

69. Grindheim (2002: 709) rightly asserts that "the Corinthians rely on a kind of rhetoric that was supposed to allow them to excel in personal status, to the detriment of others" when they should have had "their self-identity" shaped by "the word of the cross." Cf. Whitmarsh 2001: 190–91.

70. Lémonon 2001: 31 author's translation.

SOLUTIONS: THE SPIRIT AND THE MIND OF CHRIST
(2:10–16)

The Spirit is the agent of the wisdom of God within the life of the ἐκκλησία. First Corinthians 2:10 begins with δέ which contrasts Paul's previous, rather negative assertion concerning those outside the community of faith and their lack of ability with regard to understanding God's wisdom with the positive side of his identity-forming antithesis: through the agency of the Spirit, God's wisdom may be known. Paul includes himself in the ingroup and writes, "God has revealed (ἀπεκάλυψεν) these things to us by the agency of the Spirit (πνεύματος)," as opposed to the wise and powerful of the world. The verb ἀποκαλύπτω, in this context, indicates "divine revelation of certain transcendent secrets" (1 Cor 14:30).[71] Noting this usage, Adams contends that "the dominant theological perspective of 1 Corinthians is an apocalyptic one."[72] The prepositional phrase διὰ τοῦ πνεύματος indicates intermediate agency, with God as the ultimate agent of that which has been revealed.

The γάρ is explanatory and provides the reason for the agency of the Spirit: "For (γάρ) the Spirit examines (ἐρευνᾷ) all things." The verb ἐραυνάω in this context emphasizes the examining work of the Spirit and brings to the fore the idea that within the ἐκκλησία the Spirit is to be the primary epistemic agent of categorization, not those who are judging based on the world's wisdom (1 Cor 6:1–2, 11).[73] Social categorization without the guidance of the Spirit produces results similar Paul's description in 1:11–12. The examining work of the Spirit is further extended to "even the depths (βάθη) of God" (Rom 11:33) or that which is considered most "difficult to assess."[74] The evaluative work of humanity is limited in comparison to the work of the Spirit. Jewett rightly sees here "the limit of divine profundity that is barred to humans except with

71. BDAG 112.

72. Adams 2000: 106. Scroggs (1967–68: 35) stresses "that the *content* of Paul's wisdom is apocalyptic." Cf. Beker 1980: 277; Kovacs 1989: 219; Brown 1995: 139–44.

73. Scott 2006: 46; Cyss 2004: 164–65. Jenkins (2000: 22 emphasis original) furthers this by noting, "socially and epistemologically, categorization involves the invocation of similarity *within* categories, as the basis for differentiation *between* them."

74. BDAG 162. Schlier (*TDNT* 1.517) explains, "the depth of the activity of God is concealed from the world in principle; it is accessible only to the πνεῦμα τοῦ θεοῦ." LSJ 301 cites Judith 8:14 which provides an interesting conceptual parallel with Paul's words. Also, the genitive phrase here is understood as a possessive genitive.

divine assistance."[75] The presence of the Spirit provides the necessary cognitive resources for an accurate apprehension of God's wisdom.

In 2:11, Paul further explains the agency of the Spirit with regard to the revelation of God's wisdom by the use of a rhetorical question that alludes to the reflexive nature of social identity: "For who among a person knows the thoughts of a person except the person's spirit within him or her?" This question illustrates that the concept of reflexivity, which is central to the formation of identity, is not only a modern phenomenon but is, in a general manner, part of the human experience.[76] Reflection on the self is necessary for social categorization and the construction of identity, and Paul's question here provides an illustration of this within an ancient context (Rom 7:7–25).[77] Paul returns to his main point, "so also, no one knows the thoughts of God, except the Spirit of God." The means by which those within the community come to know God's wisdom is through the agency of the Spirit and not through human wisdom, a topic he emphasizes in 2:12.

Paul employs the resources of social memory to continue to construct the Corinthian Christ-followers' social identity in relation to the Spirit's agency within the community of faith. He reminds them, "Now (δέ) we (ἡμεῖς) have not received the spirit of the world (τὸ πνεῦμα τοῦ κόσμου)." The δέ connects Paul's argument with the ἀπεκάλυψεν from 2:10, and ἡμεῖς refers to the whole Pauline community in Corinth, not only to Paul and his co-workers.[78] With the entire group in view, he

75. Jewett 2007: 716.

76. Jenkins (1996: 9–10) intimates that Giddens understands reflexivity to be a modern phenomenon; however, Giddens (1991: 53), whom Jenkins references, points out that "what a person is understood to be certainly varies across cultures, although there are elements of such a notion that are common to all cultures." So, it may be that Giddens rightly notes a change in reflexivity with the rise of modernity; however, his diachronic approach, when focused broadly on reflexivity and personhood across cultures, may temper the force of Jenkins' reference, though not completely. Cf. Mauss (1938: 263–81) for a discussion of the ancient differences between personhood and selfhood.

77. Holland 1999: 264; Dodd 1999: 54–55. While one could argue for the rhetorical and literary value of the "I," the connection with self-mastery within the Roman context argues against the approach that reduces reflection on the self to a product of the Enlightenment.

78. This approach follows Stuhlmacher (1987: 334) contra Chambers who restricts the referent here to the apostles (2004: 259). Adams (2000: 116) argues that it refers to Paul "and his readers" and that "the use of the first person plurals in this verse serves to sharpen the social distinction (ἡμεῖς, ἐλάβομεν, εἰδῶμεν, ἡμῖν). Paul sets himself and his readers over against the κόσμος."

points them back to the beginning of their "new status" which was not constituted by means of the reception of "the spirit of the world" whose power is ending (1 Cor 2:8). Next, by the use of ἀλλά he reminds them, as Horrell notes, that they were "confirmed" by "the Spirit, the one who is from God (τὸ πνεῦμα τὸ ἐκ τοῦ Θεοῦ)."[79]

"The spirit of the world" is not to have normative influence within the Christ-movement. The possessive genitive most likely describes the broad system of thought or ethos which is opposed to God's work among the Corinthian Christ-followers. SIT further clarifies this idea through the use of "normative and informational influences."[80] In the current passage "the spirit of the world" would be classified as having "normative influence" because, in the Corinthian situation, Rome's political power[81] relies on *public compliance* and has "the power to threaten, punish, or enforce laws." It does not require *private acceptance or internalization* for its continuation.[82] Paul's concern is that some within the ἐκκλησία were socially identifying with, and thus internalizing, this system of power and control. On the other hand, "informational influence" is conformity to group norms based on "private acceptance" and the "internalization of beliefs, attitudes, and behaviours."[83] Some within the ἐκκλησία were in the process of internalizing "the spirit of the world" and this resulted in group norms not having their basis in an ethos of faith and love (1 Cor 2:8; 13:2, 13). Paul recognizes, to a certain extent, the need for the normative influence of Rome (Rom 13:1–7), but within the Pauline communities the imperial ideological system is a hindrance and not to be internalized. Rather, communal existence should be constructed through the agency of "the Spirit, the one who is from God."

---

79. Horrell 1996: 86.

80. Hogg and Abrams 1988: 165.

81. Rome's political power seems to be in the fore; however, this does not preclude discussion of, as Adams (2000: 117) asserts, "the Corinthians, adopting Greek, and principally Stoic, ideas about the cosmic role of πνεῦμα, regarded as the life-principle sustaining and permeating the κόσμος." Thiselton (2000: 260–61) provides an excellent summary of this Stoic concept; for example, he cites intriguing parallels by Epict. *Diatr.* 1.14.6; Sen. *Ep.* 62.12, M. Aur. *Med.* 5.27. If the Corinthian Christ-followers were identifying with the political power of Rome, it should not be surprising to find that they are also internalizing some of the philosophical concepts that are evident among the provincial elites.

82. Hogg and Abrams 1988: 166 emphasis original.

83. Hogg and Abrams 1988: 167.

The next clause further clarifies the need for the reception of the Spirit within the community. Paul uses ἵνα to introduce the purpose clause and makes this contingent epistemic reality inclusive of the entire community through the use of the subjunctive εἰδῶμεν "we might know" (1 Cor 3:1–4).[84] The purpose of the reception of the Spirit is to reveal God's wisdom among the Christ-following community. Its content is described as in 2:11 as τά, "the things," both of which refer back to God's wisdom in 2:6, but here it is further described by the passive participle χαρισθέντα as something "freely given." This is not some form of esoteric knowledge for the initiated few, but Paul says it is "to us" (ἡμῖν), i.e., the entire community, and it was given "by God."[85] If the purpose of the Spirit in this context is to reveal God's wisdom, why would those following Christ rely on the world's resources in seeking understanding and communicating truth within the ἐκκλησία? He addresses this question further in 2:13.

The communication of God's wisdom does not rely on the resources of the world's wisdom for its persuasiveness. The antecedent for the relative pronoun ἅ in 2:14 is τὰ χαρισθέντα from 2:12, and it is that which Paul says "we speak." The use of ἀλλά establishes the antithesis between the two approaches to teaching, which he further develops by saying that the speaking of followers of Christ is "not with words taught by human wisdom." He writes that theirs is instead "in (words) taught by the Spirit" (ἐν διδακτοῖς πνεύματος), thus connecting their current approach to teaching back to 2:12 and to that which was received, "the Spirit, the one who is from God." So, when teaching within the Christ-following community, the primary source of insight and inspiration is to come from the Spirit and not from "human wisdom."

---

84. The contingent nature is evident in 1 Cor 3:1–4 in that they are living as if they do not possess these epistemic resources. Jenkins (2000: 7–10, 19) rightly contends that categorization is an epistemological concern and "categoric identity" is employed in order to "orient behavior." Jenkins also describes categorization such as this as "the conjunction between power and knowledge." Paul's categorization is forming identity in his hearers.

85. Wilckens 1959: 52–96; Schmithals 1971: 151–54. Both hold to a form of the Gnostic hypothesis as the exigence in 1 Cor 2:6–16. Wilckens (1979: 513) has subsequently modified his position on this issue and now understands this passage within the framework of Hellenistic Judaism and early Christian traditions concerning the crucifixion of Christ. Winter (1975: 205) rejects the Gnostic hypothesis while acknowledging that it is only through the Spirit that this wisdom may be accessed.

The reason for this is that "human wisdom" is incapable of properly categorizing reality from God's point of view. The last three words in 2:13 are an interpretive crux for 2:6–16; they read, "categorizing spiritual people and spiritual things" (πνευματικοῖς πνευματικὰ συγκρίνοντες). The participle συγκρίνοντες[86] reveals the purpose for the speaking: to categorize, compare, and draw distinctions between two approaches to communal life and wisdom. The reason for the unfruitfulness of human wisdom and the necessity of the agency of the Spirit is that human wisdom does not function within the same epistemic situation as God's wisdom. Notice that Paul makes his boundary-marking statement clear; the problem is between "spiritual people" (πνευματικοῖς) and an implied "unspiritual people,"[87] and between "spiritual things" (πνευματικα) and a likewise implied "unspiritual things." What Paul understood as a problem within the ἐκκλησία was the manner in which social comparisons were occurring with regard to who was spiritual and who was not, as well as what was considered spiritual and what was not.[88] For Paul, the work of the Spirit is that which allows for correct categorization of social realities within the community of faith. Thus, Paul has not really been arguing against all forms of human wisdom, eloquence, or power, only asserting that they are ultimately inconsistent and unreliable epistemic resources within the ἐκκλησία without the agency of the Spirit. This Spirit-centered approach to wisdom and power becomes more evident in 2:14–16.

The cognitive-spiritual resources[89] necessary to properly assess the way to live out the social implications of the gospel and a transformed social identity are described by Paul in 2:14–16. The metaphor he employs for this purpose is "the mind of Christ" and is "focused . . .

86. BDAG 953 suggests clarifying based on a "compatible relationship." HRCS 1300 considers the compassion connections, and 1 Macc 10:71 provides a nice parallel for this usage. LSJ 1667 too quickly classifies it in the category of "interpretation," and the examples they provide are inconclusive. A better option would have been the "compare" category in that the example from Aristotle's *Rh.* 1368a21 aligns nicely with the current context.

87. This understands πνευματικοῖς as a masculine plural. See Thiselton 2000: 264–65; Schnabel 2006: 175–76; Artz-Grabner 2006: 132–33.

88. Theissen 1987: 352, 368.

89. By this we mean that which gives meaning to the lived-out social-religious experiences. It reflects on what can be known about the social situation from religious customs. A similar approach can be taken with the resources from art and funeral remains. See Gilead 1995: 136.

on community life."[90] The previous section, 2:10–13, provides a positive argument for the agency of the Spirit in revealing God's wisdom, but 2:14a describes the counterexample relating to the epistemic situation of those who have not received the Spirit. The contrast is marked by δέ which frames this aspect of Paul's argument in relation to that which he has just written. The outgroup is immediately made clear, "The unspiritual person (ψυχικὸς ἄνθρωπος) does not receive the things of the Spirit of God." First, "the unspiritual person" is one whose identity has not been transformed by the agency of the Spirit. This person is set in contrast, in 2:15, to "the spiritual person." Schnabel contends Paul's focus here is the impossibility for human beings, based on their own intellectual abilities, to comprehend God's revelation in Jesus.[91] Second, this

90. What follows is a brief summary of various approaches to understanding the "mind of Christ." Williams (2001: 226) understands the mind of Christ to be concerned with "the understanding of God's plan of salvation that is potentially available for all Christians" but downplays its significance for mission. Willis (1989: 118) argues that it "refers to believers having their outlook shaped by an awareness of Christ. He is the norm for the consciousness or 'outlook' of the Christian community." His approach tends to minimize the vital role of theology within the community. Scott (2006: 45) understands it simply to be "a new way of thinking and reasoning," an approach that often understates the eschatological work of the Spirit within the Christ-movement. Fee (1987: 120) equates the mind of Christ with the Spirit but notes, "their behavior betrays them. They do, but they don't." Munzinger (2007: 35), on the other hand, equates it with the renewed mind in Rom 8:6 and 12:2 and argues that it is "the cognitive and reflective aspect of the new creation, defined by the Christ-event and empowered by the Spirit." Thiselton (2007: 35) views the mind of Christ as a "mind-set," while Collins (1999: 138) understands it as "a constellation of thoughts and beliefs that provide criteria for judgment and action." Wilckens (1959: 36) views the mind of Christ as a completely different "value-system" (*Wertungssystem*) through which the world is understood. Munck (1959: 159) argues that possession of the mind of Christ is limited only to preachers like Paul and Apollos. Chester (2003: 288–90) connects this with the initiated and enlightened consciousness associated with the mystery cults. Welborn (2005: 220–21) sees a mystery religion background, as well, but limits the mind of Christ to Paul and argues that "Paul is the mystagogue of 'Christ crucified.'" Mitchell (1991: 78) connects it with the concept of political unity and the ideal "state of 'common mind' or ὁμόνια." Horsley (2008: 79–80) aligns it with "Hellenistic-Jewish religiosity focused on Sophia." See Philo *Deus* 143. On the cognitive aspects of metaphorical language, see Lackoff and Johnson 1980: 3–5.

91. Schnabel (2006: 179–80) writes, "Paulus wiederholt abschließend, unterstrichen mit der Autorität der Heiligen Schrift, dass kein Mensch von sich aus die intellektuellen Möglichkeiten hat, die Gedanken Gottes und damit seine Heilsoffenbarung im Kreuzestod Jesu zu erkennen." BDAG 1100 describes ψυχικός as "an unspiritual person, one who merely functions bodily, without being touched by the Spirit of God." Cf. *TDNT* 9: 663; Hays 1997: 46.

outgroup also "does not receive"; this encompasses those of "the spirit of the world" in 2:12 and "the rulers of this age" from 2:6, 8.[92] Third, the individuals in this group actively reject[93] "the things of the Spirit of God" which include God's wisdom (1 Cor 2:6), God's Spirit (1 Cor 2:12), the gospel of a crucified-Christ (1 Cor 1:18), and all that which has been freely given by God for a transformed life (1 Cor 2:12; 2 Cor 5:17). In this first clause, then, Paul describes individuals who refuse all that God offers and marks them as those without the Spirit.

In 2:14b, Paul continues to clarify the mindset of "the unspiritual person" and explains three reasons to consider them an outgroup. First, he writes, "for they are foolishness (μωρία) to him/her," which reveals the evaluation of the "unspiritual person" with regard to "the things of God." The use of μωρία at least connects back to ὁ λόγος τοῦ σταυροῦ from 1:18 but may also extend to Paul's experiences as a missionary among the nations (1 Cor 1:23).[94] Second, Paul concludes, "The person does not even have the power to know." Previously, the person was described as actively rejecting but now the individual is powerless to know the things of God. A person's epistemic situation will always result in not knowing without the agency of the Spirit. Paul is building his case, showing why those within the ἐκκλησία should not rely on the wisdom of the world, and here he asserts that those outside the Christ-following community cannot know the things associated with God. Third, he provides the reason for the lack of knowledge and insight by "the unspiritual

92. Wolff 1996: 61.

93. Thiselton (2000: 270) argues that their rejection is based on "prior horizons . . . pre-existing interests and concerns" in which "the cross and the things of the Spirit find no desired relevance or credibility."

94. Cic. *Rab. Perd.* 5.16 "But the executioner, the veiling of the head and the very word 'cross' should be far removed not only from the person of a Roman citizen but from his thoughts, his eyes and his ears." Welborn (2005: 20, 23) rightly contends that there is more to Paul's use of foolishness here than simply an "antithesis to 'wisdom.'" Paul appropriates, evaluates, and affirms the term foolishness "from the application of the term as a judgment upon his preaching, to his acceptance of the word as the truth of his life in fellowship with the suffering of Christ." Welborn also warns against interpreting Cicero's comments as a widely held view with regard to crucifixion. Hengel (1977: 41–45) takes the view that the Romans in Corinth "must have found crucifixion quite as horrific a punishment as did the simple citizens of Roman cities, freedmen and slaves at the time of the Civil War." Also, Welborn's argument for the lack of the word "foolishness" in relation to early descriptions of the cross of Christ is limited in that he looks only for occurrences of the word itself when other words he cites on page 21 would fall within the semantic domain of the μωρία; see L&N 380.

person"; it is "because they are spiritually discerned." The mindset of the "unspiritual person" is incompatible with "the mind of Christ" (1 Cor 2:16). Those who are powerful and wise (1 Cor 1:27) according to this world's standards cannot know the things of God because they are spiritually understood. Those outside the ἐκκλησία should not be relied on for guidance in social comparison, categorization, or evaluation because they lack the epistemic condition necessary for proper examination: the agency of the Spirit who produces "the mind of Christ."

Munzinger argues that this is actually "an epistemological change in which both Spirit and mind are active. While the Spirit is the prerequisite for true knowledge, it becomes active without eclipsing the function of the mind."[95] Carson rejects the notion that Paul is addressing issues of "epistemology" in this section.[96] Carson, however, is too strong here. While it is correct that the message of the cross is central, there is an implicit epistemological component to Paul's discourse related to public proclamation.

Paul again deploys this identity-forming antithesis in 2:15a, introduced by δέ, in which "the spiritual person" is presented as the counterexample ingroup-prototype[97] to "the unspiritual person" from 2:14 who could not investigate accurately the things of God. He writes, "The spiritual person accurately assesses (ἀνακρίνει) all things." Often this language is understood to argue for some type of classification of Christ-followers into categories based on levels of understanding. Paul, however, is still referring to the entire community of Christ-followers and not, as Bultmann and Käsemann held, to an elite group with privileged insight.[98] Hunt notes that Bultmann's classifications are related to his broader existential program "and sees the ethical immaturity of the Corinthians as precluding their receiving Paul's wisdom about God and the Cross."[99]

"The spiritual person" becomes the prototype for Paul within the Christ-following community especially when compared to the comportment of some of the Corinthian Christ-followers in 3:3. The verb ἀνακρίνει does not mean "to discern" but indicates a process of careful

95. Munzinger 2007: 170.

96. Carson 2003: 64.

97. Pearson (1973: 1–9) connects those "in Christ" with those whom Paul refers to as "the spiritual ones."

98. Bultmann 1969: 70–72; Käsemann 1960: 269.

99. Hunt 1996: 7; Litfin (1994: 220) comes close to Bultmann on this point.

"investigation" or "examination."[100] Paul, in describing the group proto-type, establishes the centrality of proper categorization and assessment within the ἐκκλησία, an examination that will be flawed if attempted within the context of the world's wisdom. The object of ἀνακρίνει is τὰ πάντα and includes all the things that the ψυχικὸς ἄνθρωπος in 2:14 did not receive or understand. Fee suggests, "not necessarily all things, of course, but all things that pertain to the work of salvation, matters formerly hidden in God but now revealed through the Spirit."[101] While we agree with Fee, his approach may limit the insight into the social implications of the cross for those living together in the ἐκκλησία. Paul is addressing concrete situations within this marginal community in the Roman Empire and is not primarily concerned with doctrinal matters. Campbell employs the concept of "theologizing" to describe what Paul was engaged in as he sought "solution[s] to serious social and cultural problem[s] which threatened the harmony of the Christ-movement."[102]

Those outside cannot properly assess group norms within the Christ-movement. In 2:15b, another use of δέ, "on the other hand,"[103] specifies the contrast with the prior assertion from 2:15a concerning the ability of "the spiritual person" to accurately evaluate all things. This person, Paul writes, "is not correctly evaluated by anyone." He is telling the Corinthians that those outside the ἐκκλησία cannot properly as-sess those who have the Spirit with regard to the things of God. Paul's rhetoric here is designed to resocialize the community by means of the introduction of a new ingroup prototype,[104] in relation to the inevitable pressures associated with social contact and comparison. He does this by reminding the Corinthians that they have been given all the cogni-

100. Garland 2003: 101. BDAG 66 places the current reference under the heading "to examine with a view to finding fault." This expanded definition is helpful; how-ever, the glosses provided include "judge, call into account, discern." L&N 15, 364, list ἀνακρίνω in domains that include "study thoroughly, investigate in court, criticize, and evaluate carefully" and render 1 Cor 2:15, "the spiritual person makes careful judgments about all things."

101. Fee 1987: 118.

102. Campbell 2006a: 116.

103. BDAG 213.

104. The importance of the group prototype is that, based on 1 Cor 3:1–4, they are not behaving as a "spiritual person" but as a "fleshly person" (cf. Fee 1987: 118; Garland 2003: 101). Here Paul would be taking advantage of what Hogg and Abrams (1988: 21 emphasis original) refer to as the process of "self-definition" occurring within "the defining characteristics of the group prototype."

tive, emotional, and evaluative resources necessary to properly construct a social identity that will stabilize the community and reinforce the Pauline mission.[105] The integrative metaphor for this is found in 2:16 and is described as "the mind of Christ."

The agency of the Spirit is the source for transformed cognitive processes. The "unspiritual person" from 2:14 cannot properly evaluate the "spiritual person" from 2:15 because the latter has "the mind of Christ" from 2:16, which for Paul provides the answer to living in unity within the ἐκκλησία in their transformed identities (1 Cor 1:10). This unity does not deny difference (1 Cor 7:20; 8:7–13; 12:12–13) but, as Campbell asserts, embraces "diversity not as a remaining vestige of human sinfulness, but as something perfectly in accord with the mind of Christ."[106] Paul begins with a question drawn from Israel's scriptures designed to reorient the Corinthians' thinking. He writes in 2:16, "For who has known the mind of the Lord so as to instruct him? (τίς γὰρ ἔγνω νοῦν κυρίου, ὃς συμβιβάσει αὐτόν;)." Paul quotes Isa 40:13 LXX with the exception of the middle clause which has been omitted.[107] Senft suggests the reason for this is that Paul is quoting from memory.[108] Paul also follows the LXX which translated רוח with νοῦς instead of πνεῦμα; however, his understanding of "the mind of Christ" in relation to the work of the Spirit in 2:11 actually aligns more closely with the MT reading of רוח in Isa 40:13. Lémonon asserts, "The Spirit of the God of Israel has become the mind of the Lord, the Christ."[109] For Paul, the reception of the Spirit is the basis for the cognitive transformation referred to as "the mind of Christ." Lémonon rightly warns, however, that "one must not be lured into attributing to the Spirit what are only one's personal thoughts."[110]

---

105. 1 Cor 1:12, 26; 5:9–10; 6:6; 7:17–24; 10:27–28; 14:23; Tajfel 1978a: 28.

106. Campbell 2006a: 94.

107. Wilk 1998: 287–92, 309. Paul also quotes this verse in Rom 11:34.

108. Senft (1979 : 54) writes, "Paul justifie son droit et son intransigeance par une parole de l'Écriture, Es 40:13, qu'il cite de mémoire." Cf. Heil 2005: 69–75. Allo 1956: 50–51.

109. Lémonon (2001: 26 author's translation), writes, "L'esprit du Seigneur, Dieu d'Israël, est devenu la pensée du SEIGNEUR, le Christ." Dunn (1998: 250) doubts this connection and takes the view that "not too much should be made of 1 Cor 2:16" in terms of its Christological significance.

110. Lémonon (2001: 30 author's translation), writes, "Mais il ne faut pas se leurrer en attribuant à l'Esprit ce qui n'est que pensée personnelle."

Paul writes "but we have the mind of Christ" (ἡμεῖς δὲ νοῦν Χριστοῦ ἔχομεν), that which assists the community in living out the social implications of the gospel. Jewett's description of the "mind of Christ" serves as an apt definition for what is occurring in this passage; it is "the constellation of thoughts and assumptions which makes up the consciousness of the person and acts as the agent of rational discernment and communication."[111] The "mind of Christ" requires the agency of the Spirit and may be responded to positively, rejected, or rationalized out of action. The last two of these options appear to be what some in Corinth were doing (1 Cor 3:1–4).[112]

With regard to "the mind of Christ," 2:16b provides three useful insights. First, the δέ contrasts with the previous scripture reference in that the original question, "Who has known the mind of the Lord so as to instruct him?" expects a negative answer. For Paul, however, those who have received the Spirit and "the mind of Christ" understand God's wisdom as revealed in the cross. Schrage likewise contends that the Spirit who teaches is the Spirit of the crucified-Christ and this produces a critique of all elitist understanding of wisdom.[113] Second, the pronoun ἡμεῖς refers to ὁ πνευματικός in 2:15 and continues to describe the group prototype, the one who embodies what it means to be a "spiritual person." These people have at their disposal resources for life together which the "unspiritual ones" do not have, so why would the community continue to rely on the wisdom of this world which cannot comprehend God's ways? This question relates back to 2:14–15 asking why the "unspiritual person" cannot properly evaluate the spiritual person. Paul's answer is that their

111. Jewett 1971: 450. My understanding of "the mind of Christ," in the context of 1 Cor 1–4, is that it provides the vital decision making link for negotiating the identity forming factors of wisdom and power.

112. Litfin (1994: 220) understands Paul to be establishing the model in 1 Cor 2:6–16 and then in 3:1–4 describing the actual situation in Corinth, one in which, though they had received the Spirit, they were still living as if they had not.

113. Schrage (1991: 267) writes, "Das Pneuma, das die Christen Verstehen lehrt, ist nicht irgendein Feld-, Wald- und Wiesengeist oder eine naturhaft-magische, Enthusiasmus bewirkende Potenz, sondern das Pneuma des gekreuzigten Christus, also am Kreuz zu messen und darum unausweichlich ein Kritiker aller eigenen Weisheit und ebenso aller elitären." Hays (1997: 47) argues for a synonymous understanding for the Spirit and the mind here. They have the mind of Christ because they have the Spirit. Strecker (1999: 209) contends for a holistic transformation not just a cognitive transformation, while Munzinger (2007: 173 n. 177; 87) sees an "amalgamation of cognitive and social identity."

mindsets are incompatible.[114] Third, the presence of νοῦς echoes back to the beginning of this rhetorical unit in 1:10 and provides conceptual continuity for Paul's argument.[115] Both 1:10 and 2:16 contain νοῦς and reinforce the idea that Paul is addressing the cognitive dimension of the Corinthians' social identity. Likewise, Strüder connects 1:18—2:16 with 3:1–4 and notes that the Corinthians' "new identity . . . is growing and already under construction."[116] The Corinthian Christ-followers' identity needs construction, or as Schrage describes it *Schocktherapie*, because they are too readily identifying with their old social identities, and Paul's argument seeks to address that specific issue in 3:1–4.[117]

HINDRANCE: OVER-IDENTIFICATION WITH OLD SOCIAL IDENTITIES (3:1–4)

There is a problem in the community with those who are primarily socially identifying with their old identities. Paul has been developing an identity-forming antithesis since 1:18, but in 3:1–4 it is applied in a different way. Up to this point, intergroup issues and boundary-marking with those outside the ἐκκλησία have been his focus, but now he is interested in those living as if their identity had not been transformed. These people were still identifying primarily with their old identity structures. In 3:1, Paul begins by repositioning himself in the letter with "and I (κἀγώ)." This is a continuation of the previous argument; however, Paul is personally involved in this line of reasoning. He continues his practice of describing the group in kinship terms with "brothers and

---

114. Munzinger 2007: 173 n. 177, 87.

115. Contra Conzelmann 1975: 57. Widmann (1979: 44–53) goes further than Conzelmann and understands 1 Cor 2:6–16 as an interpolation by the spiritual ones desiring to correct Paul's misrepresentation of their point of view. Murphy-O'Connor (1986: 83; cf. Fee 1987: 100) rejects Widmann's hypothesis as "less *probable*" than the idea that Paul is using the language "of his opponents." Walker (1992: 93 emphasis original), however, is convinced by Murphy-O'Connor and Fee, and thus he understands "the ideational content of 1 Cor. 2:6–16" as "significantly different" and "contradictory to" the approach of Paul elsewhere in his letters and thus "the *cumulative* impact of the various lines of evidence supporting the interpolation hypothesis" better "explain the origin of 1 Cor 2:6–16." Thiselton (2000: 224; Weiss 1910: 52) rejects the idea of a non-Pauline interpolation and believes instead that Paul "reclaim[s] the terms for the gospel" by redefining them in light of the nature of God and of the gospel."

116. Strüder (2005: 322) writes, "dass die neue christliche Identität auch in der Gemeinde am Isthmus bereits wächst und im Bau ist."

117. Schrage 1991: 279; Litfin 1994: 220; Strüder 2005: 312.

sisters" (ἀδελφοί) but then recalls a series of events which had occurred when Paul was among them. He writes, "I was unable to speak to you as spiritual (πνευματικοῖς)," that is as the prototypical group member he has just described in 2:12–16. He then includes ἀλλά to emphasize the distinction he is about to make. He writes that he had to speak to them "as people of the flesh (σαρκίνοις), as infants in Christ (νηπίοις ἐν Χριστῷ)." For Paul, this group was living as "fleshly people"; from a SIT perspective they were socially identifying with key aspects of their Roman social identity, especially in relation to prototypical leaders (1 Cor 1:12; 3:4, 22).

This group is further defined as "infants in Christ" (νηπίοις ἐν Χριστῷ) and is now rhetorically positioned as an outgroup within the ἐκκλησία in contrast to the πνευματικός from 2:15.[118] The cognitive issue in Paul's image relates to the lack of correct perception. Those in this group had failed to allow the teaching they had received from Paul to continue to transform their identity "in Christ."[119] The pressure of Paul's social influence is significant in this passage and evidences social stereotyping similar to that found in 1:23. Social categorization is necessary for intragroup discrimination, and Paul's rhetoric in this verse relies on his ongoing pedagogical role within the ἐκκλησία. So, he reminds the Corinthians that when he was with them he could not speak to them as people who were not yet capable of receiving and recognizing the social implications of God's wisdom (1 Cor 2:1–5).

Furthermore, Paul notes that the Corinthians were infants in the past but also that they continue to live as such. To address this, he employs the resources of social memory in 3:2 and writes, "I gave you milk (γάλα) to drink, not solid food (βρῶμα)." Paul could only give the Corinthians what they were capable of receiving, and thus he tells them that when he was among them, he could only give them what they were able to take in. Paul continues, "for you were not able (ἐδύνασθε)," reminding the Corinthians again of their lack of ability to receive and thus comprehend the things freely given from God. He then moves from the past to the present to reveal the actual exigence, "but even now (νῦν) you still are not able (δύνασθε)." The problem was not so much that the Corinthians could not receive Paul's teaching before but that they still do not grasp the social implications of his teaching. This is evidenced by the

118. Weiss 1910: 71.
119. Francis 1980: 57; Cyss 2004: 180.

separations among them based on their identification with certain leaders. From a social identity perspective, these are the leaders who embody the Corinthians' shared group values, affirm their already-salient social identity and enforce their agreed-upon social norms.[120]

Those within the community of Christ-followers in Corinth were placing too much focus on key aspects of their social identity, especially in their relations to prototypical leaders. These various aspects of their social identity are described by Turner as levels of abstraction in which categorization occurs; these include the "superordinate, intermediate, and subordinate."[121] The subordinate relates to personal categorization; the intermediate relates to ingroup and outgroup comparisons, while the superordinate relates to the most broadly defined categories of existence.

For Paul, these other aspects or levels of one's social identity are to be reprioritized within the ἐκκλησία, with the "in Christ" identity serving as the master identity within the hierarchy (1 Cor 7:24).[122] In Corinth, however, that which was to be reevaluated was controlling the Corinthian Christ-followers' social identifications and creating instability within the community.[123] Identities are not simply asserted. They are negotiated within the context of communal life and in the interaction between the way one views oneself and the way one is viewed within the community; as Jenkins remarks, "*Social identity is never unilateral.*"[124] They were dividing over leaders who embodied shared group values.

In 3:3a, Paul categorizes the community as "fleshly." The explanatory γάρ shows that Paul is providing a further reason for his assertion in 3:1–2. Paul's point is clear as he writes, "You are still being influenced by the flesh (σαρκικοί)." The use of σαρκικός in 3:3 indicates that the Corinthians' ongoing behavior within the community was "disappointing" to Paul.[125] The idea here is that the Corinthians' character was

120. Hogg and Abrams 1988: 174.

121. Turner 1987: 45.

122. However, one should not infer from this a corresponding decrease in diversity. "In Christ" is not a status above others; it is one among many of the discursive agents that formed early Christ-movement identity. Cf. Deaux 1991: 80–81; Sardiello 1998: 120.

123. Theissen 1982: 107.

124. Jenkins 1996: 21 emphasis original.

125. BDAG 914. Also, we understand no significant difference between σαρκίνοις in 1 Cor 3:1 and σαρκικοί here.

being compromised, and their social identifications were hindering their moral and spiritual progress.

Paul argues that jealousy and strife are evidence of a lack of spiritual maturity (i.e., salient "in Christ" social identity) within the community. In 3:3b, he begins a new sentence and writes, "for since there is still jealousy (ζῆλος) and strife (ἔρις) among you." The γάρ indicates that he is still providing evidence for his assertion concerning the Corinthians' lack of spiritual maturity. The poor cohesion within the community and the existence of divisions are indicators that there are still problems that need to be addressed, namely "jealousy and strife."[126]

Paul continues with a compound question: "Are you not fleshly (σαρκικοί) and are you not walking around (περιπατεῖτε) like humans?"[127] The lack of community stability and coherent "in Christ" identity are indications that the Corinthians were still "fleshly." In this case, he equates the Corinthians current ethical choices with the choices that those who do not have the agency of the Spirit and the mind of Christ are making. For Paul, these things ought not to be.

In 3:4, Paul's rhetoric is designed to refocus the Corinthians' attention back to 1:12 concerning their social identification and the ways it has become a hindrance to the development of maturity and identity within the ἐκκλησία. He writes, "For when one says (ὅταν γὰρ λέγῃ τις), 'I belong to Paul,' or 'I belong to Apollos,' are you not merely human?" The initial phrase (ὅταν γὰρ λέγῃ τις) is indefinite enough that Paul would not have to be addressing any one particular group. His question suggests that the Corinthians are behaving like those outside the ἐκκλησία because of their over-identification with leaders (1 Cor 1:12). So, in reality, 3:1–4 is the focus of Paul's message to the Corinthian Christ-followers, and in 3:5–23 he is going to provide them with detailed cognitive solutions.

CONCLUSION

This chapter brought together Paul's argument from 2:6—3:4 and found two primary hindrances to the formation of a salient "in Christ" social identity. First, it was discovered that some in Corinth, from Paul's per-

---

126. Clarke 2006: 99–100. Mitchell (1991: 81) explains that "Ἔρις is personified as the Greek goddess of Discord, the opposite of Ὁμόνοια." See Dio Chrys. Or. 12.72.

127. Cf. Ehrensperger 2007: 129; Tomson 1990: 74–75.

spective, were over-relying on the world's wisdom and power which in the first century was the Roman Empire. Second, a general over-identification with previous social identities was also revealed, which was hindering the Corinthians development "in Christ." Paul's solution to both of these problems was found to be the agency of the Spirit and the mind of Christ. These combined resources provided for the transformation of cognitive processes in order to categorize communal life from God's perspective and not from the world's point of view. Many of the difficulties in the text involved the Corinthians' relationship to leaders within the Christ-movement, so in 3:5–23 Paul will provide a better way to think about and identify with leaders by recognizing that they ultimately all belong to God.

8

Social Identity Formation: All Belong to God

INTRODUCTION

WE HAVE JUST ARGUED that Roman imperial ideology is a significant hindrance within the ἐκκλησία in Corinth. Paul's solution
to this problem is the agency of the Spirit and the development of the
mind of Christ. One concrete way in which over-identification with old
social identities reveals itself is in the dividing over prototypical leaders.
Thus, Paul provides the Corinthians with a new way to think about and
identify with their leaders, namely that all belong to God. This solution
is the concern of this present chapter.

The Oxford English Dictionary defines metaphor as a "figure of
speech in which a name or descriptive term is transferred to some object
different from, but analogous to, that to which it is properly applicable."[1]
Aristotle classified metaphor as a trope.[2] In the parts of a metaphor, the
first component is the "topic" and the second is the "vehicle," while the
interpretation of the metaphor is its "ground."[3] Metaphors are not simply
figures of speech used to describe an abstract concept; they are a way of
thinking. Two approaches to metaphor processing include the analogical approach and attribution approach. In the first, metaphors function
as any other analogy, and the properties of the topic and vehicle which

1. Simpson and Weiner 1989: 676.

2. Arist. *Poet.* 21–2; *Rh.* 3.2.6—4.4, 3.10.7–11. 15. Silk (1996: 967) recognizes three
functions for ancient metaphors: "to make clearer, as through a diagram, usually by
appeal to familiar experience"; second, "to make immediate, as if to the senses ... this is
less a matter of making clear than of making alien ('defamiliarizing,' in modern theoretical terminology) and thereby making listener or reader experience anew"; third, "to
exploit the associations, including the contrary associations, of the vehicle, beyond any
limited point or ground of comparison."

3. Gentner and Bowdle 2003: 18.

are similar are uncovered as a means by which to understand the underlying comparison.[4] The second approach, put forth by Glucksberg, understands metaphors as expressions of class categorizations.[5] Here, "the topic is a member of the category of which the vehicle is a prototypical member."[6] The second approach works well with SIT and its focus on social comparison and categorization. In the context of 3:5–23 we will investigate the way Paul's use of metaphorical language furthers the process of social categorization that is occurring as the Corinthian Christ-followers seek to accept Paul's teaching and apply it in the life of their community. Paul's strategy in this section of his argument is to construct the Corinthians' identity by encouraging them to think differently about their teachers and about the God of Israel.

IDENTITY-FORMATION METAPHOR: GOD'S FIELD (3:5–9B)

Paul's rhetorical goal emerges in 3:5, which is to persuade the Corinthian Christ-followers to cease boasting in their teachers and leaders (1 Cor 3:21). Yinger rightly understands the issue here as the "Corinthian proclivity to evaluate [their teachers] as competing itinerant philosophers."[7] Thus, Paul begins by asking two questions: "What (τί) then is Apollos? Or what (τί) is Paul?"[8] These questions are designed to recategorize the Corinthian Christ-followers' thinking and adjust their social comparisons with regard to their estimation of the role of teachers within the ἐκκλησία in three ways.[9]

First, he relates the general function of those such as Paul and Apollos within the Christ-movement as "servants." This term describes "one who serves as an intermediary in a transaction" and is a metaphor

---

4. Gentner 2001: 199–253. See Wanamaker 2005: 418–25 for examples of Paul's use of metaphors for the purpose of moral formation. The examples in this chapter include the ἐκκλησία as God's field (1 Cor 3:9), building (1 Cor 3:9), and temple (1 Cor 3:16–17). See also DeNeui 2008.

5. Glucksberg 1990: 3–18.

6. Gentner and Bowdle 2003: 20.

7. Yinger 1999: 206.

8. Though there are mss that contain the reading τις, Paul's emphasis is on the Corinthians' roles and not on them as individuals (Clarke 1993: 119).

9. Yinger (1999: 206) understands the issue here as one "of comparative status." He is undoubtedly correct but the comparison extends to the entire community and not only to the leaders. Paul has been addressing issues of communal evaluation since 1 Cor 1:10.

for their tasks among the community and not, as Hays argues, an official church office.[10] Clarke contends that by using διάκονος, "Paul had deliberately inverted the Graeco-Roman scale of values" with regard to patronage and "menial work."[11]

Second, by employing the resources of social memory, Paul and Apollos are described as the ones "through whom you came to believe." This emphasizes, as indicated by Chester, "the point at which [they] came to be in Christ."[12] From a social identity perspective the point of faith may be described as that point at which they committed to the norms of behavior within the Christ-movement.[13] Halbwachs argues that memories are recalled "externally, and the groups of which" one is a member provide "the means to reconstruct" those memories.[14] A religious movement assists in this with rituals and beliefs as well as myths that provide meaning for the social environment.[15] Misztal summarizes the significance of remembering within religious groups by noting that "the importance of memory lies in the identity that it shapes."[16]

Third, Paul reorients the Corinthians' perspective away from individual human agency and notes, "even as the Lord entrusted to each one,"[17] so that the social comparisons of the Corinthians' teachers would be based on God's wisdom and not on the world's wisdom (1 Cor 2:14–16). The proper categorization and evaluation of the Corinthians' leaders is the first opportunity for the community to exercise the cognitive resources of the "mind of Christ" in a mature manner and not as they have previously (1 Cor 3:3).[18]

---

10. BDAG 230; Hays 1997: 52.

11. Clarke 1993: 119–20; 2008: 67.

12. Chester 2003: 81. Cf. Schrage 1991: 291; Thiselton 2000: 300. This construes the prepositional phrase διά plus the genitive as intermediate agent.

13. Engberg-Pedersen 2000: 34–36.

14. Halbwachs 1992: 38.

15. Halbwachs 1992: 87. Myth here is understood as the narrative of the community that relates to its beginning as a group (Misztal 2003:13). Theissen (1999: 3, see also 23–27, 325–26) describes myth as that which "explain[s] in narrative form what fundamentally determines the world and life." For a more expansive use of myth in Paul, see also Bell 2007: 23–65.

16. Misztal 2003: 14.

17. BDAG 242. Thiselton (2000: 300) discusses the possible "semantic" connection with διάκονος and translates ἔδωκεν as "assigned."

18. This builds on the presence of the inferential οὖν in 3:5 pointing back to the previous argument in 1 Cor 2:6—3:4.

Paul continues by reminding the Corinthians of his work and that of Apollos, employing agricultural imagery designed to emphasize their foundational nature.[19] The use of the agricultural metaphor would have been particularly striking in light of the food shortage in Corinth, which is attested to around 51 CE.[20] In 3:6, he begins "I planted," emphasizing his arrival in Corinth prior to Apollos. Barton asserts, "The temporal primacy involved in 'planting' implies for Paul a certain primacy of authority in his relations with his converts."[21] But Barton's focus here misses the ground of the metaphor which is to emphasize that both he and Apollos are only servants of God among the Corinthians. Paul continues, "Apollos watered," which is not to be understood as a work secondary to Paul's. The comparison here is between the workers in relation to God. Horsley describes Apollos as one who "came along later and only watered" and "had invaded his territory in Corinth."[22] Clarke, on the other hand, notes that "Paul demonstrates" here "that there is no tension between him and Apollos."[23] Ker, however, argues that Paul's rhetoric is not structured as an "unmistakably open attack" but that he is still employing categorization in order to undermine Apollos.[24] While Campbell is a bit more irenic on this issue, he still conceives of "Apollos" as one who interfered in some way "with the life of the Corinthian community."[25] Which of these approaches is to be preferred?

Paul's understanding of Apollos and himself as servants belonging to God suggests that there are no personal difficulties between the two. First, Paul's argument in this section is that all belong to God (1 Cor 3:23) and that categorizations based on worldly status are inconsistent with God's wisdom. In the ἐκκλησία, for leaders, "there is but one status" and that is to be a "servant of the Lord."[26] Moreover, the strong adversative ἀλλά establishes the contrast between the status of the workers and

---

19. Mitchell 1991: 216; Keener 2005: 42.

20. Danylak 2008: 232–33; West 1931: 73.

21. Barton 2003: 36.

22. Horsley 1998: 64–65.

23. Clarke 2008: 142.

24. Ker 2000: 96; Weiss 1910: xxxii.

25. Campbell 2006a: 86; see also Welborn (2005: 105–9) for a summary of the viewpoint that there was a rivalry between Paul and Apollos.

26. Kuck 1992: 170; Mihaila (2006: 80) rightly explains that "Paul's concern thus is to remove any ground for boasting in teachers, since all belong to God, regardless of their distinct individual gift/task."

the ultimate agent who provides growth within the community: "God causes its continual growth (ηὔξανεν)," a point Paul will restate in 3:7. The elevation of teachers within the community misunderstands the nature of the growth that is actually occurring. Paul and Apollos are God's servants and are not to be evaluated in the same manner as one would assess servants in the Roman world.[27]

Second, the workers are nothing in comparison with God who allows the growth to occur.[28] Paul writes, "Neither the one who plants (ὁ φυτεύων) is anything nor the one who waters (ὁ ποτίζων)." The implication is that neither Paul nor Apollos nor any other teacher is to be the focus of social identification within the ἐκκλησία. That is reserved for God "who causes the growth (ὁ αὐξάνων) to occur." God's sovereign work has produced the ἐκκλησία and thus Schnabel rightly notes that this "unmasks the absurdity of the Corinthian fixation on rhetoric and social status."[29] With both Paul and Apollos subordinated to God, the implication follows that God is positioned as the head of the community, and thus personal animus among leaders misunderstands the hierarchical nature of work within God's field.

Third, Paul and Apollos are each entrusted with differing responsibilities by God but they work together as one. Paul continues with two substantival participles, "The one who plants (ὁ φυτεύων) and the one who waters (ὁ ποτίζων) are one." This description serves as an apt image for the type of unity Paul desires among the Corinthian Christ-followers. Horrell rightly remarks that Paul "and Apollos are only servants (3:5; 4:1), not figures who intend to be exalted as the heads of factions."[30] There is still no indication of an ongoing conflict between them, thus Horsley's view is too strong. Furthermore, Mitchell understands this relationship to be "paradigmatic" of what Paul desires for the entire community.[31] If this is correct, it undermines the approach that Paul and Apollos were rivals, and it also implies that this relationship

---

27. Plut. *Vit. Per.* 1.4—2.1, 2. "While we delight in the work [of craftsmen and artisans], we despise the workman ... it does not necessarily follow that, if the work delights you with its graces, the one who wrought it is worthy of your esteem." Originally cited in Winter 1989: 304. See Schrage 1991: 292.

28. Winter 2001: 55–56 n. 49.

29. Schnabel 2006: 195 author's translation.

30. Horrell 1996: 135.

31. Mitchell 1991: 213.

could be viewed as a group prototype in relation to social status comparisons. Mitchell's line of reasoning calls into question the approach of both Campbell and Ker. The "paradigmatic" nature of Paul's rhetoric will be discussed in 1 Cor 4:6. Thus, Paul has argued that workers such as he and Apollos are servants who belong to God, and as such, assessment of their work is left up to God and not to those within the community of Christ-followers. Moreover, there is no room for personal rivalry between servants, nor should there be divisions in the name of the servants because they all ultimately belong to God.

Paul recognizes that the complete suspension of social comparisons is not likely, so he attempts to adjust the Corinthians' cognitive framework in relation to judgment and accountability before God by continuing, "and each one will receive one's own wage (μισθόν)." The word μισθός is normally translated "wage" or "pay" and is also used in 1 Cor 3:14 "in an eschatological sense" pointing to "God's future judgment."[32] Yinger, on the other hand, argues that one "should not immediately" see here a "reference to some sort of heavenly rewards."[33] A determination between these two viewpoints is difficult; however, what is clear is that the μισθός that is to be received ultimately comes from God.[34] If one considers Preisker's view that Paul's usage of μισθός has its basis in "his ancient Pharisaic heritage," then Kuck's approach is somewhat more plausible.[35]

The agricultural metaphor continues as Paul notes that one's reward will be "according to one's own labor (κόπον)." This reinforces his previous contention that the assessment of the servants is the responsibility of God and not the Corinthian ἐκκλησία. The reason for this is that some within the ἐκκλησία were relying on the world's standards to assess their leaders and teachers. Hall sees in the use of κόπος a key concept by which to critique "aristocratic virtue in the Graeco-Roman world, particularly when linked with manual labour."[36] Paul's use of κόπος here, then, may be seen as an implicit critique of Roman social

32. Kuck 1992: 167; Shanor 1988: 469.

33. Yinger 1999: 212; VanLandingham (2006: 189) understands this section to relate to judgment in general and not specifically to one's works, without regard to salvation. BDAG 653 sees an "affirmation of laudable conduct, *receive one's reward.*"

34. Thiselton 2000: 304.

35. Preisker 1967: 720.

36. Hall 2003: 56. See Yinger 1999: 214.

identity that casts aspersions upon those who work hard. While we are
not in agreement with some of Hock's conclusions, he is correct to note
that "by working at a slavish and demeaning trade Paul sensed a considerable loss of status."[37] Kuck asserts that Paul continues the theme
of "diversity" here "by affirming that the individual differences will be
confirmed by God's future judgment."[38] Paul's point in 3:8 is that socially
identifying with one teacher over another indicates that one does not
understand the nature of God's way of evaluating workers and reveals a
lack of maturity within the community (1 Cor 3:1–4). The servants and
the ἐκκλησία in Corinth all belong to God.

In 3:9a, Paul creates rhetorical space in which to construct identity. He begins with an inferential γάρ, indicating the conclusion
concerning God's ownership which is to be drawn from the previous
arguments. He writes about himself and his co-workers, "We are co-
workers (συνεργοί) who belong to God," that is, servants working together who also belong to God, taking the genitive as a possessive.[39] As
co-workers, they labor together in the proclamation of the gospel and,
as Ehrensperger concludes, συνεργοί "stresses the cooperative rather
than the hierarchical dimension of the relationship between those
designated as συνεργοί and Paul, who is one amongst them."[40] While
this is accurate, for Paul, cooperation exists in the context of hierarchy
(1 Cor 3:23). Birge is right to argue that the field metaphor used by Paul
in 1 Cor 3:5–9 is also "the language of household kinship" with its implicit hierarchy.[41] Hierarchical and household structures are two areas

37. Hock 1978: 564.

38. Kuck 1992: 164.

39. Hays 1997: 52–53; Schnabel 2006: 201. Weiss (1910: 77) argues that this phrase
should be understood to mean that they are co-workers with God, not as emphasizing
the idea of belonging to God. Ker (2000: 87) follows Weiss in this regard. Garland (2003:
113) rightly contends that contextual factors argue against Weiss and Ker on this issue.

40. Ehrensperger 2007: 48. Ollrog (1979: 3) recognizes the importance of studying Paul's friends and supporters rather than focusing on his opponents. Ehrensperger
(2007: 47) credits Ollrog with the insight of regarding Paul as one among equals within
the early Christ-movement. Wellborn (2005: 108–9) is not convinced that one can discern such "unity and collegiality" between Paul and Apollos. Ehrensperger (2007: 147)
counters that Paul understands their relationship as one "of working together" and "not
as one of competition."

41. Birge's (2002: 14) contention that the field is also kinship language is based on
the "familial bonds of affection . . . rooted in Greco-Roman household kinship—διά
κονος, κύριος, συνεργός" connected with "θεοῦ γεώργιον, θεοῦ οἰκοδομή," which

where Paul continues to see the usefulness of Roman social identity. Both of these function within the context of kinship discourse which is the primary discourse in antiquity for identity formation. Birge concludes that Paul "effectively dissolves any basis for the Corinthians' promotion of one missionary over the other and, in doing so, he offers a model for missionary leadership based on the metaphor for cooperation found in household kinship."[42]

In 3:9b, Paul continues his use of the agricultural metaphor and directly applies it to the Corinthian Christ-followers. He writes, "You are a field (γεώργιον) that belongs to God"; this also construes the genitive as a possessive continuing the broader thought Paul has been arguing throughout this section that all belong to God. The ἐκκλησία in Corinth is described by Paul as land ready for development, land which belongs to God. Interestingly, DeNeui's research into the use of the field metaphor in Graeco-Roman sources found "no examples of the use of the field for a community" nor "of ownership of the field to God."[43] Paul is forming the Corinthians' social identity in the context of their communal relationships both with God and the servants of God.[44] The theme that both the servants of God as well as the Christ-following community belong to God emerges clearly from Paul's use of the agricultural metaphor in 3:5–9b.

IDENTITY-FORMATION METAPHOR: GOD'S BUILDING (3:9C–15)

The agricultural metaphor is abruptly disturbed in 3:9c, and Paul shifts his metaphor to the domain of building and construction but continues the thought of the community belonging to God.[45] He writes, "You are a

---

"provides a bridge from the metaphor of agriculture to building and building material found in vv. 10–15." Roman household kinship discourse (and its implicit hierarchy) provides Paul with rhetorical resources by which to form the identity of the ἐκκλησία in Corinth. Cf. *CIL* 6.9326; *CIL* 6.13738; Cic. *Q Fr.* 1.3.3; Dion. Hal. *Ant. Rom.* 2.26–27.

42. Birge 2002: 15.

43. DeNeui 2008: 219. Cf. BDAG 195; Garland 2003: 113; Thiselton 2000: 306.

44. Dunn (1998: 534–36), though focusing on Paul's construction of corporate identity in Romans, recognizes the centrality of this in Paul's work and also details the use of metaphor in this construction. In Dunn's estimation the image present in 1 Cor 3:9 is one of "the most important" of the "Pauline metaphors."

45. Hogeterp (2006: 313) understands 1 Cor 3:9 as the beginning of a new rhetorical unit designed to introduce the central metaphor—the community as the temple of God

building (οἰκοδομή) that belongs to God," taking the genitive as one of possession. Judge notes that οἰκοδομή was a term used "for the process of construction on a building site."[46] Paul's community construction was designed to transform "social realities," continues Judge, "that lay within the fabric of the old ranking system" by means of "a revolution in social values."[47] Adams understands a community like the one in Corinth, a recipient of Paul's letters, as a community whose "social world" is "in the making" and thus whose "social identity, social relations, attitudes and modes of behaviour" are being formed.[48] The building metaphor in 3:9c–15 also incorporates apocalyptic discourse designed to assist the ἐκκλησία in the maintenance of their social identity.[49]

In 3:10, Paul is not focused on his own agency in the construction of the community but on God's, which he describes in the context of a discourse of grace: "according to the grace of God (τὴν χάριν τοῦ Θεοῦ) given to me." Grace here is not focused on intellectual assent or doctrinal concerns but on the practical social implications of God's work within the community of Christ-followers.[50] Thus, it connects with 1 Cor 1:4–9 which described God's grace in the framework of the formation of the Corinthians' social identity. Moreover, Ehrensperger describes the discourse of grace as "an activity which is initiated by God to promote the life and well-being of the recipients and which, in response, demands

in 1 Cor 3:16–17. The foundation of Rome is described similarly in Plut. *Mor.* 320B, also cited in DeNeui 2008: 160.

46. Judge 2008: 173. BDAG 697 recognizes the process orientation of the word; it is "a building as [a] result of a construction process."

47. Judge 2008: 173.

48. Adams (2000: 23–24) rightly connects this with Berger's concept of the symbolic universe. In referencing this verse Adams takes the view that "Paul's letter-writing activity may be thought of as a world-constructing endeavour, an attempt to influence the social and ideological formation of the" community.

49. The combination of apocalyptic, moral exhortation, and identity formation that occurs in this section is somewhat similar to that which Wanamaker (2002: 136) observes as Paul's strategy in 1 Thessalonians.

50. Crook (2008: 34) takes the point of view that God has generously given something to Paul. Thus, Crook translates the phrase "by the benefaction given to me." This brings to the fore the idea that Paul has received "concrete good" rather than "abstract theological virtue known ephemerally as grace." However, Crook's contention (2008: 37), based on 3:11, that what was given was "the vision of Christ" ends up making this statement about Paul's agency. The communal context of 1 Cor 1:4 provides an understanding of this verse that maintains the primary focus on God's agency.

a respective activity from those who receive it."[51] In this context, grace requires Paul to be engaged in a mission to the nations and the Corinthian Christ-followers to be engaged in the maintenance of that mission in Paul's absence. Paul's initial work in Corinth is described, "Like a wise master-builder (σοφὸς ἀρχιτέκτων), I laid a foundation (θεμέλιον)." The subordinating conjunction ὡς introduces Paul's assessment of his own work as a σοφὸς ἀρχιτέκτων. The rhetorical use of σοφός is significant in the context of his discourse on wisdom in 1 Corinthians 1–2.[52] Paul relied on the wisdom of God in his work among them, so the Corinthians should likewise rely on this wisdom for the maintenance of the ἐκκλησία.

DeNeui argues that Paul is "claiming a certain authority" by the use of ἀρχιτέκτων.[53] However, we would contend that Paul is not asserting his authority or seeking to elevate his own position by the use of this term. Lanci has pointed out that its use does not imply a dominant position of authority.[54] Furthermore, DeNeui too quickly stresses Paul's claim of authority when the context emphasizes God's grace. This is not to deny that Paul was in an asymmetrical relationship with the Corinthian Christ-followers; it is just that the lexical connotations that DeNeui sees for ἀρχιτέκτων are mitigated by the literary context of 1 Cor 3:9c–15.

Paul's role as a key advisor in constructing the Christ-movement among the nations is the framework of the next clause: "but another builds on it (ἐποικοδομεῖ)." This clause lacks any sense of a critique of the fact that others are working among the ἐκκλησία in Corinth. Paul fully expects the community to continue to develop in his absence; some of this would happen under leaders (1 Cor 16:10, 12, 15–19), but most of this formation would occur within the social life of the community. While Kuck agrees with the communal focus of this section, he appears to unduly restrict the work that is occurring in relation to the social implications of the gospel when he writes that Paul is not addressing "moral actions in general but rather the quality of the church that results from the effort of each."[55] The difficulty with this point is that those "moral actions" are the specific contact zones for mission as social integration,

51. Ehrensperger 2007: 81.

52. Theissen 1999: 101–7, 275.

53. DeNeui 2008: 174–75.

54. Lanci 1997: 78.

55. Kuck 1992: 174.

and the way one might separate Paul's moral guidance from his mission guidance is unclear; they are interrelated and inseparable.[56]

Paul's concerns here should not be limited only to the teachers or leaders but should be understood more broadly. It is actually quite problematic to identify a high level of institutionalization at this early stage within the Christ-movement, though there is no doubt that diverse approaches to communal formation were in existence.[57] The entire ἐκκλησία is given guidance by Paul; he writes, "but each one must be careful (βλεπέτω) how he builds (ἐποικοδομεῖ)." Paul provides practical advice on the way this communal maintenance and this building project are to continue (1 Cor 6:12; 8:1; 10:23; 12:7; 14:3–5, 12, 26; 15:58). Kuck rightly concludes, "in 3:10–15" one should "see a reference to the work of all believers" and not only to the labors of a specific group of teachers within the community.[58] Paul's advice is that the community must pay close attention (βλεπέτω) to the way they build.

This phrase introduces the apocalyptic eschatological context of Paul's rhetoric that is to emerge in 3:13–15.[59] It should also be noted that Carter understands the presence of apocalyptic eschatology in a text to be an indicator that identity formation is occurring.[60] Kazen contends that the Son of Man typology played a central role in the creation of group identity in the early Christ-movement.[61] He suggests that in the gospels a collective understanding of the Son of Man, similar to that found in Daniel and 1 Enoch, is evident and "provided an eschatological group identity."[62] He rightly notes that Paul does not explicitly employ the phrase Son of Man, but he suggests that similar concepts are to be found in Paul's "participatory christology" including "suffering and martyrdom, serving behaviour, reversed value scales and expectations of eschatological vindication."[63] Overall, Kazen's suggestion is plausible and

56. Dickson 2003: 230 and Barram 2006: 10.

57. Cf. Clarke 2008: 12–13; Wire 1990: 80. Mount (2005: 340) recognizes the interpretive difficulty that emerged based on the charismatic nature of the community of Christ-followers, even though in the case of 1 Cor 11:3–16 his solution is not particularly convincing.

58. Kuck 1992: 174.

59. Chevallier 1980: 124.

60. Carter 2000: 10–11.

61. Kazen 2008: 98.

62. Kazen 2008: 120.

63. Kazen 2008: 122; see also Middleton 2006: 146–56.

the focus on a corporate interpretation of the Son of Man is most helpful in understanding the way textual images could form social identity.
DeNeui questions whether "eschatology" is an "overriding theme of 1 Cor
3:5–17."[64] However, his separation of eschatological and ecclesiological
categories is too fine of a distinction with regard to Paul's theologizing.

In 3:11, Paul expands on his previous idea that God's call "in Christ"
is the foundation for the Corinthians' social identity (1 Cor 1:1–2). Now
he argues that Jesus Christ is the foundation, and thus the Corinthians'
sense of belonging rightly has its basis in him and not in competing
allegiances that would diminish his role as the center of communal life.[65]
This concept is inherent in Paul's description of the call to communal
fellowship with Christ in 1 Cor 1:9. Thus, Paul writes, "For no one can
lay any foundation (θεμέλιον) other than what is being laid." Carter's
textual identity framework notes that the "central focus" for the community must be its "commitment to Jesus" as "the central feature of the
community's identity."[66] This is specifically Paul's point in 3:11; without
Christ there is no reason for the community in the first place.[67] It is often
noted that the building metaphor served as an appropriate political topos within the Roman world to encourage civic unity and peace.[68]

Paul makes the foundation clear as he writes that it "is Jesus
Christ."[69] In what sense, then, is Jesus Christ the foundation of the community? Recent work by Johnson Hodge may prove helpful here. She
understands Paul to be addressing his central theological issue, which is
"gentile alienation from the God of Israel," by offering the solution that
gentiles receive "Abrahamic heritage . . . through Christ."[70] This is accomplished through "patrilineal descent" which was "the prevailing kinship structure of the ancient world."[71] Though in general this approach
is evident in Paul, in the Corinthian correspondence Abraham is only

64. DeNeui 2008: 139.

65. Schrage 1991: 298.

66. Carter 2000: 9; Kreitzer 2005: 507.

67. Kuck 1992: 175.

68. Mitchell 1991: 99–105; Mihaila 2006: 82–83; Lanci 1997: 78–79.

69. We introduced the importance of this concept for understanding a particularistic approach to identity formation on p. 84. Hodge provides a plausible application of
that approach. Furthermore, on p. 129, the foundation of the group's social identity was
introduced in the context of God's grace and call "in Christ."

70. Johnson Hodge 2007: 117.

71. Johnson Hodge 2007: 19.

mentioned in 2 Cor 11:22 and not in a context that would immediately apply to gentiles; however, patrilineal descent is evident in 1 Cor 10:2 with regard to Moses. If one accepts the kinship discourse framework of Paul's argument, then Johnson Hodge provides a convincing reading of what it means to be "in Christ." Christ as the foundation of the community may be understood within the context of a "containment theory of descent" in which "characteristics, status, and capabilities of the descendents can be traced back to the seeds of ancestors"; these are key components of one's social identity.[72] This reading provides a plausible, concrete understanding of the foundation of the community being Jesus Christ and God's call to be in fellowship with him (1 Cor 1:1–2, 9; 3:10). He is the center of the community with regard to wisdom, power, and identity for "those whose line of descent springs from faithfulness" (Rom 4:17; Gal 3:7).[73] The reason that Jesus Christ is the only possible foundation for the Pauline community is because, as gentiles, his faithfulness provides the only means for the Corinthians to rightly relate to the God of Israel (1 Cor 1:29–31).[74]

Having established that Jesus Christ is the foundation of the community in that he provided the means by which gentiles are called to relate to the God of Israel, Paul continues in 3:12, "if anyone builds on the foundation." How can this be understood with regard to a kinship reading of being "in Christ"? Johnson Hodge's description mentioned above notes that kinship language focuses on ancestral "characteristics, status, and capabilities."[75] In this context, those aspects of one's previous identity that adversely impact the clear proclamation of the gospel, those key "characteristics, status" or "capabilities," are considered problematic within the ἐκκλησία. These are described metaphorically as "gold, silver, costly stones, wood, hay, or straw," some of which have lasting value and some of which do not,[76] especially in relation to the eschatological con-

72. Johnson Hodge 2007: 95.

73. Johnson Hodge 2007: 80. This renders the genitive ἐκ πίστεως as a subjective genitive with regard to Abraham's work.

74. Johnson Hodge's work coheres quite well with the particularistic approach to identity taken in this book and follows closely the work of Nanos and Stowers but makes little use of Campbell, though his initial work pre-dates Johnson Hodge's by close to two decades (Campbell 1991: 106–14).

75. Johnson Hodge 2007: 95.

76. This approach avoids the unnecessary categorization of the constituent parts beyond the obvious "property attribution," in this case, that which would survive fire

flagration seen in 3:13[77] and, as Hogeterp insightfully remarks, within the context of "community building upon the gospel mission."[78]

In 3:13, the apocalyptic discourse emerges as a means by which to form social identity. Brown rightly sees in 1 Corinthians the hermeneutical challenge of "applied apocalyptic" in which a text seeks "to promote a new way of *being* in the world, namely, a way characterized by unity and reconciliation, by eliciting a new way of *knowing* 'according to the cross.'"[79] The sentence from 3:12 continues, "each builder's work (τὸ ἔργον) will be plainly seen." The work referred to here is the end result of the construction and maintenance of the Christ-following community in Corinth. Kuck describes it as that which "results from the effort of each," an endeavor "not limited to missionaries and teachers," but that which is done by the entire community.[80] The results of the Corinthians' communal construction will be made clear at some point in the future (φανερὸν γενήσεται). This apocalyptic discourse draws "upon *topoi* found in the writings of the genre of apocalypse but are not themselves apocalypses."[81] In the case of 3:13, there is the focus of an imminent day of judgment and the presence of fire.

The social function of Paul's approach to apocalyptic identity formation continues in 3:13b as he writes, "for the Day (ἡ ἡμέρα) will make it clear." He is forming the community by virtue of the fact that their

---

and that which would not. This is similar to "pivot and convergence," an approach to metaphor that is evident in Aesch. *Sept.* 412f; cited in Silk 1974: 200.

77. Kuck (1992: 177) wrongly connects these with "the building of the tabernacle or temple in the OT: Exod 25:3–7; 31:4–5; 35:32–33 (gold, silver, stone, wood, among others, for the building of the tabernacle); 1 Chron 22:14–16; 29:2 (gold, silver, wood, precious stones, among others, for the building of the temple). It would seem that the OT descriptions of the building of the tabernacle provided the starting point for Paul's list in 1 Cor 3:12." Kuck's view is based on an anticipation of 1 Cor 3:16–17 being the Jewish temple; however, if the many temples that dotted the landscape of Corinth were in view, this would weaken Kuck's argument. This view is similar to that of Shanor (1988: 471) but has been critiqued by Hogeterp (2006: 320). Both offer insightful comments on this issue but a consideration of reception theory and its impact on argumentation and the way it is received provides a possible middle-path between these two approaches. Cf. Thiselton 2000: 311; Williams 2000: 818; Mihaila 2006: 85; DeNeui 2008: 179.

78. Hogeterp 2006: 320.

79. Brown 1995: 12. For a discussion of the role of apocalyptic in Paul see Martyn 1967: 264; Käsemann 1969: 131–34; Meeks 1983b: 689; Brown 1995: 4–8; Martin 1995: 62; Adams 2000: 106–7; Harink 2005: 17–19; Campbell 2006a: 144–46.

80. Kuck 1992: 174.

81. Wanamaker 2002: 134.

understanding of the reality of this future event should create present identity salience and thus provide an ongoing mechanism for social identity maintenance. The use of ἡ ἡμέρα reflects Paul's Jewish apocalyptic orientation but also serves as an implicit critique of Roman imperial eschatology.[82] The empire may claim everlasting peace and security, but Paul has already noted in 1 Cor 2:6–9 that their doom is sealed. Paul's discourse here reinforces the Corinthian Christ-followers' social identity by reorienting their eschatological horizon, something he does again in 1 Cor 6:9–10.

The reason that the day of judgment will make this clear is "because (ὅτι) it will be revealed (ἀποκαλύπτεται) by fire (πυρί)." The causal ὅτι introduces the presence of "fire" in the context of future judgment and, as Hogeterp argues, "probably stems from biblical and post-biblical Israelite traditions, since the eschatological connotations to Paul's idea are very strong."[83] Paul's focus here is on the process of community building and the accountability that marks an important boundary between those inside and outside the community, a distinction that the Christ-followers in Corinth appear to have overlooked (1 Cor 5:11–13).[84] Paul continues, "and the fire will test what kind of work each has done." This future "fiery judgment"[85] refers to a future judgment upon the works of the community of Christ-followers. Paul's purpose in reminding the Corinthians of this future judgment is not to alienate them but to reinforce their identification with Paul and his co-workers. This constant future orientation provides the cognitive, ethical, and emotional resources necessary for the maintenance of the Corinthians' social identity. Later in the letter, Paul describes this communal ethos as "faith, hope, and love" (1 Cor 13:13).[86]

In 3:14, Paul provides a communally empowering aspect of his teaching; he writes, "if what someone has built (ἐπῳκοδόμησεν) survives," indicating that the future judgment does not necessarily require a sense of

---

82. Others have argued that Stoicism is in the background of Paul's argumentation here (Hogeterp 2006: 321). Cf. Héring 1949: 31.

83. Hogeterp (2006: 320–21) provides helpful references in this regard: Amos 4:11; LXX Sir 39:28; 1QpHab X, 2–13; 1QS II, 4–8; 1QS VIII, 4–9. Contra DeNeui 2008: 139–40.

84. Ivarsson 2008: 188–90.

85. Adams 2007: 200.

86. Wanamaker (2002: 142) describes these, in the context of 1 Thess 1:3, as "the three cardinal Christian virtues" of the Christ-following community.

communal dread but that if the results are acceptable, "he will receive a reward" (μισθὸν λήμψεται). Paul's purpose is to shape the Corinthians' identity, and he includes both positive and negative rhetorical elements to accomplish his task. This is part of his larger mission to further the gospel and assure the continuance of the Christ-movement throughout the Roman Empire. The formation process, would involve, as noted by Wanamaker, "a change of identity that was accomplished through a re-socialization process in which Paul and his missionary colleagues served as the agents of socialization."[87] To this, however, one should add that the community itself was a key component in this resocialization process, as was their interaction with their cultural and civic environment.[88] This takes into consideration the post-colonial concept of hybridization in which there is a constant dialogical process occurring between the colonizer and the colonized. This may fruitfully be extended to the process of conversion and the interaction that emerges between the converted and the non-converted. This does not minimize the agency of the Spirit but expands the understanding of the Spirit's work to include all aspects of one's social identity.[89]

In 3:15, Paul reassures those within the community that their eternal status is not endangered in this judgment. He writes, "If someone's work is burned up (κατακαήσεται), he will suffer loss (ζημιωθήσεται)." At this point in his argument he is clear; the ongoing formation of the community of Christ-followers is vital, and if a reorientation does not occur then something will be lost. Lest the community give up in light of the difficulties, he reminds them, "he himself will be saved (σωθήσεται)" and then concludes, "but only as through fire (πυρός)." In other words, this is so important that the community will survive but just barely. This type of community is not part of Paul's rhetorical vision, but it is a possibility unless their social identifications are realigned, producing a distinct ethos which results in an alternative community within the Roman Empire. Paul's rhetorical vision for the Corinthians comes into view in 3:16–17; they are sanctuaries of God, and this way of naming the Corinthians should transform their spatial and social relations.

The imagery of the building emphasizes the corporate nature of Paul's construction and is a motif often employed to encourage unity

---

87. Wanamaker 2002: 133; but see Pickett 1997: 98–99.

88. Wright 2005: 59.

89. Leander 2008: 225–32

among a body of people.[90] Mitchell recognizes the identity-forming power of this metaphor; she notes that the description of the ἐκκλησία as God's building is "a call to the Corinthians to live in the unity which that identity implies" and is further emphasized in 3:16–17 where the community of Christ-followers is described as God's temple.[91]

IDENTITY-FORMATION METAPHOR: GOD'S TEMPLE
(3:16–17)

Paul begins in 3:16 by asking the Corinthian Christ-followers, "Do you not know that you are the temple of God (ναὸς Θεοῦ) and the Spirit of God (τὸ πνεῦμα τοῦ Θεοῦ) dwells in you?" The term ναός is used by Paul to describe his vision for the Corinthians' social identity, and he relies on a metaphor that was culturally and civically significant in Roman Corinth.[92] The metaphor suggests the Corinthian Christ-followers belong to God and are "indwelt" (οἰκεῖ) by "the Spirit of God" (τὸ πνεῦμα τοῦ Θεοῦ). Paul has focused on the Corinthians' social identity since 1 Cor 1:2, and now the temple imagery in 1 Cor 3:16 creates a spatial[93] location for the Spirit within the community as a group; the use of the second person discursively establishes this.[94]

Paul is now concerned with those who would work against the construction and maintenance of the community of Christ-followers.

90. Thiselton 2000: 307; Mitchell 1991: 99–100.

91. Mitchell 1991: 102–3; Campbell 2006a: 153; but see DeNeui 2008: 153–54.

92. Bookidis 2003: 247–60; 2005: 163. Fotopoulos (2006: 50) argues that "the Asklepieion's dining rooms are a very probable location in which Corinthian Christians could have eaten food offered to a pagan god when reclining in the 'idol's temple,' such as Paul describes in his instructions on sacrificial food in 1 Cor 8:1—11:1." Bookidis (2005: 163) provides convincing arguments for three different levels of religious operation in Roman Corinth: official Roman cults, cults with Greek roots (e.g., Apollo, Aphrodite, Asklepios, and Demeter and Kore), and fringe Greek cults (e.g., Medea). See further Bookidis 2003: 247–60.

93. Flanagan (1999: 26–30) provides the theoretical construct used on these pages for critical spatial analysis. Sacred space is not limited to materiality. Newsom (2004: 7) reflects on the nature of discourse: "language is always socially stratified and socially stratifying."

94. De Fina, Schiffrin, and Bamberg 2006: 9; Tellbe 2008: 118–20. In 1 Cor 3:16 Paul employs both ἐστε and ὑμῖν, though Cranfield has warned against making too much of the use of second person plurals and singulars (1982: 280). Thiselton (2000: 316 emphasis original) takes the view "that the Spirit of God dwells in the Christian community *corporately as a community*."

In 3:17a Paul writes, "If anyone destroys (φθείρει) God's temple, God will destroy (φθείρει) that person." The chiastic structure of the verse is noted by Käsemann, and the repetition of the verb φθείρω in "the protasis and the apodosis" clearly and cogently describes God as the one who "rewards every man [sic] according to his [sic] works."[95] Käsemann also connects Paul's argument here with Gen 9:6 and reinforces the eschatological framework of the larger discourse unit by noting that for Paul "the Last Day is immediately imminent."[96] Käsemann is useful for understanding Paul's strategy of apocalyptic identity formation, and his reflection on the charismatic and communal nature of the judgment context indicates the ongoing function of Paul's argument in the formation and maintenance of the community. Käsemann explains that "the proclamation of the judgment is therefore more than a threat. In it a process of being judged is already under way."[97] Though it is unclear whether Käsemann would concede such a point, it may well be that Paul's rhetoric in this passage functions from an apocalyptic perspective which in turn has ethical implications for social identity.[98]

In 3:17b, Paul makes the necessity of this judgment clear: "for God's temple is holy (ἅγιός), which you are." Paul again names the community, which is another of the means by which Carter notes that a text forms identity.[99] Paul's metaphor is designed to indicate that the groups that exist within the community (1 Cor 1:12–13) are incompatible with the Corinthian Christ-followers' social identity as God's temple.[100]

Paul continues to engage in apocalyptic identity formation and builds on the imagery of the temple to construct embodied ritual space which may transform social space into sacred space.[101] In the Roman Empire, sacred space existed within Roman homes, outside temples, and within the broader civic structures, which combined to produce Roman civic identity.[102] The complexity of the interpenetration of Greek

95. Käsemann 1969: 67.

96. Käsemann 1969: 67.

97. Käsemann 1969: 68.

98. The legal issues in Käsemann's argument have not been completely persuasive; see Thiselton (2000: 318).

99. Carter 2000: 9.

100. Berger 2003: 63.

101. Økland 2004: 37–38; Samra 2006: 144.

102. Alcock 1994: 259.

domestic space and the Roman *domus* is clear from Hales' work, but she does conclude that the Roman homes were involved "in the battle between the extremes of belonging and of transgression."[103] The Roman villa in Corinth reveals a similar interaction between Greek and Roman identity. The Hellenistic floor mosaics were retained in the Roman era home, although no effort was made to align the architecture with them. There was at least an interest in maintaining them in the rebuilt domestic space.[104] Grahame's analysis of Roman identity in the context of domestic space is that the material remains indicate differing expressions of Roman social identity that were impacted by "local" tastes and "processes of 'self-assimilation' and social competition."[105] Paul seeks, however, to situate sacred space in one location thus transforming a key aspect of the Corinthians' civic identity. This one sacred place was positioned in the life of the community rather than in topography or materiality since as God's temple they belong to God.

THE GROUP BELONGS TO GOD (3:18–23)

Some within the community were in the process of self-deception. In 3:18, Paul writes, "Let no one deceive ($\overset{\text{'}}{\epsilon}\xi\alpha\pi\alpha\tau\acute{\alpha}\tau\omega$) himself or herself," employing the first of two third person plural imperatives, which indicates that his guidance extends to the entire community.[106] The role of self-deception in the context of the Corinthian situation has been pointed out by Theissen, but Sampley is correct in noting that "Paul expects believers to be self-reflective."[107] The concept of reflexivity is central to the way in which people encounter themselves in a group and to the construction of social identity.[108] Paul, in 3:18–23, is addressing many of the same issues that Turner addressed in his SCT and suggests that some within the community are not just mistaken but are actually in the pro-

---

103. Hales 2003: 243.

104. Shear 1930: 19–22.

105. Grahame 1998: 176.

106. The present tense here functions as a gnomic present providing a sapiential understanding of communal life. Wallace (1996: 486–87) contends that the use of the third person imperative is "engaging the volition and placing a requirement" upon the addressees. This clause also introduces a first class conditional which is assumed to be true (BDF §371).

107. Theissen 1987: 59–66; Sampley 2002: 833.

108. Mead 1934: 144–64; Jenkins 1996: 20.

cess of deceiving themselves by means of their social categorization and thought processes. The aspects of Turner's approach that are in view here include "group cohesion, interpersonal attraction, and ethnocentrism."[109]

Paul's critique of imperial ideology and the wisdom of this age continues as he writes, "if any person among you thinks (δοκεῖ) he or she is wise (σοφός) in this present age." Hays refers to this as a "self-diagnostic test."[110] He then notes a similar approach to wisdom by Socrates who argues that one must discount one's wisdom if one is to be considered wise (Pl. *Ap.* 23B), but for the Christ-follower the goal is not "epistemological humility" or "the cultivation of an inquiring mind" but "the obedience of faith" (Mark 8:34–35).[111] The phrase "in this present age" picks up Paul's argument from 2:6–9 concerning the political powers of his day and, in the context of Roman Corinth, may extend to an overestimation of the power and wisdom of the Roman Empire.[112]

Paul then provides a description of the type of transformation he has in mind, "let him or her become foolish (μωρός) for the purpose of becoming wise (σοφός)." The cognitive reversal is now complete; those who rely on the resources of imperial ideology are self-deceived and fail to understand reality, but those who respond to Paul's imperative can avoid self-deception and come to realize the lack of wisdom inherent in the world's system and decide to become foolish in order to actually become wise.[113] An ethos of foolishness would emerge if this social identity became salient within the ἐκκλησία. Welborn notes three social implications of becoming a fool. First, a fool would "recognize the tyranny of conventional wisdom." Second, a fool would understand the

109. Turner 1987: 57.

110. Hays 1997: 59.

111. Pl. *Ap.* 23B "This one of you, O human beings, is wisest, who, like Socrates, recognizes that he is in truth of no account in respect to wisdom"; cited in Hays 1997: 58–59. Welborn (2005: 224) contends with regard to Socrates and this view of him as one who was unwise that he "did not attempt to correct the impression that he was a foolish, comic figure. Plato *Apol.* 21A–24A."

112. Middleton (2006: 151), remarking on Mark 8:35, 38, concludes that "the world is divided into two distinct camps: those on the side of Jesus and the gospel . . . and those who belong to Satan."

113. Welborn (2005: 223–24) asserts that "3:18–19a, and the paragraph which these verses introduce (3:18–23), is the summation of the argument developed since 1:10." Further he refers to this as "a rhetorical *inclusio.*" While agreeing with Welborn with regard to the presence of some sort of *inclusio,* Bird (2008: 379) argues that this is "a *functional* rhetoric" and "not a *formal* rhetoric."

"paradoxical nature of wisdom in the present age." Third, a fool would then comprehend that Paul's public presentation as a fool has a "pedagogical purpose" which is seen in 3:18b, (ἵνα) that they "may become wise."[114] In this verse Paul is calling the community to a position of cultural criticism and not civic acculturation; Welborn's work here is most convincing in that the tradition of the fool or the comic mime was one in which "cultural criticism" could safely exist within the empire.[115] Paul's call to reject the world's wisdom carried with it an implicit critique of the status quo and the Roman Empire.

In 3:19, Paul further explains the rationale for his assertion by writing, "For the wisdom (σοφία) of this world is foolishness (μωρία) to God." Paul clearly renders his verdict on the epistemic condition of the world's system—it is foolishness to God, and thus it should be viewed as such within the ἐκκλησία. To explain what he means by this he turns from a Roman concept of cultural criticism to Israel's scriptures.[116] He continues through the use of the citation formula, γέγραπται γάρ "for it is written," which references Job 5:13,[117] as a reminder that they are not to boast in leaders but "in the Lord" (1 Cor 1:31).[118] He writes, "He is the one who catches the wise in their craftiness." Here the critique is that human ingenuity will eventually result in human failure. In the context of Roman political power, the difficulties in maintaining an empire (Cass. Dio 69.5.2–3)[119] so vast will eventually lead to its undoing no matter what the exalted claims of an eternal kingdom provide in terms of social cohesion (*Aen.* 1.223–38).

In 3:20, Paul adds a second quotation, this time from Ps 93:11 LXX (Ps 94:11); he writes "The Lord knows the thoughts of the wise, that they are futile." The context of Ps 93 LXX further supports taking Paul's usage

114. Welborn 2005: 228–29.

115. Welborn 2005: 227.

116. Sampley 2002: 833.

117. Although we are not completely convinced of the broader contextual connections with this reference in Job, Garland (2003: 123) plausibly contends that "this quotation proves its point, since it comes from Eliphaz, whose 'wise' counsel is ultimately discredited." Thiselton (2000: 322) takes the view that Paul rather extensively reworks the Job reference, and Stanley (1992: 190) convincingly argues that the differences reflect two different interpretive choices.

118. Hays (1997: 60) understands this as the principle that connects both citations from the Hebrew Bible.

119. Boatwright 2000: 4.

as an imperial critique. Hays concludes that Ps 93 LXX "is an extended prayer for God to overthrow wicked oppressors," and in Roman Corinth it may be seen as an implicit critique of Roman imperialism, responding to an overestimation of Rome's power by some within the community of Christ-followers (1 Cor 6:1–8).[120]

In 3:21a, Paul writes, "So then let no one boast (καυχάσθω) in humankind," employing the second of two third person imperatives in this section of his argument. Now it becomes evident that Paul's concern is not with wisdom in general but with boasting associated with a pretentious approach to wisdom that is contrary to the ways of God. This boasting reveals a posture of self-sufficiency and independence from God that is counter-productive in the construction and maintenance of a Christ-following community. Boasting is not to exist because the Corinthians' relationship to the God of Israel is based on the faithfulness of Christ (1 Cor 1:30). Barrett insightfully summarizes this by noting that "it was the obedience of Christ unto death that won their freedom for them, and it is in him that they enjoy their new relation with God."[121]

A particularistic approach to identity argues that key aspects of one's social identity are still relevant when following Christ. Paul, from a rhetorical point of view, has argued against the over-reliance on the world's wisdom; however, he does not dismiss this *in toto*.[122] To illustrate his point he does not employ the resources of Israel's scriptures but those from Roman philosophy (Cic. *Fin.* 3.22.75; Sen. *Ben.* 7.3.2—7.4.3) which would declare that "the wise man possesses all things."[123] The idea that all things belong to a specific, identifiable group is also evident in Diog. Laert. 6.37 and 6.72: "The wise are friends of the gods, and friends share what they have. The gods own all things; therefore, the wise have full access to all things." This self-categorization is similar to what Paul has been doing since 1 Cor 3:5; however, the former practice this from a different world-view.[124] Paul writes, in 3:21b, "For all are yours,"

120. Hays 1997: 60; Saunders 2005: 233–34.

121. Barrett 1968: 97.

122. Scott 2006: 24–25.

123. Hays 1997: 60–61.

124. Barrett 1968: 96. Garland (2003: 124) takes the view that these "philosophers appealed to it to affirm human self-sufficiency and mastery over all circumstances. Paul uses it to affirm the Christian's complete dependency on God." Fitzmyer (2008: 208), in discussing the way Paul takes over this maxim, contends that Paul "makes it a principle for Christian faith and for the acceptance of 'the message of the cross,' which is other-

which echoes back to the initial concern over the community's social identification with various leaders or ideologies[125] within the ἐκκλησία (1 Cor 1:10–12). He is reprioritizing the Corinthians' current social categorizations away from their focus on personalities to a focus on God as the center of communal life. Sampley understands Paul's rhetorical moves in 1 Cor 3:21–23 as "all things are yours . . . [quite a list occurs] . . . all belong to Christ, and Christ belongs to God." Thus, he concludes, "Boasting in human associations is out of order, showing as it does a lack of proper understanding and perspective."[126] We would suggest that instead of a "lack of proper understanding," it was a lack of correct social categorization.

In 3:22, Paul provides concrete examples of what actually belongs to the community of Christ-followers (πάντα ὑμῶν). First, he alludes back to 1 Cor 1:12 and 1 Cor 3:4–6 by writing, "whether Paul or Apollos or Cephas" and reminds the ἐκκλησία that even these leaders are not to be elevated as ideological focal points but are to be understood as servants in their midst. Second, he uses words that are often employed within the context of the Roman concept of ἀδιάφορα.[127] Campbell has rightly suggested that ἀδιάφορα provides a useful conceptual framework for the continued relevance of social identity within the Christ-movement but also cautions that this indifference does not extend to Jewish identity.[128] Paul concludes by stating, "All things belong to you."[129]

wise folly in ordinary human eyes." Cf. Gen 1:26–28; Ps 8:6–8 for the view that a similar understanding of reality is found in Israel's scriptures.

125. Eagleton (1991: 28) asserts that ideology and culture are closely related; however, ideology is more interested in "signs, meanings, and values encoded" in culture. See Hogg and Abrams on n. 180 p. 31.

126. Sampley 2002: 833.

127. Sampley 1991: 77–82. We are not arguing that Paul has developed a *topos* of ἀδιάφορα, only that in a general way he allows for freedom in matters that are morally neutral (1 Cor 7:17–24 and 1 Cor 8–10; Jaquette 1995: 30–54, with caution). Also, the way Paul's apocalyptic discourse, with its penchant for totalizing language, functions rhetorically within the context of ἀδιάφορα is not quite clear. Campbell, on the other hand, has recently argued that "abiding difference at the point of call" is the key principle when thinking about ἀδιάφορα, and thus one's state when called may not be classified as indifferent; that still matters to Paul (2008a: 2).

128. Campbell 2006a: 89–90.

129. Holmberg's (2008b: 5) definition of identity focuses on the recognition of one's "belonging to the Lord Jesus Christ" and sees the focus of scholarship on the early Christ-movement to be on addressing "the degree of concreteness of early Christian identity." Holmberg, however, understands identity to be construed, and what we un-

Things that are significant as well as morally indifferent belong to the community, but he does not conclude his argument there. Instead, in 3:23 Paul argues, "All things belong to you, and you belong to Christ." Barrett likewise concludes that "Christ achieved this benefit for them only because he belongs to God."[130] This hierarchical concept of belonging provides the acceptable means by which these gentiles "in Christ" now relate to the God of Israel. In this way, Sampley notes, "Only God can establish a person's worth."[131]

In 3:23, Paul further describes the hierarchical structure of identity that he considers necessary to reorient the Corinthians' social identity and to reinforce the Pauline mission; he writes, "and you belong to Christ and Christ belongs to God." Christ as a fellow-sibling becomes the model of a delegated submission and ownership that allows for the development of the Corinthians' social identity and the furtherance of God's mission among the nations. The end result of Paul's argument here is that the elevation of leaders or ideological perspectives is inconsistent with the concept of hierarchical ownership. The Corinthian Christ-followers' social identification with various personalities within the community or their reliance on the world's wisdom or ideological resources cannot produce an alternative community with a distinct ethos. Instead, what results is a voluntary association similar to those throughout the Roman Empire. Sampley concludes, "Belonging to God is foundational, that is what matters. All other associations are at best indifferent matters and at least idolatrous."[132] While Sampley's statement may be too stark with regard to idolatry, Paul is clear that the community of Christ-followers belongs to God, whether as God's field, building, or temple.[133] The Corinthians' social identity first and foremost has its basis in God's work through Christ, applied to the community by God's call and through the agency of the Spirit. God's wisdom supports and sustains the Corinthians' social identity while the world's approach to wisdom is futile in this regard. That has been Paul's argument in 3:18–23.

---

derstand as identity he describes as self-understanding. Holmberg's view of identity was discussed on p. 69.

130. Barrett 1968: 97.

131. Sampley 2002: 833.

132. Sampley 2002: 833.

133. Hays 1997: 61.

CONCLUSION

This chapter uncovered Paul's approach to social identity formation in 3:5–23, which relied on the categorizing resources of metaphor to create a transformed understanding of group belonging. This occurred through the use of kinship discourse to encourage a sense of family and coopera-tion. Next, it was shown that Paul's vision for social formation included apocalyptic eschatology. The community was described as God's temple, a metaphor that further transformed the Corinthians' social relations. Paul's approach to identity formation drew from both the scriptures of Israel and Roman moral philosophy. Paul concluded his argument by reminding the Corinthians that all things belong to God, even their Roman social identity. This transformed understanding of belonging was necessary for the continuation of the Pauline mission in Corinth. What was Paul's strategy for applying his teaching from 1:1—3:23 con-cerning the formation of a salient "in Christ" social identity? That is the focus of chapter nine.

9

Paul's Strategy of Social Identity Formation

INTRODUCTION

Tнıs снартеr ınquires ınто the way Paul attempts to disentangle the adverse impact of Roman social identity within the ἐκκλησία in 1 Cor 4:1–21. In 4:1–5, Paul believes that the Corinthians' current practice of self-examination and social categorization is in need of further transformation. In 4:6–13, Paul's pedagogical approach is evident as he reveals specific aspects of Roman social identity responsible for the conditions within the ἐκκλησία. Moreover, it will be argued that Paul views suffering as one possible indication of salient "in Christ" social identity.[1] In 4:14–17, it will be shown that Paul continues to use kinship discourse to address educational concerns. Finally, in 4:18–21, Paul's strategy is evident as the opening rhetorical unit of the letter comes to a close by means of a discourse of empowerment.[2]

---

1. Paul understands suffering in other ways as well. For example, in this section, Paul brings to the fore the idea that suffering is part of the experience of being "in Christ" (1 Cor 4: 9–13; cf. 2 Cor 1:8–10; Rom 8:16–18). Alternatively, Paul understands that God's power is manifested in suffering and in spite of suffering (2 Cor 4:7–12; Gal 3:3–4). Furthermore, Paul is able to recognize that those "in Christ" may suffer because of the powers of evil that fight against those who are in union with Christ (2 Cor 12:7; Phil 1:27–30; Rom 8:17–30). Finally, Paul understands suffering as a manifestation of God's wrath (Rom 1:18–32). See Lim 2007: 52, 56–62.

2. We understand 1 Cor 4:1–21 as Paul's immediate application of his arguments concerning identity formation put forth in 1 Cor 1:1—3:23. Thus, the reading that follows assumes the exegetical choices made in the previous chapters of this book. At the beginning of this work, it was stated that one of our goals is to determine whether a particularistic approach to Christ-movement identity is sustainable over a large passage of scripture, and that aim continues to guide our analysis. Thus, this chapter sets out to provide a reading of 4:1–21 informed by the findings concerning Paul's strategy of identity formation found in the previous chapters and, despite the contested nature

SELF-EXAMINATION AND SOCIAL CATEGORIZATION
IN THE CHRIST-MOVEMENT (4:1–5)

Paul's approach to identity formation has a limited role for self-examination and social categorization.[3] He recognizes that one's conscience may be helpful in assessing one's life; however, it is also quite unreliable in that regard. Paul, as a Jew, required minimal adjustment in his social engagements after his conversion,[4] but the same was not true for the gentiles in Corinth. Paul's purpose here is to remind the Corinthians that Christ is the only reliable guide for proper assessment of communal life within the Christ-movement.[5]

In 4:1, Paul provides specific guidance with regard to the thought processes of the community. He writes, "Let each person think about (λογιζέσθω) us in this manner," which provides specific directions for the social categorization of those within the community. He continues, "as servants (ὑπηρέτας) of Christ," which makes plain his previous description in 3:5, though διάκονος was employed in the context of a description of the particular ministries to which each servant was called. Next he writes, "and as stewards (οἰκονόμους) of God's mysteries (μυστηρίων)," which refers back to 1 Cor 2:1, 7, reinforcing the manner of the original proclamation of the gospel among the Corinthians.

In 4:2, Paul rhetorically establishes a group norm by writing, "so then it is required of servants (οἰκονόμοις)" in whom a transformed understanding of accountability and assessment is to be part of their social categorization. He completes his thought with a ἵνα clause which adds a sense of contingency into his argument and writes, "that they might be judged (εὑρεθῇ) faithful (πιστός)." The aorist subjunctive εὑρεθῇ introduces the judgment language that is to be prominent in this discourse unit (see Gal 2:17). Paul establishes a group norm

---

of some exegetical choices, will seek to engage with secondary scholarship only when within the scope of these issues.

3. Seneca is an example of a Roman who over-estimated the ability of one to master the conscience. Cf. Sen. *De ira* 3.36.1–4; Sen. *De vita beata* 20.4; Sen. *Ep.* 97.12–16; see also, from a later period, M. Aur. *Med.* 5.11. Cf. Chester 2003: 197; Hays 1997: 66.

4. Chester (2003: 199), dealing with Jewish conversion, takes the view that "Conversion is in a sense a process of judgement which anticipates the final one, but which leads to the possibility of a new life rather than to condemnation."

5. Chester 2003: 202.

of faithfulness (πιστός) which will characterize Timothy as a group prototype in 4:17.[6]

In 4:3, Paul's argument takes an unexpected turn when he writes, "Now for me it is a small matter." One might have expected Paul to emphasize the importance of communal assessment; instead he appears to be minimizing its function. He continues, "that I might be judged (ἀνακριθῶ) by you or by a human court." He now describes two types of social influence and power, one which operates within the community of faith and one which is controlled by those outside the community of Christ-followers (i.e., the law courts; 1 Cor 6:1–11). The verb ἀνακρίνω is used twice in this verse and once in 4:15. Paul provides a concrete application of his teaching in 2:14–15 which employs forms of ἀνακρίνω three times. In 2:14–15, Paul is clear that those outside the community do not have the epistemic resources to properly assess communal life within the Christ-movement, while those within the community of faith are not subject to the evaluation of others.[7] To make this earlier point more poignant, in 4:3 he concludes with "but I do not even judge (ἀνακρίνω) myself." Now Paul is clear; his own self-categorizations and assessments are not trustworthy forms of evaluation. Paul has called into question three of the primary means of social identity formation: the individual, in this case Paul himself; the ingroup, in this situation those within the ἐκκλησία; and the outgroup, the Roman Empire described by means of the law courts. Paul is not confident in any of these resources to properly assess the social implications of the gospel (1 Cor 2:14–15; 1 Cor 4:3–4).

Paul's rhetoric here, however, is somewhat tempered by his arguments later in the letter. For example, in 1 Cor 9:3 he employs a participial form of ἀνακρίνω as he lays out his defense for those who will examine him.[8] In 1 Cor 10:25, 27, he again uses participial forms of ἀνακρίνω in the context of judgment with regard to meat offered to idols, but there

---

6. Roitto (2008a: 114) employs the resources of cognitive psychology to explain the emergence of group norms and Christ-movement identity. He concludes that the movement, "integrated narrative, identity, prototypical attributes and behavior norms into a (more or less) shared web of cognitive schemata."

7. Scott 2006: 46–47.

8. Cf. Butarbutar 2007: 107–10; Mitchell 1991: 246–47.

he includes the concept of συνείδησις.[9] Also, Paul uses ἀνακρίνω in the context of mission; in 1 Cor 10:27 and 1 Cor 14:24 he provides guidance concerning the way ἀνακρίνω functions with regard to those outside the community of faith, those who are ἄπιστος.

In 4:4, Paul uses himself as an example and declares, "For I am not aware of anything against myself." The propensity for improper self-assessment adversely impacts communal life within the Christ-movement, so Paul quickly adds, "but I am not acquitted by this."[10] Paul recognizes that he is incapable of accurately assessing his social involvements, and if those in the ἐκκλησία follow his example they will likely think less of their ability to properly assess communal life. Paul then focuses the Corinthians' social categorizations upon the one in whom the community is founded. He writes, "The one who judges (ὁ ἀνακρίνων) me is the Lord." He now employs the resources of ἀνακρίνω with regard to the Lord as the one who can be relied on to properly assess the communal life of the ἐκκλησία. This step in Paul's rhetoric anticipates a shift in temporal orientation from this age to the age to come, which forms the Corinthians' identity by recontextualizing the sphere of judgment from their present social situation into a future context of judgment.[11]

In 4:5, Paul's apocalyptic identity discourse begins, "So then, do not judge (κρίνετε) anything before its time." The issue here is one of temporal orientation. The over-identification with the political power of Rome evidently led to an orientation that minimized a significant role for future judgment. This is not to argue that the community had a full-blown "over-realized eschatology" but an "over-identification with Roman imperial eschatology."[12] Paul's lack of confidence in the Corinthians' ability to evaluate appropriately the social implications of the gospel is evident in 1 Cor 1:10–12; 2:5; 3:1, 18. Chester underscores this by writing, "In line with Paul's positive estimation of Judaism there are fewer changes required in how behaviour is assessed than in the case of Gentile converts."[13] Next, Paul further defines the future timeframe

9. Gooch 1993: 78.

10. Gooch 1987: 252.

11. We are not arguing that this excludes present implications (see Godet 1898: 210). Chester (2003: 200) rightly recognizes that Paul's statement looks "to the parousia" while also indicating "a present orientation."

12. Witherington 1995: 295–98.

13. Chester 2003: 201.

by writing, "Wait until the Lord (ὁ κύριος) comes," which introduces a specific time when proper judgment, assessment, and evaluation will be made by the only one who can accurately judge the community and its leaders.

Paul continues to employ apocalyptic motifs, in this case light and darkness, by writing, "who will bring to light those things hidden in the darkness." The abstract, apocalyptic imagery gives way to a concrete application of this imagery as he continues, "and he will reveal the purposes of the heart." Those internal motivations, categorizations, and identifications which impact behavior and belief will be exposed by the Lord's judgment. Paul, however, does not leave the community there; instead he concludes, "and then each one will receive praise from God." Paul's apocalyptic identity formation leaves the community ennobled and confident in the future judgment before God. This last clause functions to strengthen the community through a reorientation of their temporal horizon. This is accomplished by adjusting the relative importance the Corinthians place on their current social categorization. This transformed comparison now becomes a motivating force which emerges from the Corinthians' confidence that they will one day receive praise from the God of Israel.[14] In this opening section of chapter 4, Paul argues that for a salient "in Christ" social identity to emerge the Corinthians cannot rely on the world's system of social categorization with regard to their leaders and their communal life. Next he addresses the importance of suffering in the formation of social identity.

PAUL'S IDENTITY, SUFFERING, AND MISSION (4:6-13)

Ingroup bias and stereotypes are evident in 4:6-13. There is a correlation between salient social identity and ingroup bias, especially as it relates to "*decision-making*" along the "*intergroup division*."[15] Group dynamics similar to these are evident within the various divisions in the ἐκκλησία. This section also correlates stereotypes between imperial, civic concepts of leadership and the representation of anti-stereotypes within the leadership of the Christ-movement.

In 4:6a, Paul presents the application of his argument, which began in 3:5, by writing, "now these things, brothers and sisters (ἀδελφοί),"

14. Chow 1992: 173.
15. Wetherell 1987: 163 emphasis original.

with a linking use of δέ and ἀδελφοί as kinship language. The word ταῦτα refers back to 3:5 where Paul began to use Apollos and himself as literary foils for communal life with regard to leadership, mission, faithfulness, and identity maintenance.[16] Paul makes this evident in the next clause as he writes, "I have figuratively applied (μετεσχημάτισα)[17] my teaching to myself and Apollos because of you." Here he employs an aorist verb μετεσχημάτισα which is translated as "transform" in the context of the "false apostles" and "Satan" in 2 Cor 11:13–15, while in Phil 3:21 Paul uses it with regard to the future "transformation" of the body.[18] The use of this term in the context of righteous suffering at the hands of an imperial power in 4 Macc 9:22 provides an interesting inter-texture with Paul's catalog of hardships that is to come in 4:9–13. Also, the prevailing stereotype of leaders within the community and Paul's lack of confidence of the world's approach to self-examination and social categorization (1 Cor 4:1–5) support the contention that there were no personal difficulties between Paul and Apollos.[19] Paul employs himself and Apollos as rhetorical figures for the benefit of his audience in or-der to reveal the ingroup bias that was destabilizing the community of Christ-followers in Corinth and hindering the Pauline mission.

The purpose for the extended illustration is made evident through the use of pedagogical language as Paul writes, "so that in us you may learn not to go beyond what is written" (ἵνα ἐν ἡμῖν μάθητε τὸ μὴ ὑπὲρ ἃ γέγραπται). The ἵνα clause indicates the purpose for the reference to the two communal leaders (ἐν ἡμῖν), which was to teach the community. The use of μάθητε is similar to Phil 4:9 which combines teaching and

16. Fowler (2004: 155) would describe this in the context of personhood: "some-times an entity is perceived as a person, sometimes not, sometimes individual biogra-phy might be brought to the fore, while at other times the person is thrown into relief as highly dividual, and even as a 'stereotypical' social figure playing a role." This closely approximates what Paul has been doing with Apollos and himself in 1 Cor 3:5—4:5.

17. Paul's meaning here is somewhat dissimilar to the word's meaning in the extra-biblical context. In the classical era, the noun σχημα could be used to indicate a figure of speech. This insight combined with the prepositional prefix μετά may plausibly imply the translation "to transfer by a figure." In this case, Paul may be indicating that he used himself and Apollos in place of those within the community of faith who were actually creating the instability through their ingroup bias and stereotyping (1 Cor 3:5—4:5). Cf. Robertson and Plummer 1911: 81; Fiore 1985: 89 notes the "parenetic purpose" of this section.

18. Doble 2002: 13.

19. Mihaila 2006: 369.

learning discourse (1 Cor 14:31, 35). The direct object of μάθητε is the entire clause τὸ μὴ ὑπὲρ ἃ γέγραπται. This phrase is notoriously difficult to interpret and closely approximates a citation formula for a reference from Israel's scriptures; however, no reference follows. In the context of the Corinthian correspondence and the ongoing exchange of letters between the community and Paul, this clause may refer to Paul's writing itself.[20] In 1 Cor 14:37, Paul categorizes the community and then writes that they are to come to understand that what Paul "writes" (γράφω) "is

20. Many scholars would disagree with this claim. For example, Legault (1972: 230) argues that it is not part of the original text. However, there is no clear evidence that τὸ μὴ ὑπὲρ ἃ γέγραπται was not originally there. Also, it is not apparent how a gloss of this nature would have made it into "all the extant manuscripts and versions" (Ross 1971: 216). Hanges (1998: 287) contends that the referent for τὸ μὴ ὑπὲρ ἃ γέγραπται is a written document similar to "the Greek *leges sacrae*" which contained "published bylaws or proceedings of civic and private cults." The legal bylaws approach of Hanges fails for a couple of reasons. First, Donahoe (2008: 146) rightly notes, "if there were specific rules being broken, then it would seem improbable that Paul would not cite them specifically." Second, Hanges provides insightful examples of how both τὰ γεγραμμένα and ἃ γέγραπται were used to refer to other sacred documents; however, he fails to see the potential for the self-referential nature of both τὰ γεγραμμένα and ἃ γέγραπται. Welborn (1987a: 327) argues that μὴ ὑπὲρ ἃ γέγραπται represents a well-known saying among the ἐκκλησία in Corinth and that the presence of τό prior to the phrase serves as evidence that Paul is quoting an already existing saying (cf. Rom 13:9; Gal 5:14; 6:9). Garland (2003: 134) rightly asserts that "the problem with this view is that this adage is not found anywhere else, which weakens the argument that it was a well-known cliché." Second, from a syntactical standpoint τό functions as the direct object of μάθητε referring to Paul's writing and thus does not have to be understood as introducing a maxim. Ciampa and Rosner (2007: 705; Schrage 1991: 334–35) argue that μὴ ὑπὲρ ἃ γέγραπται refers "most naturally" to Israel's scriptures and thus "4:6 instructs the Corinthians not to transgress the exhortations found in and constructed from the Scriptures." Ciampa and Rosner (2007: 705) do not argue that Paul is referring to a specific text in 4:6; but, following Hays (1997: 69), they argue that the scriptural references Paul has made thus far in 1 Cor 1–4 (i.e., 1:19, 31; 2:9, 16; 3:19, 20) are in view and that these taken together argue that the community is "to boast exclusively in the Lord (not in human leaders)." First, it is not clear that the hearers would have been able to make that connection nor how such a string of conceptual allusions to Israel's scriptures is relevant to Paul's argument, not to mention some of the difficulties in recovering the scriptural reference that might have been in view (e.g., 1 Cor 2:9). Second, since Paul does not normally refer to scripture in this way (note the presence of ἃ before γέγραπται), and since there is no obvious scriptural referent for γέγραπται, it seems that a reference to Israel's scripture may not primarily be in view in 4:6 (see Welborn 1987a: 331), though it does not exclude a general reference to the scriptural tradition. In light of these critiques, scholars should consider the possibility that Paul was referring to his own writing in this context. See Tyler (2001: 243–42) for a further summary of the various scholarly views.

a command of the Lord" (κυρίου ἐστὶν ἐντολή).[21] The benefit of this interpretive choice includes, first, that it provides a plausible reason for the lack of a scriptural reference after the introductory formula. Second, it supports the contention that Paul and those within the community were in a hierarchical, asymmetrical relationship and that Paul's letter writing was to emerge as authoritative within the community. Third, it does not require the collation of the various scriptural references from 1 Corinthians 1–4 as the referent of the Corinthians' misunderstanding though it does not preclude an allusion to those references.[22]

A further purpose (ἵνα) for Paul's teaching becomes apparent as he addresses the issue of arrogance that is the cause of many of the difficulties within the community; he continues, "in order that none of you might become arrogant (φυσιοῦσθε) in favor of one against the other." Ingroup favoritism and outgroup stereotyping[23] had resulted in an inflated sense of one's ingroup while providing the impetus for intragroup discrimination, and Paul's teaching here is designed to address these communal issues. The phrase "one against another" indicates the manner in which social identification was occurring within the community, an identification which produced arrogance.[24] The Corinthians' ingroup bias is specified by the use of the prepositional phrase κατὰ τοῦ ἑτέρου and results in "othering" the outgroup. The social categorization that was occurring within the community resulted in a lack of "in Christ" social identity salience, and Paul's purpose for writing (1 Cor 1:10) is to restore the Corinthians' communal focus in their shared relationship to the God of Israel through the crucified messiah.[25]

In 4:7, Paul asks the first of three rhetorical questions; he writes "For who makes a distinction (διακρίνει) among you?" The verb διακρίνει in this context means "to make a distinction or separate"; thus Paul wants the Corinthians to think about those whose social cat-

21. Calvin 1960: 90; Thiselton 2000: 352–55.

22. Cf. Swancutt 2006: 9; Gladd 2008: 186–90; Welborn 1987a: 327–28; Ciampa and Rosner 2007: 705.

23. In the context of 1 Corinthians 1–4, the outgroup stereotyping within the community related to ministry comportment, while within the civic community the outgroup stereotyping revolved around social identifications with key components of Roman identity most acutely expressed with regard to the political identification with Rome and the patron-client system.

24. Epic. *Diatr* 2.16.5–10, cited in Nguyen 2008a: 100.

25. Feuillet 1966: 398–99.

egorization is influencing communal life and to identify those people. This question may allude to 1 Cor 1:26 and the social categorization that is evident in that reference. Here it is designed to point out that the Corinthians' socially constructed ingroup misunderstands a fundamental social implication of their calling "in Christ." Paul extends his argument as he asks, "And what do you have that you did not receive?" This question implies the answer—nothing. It also introduces Paul's concern with the Corinthians' current practice as regards the patron-client system in the ἐκκλησία.[26]

Paul concludes this section of his argument by writing, "But if you did receive it, why do you boast (καυχᾶσαι) as if you had not received it?" It would have been unacceptable to boast about the actual gifts one received from a patron; the boasting was only to be directed to the patrons for their beneficence and graciousness. The literary works of Virgil and Horace were written primarily for the purposes of forming and maintaining the social identity of their patron, Maecenas, within the empire and not primarily for their own personal advancement.[27] Paul appears to be arguing that the Christ-following community's current practice with regard to social organization reflects too closely that of the broader culture, whereas the ἐκκλησία has been called to be an alternative community with a distinct ethos. Though social identities are important, they are not to be the source for boasting (καυχᾶσαι) or separation (διακρίνει) since everything the Corinthians have received ultimately comes from God (1 Cor 3:22–23).[28]

In 4:8, Paul is often thought to be addressing issues related to "over-realized eschatology" in Corinth (see also 1 Cor 15:12). Horrell describes this as "the belief that the future promises of God are fulfilled and experienced in the present."[29] Thiselton's seminal article on this topic is frequently referenced, though in his commentary he has sought "to qualify this in spite of reaffirming this emphasis."[30] Hays, on the other hand, argues that "the Corinthians did not have an 'overrealized eschatology.' Instead, they employed categories of self-understanding derived from

26. Clarke 1993: 33.

27. Gold 1987: 3–4.

28. Barclay 1992: 57.

29. Horrell 1996: 120; cf. Käsemann 1969: 126; Barrett 1968: 109; Campbell 2006a: 93.

30. Thiselton 1978: 510–26; 2000: 40.

a decidedly noneschatological Greco-Roman cultural environment."[31] For Hays, the presence of apocalyptic eschatological language reveals a rhetorical purpose "to gain critical language against various problematic practices of the Corinthians."[32] Hays may go too far in suggesting that there is no eschatological problem within the ἐκκλησία. Perhaps the problem related to an over-identification with Roman imperial eschatology. This would account for the eschatological language in Paul's argument pointed out by Thiselton, while giving full attention to the Roman influences pointed out by Hays. It should also be noted that this suggestion is broadly in view with both scholars, but that imperial eschatology provides a more focused interlocutor for Paul in the Corinthian correspondence.[33]

In 4:8, Paul begins by writing, "Already you are filled! Already you have become rich! Without us you have become kings!" These are examples of social identifications of some within the ἐκκλησία, at least from Paul's perspective. These descriptors all reflect a positive ingroup bias on the Corinthians' part, but Paul redeploys these categorizations to reveal their intragroup discrimination. Paul's desire to re-establish the foundation of the Corinthians' social identity becomes evident in these statements—they actually had a salient social identity but, from Paul's perspective, it was misplaced. They understood themselves as kings. Language associated with the patron-client relationship may indicate that some of the difficulties within the ἐκκλησία related to the patron-client social structure within the Christ-movement.[34]

The use of economics as a means of ingroup bias accords well with scholarly reconstructions that point to a disparity between the financial resources of some of the groups within the community of faith.[35] The

31. Hays 2005: 6.

32. Hays 2005: 6. Jenkins (1996: 38) argues that the presence of "language" is necessary for the construction of an "interior world" and results in "a social view of (the) mind" which "is vital for an understanding of social identity."

33. Cf. Thiselton 2000: 40; Hays 2005: 6.

34. Chow (1992: 130) understands this to be the case with regard to the issue of the immoral brother in 1 Cor 5:1–13. The man, in this case, contends Chow (1992: 170), "could have been one of the rich and powerful patrons in the church. If this was so, it would be easy to imagine that he was an influential patron in the church, and that not many would dare to take any action against him." (Clarke 2000: 182; see Sen. *Ben.* 5.4.2).

35. Theissen 1982: 33–36; Friesen 2005: 352–54.

inference from the idea of satiation may align well with the social implications of table fellowship and eating in general.[36] Horrell is right to recognize the importance of food and meals in "the process of forming and maintaining Christian identity."[37] With these statements, Paul has summarized significant social issues within the community: patron-client relations, economic disparity, and disagreements with regard to meals. The idea that the rhetorical vision of the community had diverged from that of Paul is highlighted by his use of the phrase χωρὶς ἡμῶν. In light of 4:6b, the idea here may be that the community has developed collective behaviors which have moved beyond the social influence of Paul's writing.[38] Tuckett has drawn attention to this with regard to the negotiation and self-presentation that has emerged within the Christ-following community in Corinth subsequent to their conversion.[39] Paul's focus on the Corinthians' call is central to his configuration of social presence and performance—they are to remain in the state in which they were when they were called (1 Cor 7:20). The difficulty within the community of faith was a misunderstanding of the nature of particularistic identity and specifically the social implications that follow from "the word connected with the Cross" (1 Cor 1:18) which has the power to transform identity.[40]

Paul continues, "I wish you had become kings (ἐβασιλεύσατε), so that we could reign (συμβασιλεύσωμεν) also with you!" He uses an unaugmented aorist verb ὄφελόν, which functions as a particle indicating "an unfulfilled wish."[41] Next he employs an ingressive aorist

36. Gooch 1987: 247.

37. Horrell 2008: 201.

38. The degree to which these ἐκκλησιαί followed Paul's rhetorical vision is one of the reasons that Horrell questions whether or not scholars may speak of "Pauline" assemblies. Horrell (2008: 203) concludes that "there seems no clear justification for speaking of 'Pauline churches', or at least, not without heavily qualifying exactly what that might mean." Horrell relies on a universalistic approach to Christ-movement identity which he presupposes as he argues for the lack of a contextualized, discernible, Pauline ethos. His essay raises an important issue in that we should not envision multiple assemblies divided along ideological lines; however, the solution is not to downplay the impact of Paul's influence in those communities but rather to see the existence of diversity as an example of the ἐκκλησιαί following Paul's rule in his assemblies that each is to stay in the situation in which he or she was called (1 Cor 7:17–24).

39. Tuckett 2000: 420.

40. Brown 1995: 12.

41. Wolff 1996: 87.

ἐβασιλεύσατε, for the second time in this verse. Paul writes this clause idiomatically and, as Didier notes, "wielded irony with such assurance."[42] It does not follow that the recipients did not understand themselves in such a way; it is plausible that this is exactly their self-understanding—thus the heightened rhetorical effect of the clause. Paul's purpose in desiring such a status for the Corinthians was, "so that we could reign (συμβασιλεύσωμεν) also with you." In this clause, Paul uses another form of βασιλεύω, this time as a compound verbal form συμβασιλεύσωμεν with an attached prepositional prefix. Thiselton notes that this, when "coupled with χωρὶς ἡμῶν . . . sharpens and heightens the pathos of the illusion."[43] Although correct, Thiselton somewhat overlooks the expectation of reciprocity evident in the patronage system,[44] which may be the sense of what Paul is arguing at this point.

Clarke notes the presence of secularized concepts of leadership in 4:6–8; however this section also resonates with a number of allusions to political power and social identification with Rome.[45] The patron-client social structure functioned as an ongoing resource for social identity formation and friendship and was often expressed in Latin as *amicitia*.[46] Evidence for the patron-client system and its role in identity formation is apparent in an inscription found in Corinth; it reads, "Marcus Antonius Promachus (set up this monument to honor) his friend and patron [----] because of his fine character and trustworthiness."[47] The patron-client

42. Didier 1955: 41 author's translation.

43. Thiselton 2000: 359.

44. The reciprocity was asymmetrical with regard to the Emperor, cf. Sen. *Ben.* 5.4.2, but Saller (1982: 78) argues that delegated patronage provided a framework for loyalty throughout the empire. Still it remains asymmetrical throughout.

45. Clarke 1993: 123. The emperor was the head of the entire patron-client system. Winter (2003a: 191) rightly notes that "Corinth had long understood the importance of civic patrons"; see especially n. 68 for a listing of "imperial patrons." Clarke (1993: 36; cf. 31–36) provides an insightful discussion on this topic with regard to friendship but concludes that the concepts associated with the patron-client system "formed the basis of Graeco-Roman society."

46. Saller 1982: 13–15, 78; Robertson 2001: 71. Judge addresses concerns over the use of the Roman "patron-client system in the Greek states" and rightly points out that many of these were actually "Roman colonies" as was Corinth. Judge (2008: 165, 167) understands that a form of patron-client system existed within the Christ-movement but that the innovations which emerged related to the rejection "of status conventions which permitted people to exploit the system for private advantage."

47. Kent (1966: 107) also notes that the phrase "τὸν φίλον καὶ προστάτην" is "the equivalent of *amicum et patronum*." This inscription is also referenced by Winter 2003a:

system functioned within the context of asymmetrical friendships and may have served as a model through which the arrogance, competition, and dissension within the ἐκκλησία could have arisen.[48] It is quite plausible that the early Christ-movement developed within the framework of some form of *clientele*, but there is a lack of evidence for the way it actually functioned (see Philemon 8–19). Schüssler Fiorenza slightly overstates the case but still provides some insight: "The rich convert to Christianity, therefore, probably understood herself/himself as entering a club, and expected to exercise the influence of the patron on this club. Without question the house church, as a voluntary organization, was structured according to this patron-client relationship."[49] An example of this would be Phoebe who served as a patron to Paul (Rom 16:1–2),[50] while Paul functioned as a "patron," argue Osiek and Balch, "to those he baptized personally, such as Gaius, Crispus, and Stephanas."[51] However, the practice of "double reciprocity" and "service-oriented ministry," as pointed out by Joubert, may indicate that these roles could shift and that one could equally see Paul, Phoebe, Gaius, Crispus, and Stephanas in the alternate position as well.[52] Paul, in 4:8, addresses political power and

194. One should note the combination of friendship and patronage language in this inscription; but see Winter 2003a: 196.

48. Saller (1982: 78) asserts that "an emperor could create divisions most effectively by encouraging *delatores* with rewards of offices and honors." This created a situation in which relationships could prove beneficial but could also be dangerous if the political situation changed (see Sen. *Ep.* 55.3). Saller notes, "struggling factions did not divide along class or *ordo* lines" and "manipulating *beneficia* to encourage tensions and divisions" was not an effective practice (1982: 78; Hales 2003: 16). Theissen (1982: 95–96) understands a similar context but relates it primarily to the communal meal in 1 Cor 11:22, 34–35. Meeks (1983a: 57–58) argues that those mentioned above provided services that are consonant with those of patrons (1 Cor 16:15, 23). Marshall (1987: 38) understands this as the social context for the conflict between Paul and the Corinthian Christ-followers, though he overstates the level of conflict.

49. Schüssler Fiorenza 1994: 181.

50. Patronage functioned within the context of mission; Jewett (2007: 947) more correctly describes Phoebe as the "missionary patroness" with regard to "the Spanish mission."

51. Osiek and Balch 1997: 99.

52. Joubert 2001: 24. Osiek, Macdonald, and Tulloch (2006: 195–98) provide a concise summary of the social function of the patronage system in the Roman empire. Later in the book (212) they argue that "Crispus, Gaius, and the household of Stephanas" were the patrons of Paul so that he "could carry out his mission and the church could thrive." Even though Osiek's name is on books in which two different positions are presented, the conflict may be resolved through the concept of reciprocity in that obligations went

patronage issues related to Roman social identity. The embodiment of this transformation of identity is described with regard to Paul and the other apostles in 4:9.

In 4:9, Paul introduces a metaphor which is meant to convey the necessity of suffering for ongoing mission. Lim has recently argued that suffering is essential to Paul and that his experience with suffering is interpreted in the context of the life of Jesus.[53] From an identity formation perspective, what is the function of a catalog of suffering? Its purpose is to make clear that as the "in Christ" identity emerges as the master social identity—suffering will follow. In this case, Paul is not defending his apostleship but is revealing a significant social implication for a community who has "the mind of Christ" (1 Cor 2:16). Earlier, the lack of evidence of conflict with the civic authorities in Corinth like that experienced by the Thessalonians was noted.[54] If suffering is an integral aspect of mission, then the Corinthians' increased identification with the Pauline mission will likely result in an increase in suffering at the hands of those aligned against God's kingdom.

The story of Paul's suffering in 4:9–13 forms the identity of the community. Emplotment is defined by Ricoeur as "a synthesis of heterogeneous elements." [55] It is what turns unconnected information into a story with which an audience identifies. This social identification pro-

---

both ways. Winter (2003a: 196) notes that the Corinthian inscription referenced above includes friendship language but that Paul normally avoids this because of the fiscal implications that its inclusion requires, though this distinction may be too fine. Even though Winter references Saller in support of his contention, Saller's broader thesis relates to the fluidity of the borders between the traditional understanding of patronage and friendship.

53. Lim (2007: 247) employs the analytical tools of the narrative substructure approach to provide a thoroughly convincing reading of 2 Corinthians with regard to the purpose of suffering in the mission of Paul (see Longenecker 2002: 3–16). For the significance of Paul's story, see Horrell (2002d: 171) who rightly concludes, "the story that matters is not that of Paul but the identity-forming story of Christ, the story of the gospel."

54. Clarke (2000: 185) argues that the assembly in Corinth "finds itself in little conflict with the surrounding Greco-Roman culture."

55. Ricoeur 1991: 21. Brawley (2005: 17) contends that "for Ricoeur discrete events of human life are held together by our own narrative, in which our emplotment integrates diverse experiences into a person who is identified as a unified character." The emplotment evident in 1 Cor 4:9–13 is not the same as in e.g., 2 Cor 11:22–33 which contains a specific incident of narrative suffering. While 1 Cor 4:9–13 leaves out the actual narrative, it may be described as narrative emplotment by ellipsis.

vides the interpretive grid for identity formation; the past events within the narrative are given significance and power in order to participate in the present negotiation of identity. Misztal refers to these episodes as "frames of meaning" which are correlated with "the group's common view of the world."[56] As Paul emplots this narrative of suffering, he is ascribing an identity to the community through his experience with suffering. Lawler notes that narrative may be used in this manner to "break down the dividing line between self and other and thus to see selves and identities as embedded in the social world."[57] One of the primary ways this occurs is, as Steedman asserts, "through the use of *someone else's* story of suffering, loss, exploitation, [and] pain."[58] Paul is seeking to form the social identity of the Corinthian Christ-followers through identification with his and others' sufferings. In the same way, Paul will write to them later (see 2 Cor 1:5), he has learned to identify with the story of Jesus, and his sufferings are a key source of his identity as an apostle.

In 4:9, Paul begins his narrative by writing, "For I think (δοκῶ) God has exhibited (ἀπέδειξεν) us apostles last of all," in which the γάρ further explains the implication of his previous assertion with regard to patronage within the ἐκκλησία. The use of δοκῶ indicates the cognitive framework of this discussion and further extends the social implications of the "mind of Christ" from 1 Cor 2:16. In other words, Paul is providing another example of the way the "mind of Christ" functions, in this instance to interpret the suffering of those within the Christ-movement as vital to their ongoing existence as a community of faith. God is presented as the sovereign, patron, and benefactor in this passage.[59] As the grammatical subject of the rarely employed main verb ἀπέδειξεν, ὁ Θεός indicates that "God has made/exhibited us (as) the last ones perhaps in a triumphal procession."[60] The specific group that is exhibited "last" is described as "the apostles," which socially categorizes them "at

---

56. Misztal 2003: 82.

57. Lawler 2008: 19. Lawler also cites Ricoeur, Misztal, and Steedman in her broader discussion (2008: 10–30). Stiver (2001: 66–68) describes the way in which texts may form identity using Ricoeur's "mimesis" or "figuration" framework (e.g., "prefiguration," "configuration," and "refiguration").

58. Steedman 1996: 107.

59. Neyrey 2005: 490–91.

60. BDAG 108. See also 4 Macc 1:8 in which ἀποδείκνυμι is employed in the context of patron-client language, specifically ἀρετή.

the bottom of the scale of social prestige."[61] The reference to apostles is plural whereas the previous reference in 1:1 referred only to Paul. In the context of social identity formation, Paul's example is important but so is the example of his co-workers (1 Cor 1:1; 4:9; 9:1, 2, 5; 12:28, 29; 15:7, 9).[62] Here, two identity-forming concepts from the work of Ehrensperger are important. First, the "leadership roles in this early Christ-movement were far from being firmly established"; this is important if one considers the function of an apostle and the implicit power claims inherent in statements of weakness.[63] Second, and more important for this book, Paul's emphasis here is "in stark contrast to the Roman elite value system"; the audience undoubtedly would have understood the rhetorical position in which Paul was placing himself and the other apostles with regard to Roman imperial practice.[64]

These are brought into relief in the next phrase, "as ones sentenced to death." Nguyen has persuasively argued that the most appropriate context for interpreting 4:9–13 is "the Roman spectacle of executing condemned criminals (*noxii*) within the arena, which was a significant social event in Roman society."[65] Seneca describes one of these afternoon affairs: "the previous combats were the essence of compassion; but now all the trifling is put aside and it is pure murder. The men have no defensive armour. They are exposed to blows at all points, and no one ever strikes in vain . . . the outcome of every fight is death."[66] The *noxii* were exhibited publicly as a means of social control within the empire; their deplorable situation and their dishonorable deaths all sup-

---

61. Theissen 1982: 72–73.

62. Hafemann (1986: 57–58) is not convincing in arguing that the first person plurals are rhetorical in 1 Cor 4:9–13 and that Paul is actually only referring to his own experience here. Paul's use of pronouns is too inconsistent to make any exegetical decisions based primarily on the use of singular or plural numbers (see Cranfield 1982: 280).

63. Ehrensperger 2007: 111. The primary issue is not weakness alone but weakness in which the power of God is manifested.

64. Ehrensperger 2007: 112.

65. Nguyen 2007: 489. The three main options to this reading include: Welborn's theatrical setting (2005: 52, 55–57), Fee's Roman triumphal procession in general (1987: 174–75), and Thiselton's closely related gladiatorial setting (2000: 259–60). Cf. Nguyen 2007: 493–97 for a critique of each of these viewpoints (Garland 2003: 140 combines Fee and Thiselton). Nguyen (2008b: 33–48) has also argued that the significance of the Roman Arena has been overlooked by scholars, but Middleton (2006: 141) considers a similar context.

66. Sen. *Ep.* 7.3–5, cited in Nguyen 2007: 498.

port the ground of the metaphor and serve to recategorize the cognitive framework within the ἐκκλησία by means of an image that emplots new meaning for the community. Nguyen's work is helpful in two other ways. First, he rightly details the importance of "Paul's self-identification with the Christ who suffered a criminal's death of crucifixion," though Paul's identification, as pointed out by Lim, extends to "the entire incarnate life of Jesus, and not just the crucifixion."[67] Second, Paul's metaphor is a "vivid and stark expression of his cruciform identity."[68] That statement may be extended to include the necessity of suffering for the ongoing mission of God throughout the Roman Empire.[69]

The final clause of the metaphor provides the purpose for the exhibition, "because we have become a spectacle (θέατρον) to the world, both to angels and to humankind." Nguyen, based on this clause, argues that the actual purpose of the metaphor is "to depict the lowliness of the apostles," but as mentioned above the necessity of suffering in mission is its primary ground and only secondarily is it concerned with the empirical characters in the narrative.[70] This understanding connects with Paul's previous comments with regard to himself and Apollos in 4:6.[71] Also, the apocalyptic nature of the language here indicates that identity formation is occurring.

The noun θέατρον in the context of ἐπιθανατίους suggests that the exhibition of the apostles is not to be understood in a positive light. Adams contends that τῷ κόσμῳ is not used in a "bad sense" but that "since the apostles are linked to the κόσμος in a negative way . . . as objects of shame, disgrace, and dishonour" the presentation of the κόσμος was most likely not consonant with the Corinthians' understanding of the world.[72] The population of the κόσμος are described as καὶ ἀγγέλοις καὶ ἀνθρώποις. The angels indicate apocalyptic discourse as does the broader cosmic spectacle. Paul is attempting to expand the Corinthians' horizon of social identification. He accomplishes this through the use of the passive verb ἐγενήθημεν which indicates that God is the agent of the exhibition. This imagery also correlates well with

67. Nguyen 2007: 501; Lim 2007: 148.
68. Nguyen 2007: 501.
69. Lim 2007: 161.
70. Nguyen 2007: 499.
71. Adams 2000: 120.
72. Adams 2000: 122.

Mark's account of Jesus, that he would be "delivered over to the hands of men" (Mark 9:31; 8:31; 10:33–34)[73] and with Paul's own experience, seen in Phil 1:29–30.[74] Suffering is central to the Pauline mission, and the lack of it in Corinth may have contributed to the ongoing social identification with key aspects of Roman identity.

In 4:10, Paul continues by means of binary categorizations the metaphor he introduced in 4:9. He begins, "We are fools (μωροί) on account of Jesus," which indicates the first of three social identifications that would have been rejected by most within the Roman world (i.e., foolish, weak, and dishonored). Paul only employs μωρός in the context of 1 Corinthians 1–4, e.g., 1:25, 27, 3:18, and 4:10.[75] Thus, his use of this term should be uncovered in the immediate literary context. First Corinthians 1:25 is closely connected to 4:10 in that two of the three binaries are included. First Corinthians 1:27 reinforces the close conceptual link with 4:10 by including shame language as well as the agency of God which is evident in 4:9. Finally in 3:18, Paul is more pre-scriptive in that he provides guidance as to the way one should address issues related to wisdom, foolishness, and self-deception. A contextually informed reading of μωρός argues that Paul's meaning here is an extension of his previous usage which focused on the incompatibility of the world's cognitive resources with "the word connected with the cross" (1 Cor 1:18). Nguyen is correct to assert that "convinced of the scandalous and foolish message of a crucified Christ, Paul uses the metaphor of the Roman execution of *noxii* to identify himself and the other apostles as similarly condemned to death and foolishly displayed as a spectacle by God to the world."[76]

Paul's use of the fool motif may have its basis in Israel's scriptures and his mission. His prophetic identity emerges from within the context of Jeremiah. For example, Jeremiah 5:21 compares nicely with 1 Cor 2:9 and addresses similar epistemic issues: "Hear this, you foolish people

73. Middleton 2006: 83, 150.

74. Lim 2007: 153–54.

75. Thiselton 2000: 361.

76. Nguyen 2007: 501. Welborn (2005: 3) argues that the context of the fool is sourced in "the genre of the 'fool's speech' (2 Cor. 11.1—12.10) from the Greek and Roman mime." Nguyen (2007: 493) offers four critiques of Welborn's view. The most substantial relates to the difficulty of sustaining the entertainment focus of the theater without fully recognizing that "spectacles of death were another form of popular entertainment."

who have no understanding, who have eyes but do not discern, who have ears but do not perceive."[77] Finally, becoming a fool is "on account of Jesus (διὰ Χριστόν), which Lim shows, "functions as the cause and motivational factor behind suffering. Commitment to the gospel of Jesus requires that one also embrace the hardships that come with it."[78]

Next, Paul writes, "but you are wise (φρόνιμοι) in Christ," which establishes the "negative" binary relationship with regard to the previous clause; however, the contrast is not all-inclusive. Notice that Paul includes the prepositional phrase ἐν Χριστῷ, and, instead of σοφός which is employed throughout 1 Corinthians 1–4, he uses φρόνιμος. This alteration may be for stylistic purposes, but more likely it was used to avoid confusion with regard to his argument concerning σοφός in 1 Cor 1:18—3:23. Here the focus of the contrast appears to be: first, the connotation of "understanding associated with insight" and "prudence"; second, connected with the Corinthians' understanding of ἐν Χριστῷ, simply a cumulative identity that provides "prudence" and "insight" for life in general (1 Cor 10:15).[79] Paul, however, in this context, argues that being rightly related to the God of Israel through Christ results in suffering, not in an increased acumen for business or social relations.[80]

The second binary contrasts the Roman ideology of power with God's view. Paul writes, "We are weak (ἀσθενεῖς), but you are strong (ἰσχυροί)." Fitzmyer is correct to take the view that Paul's use of "strong" here is the way the Corinthian Christ-followers saw themselves, as did their "contemporaries."[81] The use of ἀσθενής, ἰσχυρός, and similar words from their semantic domains is often associated with patron-

77. Beker (1980: 115) also references Gal 1:15 and Rom 1:1 but rightly notes that there are literary parallels with "the *Ebed* [עֶבֶד]" (1980: 115; see Ps 93:8 LXX (94:8) and the servant of the Lord texts: Isa 42:1–7; 49:1–9a; 50:4–9; 52:13—53:12).

78. Lim 2007: 154.

79. BDAG 1066.

80. Fee (1987: 176) suggests that "in one sense Paul would allow that they are [wise], since they are 'in Christ'. But they are all of these things [wise, powerful, or honoured] in the wrong way."

81. Fitzmyer 2008: 219. The challenge here relates to the presence of irony in Paul's descriptions in 1 Cor 4:6–13. Furthermore, if one reads Paul's claims in a straightforward manner, then this raises the issue of the relation between the parallel expressions "wise in Christ" and "you are strong." Read this way, Paul would be arguing that the Corinthians had, in fact, experienced the power of God. We think, based on 1 Cor 9:22, that Paul had the contrasting relationship in view (see 2 Cor 13:4; Garland 2003: 141).

client relationships,[82] the Greek concept of ἀρετή, or the Roman concept of *virtus*.[83] Paul's argument in this section focuses on those aspects of social identity that are likely to be in conflict with an "in Christ" identity which transforms the status quo with regard to power (1 Cor 1:25, 27). The social contrasts in 4:10 emerge, as Ehrensperger argues, as "an alternative power and leadership discourse in the context of a society which was dominated by competition for status, domination and control."[84]

The final binary relationship is described within the context of the honor and shame framework, "You are honored (ἔνδοξοι), but we are dishonored (ἄτιμοι)." This comparison is conceptually linked to 4:13 and the practice of dishonorably disposing of certain classes of people within the empire. Burial practices in general are a vital means of forming and maintaining social identity[85] and Nguyen, though not making that connection, rightly explains that often after the death of the *noxii* their "corpses" were left "unburied" as a "symbolic" way of "securing their damnation."[86] The honor of proper burial or funerary rites was withheld from the *noxii* in order to reinforce social control throughout the empire. Kyle explains this social function: as "a public warning for potential offenders, punishment was taken beyond death to despoiling the corpse, and even further."[87] For Paul, this imagery serves to teach the ἐκκλησία that those within the Christ-movement are interconnected and, building on the work of Williams, that "they are enmeshed in relationships of interdependence . . . in terms of a shared fate."[88] The notion of fate is foreign to Paul's approach, which would more appropriately be referred to as a "shared calling and fellowship" (1 Cor 1:9; 7:20). Williams

---

82. Winter 2001: 197.

83. *Aen.* 11.27 employs *virtus* in the context of martial courage, cited by McDonnell (2006: 44). McDonnell (2006: 40) also explains that when "*virtus* and ἀρετή are found in bilingual honorary inscriptions, the contexts are usually military in nature."

84. Ehrensperger 2007: 97.

85. Hope's work relates to the cemetery in Roman Nîmes, which contains the remains of gladiators. She (1998: 179) concludes, "a funerary memorial is an aid to memory," and "simultaneously it may also memorialise chosen features of the identity of the deceased." Stone (2007: 138) notes that those in political power employed certain burial practices to establish an "élite identity in order to create hegemony over people, resources, and regions."

86. Nguyen 2007: 500–501.

87. Kyle 1998: 133.

88. Williams 2007: 228.

argues that disparate political identifications may be united through the "shared deliberation over a common good, including the common good of justice or of legitimacy" which will "generate a strong sense of shared identity, loyalty, or mutual affection."[89] Paul argues for this in 1 Cor 7:17 where his guidance for social interaction is correlated with a reminder that other groups within the Christ-movement are following a similar set of teachings (1 Cor 11:16; 14:33; 16:1). Paul's purpose is not to shame the Corinthian Christ-followers into submission (1 Cor 4:14) but to encourage them to develop a mutual sense of "in Christ" identity and dependence in order to further the Pauline mission (1 Cor 16:1, 9) and stabilize their own internal situation (1 Cor 1:10; 11:18; 12:25).[90]

For Paul, this imagery serves to teach the ἐκκλησία that those within the Christ-movement are interconnected and are part of a "shared calling and fellowship" that includes a shared destiny (1 Cor 1:8–9; 3:13). Paul's peristasis catalog is intended to be an identity-forming narrative "in which [the] 'suffering other' is appropriated."[91] He wants to move the Corinthian Christ-followers away from their current ingroup bias so they will think and behave differently with regard to groups that are currently conceived of as outgroups by the world's standards, in this case those enduring great suffering.

In 4:11, Paul continues to teach the Corinthians by writing, "To this present hour we are hungry and thirsty." The first phrase, "to this present hour," indicates that this is an ongoing experience of pain. Both πεινάω and διψῶμεν are present in Matt 25:35, 37 and resonate with the *gestalt* of the Jesus tradition.[92] Social identification with those in need appears to be an early social implication of the gospel. In Corinth, participation in the Jerusalem collection was a practical expression of social identifi-

89. Williams 2007: 228–29.

90. Schneider (1971: 2) takes the view that "concern for honor arises when the definition of the group is problematic; when social boundaries are difficult to maintain, and internal loyalties are questionable. Shame, the reciprocal of honor, is especially important when . . . resources" are "contested." In the context of a discussion on gender identity, she continues, "comportment defines the honor of social groups. Like all ideologies, honor and shame complement institutional arrangements for the distribution of power and the creation of order."

91. Lawler 2008: 23.

92. Georgi 1992: 52.

cation with the larger Christ-movement (1 Cor 16:1–4) and a critique of Roman economic exploitation.[93]

Next, Paul further describes the situation, "We are poorly clothed, beaten, and homeless," all of which indicate the exposure to danger that those who do not have political power would have experienced.[94] The first descriptor, γυμνιτεύω, is a *hapax legomenon* but is understood as "lightly clad" based on its use by Dio Chrysostom 25.3. It also echoes the Jesus tradition in Matt 25:36, 38, 43, 44.[95] The next descriptor, κολαφίζω, includes in its definition the violence of being "struck by a fist" or "roughly treated" and reinforces the contention that the story of Jesus is central to the life of the ἐκκλησία (see Matt 26:67). The final descriptor, also a *hapax legomenon*, ἀστατέω, which means "homeless," is similar to the situation of Jesus in Matt 8:20 (parallel Luke 9:58).

In 4:12, Paul reminds the Corinthian Christ-followers, "and we labor, working with our own hands." It is well established that most of the elites throughout the empire considered the life of an artisan beneath them. For Paul, however, it becomes a point of social identification. All the descriptors within this catalog are to be classified as contact zones of identity formation.[96] Paul has been emploting a narrative of social identification in which the ingroup will appropriate the narrative of suffering of the stereotyped outgroup and "behave ethically" because they see themselves as part of the others' story.[97]

This ethical narrative emplotment continues as these prototypical figures now model a proper response to their suffering: "When we are despised (λοιδορούμενοι), we bless; when persecuted, we endure." This model is based on the teaching (Luke 6:28) and example (Luke 23:34) of Jesus. The verb λοιδορέω is employed later in John 9:28 and 1 Pet 2:23, the latter providing significant conceptual overlap with the current context. In this model, those wronged, instead of retaliating, should "bless." When "persecuted," the community should "endure." In 4:13, those "slandered," instead of speaking in kind, should "speak kindly." There is no evidence that the community was being despised, persecuted, or slandered, so Paul's narrative of other-identification is preparing for the

93. Horsley 1997: 251.

94. Friesen 2005: 364–66.

95. Carter 2000: 495–97.

96. Pratt 2008: 7.

97. Lawler 2008: 24.

real possibility that, as they re-orient communal life around "the word of the cross" (1 Cor 1:18) and not "the wisdom of this world" (1 Cor 1:20), suffering will occur.

The earlier reference to the *noxii* re-emerges as Paul starkly concludes, "We have become the rubbish (περικαθάρματα) of the world, the waste (περίψημα) of all things, even now." The appropriation of a narrative identity is always susceptible to "the breach of sociality" known as "fraudulent identity." The primary reason for this is "that no narrative identity belongs to the teller alone; they also incorporate the narratives of others."[98] As Paul describes the experience of himself and the other apostles, he is inscribing an identity for the community of Christ-followers. He concludes with two images, περικάθαρμα and περίψημα, which serve as the trigger mechanisms for the emplotment, internalization, and appropriation of a social identity. Those not "in Christ" will not appropriate this type of suffering (1 Cor 12:2–3). So, as "the body of Christ" they should not be surprised when they suffer like Christ, nor should they be amazed when others within "the body of Christ" suffer. In the context of suffering, they should embody their "in Christ" identity and not respond to suffering in a manner similar to those who do not understand the ways of God (1 Cor 2:6–8; 12:2).

PAUL'S KINSHIP-FORMATION (4:14–17)

This (4:14–17) and the next section (4:18–21) together form the final step of the opening rhetorical unit which encompasses chapters 1–4. Paul has made his case concerning the proper use and function of wisdom, power, and speech and has concluded his discussion with the way this is applied in the Pauline mission. In 4:14–21, Paul's identity-forming work may be described as kinship-formation[99] which is designed to empower the ἐκκλησία while also subverting key educational aspects of Roman social identity. Paul uses several *paideia*-related concepts, the Greek equivalent of *humanitas*, which Whitmarsh contends is a significant part of "elite . . . identity in this period."[100]

What constituted the Roman educational focus with regard to social identity? For the elites, it may be plausibly summarized in Cicero's

---

98. Lawler 2008: 29.

99. Ehrensperger 2007: 58; Lieu 2004: 166; Aasgaard 2004: 297–98.

100. Whitmarsh 2004: 176.

understanding of *humanitas*. Even if the Pauline communities had few if any elites, *humanitas* would have indirectly influenced non-elites throughout the Roman Empire by means of their patronage relationships, business dealings, and civic engagements.[101] First, the ability to control one's appetites and follow the guidance of reason identifies one as possessing *humanitas* (*Off.* 1.28.101; 3.10.41). Second, a sense of duty to other human beings contributes according to Cicero (*Off.* 3.11.47). Third, closely associated with the previous two concepts is a preference for education instead of tyranny. For Cicero, *humanitas* flows from a life that takes seriously the cultivation of the mind and the virtues associated with such a lifestyle (*Tusc.* 5.23.66–67). Fourth, Cicero conceives of *humanitas* also within the context of skill development, especially with regard to oratory and rhetoric (*De or.* 2.72; 2.86), and even philosophy (*De. or.* 1.21). The concept of *humanitas* encompasses both civic and social responsibilities to humankind which, if practiced, contribute to an ordered, civilized communal existence. Moral development was central to Roman education, and this "was expressed in the virtues admired by the Roman people, virtues which the *vir bonus* had to possess: *gravitas, pietas, justitia, fortitudo, constantia,* and *prudentia.*"[102]

Paul offers an alternative formation approach to the Roman concept of *humanitas*. He uses kinship-formation similar to Jewish teaching and learning discourse in order to transform aspects of educational life within the ἐκκλησία in Corinth.[103] Where is the concern for educational identity in 4:14–21? It is evident in Paul's use of νουθετέω in 4:14, παιδαγωγός in 4:15, μιμητής in 4:16, διδάσκω in 4:17, and ῥάβδος in 4:21. The significance of these terms will emerge as we discuss these verses in what follows.

101. Revell 2009: 36–39.

102. Pascal 1984: 353; Elliott 2008a: 59, 87, 121. Paul would not seek to eliminate these aspects of Roman social/educational identity, rather he would argue that they are to be reprioritized in Christ. He would, however, disagree with the general approach to teaching/formation within the Roman educational "system." Cf. Brawley 2007: 117.

103. Ehrensperger (2007: 117–36) argues for five characteristics of Jewish teaching and learning discourse: (1) it resists Hellenic influences (Deut 6:4–25); (2) it draws on the insight of both the Father and the Mother (Prov 1:8); (3) the Jewish Father did not have rights over the life of the child (Deut 21:18–21; cf. *pater familias*); (4) its teaching is based on Israel's scriptural tradition; (5) it encourages walking in the ways of the received tradition (cf. Deut 28:9; 1 Cor 4:16).

Paul's approach to kinship-formation emerges in 4:14 where he uses honor-shame and educational language to persuade his auditors. Paul begins in 4:14, "I do not write this to shame (ἐντρέπων) you." He is not seeking to dominate the Corinthian Christ-followers or to use language like that of Roman politics, as is evidenced by the next clause, "but as my beloved children (τέκνα)—to teach (νουθετῶν) you." The type of teaching Paul has in mind is similar to that of Rom 15:14 (ἀλλήλους νουθετεῖν), where the semantic range of νουθετέω allows for the concept of formation.[104] Within the ἐκκλησία teaching is not to rely on the status-oriented honor-shame discourse, nor is it to be understood as an obligation associated with civic life; rather it is to be practiced in a manner similar to the way Jewish parents formed their children: "Hear, my son, your father's instruction, and forsake not your mother's teaching" (Prov 1:8). Paul's alternative approach to community formation will be further evident in this section.

Paul begins in 4:15, "for though you have ten thousand guides (παιδαγωγούς) in Christ," which provides a foil for his approach to kinship-formation. The παιδαγωγός was normally an older, foreign slave[105] who walked the Roman son[106] to school and guarded him as he developed Roman social values.[107] Greek households normally had one παιδαγωγός, but Young notes that Roman households could contain multiple "attendants."[108] The child often formed a kinship bond with the παιδαγωγός; Cicero remarked, "In general, decisions about friend-

104. BDAG 679; Wis 11:10 connects the parental role in formation by the use of νουθετέω, cf. Ps Sol 13:9; *EDNT* 478; M&M 430 note that the idea of "pressure" being exerted on someone is in view; Arzt-Grabner (2006: 185–86) points out uses in the documentary papyri that also indicate that a threat may be in view in the use of νουθετέω. He concludes: „Eine übermäßige Unterscheidung zwischen biblischem und nicht-biblischem Gebrauch des Wortes ist nicht nahe liegend." Ehrensperger (2007: 129), however, notes "the use of the term νουθετῶν indicates that what Paul has written so far in the letter is part of a discourse which aims at the growth and maturity of the ἐκκλησία." It appears that the Hebrew educational discourse is a closer context for Paul's use than that which is attested in the Graeco-Roman sources (see also 1 Sam 3:13; Wis 12:26; Deut 8:5).

105. Plut. *Mor.* 4ab.

106. Plut. *Mor.* 439f.

107. Witherington (1998: 265), referencing Aristides *Or.* 2.380, proposes "self-control, honor, respect, discipline, putting one's best foot forward in public and the like" as examples of Roman social values.

108. Young 1987: 170, citing *CIL* 6.1052.

ships should not be made until we have developed maturity of age and strength of mind ... Otherwise ... our pedagogues ... will claim the largest share of our affections."[109] In 4:15, Paul uses an image associated with Roman education in order to destabilize some within the ἐκκλησία with regard to their primary kinship identification (see Gal 3:24–25).[110] It is not that παιδαγωγοί are rejected; rather their significance is re-cast within the Christ-following community.

The next step in Paul's rhetoric continues this repriorization of Roman social identity; he writes, "but you do not have many fathers (πατέρας)." Paul employs kinship language to establish that Roman imperial ideology with the emperor as the "father of the fatherland"—or any other father—is an unacceptable substitute for Paul.[111] Furthermore, Ehrensperger explains that "the exclusive use of father language in relation to God could be an indication of a subversive discourse in the Pauline letters, in conjunction with other terms such as κύριος, δικαιοσύνη, εἰρήνη."[112] Paul continues with a series of prepositional phrases, starting with "for in Christ Jesus" (ἐν γὰρ Χριστῷ Ἰησοῦ), which reframes the center of experience and reinforces the "in Christ" kinship group.[113] He then reminds the Corinthian Christ-followers that the intermediate agent responsible for this transformed identity was not the Roman Empire with its declaration of "good news," but that "through the gospel" Paul had "birthed" them.[114] This recognition by the Corinthian Christ-followers will allow them to place Paul in his proper role—as their "father" but only in a relative sense. Thus, he may be understood in asymmetrical terms; however, he is not to be conceived of as the *pater familias*.

Paul continues in 4:16, "I encourage (παρακαλῶ) you, then, be imitators (μιμηταί) of me." The concept of imitation or *mimēsis* was employed early in the educational experience of Roman children. Quintilian notes that something as mundane as copying lines from an

---

109. Cic. *De. Amic.* 20.74.

110. While Paul was not strictly "anti-pedagogues" (Young 1987: 169–70), it is very possible that some within the Corinthian ἐκκλησία were παιδαγωγοί (Meggitt 1998: 97–103).

111. Lassen 1991: 131.

112. Ehrensperger 2007: 127.

113. Johnson Hodge 2007: 131–32.

114. Jewett 2007: 138. Ehrensperger (2007: 128) rightly recognizes the presence of maternal imagery that tempers the paternal imagery in this verse.

exemplar "should convey some moral lesson."[115] At this stage the pupil "cannot as yet produce anything on its own" and thus the "teacher" has the opportunity "to develop" the student's ability.[116] The increasing exposure to literature reinforces the identity formation inherent in *paideia*. Whitmarsh notes, "Literature is an ever incomplete, ever unstable process of self-making."[117] As the students were learning to read and write, the models they were given reinforced Roman social values.

Ehrensperger discerns in Paul's use of *mimēsis* an implicit critique of Roman imperial ideology and a call to follow those who "embody the message of the gospel and its alternative values."[118] Paul subverts Roman social identity transmitted by educational patterns. It appears that one of the contact zones between Paul and the Corinthian Christ-followers concerned his vision for a community life which had its roots in Israel's scriptures over one which was influenced by Roman civic life. The Roman society of which these gentiles "in Christ" were a part, as mentioned above, would have been rooted in epic narratives such as Homer's *Iliad* and *Odyssey* or Vergil's *Aeneid*,[119] while Paul's identity-formation narrative was rooted in the Torah interpreted in light of the cross. Brawley recognizes the importance of an identity narrative by suggesting that people must "make themselves part of a narrative that holds past, present, and future together."[120] First Corinthians 1–4 provides evidence of competing identity narratives within the Christ-movement.

What was Paul's solution for these competing identity narratives? He continues in 4:17, "Because of this, I sent Timothy to you." Paul's solution was Timothy, who would embody Paul's vision for Christ-movement social identity (1 Cor 16:10). Timothy was uniquely qualified to help guide the Corinthian Christ-followers through the vagaries of life "in

115. Quint. *Or.* 1.1.36.

116. Quint. *Or.* 1.1.36.

117. Whitmarsh 2001: 2.

118. Ehrensperger 2007: 154; Clarke 1998: 359, 2008: 173–82; Castelli 1991: 95–117. Clarke (1998: 359) rightly points out that "the imitation of Christ is primary," and "the fact that Paul also enjoins imitation of other named believers presupposes that he does not consider his, albeit apostolic, role as example unique." Cf. *EDNT* 429; *TDNT* 4.668.

119. Knauer (1964: 64, 84) provides numerous examples of verbal and conceptual parallels as well as the significance of these for Augustan ideology. MacDonald (2001: 14) reflects on an intertexture between Homer's *Odyssey*, books 1–4 and Tobit, as well as other biblical "analogies."

120. Brawley 2007: 110.

Christ"; he would serve as a prototypical member for the group (Acts 16:1–3). Paul continues to describe Timothy with kinship language similar to that used in 4:14 to refer to the Corinthians, "my beloved and faithful child (τέκνον) in the Lord (ἐν κυρίῳ)."[121] Paul relies on the resources of social memory, and Jewish learning and teaching discourse (e.g., ἀναμιμνήσκω, ὁδός, and διδάσκω), as he describes his reason for Timothy's coming, "to remind you of my ways in Christ."[122] Paul had preached the gospel to the Corinthians, had written them a previous letter, but in the process of interpretation, they misunderstood Paul's message. Thus, Paul intends to mediate the Corinthians' socio-cultural practice through the discursive agency of Timothy.[123]

This use of Timothy functions as a corrective to the *paideia*-related practices in Corinth. Paul's role as a teacher is brought out in 4:14. Longenecker notes the "*didaskalos*" was primarily an educator or an instructor, as compared to the παιδαγωγός.[124] The teacher could function in a manner that resembled kinship-formation.[125] Epictetus notes that teachers, though he uses γραμματικοῦ (1 Cor 1:20), employed se-

---

121. Here, Paul uses ἐν κυρίῳ instead of ἐν Χριστῷ but there is no difference in meaning. Peter Oakes (2001: 149) explains, referring to Philippians 2, that "Jesus receives the Name above every name. All knees bow to him. Every tongue acknowledges him as Lord. A Graeco-Roman hearer would probably hear this as a comparison with the Emperor." Oakes (2005: 304) also remarks that this term could have been employed even if Rome did not use it; "all Christians had, in reality, experienced Roman κύριοι. The experience must have stamped Christians' usage." Cf. Middleton 2006: 61.

122. Ehrensperger (2007: 129) contends that "The three key terms Paul uses here, ἀναμνήσει, ὁδοί, and διδασκείν, are terms which in Jewish tradition have specific meanings in relation to teaching and learning. To 'remind' them, resonates with the repeated and frequent exhortation of the Scriptures to remember the deeds and words of God on behalf of his people, to remember his guidance through the Torah. The things Timothy is sent to remind them of are 'the ways of Christ' Paul had taught them. 'ὁδός' seems to have become an early 'label' for the Christ-movement (Acts 9.2; 19.23; 22.4 etc.) but also resonates with the widespread terminology of 'walking in the ways of the Lord' in the Scriptures, as, for example, Exod. 18.20 'teach them the statutes and instructions and make known to them the way they are to go and the things they are to do'; Ps. 25.4, Deut. 26.17, 28.9. This is what Paul had been doing when he was with them."

123. Fairclough's (1992: 62–63; 71–72) three layers of discourse are in view here. Layer one is the actual letter, layer two is the discursive practice (interpretation), and the final layer is the broader discursive environment (in this case, sending Timothy to impact the environment).

124. Longenecker 1982: 53.

125. Epic. *Diatr.* 3.22.81–82.

lections from Homer to teach students.[126] These epics would have been internalized and formative in the construction of a worldview. During the imperial period, the focus of the tertiary level of education was primarily on rhetoric but could also include philosophy. In a general way, 1 Corinthians 1–4 calls into question the epistemic value of worldly wisdom within the ἐκκλησία through the cultivation of "the mind of Christ" in 2:16 and the elevation of Paul's teaching role within the community.

Paul continues by attempting to connect the ἐκκλησία in Corinth with the superordinate group, i.e., members of the Christ-movement throughout the Roman Empire (1 Cor 16:1–4).[127] He writes, "as I teach (διδάσκω) them everywhere in every assembly." This clause indicates that his mission and strategy for the Corinthians requires an adjustment in the recognition of their social identity. "In Christ" they are part of the larger "body of Christ" and are not capable of existence as an autonomous group of Christ-followers; they are part of something larger than their provincial expression of the "body of Christ."[128] This "in Christ" hybrid identity interpenetrates the Corinthians' existing Roman social identities and reprioritizes them, which then may result in an alternative community with a distinct ethos, a key goal in Paul's kinship-formation.

PAUL'S EMPOWERMENT OF THE COMMUNITY (4:18–21)

First Corinthians 4:18–21 is often understood as an example of a discourse of domination.[129] However, it may be preferable to understand it as a discourse of empowerment and transformation as has been argued recently by Ehrensperger.[130] Paul begins in 4:18, "Some of you have become arrogant (ἐφυσιώθησάν), as though I were not coming to you." How can this be understood as empowering kinship-formation? Paul does not point out the offending group. Instead, he simply uses the indefinite pronoun τίς, which allows him to address his concerns without putting unnecessary pressure on the offending member(s).

The term φυσιόω, here used in the passive "become arrogant," is rarely used outside the NT, and Arzt-Grabner finds no use of it in

---

126. Epic. *Diatr.* 2.19.7.

127. Tajfel and Turner 1979: 33–47.

128. Thiselton 2000: 375–76.

129. Birge 2002: 182.

130. Ehrensperger 2007: 179, 188.

the documentary papyri.[131] A form of φυσιόω is employed in Herodas *Mime* 2.32 which records, "those who may vaunt their birth (τῇ γενῇ φυσῶντες) with better cause."[132] Welborn, who understands this mime to be in the background of 4:14–21, describes this group as those who "are inattentive to their studies, and full of youthful arrogance."[133] This is a plausible solution in that the larger context of the mime includes discussions with the student's father, teacher, and pedagogue.[134] While we are not comfortable in going as far as Welborn with regard to this intertexture, there are close lexical connections between 1:26, "not many were of noble birth" (οὐ πολλοὶ εὐγενεῖς), and Herodas 2.32. Thus, it is possible that those who were becoming arrogant were identifying primarily with aspects of their Roman social identity rather than with their "in Christ" identity.

The verb φυσιόω used by Paul in 1 Corinthians appears to be related to aspects of the Christ-followers' Roman identity that are in need of transformation. For example, in 4:6 (φυσιοῦσθε), 18 (ἐφυσιώθησάν), 19 (πεφυσιωμένων), educational discourse is in view, thus the arrogance may result from asymmetrical educational backgrounds, differing views of wisdom, and the role of teachers. In 5:2 (πεφυσιωμένοι), it is likely that a Roman understanding of masculinity has impacted the communal decision-making process with regard to aspects of their sexual identity and group norms. In 8:1, differences that are based in a Roman ethos concerning the continued relationship to idols within the ἐκκλησία may be a contributing factor.[135] Note that Paul's alternative group ethos is introduced in 8:1 in the context of this concept, "Knowledge puffs up (φυσιοῖ), but love builds up," and in 13:4, "Love is not boastful (οὐ φυσιοῦται)." Paul's concern for arrogance within the community is really a concern with power discourse—the site at which he rejects Roman enculturation.

Paul shifts the discourse from reported speech to first person speech and provides a firmer assessment of the Corinthians' attitude: "But I will come to you soon, if the Lord wills." Then he describes the way he intends to address the situation when he does arrive, "and I will find out not the

131. Arzt-Grabner 2006: 172.
132. Sharpley 1906: 11.
133. Welborn 2005: 88.
134. Welborn 2005: 87.
135. Börschel 2001: 98.

talk of these arrogant people (τῶν πεφυσιωμένων) but their power (δύναμιν)." Paul is establishing ingroup/outgroup identity to further his broader purpose in 1 Corinthians 1–4, to provide the cognitive resources necessary to understand and apply the social implications of the gospel. Tajfel and Turner claim that an individual's self-concept is derived from his or her perceived membership within a social group.[136] SCT argues that, once this ingroup identity is established, outgroup stereotyping occurs, which results in further ingroup salience.[137] Paul's use of outsider language, i.e., "become arrogant" (φυσιόω), and his re-inscribing the Corinthians' narrative substructure/discourse from their "talk" (λόγος) to their "power" (δύναμις) redefines the Corinthians' identification categories and seeks to strengthen ingroup identity.

Paul's apocalyptic worldview is the foundation for his kinship-formation. The next step in his rhetoric declares, "The kingdom of God (ἡ βασιλεία τοῦ Θεοῦ) does not consist in talk but in power." This anti-imperial polemic reminds the Corinthian Christ-followers who have put their trust in the Roman Empire that in comparison to God's kingdom, Rome is not so powerful. In Rom 14:17, one of the few places where Paul employs the descriptive genitive phrase ἡ βασιλεία τοῦ Θεοῦ, he similarly redefines the nature of the kingdom as compared to the Roman Empire. Paul rarely uses kingdom language because of the possibility of its being misunderstood in the context of Roman imperial ideology.

The final term associated with Roman educational identity, the "stick" (ῥάβδος) which is connected with the pedagogue from 4:15 is found in 4:21.[138] Bartchy, in considering this connection, suggests that it shows the extent to which Paul's approach to formation differed from the Roman pedagogues.[139] Dutch, while not dismissing this connection, has made a case for a multi-faceted understanding of "the stick." He notes, "Paul's language of 'the stick' can be read within the social context of family, schools, gymnasia, and games."[140] This understanding provides a more expansive context for the formation of Roman social identity. However, Dutch's contribution to this discussion is that in each

---

136. Tajfel 1978b: 63; Hogg 2006: 111.

137. Stryker and Burke 2000: 286.

138. Fitzmyer 2008: 226.

139. Bartchy 2003: 135–47.

140. Dutch 2005: 263.

of these educational contexts physical punishment was commonplace.[141] Furthermore, Aasgaard sees a threat of physical punishment in this verse. He remarks: "Very often, then, Paul deals with Christians with the traditional authority of a *pater familias*, even threatening them with physical punishment if they disobey (1 Cor. 4:21)."[142] Aasgaard's argument may fail for two reasons: it is not clear how unilateral the *pater familias* was in the mid-first century CE.[143] Second, physical punishment may not be the main point of this passage but a ringing critique of *paideia* as practiced among those in Corinth.[144]

Thiselton may be closer to Paul's use here. He argues for "the 'rod of correction' of OT and LXX traditions."[145] He does not, however, provide examples for this use, except for 1 Sam 17:43 referring to David coming to Goliath with a "stick" (ῥάβδῳ).[146] We would like to suggest that Proverbs 22:15 forms the basis for Paul's rhetoric because it contains significant kinship-formation language. The synthetic parallelism of the proverb begins in the LXX, "Folly is found in the heart of a child (νέου)"; then it concludes, "but the stick (ῥάβδος) of training (παιδεία) will drive it far from him." Proverbs 22:15 echoes key indicators for Paul's kinship-formation. It contains kinship language, in this case "child" (νέος), and formation language, "training" (παιδεία). Paul's kinship-formation required more than, e.g., Martial's "sinister rod" or "scepter" from a Roman pedagogue (*Epig.* 10.62.10). It required a "stick of training" (Prov 22:15; 1 Cor 4:21).

First Corinthians 4:21 opened with the question, "What do you wish (τί θέλετε;), shall I come to you with a stick (ἐν ῥάβδῳ)?" Though we have suggested that the "stick of training" is in view, Paul's main purpose is not to threaten them with physical violence; rather, he was furthering his anti-Roman imperial polemic. He was saying, "In light of all I have just said, would you want me to come to you as the Roman

---

141. Lassen (1991: 136 n. 40; cited in Dutch 2005: 262 n. 37), on the other hand, notes "the possibility that the rod refers to that carried by the lectors on an assize."

142. Aasgaard 2007: 156.

143. Aasgaard acknowledges this in his earlier work (2004: 49–51; but see 2007: 142, 152, 156).

144. Ehrensperger 2007: 126–28.

145. Thiselton 2000: 378.

146. This seems to contradict Thiselton's argument that 1 Cor 4:21 is not a threat but a warning, in that violence is in view in the 1 Samuel passage.

pedagogue or shall I come to you 'with love (ἀγάπη) in a spirit of humility(πραΰτητος)?' You decide" (2 Cor 10:1).[147] Paul's rhetoric is far from the dominating propaganda of the Roman Empire; it is a rhetoric of empowerment that has its basis in a salient "in Christ" social identity.

CONCLUSION

This chapter brought together Paul's argument from 4:1–21 in which he sought to disentangle the adverse impact of Roman social identity within the ἐκκλησία. It was discovered that Paul sought to adjust the Corinthian Christ-followers' thinking with regard to self-examination and social categorization. This was accomplished by a focus on God's future judgment. Paul then addressed concerns related to the Corinthians' practices with regard to the patron-client system that had caused many of the difficulties within the community. It was determined that the Corinthians' current lack of suffering had formed their social identity, and Paul emploted a narrative identity that included suffering as a vital aspect of communal life. Next, Paul corrected the Corinthian Christ-followers' social identification with imperial ideology in the context of honor and shame discourse and redeployed the resources of *mimēsis* and group prototypes within the community. Finally, Paul's rhetoric of empowerment focused on issues of power, apocalyptic, and social categorization, and revealed the application of his overall approach in the formation of a salient "in Christ" social identity within God's ἐκκλησία in Corinth.

147. Bartchy 2003: 142.

10

Conclusions

PAUL WAS CONCERNED WITH the continuation of gentile identity "in Christ" just as he was with the continuation of Jewish identity "in Christ." This finding substantiates William S. Campbell's general understanding of Paul's approach to identity formation and further calls into question the accepted view that Paul was disinterested in or sought to obliterate social, ethnic, or cultural identities in his definition of the Christ-movement. Thus, in 1 Corinthians 1–4 Paul was found to be arguing for an "in Christ" identity in which being "in Christ" functioned as the salient identity position within the identity hierarchy. Existing social identities were to be reevaluated and reprioritized based on the social implications of the gospel, but were not to be opposed or dismissed as insignificant "in Christ" unless they contradicted it.

Paul's approach to the Roman Empire was found to be more differentiated than is often thought. He was neither completely subversive nor completely disinterested in the Roman Empire. Thus, while it may be accurate to claim that Paul was, in some respects, counter-cultural, he was by no means universally so in relation to Roman identity. The goal for his mission and strategy could be described as the formation of alternative communities with a distinct ethos, within and at some points in some tension with the emerging ethos of the Roman Empire. This finding is significant during a time when scholars are stressing Christ *or* Caesar in relation to Paul. For Paul, it was Christ *and* Roman identity except in those areas where ideological positions conflicted. In those areas it was Christ whose lordship was adhered to because the community belonged to God through Christ.

Paul was found to be concerned with the transformation of cognitive and rational capacities with regard to social identity. This nuanced understanding contributes to the discussion in Pauline anthropology which often dismisses epistemic concerns or provides a mystical understanding of the Spirit's agency that appears to bypass normal cognitive processes. Paul was not rejecting Roman or Greek approaches to wisdom as such; rather he was calling into question those cognitive processes which contradicted the social implications of the gospel. Thus Paul may be seen as providing insight into the way already existing cognitive processes might be transformed "in Christ." So, one should not isolate one's social identity from one's communal spiritual experience. For Paul, these are both necessary for salient "in Christ" social identity.

In 1 Corinthians 1–4, Paul addressed many of the problems within the Christ-movement as group-related issues, and thus the group-focused research of Henri Tajfel and John Turner (i.e., SIT/SCT) were found to be helpful in identifying them. This substantiates their continuing use in New Testament studies. Furthermore, this research found that these theories were strengthened when they were combined with others from the field of social identity and New Testament studies (e.g., Sheldon Stryker, Peter Burke, Richard Jenkins, Kathy Ehrensperger, and Warren Carter). These combined resources, when applied to 1 Corinthians 1–4, indicated that the problems Paul addressed could be described as relating to Roman social identity.

Paul's concern in Corinth was with civic identity which is understood as a significant component of social identity in antiquity. Corinth, as a Roman colony, was susceptible to the ongoing transition in *polis*-religion that was occurring throughout the first century CE. This cultural dynamic may have contributed to a lack of conflict with the local governing authorities. It also may have allowed for an openness to those outside the Christ-movement that inadvertently added to difficulties related to this over-identification with key aspects of Roman social life in Corinth. This finding emerged from a study of archaeological, numismatic, epigraphic, and literary artifacts that are sometimes neglected by social theorists. Thus this book found that by combining the resources of the social theoretical and social historical approaches one can arrive at a more firm conclusion than might otherwise be expected if only one of these approaches was utilized.

This book also opens up a number of areas for future research. In the introductory section, we briefly surveyed ancient authors and identity formation; it would be useful to do a complete concept analysis on their work to further substantiate the comparisons with Paul's writing.

The identity theory of Stryker and Burke has been underutilized in New Testament studies, and their approach could prove useful in addressing issues of identity in Romans and Galatians. Finally, this research could be expanded to include 1 Corinthians 5–16 in order to determine the extent of Paul's focus on the continuing influence of previous social identities "in Christ" and the alternative nature of his approach to communal formation.

1 Corinthians 1–4 shows that some in Corinth were continuing to identify primarily with key aspects of their Roman social identity rather than their identity "in Christ," and this confusion over identity positions contributed to some of the problems within the ἐκκλησία. Paul seeks to realign their identity hierarchy in order to create an alternative community with a distinct ethos in comparison with the Roman Empire. The approach taken in this book distinctively asserts that previous gentile social identities are relevant and not extraneous "in Christ." The tensions within the community thus derive from conflicting understandings concerning the social implications of the gospel received from Paul.

Bibliography *

Aasgaard, R. 2004. *"My Beloved Brothers and Sisters": Christian Siblingship in Paul.* Early Christianity in Context 265. London: T. & T. Clark.

———. 2007. "Paul as a Child: Children and Childhood in the Letters of the Apostle." *JBL* 126:129–59.

Adams, E. 2000. *Constructing the World: A Study in Paul's Cosmological Language.* SNTW. Edinburgh: T. & T. Clark.

———. 2007. *The Stars Will Fall from Heaven: 'Cosmic Catastrophe' in the New Testament and its World.* LNTS 347. London: T. & T. Clark.

———. 2009. "First-Century Models for Paul's Churches: Selected Scholarly Developments Since Meeks." Pages 60–78 in *After the First Urban Christians,* edited by T. D. Still and D. G. Horrell. New York: T. & T. Clark.

Adams, E., and D. G. Horrell, editors. 2004. *Christianity at Corinth: The Quest for the Pauline Church.* Louisville: Westminster John Knox.

Adams, J. N. 2003a. *Bilingualism and the Latin Language.* New York: Cambridge University Press.

———. 2003b. "'Romanitas' and the Latin Language." *Classical Quarterly* 53:184–205.

Alcock, S. E. 1993. *Graecia Capta: The Landscapes of Roman Greece.* Cambridge: Cambridge University Press.

———. 1994. "Minding the Gap in Hellenistic and Roman Greece." Pages 247–61 in *Placing the Gods: Sanctuaries and Sacred Space in Ancient Greece,* edited by S. E. Alcock and R. Osborne. Oxford: Clarendon.

Allo, E.-B. 1956. *Saint Paul, première épître aux Corinthiens.* Paris: Gabalda.

Amandry, M. 1988. *Le monnayage des duovirs Corinthiens.* Bulletin de correspondance hellénique 15. Athens: École française d'Athènes, Paris.

Ando, C. 2000. *Imperial Ideology and Provincial Loyalty in the Roman Empire.* Berkeley: University of California Press.

Appiah, K. A. 2005. *The Ethics of Identity.* Princeton: Princeton University Press.

Arafat, K. W. 1996. *Pausanias' Greece Ancient Artists and Roman Rulers.* Cambridge: Cambridge University Press.

Arzt-Grabner, et al. 2006. *1 Korinther.* Papyrologische Kommentare zum Neuen Testament. 2. Göttingen: Vandenhoeck & Ruprecht.

Ascough, R. S. 2002. "Greco-Roman Philosophic, Religious, and Voluntary Associations." Pages 4–19 in *Community Formation in the Early Church and the Church Today,* edited by R. N. Longenecker. Peabody, MA: Hendrickson.

———. 2003. *Paul's Macedonian Associations: The Social Context of Philippians and 1 Thessalonians.* WUNT, 161. Tübingen: Mohr Siebeck.

---

* All translations of classical texts in this book have been taken from the Loeb Classical Library (Cambridge: Harvard University Press) unless noted otherwise.

Asher, J. R. 2000. *Polarity and Change in 1 Corinthians 15: A Study of Metaphysics, Rhetoric, and Resurrection*. Hermeneutische Untersuchungen zur Theologie 42. Tübingen: Mohr Siebeck.

Ashforth, B., and F. Mael. 1989. "Social Identity Theory and the Organization." *The Academy of Management Review* 14:20–39.

Atherton, C. A. 1988. "Hand over Fist: The Failure of Stoic Rhetoric." *Classical Quarterly* NS 38:392–427.

Austin, J. L. 1962. *How to Do Things with Words*. Oxford: Clarendon.

Bailey, K. G. 2004. "Recognizing, Assessing, and Classifying Others: Cognitive Bases of Evolutionary Kinship Therapy." Pages 45–66 in *Evolutionary Theory and Cognitive Therapy*, edited by P. Gilbert. New York: Springer.

Baird, W. 1987. "Review of Wisdom and Spirit: An Investigation of 1 Corinthians 1:18—3:20 against the Background of Jewish Sapiential Traditions in the Greco-Roman Period." *JBL* 106:150–51.

Baker, J. C. 2008. "New Covenant, New Identity: A Social-scientific Reading of Jeremiah 31:31–34." *Bible and Critical Theory* 4.1:5.1—5.11.

Balsdon, J. P. V. D. 1979. *Romans and Aliens*. Chapel Hill: University of North Carolina Press.

Bannon, C. J. 1997. *The Brothers of Romulus: Fraternal Pietas in Roman Law, Literature, and Society*. Princeton: Princeton University Press.

Barclay, J. M. G. 1987. "Mirror-reading a Polemical Letter: Galatians as a Test Case." *JSNT* 31:73–93.

———. 1992. "Thessalonica and Corinth: Social Contrasts in Pauline Christianity." *JSNT* 47:49–74.

———. 1993. "Conflict in Thessalonica." *CBQ* 55:512–30.

———. 1996. *Jews in the Mediterranean Diaspora: From Alexander to Trajan. 323 B.C.E.–117 C.E.* Edinburgh: T. & T. Clark.

———. 2004. "Poverty in Pauline Studies: A Response to Steven Friesen." *JSNT* 26:363–66.

———. 2007. "Constructing Judean Identity after 70 C.E.: A Study of Josephus's *Against Apion*." Pages 99–112 in *Identity and Interaction in the Ancient Mediterranean: Jews, Christians and Others*, edited by Z. A. Crook, and P. A. Harland. New Testament Monographs, 18. Sheffield: Sheffield Phoenix.

Barram, M. D. 2006. *Mission and Moral Reflection in Paul*. Studies in Biblical Literature 75. Frankfurt: Lang.

Barrett, C. K. 1968. *A Commentary on the First Epistle to the Corinthians*. Harper's New Testament Commentaries. New York: Harper & Row.

Bar-Tal, D. 1990. *Group Beliefs: A Conception for Analyzing Group Structure, Processes, and Behavior*. New York: Springer.

———. 2000. *Shared Beliefs in a Society: Social Psychological Analysis*. London: Sage.

Bartchy, S. S. 2003. "Who Should Be Called Father? Paul of Tarsus between the Jesus Tradition and Patria Potestas." *BTB* 33:135–47.

Barth, F. 1969. "Introduction." Pages 9–38 in *Ethnic Groups and Boundaries: Reflection on the Origin and Spread of Nationalism*, edited by F. Barth. London: Verso.

———. 2000. "Boundaries and Connections." Pages 17–35 in *Signifying Identities: Anthropological Perspectives on Boundaries and Contested Values*, edited by A. P. Cohen London: Routledge.

Barton, S. C. 1995. "Historical Criticism and Social-scientific Perspectives in New Testament Study." Pages 61–89 in *Hearing the New Testament*, edited by J. B. Green. Grand Rapids: Eerdmans.

———. 1997. "Social-scientific Criticism." Pages 277–89 in *A Handbook to the Exegesis of the New Testament*, edited by S. E. Porter. Leiden: Brill.

———. 2003. "Paul as Missionary and Pastor." Pages 34–48 in *The Cambridge Companion to St. Paul*, edited by J. D. G. Dunn. Cambridge: Cambridge University Press.

———. 2005. "Social-scientific Criticism." Pages 753–55 in *Dictionary for Theological Interpretation of the Bible*, edited by K. J. Vanhoozer. Grand Rapids: Baker Academic.

Baur, F. C. 1831. "Die Christuspartei in der korinthischen Gemeinde, der Gegensatz des paulinischen und petrinischen Christentums in der ältesten Kirche, der Apostel Petrus in Rom." *Tübinger Zeitschrift für Theologie* 4:61–206.

Baynham, M. 2006. "Performing Self, Family and Community in Moroccan Narratives of Migration and Settlement." Pages 376–97 in *Discourse and Identity*, edited by A. De Fina, D. Schiffrin, and M. Bamberg. Studies in Interactional Sociolinguistics. Cambridge: Cambridge University Press.

Beard, M., and M. Crawford. 1985. *Rome in the Late Republic*. Ithaca, NY: Cornell University Press.

Beard, M., J. A. North, and S. R. F. Price. 1998. *Religions of Rome*. 2 vols. Cambridge: Cambridge University Press.

Becker, H. S. 1963. *Outsiders: Studies in the Sociology of Deviance*. London: Free Press of Glencoe.

Beker, J. C. 1980. *Paul the Apostle: The Triumph of God in Life and Thought*. Philadelphia: Fortress.

Bell, R. H. 2007. *Deliver Us from Evil*. WUNT 216. Tübingen: Mohr Siebeck.

Belleville, L. 1996. "'Imitate Me, Just as I Imitate Christ': Discipleship in the Corinthian Correspondence." Pages 120–42 in *Patterns of Discipleship in the New Testament*, edited by R. N. Longenecker. Grand Rapids: Eerdmans.

Berger, K. 1978. "Zur Diskussion über die Herkunft von 1 Kor 2:9." *NTS* 24:270–83.

———. 2003. *Identity and Experience in the New Testament*. Minneapolis: Fortress.

Berger, P. L., and T. Luckmann. 1966. *The Social Construction of Reality: A Treatise in the Sociology of Knowledge*. Garden City, NY: Doubleday.

Betz, H. D., and M. Mitchell. 1992. "Corinth." Pages 1139–48 in vol. 6 *Anchor Bible Dictionary*, edited by D. N. Freedman. New York: Doubleday.

Bhabha, H. K. 1994. *The Location of Culture*. London: Routledge.

Biers, J. C. 1985. *The Great Bath on the Lechaion Road*. Corinth, 17. Princeton: ASCSA.

———. 2003. "Lavari est vivere: Baths in Roman Corinth." Pages 303–19 in *Corinth, the Centenary, 1896–1996*, edited by C. K. Williams and N. Bookidis. Corinth 20. Princeton: ASCSA.

Billig, M. 1986. *Arguing and Thinking: A Rhetorical Approach to Social Psychology*. Cambridge: Cambridge University Press.

———. 1995. *Banal Nationalism*. London: Sage.

Bird, M. 2008. "Reassessing a Rhetorical Approach to Paul's Letters." *ExpT* 119:374–79.

Birge, M. K. 2002. *The Language of Belonging: A Rhetorical Analysis of Kinship Language in First Corinthians*. Contributions to Biblial Exegesis and Theology 31. Leuven: Peeters.

Bjerkelund, C. J. 1967. *Parakalô: Form, Funktion und Sinn der parakalô-Sätze in den paulinischen Briefen.* Oslo: Universitetsforlaget.

Blasi, A. J., P. A. Turcotte, and J. Duhaime, editors. 2002. *Handbook of Early Christianity: Social Science Approaches.* Walnut Creek, CA: AltaMira.

Blumer, H. 1968. *Symbolic Interactionism: Perspective and Method.* Englewood Cliffs, NJ: Prentice-Hall.

Boatwright, M. T. 2000. *Hadrian and the Cities of the Roman Empire.* Princeton: Princeton University Press.

Bock, D. L. 2007. *Acts.* BECNT. Grand Rapids: Baker.

Bockmuehl, M. N. A. 2000. *Jewish Law in Gentile Churches: Halakhah and the Beginning of Christian Public Ethics.* Edinburgh: T. & T. Clark.

Bookidis, N. 1987. *Demeter and Persephone in Ancient Corinth.* Meriden, CT: Meriden-Stinehour.

———. 2003. "The Sanctuaries of Corinth." Pages 247–60 in *Corinth, the Centenary, 1896–1996,* edited by C. K. Williams and N. Bookidis. Corinth 20. Princeton: ASCSA.

———. 2005. "Religion in Corinth: 146 B.C.E. to 100 C.E." Pages 141–64 in *Urban Religion in Roman Corinth: Interdisciplinary Approaches,* edited by D. N. Schowalter and S. J. Friesen. Harvard Theological Studies 53. Cambridge: Harvard University Press.

Borg, M. J., and J. D. Crossan. 2007. *The First Christmas: What the Gospels Really Teach about Jesus' Birth.* New York: Harper One.

Borkowski, J. A., and P. J. du Plessis. 2005. *Textbook on Roman Law.* 3rd ed. Oxford: Oxford University Press.

Börschel, R. 2001. *Die Konstruktion einer christlichen Identität: Paulus und die Gemeinde von Thessalonich in ihrer hellenistisch-römischen Umwelt.* Bonner biblische Beiträge, Bd. 128. Berlin: Philo.

Botterweck, G. J., H. Ringgren, and H. J. Fabry, editors. 2006. *Theological Dictionary of the Old Testament.* Vol. 15. Grand Rapids: Eerdmans.

Bourdieu, P. 1984. *Distinction: A Social Critique of the Judgement of Taste.* Cambridge: Harvard University Press.

Boyarin, D. 1994. *A Radical Jew: Paul and the Politics of Identity.* Contraversions 1. Berkeley, University of California Press.

———. 2004. *Border Lines: The Partition of Judaeo-Christianity.* Divinations. Philadelphia: University of Pennsylvania Press.

Brawley, R. L. 2005. "Social Identity and the Aim of Accomplished Life in Acts 2." Pages 16–33 in *Acts and Ethics,* edited by T. E. Phillips. Sheffield: Sheffield Phoenix.

———. 2007. "Identity and Metaethics: Being Justified and Ethics in Galatians." Pages 107–23 in *Character Ethics and The New Testament Moral Dimensions of Scripture,* edited by R. L. Brawley. Louisville: Westminster John Knox.

Brewer, M. B. 2001. "The Social Self: On Being the Same and Different at the Same Time." Pages 245–53 in *Intergroup Relations, edited* by M. A. Hogg, and D. Abrams. Philadelphia: Psychology Press.

Broneer, O. 1941. "Colonia Laus Iulia Corinthiensis." *Hesperia* 10:388–90.

———. 1954. *The South Stoa and Its Roman Successors.* Corinth, 1.4. Princeton: ASCSA.

———. 1971. *Temple of Poseidon.* Isthmia, 1. Princeton: ASCSA.

Brown, A. R. 1995. *The Cross and Human Transformation: Paul's Apocalyptic Word in 1 Corinthians.* Minneapolis: Fortress.

Brown, R. J., and J. C. Turner. 1981. "Interpersonal and Intergroup Behaviour." Pages 33–65 in *Intergroup Behavior*, edited by J. C. Turner, and H. Giles. Chicago: University of Chicago Press.

Brueggemann, W. 2001. *The Prophetic Imagination*. Minneapolis: Fortress.

Brunt, P. A. 1990. *Roman Imperial Themes*. Oxford: Clarendon.

Bryan, C. 2005. *Render to Caesar: Jesus, the Early Church, and the Roman Superpower*. Oxford: Oxford University Press.

Buell, D. K. 2005. *Why This New Race: Ethnic Reasoning in Early Christianity*. Gender, Theory, and Religion. New York: Columbia University Press.

Buell, D. K., and C. J. Hodge. 2004. "The Politics of Interpretation: The Rhetoric of Race and Ethnicity in Paul." *JBL* 123:235–51.

Bullmore, M. A. 1995. *St. Paul's Theology of Rhetorical Style: An Examination of I Corinthians 2:1–5 in Light of First Century Graeco-Roman Rhetorical Culture*. San Francisco: International Scholars.

Bultmann, R. K. 1947. *Exegetische Probleme des zweiten Korintherbriefes: zu 2 Kor 5:1–5; 5:11–6, 10; 10–13; 12:21*. Symbolae Biblicae Upsalienses, 9. Uppsala: Wretmans.

———. 1969. *Faith and Understanding*. Translated by L.P. Smith, 1. New York: Harper & Row.

Bünker, M. 1984. *Briefformular und rhetorische Disposition im 1 Korintherbrief*. Göttinger theologische Arbeiten 28. Göttingen: Vandenhoeck & Ruprecht.

Burke, P. J. 1980. "The Self: Measurement Implications from a Symbolic Interactionist Perspective." *Social Psychology Quarterly* 43:18–29.

———. 2004. "Identities and Social Structure: The 2003 Cooley-Mead Award Address." *Social Psychology Quarterly* 67:5–15.

Burke, P. J., editor. 2006. *Contemporary Social Psychological Theories*. Stanford: Stanford University Press.

Burke, P. J., et al., editors. 2003. *Advances in Identity Theory and Research*. New York: Kluwer Academic/Plenum.

Burnett, G. W. 2001. *Paul and the Salvation of the Individual*. BIS 57. Leiden, Brill.

Burridge, R. A. 1992. *What Are the Gospels? A Comparison with Graeco-Roman Biography*. Cambridge: Cambridge University Press.

Butarbutar, R. 2007. *Paul and Conflict Resolution: An Exegetical Study of Paul's Apostolic Paradigm in 1 Corinthians 9*. Paternoster Biblical Monographs. Eugene, OR: Wipf & Stock.

Byrskog, S. 2008. "Christology and Identity in an Intertextual Perspective: The Glory of Adam in the Narrative Substructure of Paul's Letter to the Romans." Pages 1–18 in *Identity Formation in the New Testament*, edited by B. Holmberg and M. Winninge. WUNT 227. Tübingen: Mohr Siebeck.

Calvin, J. 1960. *The First Epistle of Paul the Apostle to the Corinthians*. Translated by J. W. Fraser. Grand Rapids: Eerdmans.

Campbell, W. S. 1991. *Paul's Gospel in an Intercultural Context: Jew and Gentile in the Letter to the Romans*. Frankfurt: Lang.

———. 1993. "Covenant and New Covenant" Pages 179–83 in *Dictionary of Paul and His Letters*, edited by G. F. Hawthorne, R. P. Martin, and D. G. Reid. Downers Grove, IL: InterVarsity.

———. 2005. "Perceptions of Compatibility between Christianity and Judaism in Pauline Interpretation." *BibInt* 8:298–316.

———. 2006a. *Paul and the Creation of Christian Identity.* LNTS 322. London. T. & T. Clark.

———. 2006b. "'As Having and As Not Having': Paul and Indifferent Things in 1 Corinthians 7:17–32a." Paper presented at the General Meeting of *Studiorum Novi Testamenti Societas,* Aberdeen, Scotland.

———. 2008a. "'I Rate All Things as Loss': Paul's Rhetoric of Comparison in Phil 3:3–8 Read in Light of 1 Cor 7:17–24 and Gal. 6:11–16." Paper presented at the General Meeting of *Studiorum Novi Testamenti Societas,* Lund, Sweden.

———. 2008b. *Paul and the Creation of Christian Identity.* T. & T. Clark Biblical Studies. London: T. & T. Clark.

———. 2008c. "Gentile Identity and Transformation in Christ according to Paul." Unpublished paper, Lampeter.

Carson, D. A. 2003. *The Cross and Christian Ministry: Leadership Lessons from 1 Corinthians.* Grand Rapids: Baker.

Carter, W. 2000. *Matthew and the Margins: A Sociopolitical and Religious Reading.* London: T. & T. Clark.

———. 2001. *Matthew and Empire: Initial Explorations.* Harrisburg, PA: Trinity.

Castelli, E. A. 1991. *Imitating Paul: A Discourse of Power.* Literary Currents in Biblical Interpretation. Louisville: Westminster/ John Knox.

———. 2007. *Martyrdom and Memory: Early Christian Culture Making.* Gender, Theory, and Religion. New York: Columbia University Press.

Chambers, S. L. 2004. "Paul, His Converts, and Mission in First Corinthians." PhD diss., University of St. Michael's College.

Chance, J. B. 1982. "Paul's Apology to the Corinthians." *Perspectives in Religious Studies* 9:144–55.

Chester, S. J. 2003. *Conversion at Corinth: Perspectives on Conversion in Paul's Theology and the Corinthian Church.* SNTW. London: T. & T. Clark.

Chevallier, M. -A. 1980. "La Construction de la communauté sur le fondement du Christ. 1 Cor 3:5–17." Pages 109–36 in *Paolo e una chiesa divisa (1 Co 1–4),* edited by E. Best, et al. Serie Monografica di 'Benedictina,' 5. Roma: Abbazia di S. Paolo Fuori le Mura.

Chow, J. K. 1992. *Patronage and Power: A Study of Social Networks in Corinth.* JSNTSup 75. Sheffield: JSOT Press.

———. 1997. "Patronage in Roman Corinth." In R. A. Horsley, editor. 1997:104–125.

Ciampa, R. E., and B. S. Rosner. 2006. "The Structure and Argument of 1 Corinthians: A Biblical/Jewish Approach." *NTS* 52:205–18.

———. 2007. "I Corinthians." Pages 695–752 in *Commentary on the New Testament Use of the Old Testament,* edited by G. K. Beale, and D. A. Carson. Grand Rapids: Baker. 2007.

Clarke, A. D. 1991. "Another Corinthian Erastus Inscription." *TynBul* 42:146–51.

———. 1993. *Secular and Christian Leadership in Corinth: A Socio-historical and Exegetical Study of 1 Corinthians 1–6.* Arbeiten zur Geschichte des antiken Judentums und des Urchristentums 18. Leiden: Brill.

———. 1998. "'Be Imitators of Me': Paul's Model of Leadership." *TynBul* 49:329–60.

———. 2000. *Serve the Community and the Church: Christians as Leaders and Ministers.* Grand Rapids: Eerdmans.

———. 2002. "Jew and Greek, Slave and Free, Male and Female: Paul's Theology of Ethnic, Social and Gender Inclusiveness in Romans 16." In P. Oakes, editor. 2002:103–25.

———. 2006. *Secular and Christian Leadership in Corinth*. Eugene, OR: Wipf and Stock Publishers.

———. 2008. *A Pauline Theology of Church Leadership*. LNTS 362. London: T. & T. Clark.

Code, L. 1995. *Rhetorical Spaces Essays on Gendered Locations*. New York: Routledge.

Cohen, A. P. 1974. *Two-dimensional Man: An Essay on the Anthropology of Power and Symbolism in Complex Society*. London: Routledge and Kegan Paul.

———. 1994. *Self Consciousness: An Alternative Anthropology of Identity*. London: Routledge.

———. 2000a. "Introduction: Discriminating Relations—Identity, Boundary, and Authenticity." Pages 1–13 in *Signifying Identities: Anthropological Perspectives on Boundaries and Contested Values*, edited by A. P. Cohen. London: Routledge.

———. 2000b. "Peripheral Vision: Nationalism, National Identity and the Objective Correlative in Scotland." Pages 145–69 in *Signifying Identities: Anthropological Perspectives on Boundaries and Contested Values*, edited by A. P. Cohen. London: Routledge.

Cohen, A. P., editor. 2000. *Signifying Identities: Anthropological Perspectives on Boundaries and Contested Values*. London: Routledge.

Cohen, S. J. D. 1999. *The Beginnings of Jewishness: Boundaries, Varieties, Uncertainties*. Hellenistic Culture and Society 31. Berkeley: University of California Press.

Cole, G. 2007. *He Who Gives Life*. Wheaton, IL: Crossway.

Colish, M. L. 1985. *The Stoic Tradition from Antiquity to the Early Middle Ages*. Studies in the History of Christian Thought 34. Leiden: Brill.

Collins, R. F. 1999. *First Corinthians*. Sacra Pagina 7. Collegeville, MN: Liturgical.

Conley, T. M. 1997. "Philo of Alexandria." Pages 695–713 in *Handbook of Classical Rhetoric in the Hellenistic Period, 330 B.C.–A.D. 400*, edited by S. E. Porter. Leiden: Brill.

Conzelmann, H. 1975. *1 Corinthians: A Commentary on the First Epistle to the Corinthians*. Hermeneia. Philadelphia: Fortress.

Cooley, C. H. 1902. *Human Nature and the Social Order*. New York: Scribner.

Cousar, C. B. 1990. *A Theology of the Cross: The Death of Jesus in the Pauline Letters*. Minneapolis: Fortress.

———. 1993. "The Theological Task of 1 Corinthians: A Conversation with Gordon D. Fee and Victor Paul Furnish." Pages 90–102 in *Pauline Theology: 1 & 2 Corinthians*, edited by D. M. Hay. Vol. 2 of *Pauline Theology*. Minneapolis: Fortress.

———. 1996. *The Letters of Paul*. Interpreting Biblical Texts. Nashville: Abingdon.

Coutsoumpos, P. 2006. *Community, Conflict, and the Eucharist in Roman Corinth: The Social Setting of Paul's Letter*. Lanham, MD: University Press of America.

———. 2008. "Paul, the Cults in Corinth, and the Corinthian Correspondence." Pages 171–80 in *Paul's World*, edited by S. E. Porter. Pauline Studies 4. Leiden: Brill.

Cranfield, C. E. B. 1982. "Changes of Person and Number in Paul's Epistles." Pages 280–89 in *Paul and Paulinism: Essays in Honour of C. K. Barrett*, edited by M. D. Hooker and S. G. Wilson. London: SPCK.

Crook, Z. A. 2008. "Grace as Benefaction in Galatians 2:9, 1 Corinthians 3:10, and Romans 12:3; 15:15." Pages 25–38 in *The Social Sciences and Biblical Translation*, edited by D. Neufeld. Atlanta: Society of Biblical Literature.

Cyss, C. C. 2004. *Reading 1 Corinthians in the Twenty-first Century*. New York: T. & T. Clark.

Dahl, N. A. 1967. "Paul and the Church at Corinth according to 1 Corinthians 1:10— 4:21." Pages 313–35 in *Christian History and Interpretation: Studies Presented to John Knox*, edited by W. R. Farmer, C. F. D. Moule, and R. R. Niebuhr. Cambridge: Cambridge University Press.

Damon, W. 2001. "To Not Fade Away: Restoring Civil Identity Among the Young." Pages 122–40 in *Making Good Citizens: Education and Civil Society*, edited by D. Ravitch, and J. P. Viteritti. New Haven, CT: Yale University Press.

Danker, F. W., W. Bauer, and W. Arndt. 2000. *A Greek-English Lexicon of the New Testament and Other Early Christian Literature*. 3rd ed. Chicago: University of Chicago Press.

Danylak, B. N. 2008. "Tiberius Claudius Dinippus and the Food Shortages in Corinth." *TynBul* 59:231–70.

Davies, W. D. 1978. "Paul and the People of Israel." *NTS* 24:4–39.

———. 1980. *Paul and Rabbinic Judaism*. Philadelphia: Fortress.

———. 1999. *Christian Engagements with Judaism*. Harrisburg: Trinity.

Davis, J. A. 1984. *Wisdom and Spirit: An Investigation of 1 Corinthians 1:18—3:20 against the Background of Jewish Sapiential Traditions in the Greco-Roman Period*. Lanham, MD: University Press of America.

De Fina, A., D. Schiffrin, and M. Bamberg, editors. 2006. *Discourse and Identity*. Studies in Interactional Sociolinguistics. Cambridge, UK: Cambridge University Press.

de Ste. Croix, G. E. M. 1981. *The Class Struggle in the Ancient Greek World: From the Archaic Age to the Arab Conquests*. Ithaca, NY: Cornell University Press.

De Vos, C. S. 1999. *Church and Community Conflicts: The Relationships of the Thessalonian, Corinthian, and Philippian Churches with Their Wider Civic Communities*. SBL Dissertation Series 168. Atlanta: Scholars.

Deaux, K. 1991. "Social Identities: Thoughts on Structure and Change." Pages 77–93 in *The Relational Self: Theoretical Convergences in Psychoanalysis and Social Psychology*, edited by R. C. Curtis. New York: Guilford.

Degrassi, A. 1965. *Inscriptiones Latinae liberae rei publicae, imagines*. Corpus inscriptionum Latinarum. Berlin: de Gruyter.

Deissmann, A. 1957. *Paul: A Study in Social and Religious History*. New York: Harper.

DeMaris, R. 2008. *The New Testament in Its Ritual World*. London: Routledge.

Deming, W. 1995. *Paul on Marriage and Celibacy: The Hellenistic Background of 1 Corinthians 7*. SNTS Monograph Series 83. Cambridge: Cambridge University Press.

Dench, E. 2005. *Romulus' Asylum: Roman Identities from the Age of Alexander to the Age of Hadrian*. Oxford: Oxford University Press.

DeNeui, M. 2008. "The Body, the Building and the Field: Paul's Metaphors for the Church in 1 Corinthians in Light of Their Usage in Greco-Roman Literature." PhD diss., University of Aberdeen.

deSilva, D. 1995. *Despising Shame: Honor Discourse and Community Maintenance in the Epistle to the Hebrews*. SBL Dissertation Series 152. Atlanta: Scholars Press.

———. 1999. *The Hope of Glory: Honor Discourse and New Testament Interpretation*. Collegeville, MN: Liturgical.

———. 2000. *Honor, Patronage, Kinship & Purity: Unlocking New Testament Culture*. Downers Grove, IL: InterVarsity.

———. 2002. *Introducing the Apocrypha Message, Context, and Significance*. Grand Rapids: Baker Academic.

Dickson, J. P. 2003. *Mission-commitment in Ancient Judaism and in the Pauline Communities: The Shape, Extent and Background of Early Christian Mission.* WUNT 159. Tübingen: Mohr Siebeck.

Didier, G. 1955. *Désintéressement du chrétien: La rétribution dans la morale de saint Paul.* Théologie 32. Paris: Aubier.

Doble, P. 2002. "'Vile Bodies' or Transformed Persons? Philippians 3:21 in Context." *JSNT* 86:3–27.

Dodd, B. 1999. *Paul's Paradigmatic 'I': Personal Example As Literary Strategy.* JSNTSup 177. Sheffield: Sheffield Academic.

Donahoe, K. C. 2008. "From Self-praise to Self-boasting: Paul's Unmasking of the Conflicting Rhetorico-linguistics Phenomena in 1 Corinthians." PhD diss., University of St. Andrews.

Dormeyer, D. 1998. *The New Testament Among the Writings of Antiquity.* Sheffield: Sheffield Academic.

Douglas, M. 1966. *Purity and Danger: An Analysis of Concepts of Pollution and Taboo.* London: Routledge.

———. 1973. *Natural Symbols: Explorations in Cosmology.* Harmondsworth: Pelican.

Downing, F. G. F. 1998. *Cynics, Paul, and the Pauline Churches.* Cynics and Christian Origins II. London: Routledge.

Duff, T. 1999. *Plutarch's Lives: Exploring Virtue and Vice.* Oxford: Clarendon.

Dugan, J. 2005. *Making a New Man: Ciceronian Self-fashioning in the Rhetorical Works.* New York: Oxford University Press.

Dunn, J. D. G. 1970. *Baptism in the Holy Spirit.* London: SCM.

———. 1990. *Jesus, Paul, and the Law: Studies in Mark and Galatians.* Louisville: Westminster John Knox.

———. 1991. *The Partings of the Ways: Between Christianity and Judaism and their Significance for the Character of Christianity.* London, SCM.

———. 1995. *1 Corinthians.* New Testament Guides. Sheffield: Sheffield Academic.

———. 1998. *The Theology of Paul the Apostle.* Grand Rapids: Eerdmans.

———. 1999. "Who Did Paul Think He Was? A Study of Jewish-Christian Identity." *NTS* 45:174–93.

———. 2006. "Towards the Spirit of Christ: The Emergence of the Distinctive Features of Christian Pneumatology." Pages 3–26 in *The Work of the Spirit: Pneumatology and Pentecostalism,* edited by M. Welker. Grand Rapids: Eerdmans.

Dutch, R. S. 2005. *The Educated Elite in 1 Corinthians: Education and Community Conflict in Graeco-Roman Context.* JSNTSup 271. London: T. & T. Clark.

Eagleton, T. 1991. *Ideology: An Introduction.* London: Verso.

Ebel, E. 2004. *Die Attraktivität früher christlicher Gemeinden: die Gemeinde von Korinth im Spiegel griechisch-römischer Vereine.* WUNT 2, 178. Tübingen: Mohr Siebeck.

Edwards, K. N. 1933. *The Coins, 1896–1929.* Corinth 6. Cambridge, MA. Harvard University Press.

Ehrensperger, K. 2004. *That We May Be Mutually Encouraged: Feminism and The New Perspective in Pauline Studies.* New York: T. & T. Clark.

———. 2007. *Paul and the Dynamics of Power.* LNTS 325. New York: T. & T. Clark.

———. 2008a. "Paul and the Authority of Scripture: A Feminist Perception." Pages 291–319 in *As It Is Written: Studying Paul's Use of Scripture,* edited by S. E. Porter, and C. D. Stanley. Society of Biblical Literature Symposium Series 50. Atlanta: SBL.

———. 2008b. "'. . . so that by steadfastness and by the encouragement of the scriptures we might have hope': What Does Paul Refer to When He Refers to 'the Scriptures'?" Paper presented at SBL Annual Meeting, Boston, MA.

———. 2010. "Paul: The First Personal Witness to Jesus." In *Methodological Approaches to the Historical Jesus,* edited by J. H. Charlesworth. The Second Princeton-Prague Symposium on Jesus. Grand Rapids: Eerdmans.

Ehrensperger, K., and J. B. Tucker, editors. 2010. *Reading Paul in Context: Explorations in Identity Formation.* London: T. & T. Clark.

Eisenbaum, P. 2004. "A Remedy for Having Been Born of Woman: Jesus, Gentiles, and Genealogy in Romans." *JBL* 123:671–702.

Elliott, J. H. 1993. *What is Social-scientific Criticism?* Guides to Biblical Scholarship. Minneapolis: Augsburg Fortress.

———. 1996. "Patronage and Clientage." Pages 144–56 in *The Social Sciences and New Testament Interpretation,* edited by R. L. Rohrbaugh. Peabody: Hendrickson.

Elliott, N. 1994. *Liberating Paul: The Justice of God and the Politics of the Apostle.* Maryknoll, NY: Orbis.

———. 2000. "Paul and the Politics of Interpretation." Pages 17–39 in *Paul and Politics: Ekklesia, Israel, Imperium, Interpretation; Essays in Honor of Krister Stendahl,* edited by R. A. Horsley. Harrisburg, PA: Trinity.

———. 2004a. "The Apostle Paul's Self-presentation as Anti-imperial Performance." Pages 67–88 in *Paul and the Roman Imperial Order,* edited by R. A. Horsley. Harrisburg, PA: Trinity.

———. 2004b. "Strategies of Resistance and Hidden Transcripts in the Pauline Communities." 97–122 in *Hidden Transcripts and the Arts of Resistance: Applying the Work of James C. Scott to Jesus and Paul,* edited by R. A. Horsley. Leiden: Brill.

———. 2008a. *The Arrogance of Nations: Reading Romans in the Shadow of Empire.* Paul in Critical Contexts. Minneapolis: Fortress.

———. 2008b. "The Apostle Paul and Empire." Pages 97–116 in *In the Shadow of Empire,* edited by R. A. Horsley. Louisville: Westminster John Knox.

Elsner, J. 2007. *Roman Eyes: Visuality and Subjectivity in Art and Text.* Princeton: Princeton University Press.

Engberg-Pedersen, T. 1987. "The Gospel and Social Practice according to 1 Corinthians." *NTS* 33:557–84.

———. 2000. *Paul and the Stoics.* Louisville: Westminster John Knox.

———. 2002. "Response to Martyn." *JSNT* 86:103–14.

Engberg-Pedersen, T., editor. 2001. *Paul Beyond the Judaism/Hellenism Divide.* Louisville: Westminster John Knox.

Engels, D. W. 1990. *Roman Corinth: An Alternative Model for the Classical City.* Chicago: University of Chicago.

Erikson, E. H. 1968. *Identity, Youth, and Crisis.* New York: Norton.

Esler, P. F. 1994. *The First Christians in Their Social Worlds: Social-scientific Approaches to New Testament Interpretation.* London: Routledge.

———. 1996. "Group Boundaries and Intergroup Conflict in Galatians: A New Reading of Gal. 5:13—6:10." Pages 215–40 in *Ethnicity and the Bible,* edited by M. G. Brett. Biblical Interpretation Series 19. Leiden: Brill.

———. 1998. *Galatians.* New Testament Readings. London: Routledge.

———. 2002. "Models in New Testament Interpretation: A Reply to David Horrell." *JSNT* 78:107–13.

———. 2003a. *Conflict and Identity in Romans: The Social Setting of Paul's Letter*. Minneapolis: Fortress.

———. 2003b. "Social Identity, the Virtues, and the Good Life: A New Approach to Romans 12:1—15:13." *BTB* 33:51–63.

———. 2004. "Paul and Stoicism: Romans 12 as a Test Case." *NTS* 50:106–24.

———. 2005. *New Testament Theology: Communion and Community*. Minneapolis: Fortress.

———. 2007a. "From *Ioudaioi* to Children of God: The Development of a Non-ethnic Group Identity in the Gospel of John." Pages 106–37 in *In Other Words: Essays on Social Science Methods and the New Testament in Honor of Jerome H. Neyrey*, edited by A. C. Hagedorn, Z. A. Crook, and E. Stewart. Social World of Biblical Antiquity 2/1. Sheffield: Sheffield Phoenix.

———. 2007b. Review of *Reconceptualising Conversion: Patronage, Loyalty, and Conversion in the Religions of the Ancient Mediterranean* by Zeba A. Crook. *BTB* 37:132–34.

Esler, P. F., and R. A. Piper. 2006. *Lazarus, Mary and Martha: Social-scientific Approaches to the Gospel of John*. Minneapolis: Augsburg Fortress.

Fairclough, N. 1992. *Discourse and Social Change*. Cambridge: Polity.

Farmer, W. R., C. F. D. Moule, and R. R. Niebuhr, editors. 1967. *Christian History and Interpretation: Studies Presented to John Knox*. Cambridge: Cambridge University Press.

Fay, R. 2008. "Greco-Roman Concepts of Deity." Pages 51–79 in *Paul's World*, edited by S. E. Porter. Pauline Studies 4. Leiden: Brill.

Fearon, J. D., and D. D. Laitin. 2000. "Review: Violence and the Social Construction of Ethnic Identity." *International Organization* 54:845–77.

Fears, J. R. 1981. "The Cult of Virtues and Roman Imperial Ideology." *ANRW* II. 17:827–947.

Fee, G. D. 1987. *The First Epistle to the Corinthians*. NICNT. Grand Rapids: Eerdmans.

Festinger, L. 1954. "A Theory of Social Comparison Processes." *Human Relations* 7:117–40.

Feuillet, A. 1966. *Le Christ, sagesse de Dieu: d'après les épîtres pauliniennes*. Etudes bibliques. Paris: Gabalda.

Finney, M. T. 2005. "Christ Crucified and the Inversion of Roman Imperial Ideology in 1 Corinthians." *BTB* 35:20–33.

———. 2006. "Conflict and Honour in the Ancient World: Some Thoughts on the Social Problems behind 1 Corinthians." *Proceedings of the Irish Biblical Association* 29:24–56.

Fiore, B. 1985. "'Covert Allusion' In 1 Corinthians 1–4." *CBQ* 47:85–102.

Fischer, D. H. 1970. *Historians' Fallacies: Toward a Logic of Historical Thought*. New York: Harper & Row.

Fiske, S. T., and S. E. Taylor. 1984. *Social Cognition*. Topics in Social Psychology. Reading, MA: Addison-Wesley.

Fitzgerald, J. T. 1988. *Cracks in an Earthen Vessel: An Examination of the Catalogues of Hardships in the Corinthian Correspondence*. SBLDS 99. Atlanta: Scholars.

Fitzmyer, J. A. 2008. *First Corinthians: A New Translation with Introduction and Commentary*. New Haven: Yale University Press.

Flanagan, J. W. 1999. "Ancient Perceptions of Space/Perceptions of Ancient Space." *Semeia* 87:26–30.

Foster, G. M. 1965. "Peasant Society and the Image of Limited Good." *American Anthropologist* 67:293–315.

Fotopoulos, J. 2003. *Food Offered to Idols in Roman Corinth: A Social-rhetorical Reconsideration of 1 Corinthians 8:1—11:1.* WUNT 151. Tübingen: Mohr Siebeck.

———. 2006. "The Misidentification of Lerna Fountain at Corinth: Implications for Interpretations of the Corinthian Idol-food Issue 1 Cor 8:1—11:1." Pages 37–50 in *The New Testament and Early Christian Literature in Greco-Roman Context: Studies in Honor of David E. Aune,* edited by J. Fotopoulos. NovTSup 122. Leiden: Brill.

Foucault, M. 1972. *The Archaeology of Knowledge.* Translated by A. M. Sheridan Smith. New York: Pantheon.

Fowler, C. 2004. *The Archaeology of Personhood: An Anthropological Approach.* London: Routledge.

Fowler, H. N., and R. Stillwell. 1932. *Introduction, Topography, Architecture.* Corinth 1. Princeton: ASCSA.

Francese, C. 2007. *Ancient Rome in So Many Words.* New York: Hippocrene.

Francis, J. 1980. "'As Babes in Christ': Some Proposals Regarding 1 Cor 3:1–3." *JSNT* 7:41–60.

Freedman, D. N., editor. 1992. *Anchor Bible Dictionary.* 6 vols. New York: Doubleday.

Freud, S. *Group Psychology and the Analysis of the Ego.* New York: Norton.

Frey, J. 2007. "Paul's Jewish Identity." Pages 285–321 in *Jewish Identity in the Greco-Roman World: Jüdische Identität in der griechisch-römischen Welt,* edited by J. Frey, D. R. Schwartz, and S. Gripentrog. Ancient Judaism and Early Christianity 71. Leiden: Brill.

Frey, J., D. R. Schwartz, and S. Gripentrog, editors. 2007. *Jewish Identity in the Greco-Roman World: Jüdische Identität in der griechisch-römischen Welt.* Ancient Judaism and Early Christianity 71. Leiden: Brill.

Frid, B. 1985. "The Enigmatic ἀλλά in 1 Cor 2:9." *NTS* 31:603–11.

Friesen, S. J. 2004. "Poverty in Pauline Studies." *JSNT* 26:323–61.

———. 2005. "Prospects for a Demography of the Pauline Mission: Corinth among the Churches." Pages 352–70 in *Urban Religion in Roman Corinth: Interdisciplinary Approaches,* edited by D. N. Schowalter and S. J. Friesen. Harvard Theological Studies 53. Cambridge: Harvard University Press.

Furnish, V. P. 1961. "Fellow Workers in God's Service." *JBL* 80:364–70.

Gager, J. G. 2000. *Reinventing Paul.* Oxford: Oxford University Press.

Galinsky, G. K. 1967. "The Cipus Episode in Ovid's Metamorphoses 15.565–621." *Transactions and Proceedings of the American Philological Association* 98:181–91.

Garland, D. E. 2003. *1 Corinthians.* BECNT. Grand Rapids: Baker Academic.

Garnsey, P., and R. P. Saller. 1987. *The Roman Empire: Economy, Society, and Culture.* Berkeley: University of California Press.

Garrett, S. R. 1992. "Sociology of Early Christianity." Pages 89–99 in vol. 6 *Anchor Bible Dictionary,* edited by D. N. Freedman. New York: Doubleday.

Gaventa, B. R. 2007. *Our Mother Saint Paul.* Louisville: Westminster John Knox.

Gebhard, E. H. 1994. "The Isthmian Games and the Sanctuary of Poseidon in the Early Empire." Pages 78–94 in *The Corinthia in the Roman Period,* edited by T. E. Gregory. Journal of Roman Archaeology Supplementary Series 8. Ann Arbor, MI: Journal of Roman Archaeology.

Gebhard, E. R., and M. W. Dickie. 2003. "The View from the Isthmus, ca. 200 to 44 B.C." 261–78 in *Corinth, the Centenary, 1896–1996*, edited by C. K. Williams II, and N. Bookidis. Corinth 20. Princeton: ASCSA.

Geertz, C. C. 1973. *The Interpretation of Cultures: Selected Essays*. New York: Basic.

Gehring, R. W. 2004. *House Church and Mission: The Importance of Household Structures in Early Christianity*. Peabody, MA: Hendrickson.

Geiger, J. 2002. "Language, Culture and Identity in Ancient Palestine." Pages 233–46 in *Greek Romans and Roman Greeks: Studies in Cultural Interaction*, edited by E. N. Ostenfeld, K. Blomqvist, and L. C. Nevett. Aarhus Studies in Mediterranean Antiquity 3. Aarhus: Aarhus University Press.

Gentner, D., and B. Bowdle. 2003. "Metaphor processing, psychology of." Pages 19–21 in *Encyclopedia of Cognitive Science*, edited by L. Nadel. London: Nature.

Gentner, D., et al. 2001. "Metaphor is like Analogy." Pages 199–253 in *The Analogical Mind: Perspectives from Cognitive Science*, edited by D. Gentner, K. J. Holyoak, and B. N. Kokinov. Cambridge: MIT Press.

Georgi, D. 1992. *Remembering the Poor: The History of Paul's Collection for Jerusalem*. Nashville: Abingdon.

Giddens, A. 1984. *The Constitution of Society: Outline of the Theory of Structuration*. Cambridge: Polity.

———. 1991. *Modernity and Self-identity in the Late Modern Age*. Stanford, CA: Stanford University Press.

Gilbert, G. 2004. "Roman Propaganda and Christian Identity in the Worldview of Luke-Acts." Pages 233–56 in *Contextualizing Acts: Lukan Narrative and Greco-Roman Discourse*, edited by T. Penner, and C. Vander Stichele. SBL Symposium Series 20. Leiden: Brill.

Gilead, I. 1995. "The Foragers of the Upper Paleolithic Period." Pages 124–40 in *The Archaeology of Society in the Holy Land*, edited by T. E. Levy. London: Leicester University Press.

Gill, D. W. J. 1989. "Erastus the Aedile." *TynBul* 40:293–300.

———. 1993a. "In Search of the Social Élite in the Corinthian Church." *TynBul* 44:323–37

———. 1993b. "Corinth: A Roman Colony of Achaea." *BZ* 37:259–64

Given, M. D. 2001. *Paul's True Rhetoric Ambiguity, Cunning, and Deception in Greece and Rome*. Emory Studies in Early Christianity 7. Harrisburg, PA: Trinity.

Gladd, B. 2008. *Revealing the* Mysterion: *The Use of* Mystery *in Daniel and Second Temple Judaism with its Bearing on First Corinthians*. Beihefte zur Zeitschrift für die neutestamentliche Wissenschaft 160. Berlin: de Gruyter.

Gleason, M. 1995. *Making Men: Sophists and Self-presentation in Ancient Rome*. Princeton: Princeton University Press.

Glucksberg, S., and B. Keysar. 1990. "Understanding Metaphorical Comparisons: Beyond Similarity." *Psychological Review* 97:3–18.

Godet, F. L. 1898. *Commentary on the First Epistle of St. Paul to the Corinthians*. Vol 1. Translated by A. Cusin. Edinburgh: T. & T. Clark.

Goffman, E. 1959. *The Presentation of Self in Everyday Life*. Garden City, NY: Doubleday.

Gold, B. K. 1987. *Literary Patronage in Greece and Rome*. Chapel Hill: University of North Carolina Press.

Gooch, P. D. 1987. "'Conscience' In 1 Corinthians 8 and 10." *NTS* 33:244–54.

———. 1993. *Dangerous Food: I Corinthians 8–10 in Its Context*. Waterloo, ON: Published for the Canadian Corp. for Studies in Religion by Wilfrid Laurier University Press.

Goodman, M. 2007. *Judaism in the Roman World: Collected Essays*. Ancient Judaism and Early Christianity 66. Leiden: Brill.

Goulder, M. D. 1991. "Σοφία in 1 Corinthians." *NTS* 37:516–34.

———. 2001. *Paul and the Competing Mission in Corinth*. Library of Pauline Studies. Peabody, MA: Hendrickson.

Gouldner, A. W. 1957. "Cosmopolitans and Locals: Toward an Analysis of Latent Social Roles. Part I." *Administrative Science Quarterly* 2:281–306.

Gräbe, P. J. 2000. *The Power of God in Paul's Letters*. WUNT 2, 123. Tübingen: Mohr.

Grahame, M. 1998. "Material Culture and Roman Identity." Pages 156–78 in *Cultural Identity in the Roman Empire*, edited by R. Laurence and J. Berry. London: Routledge.

Gregory, T. E., editor. 1994. *The Corinthia in the Roman Period*. Journal of Roman Archaeology Supplementary Series 8. Ann Arbor, MI: Journal of Roman Archaeology.

Grindheim, S. 2002. "Wisdom for the Perfect: Paul's Challenge to the Corinthian Church 1 Corinthians 2:6–16." *JBL* 121:689–709.

Gruen, E. S. 2002. *Diaspora Jews amidst Greeks and Romans*. Cambridge: Harvard University Press.

Gruenwald, I. 2008. "Paul and the Nomos in Light of Ritual Theory." *NTS* 54:398–416.

Guijarro, S. 2007. "Cultural Memory and Group Identity in Q." *BTB* 37:90–100.

Gumperz, J. J., and J. Cook-Gumperz. 1982. "Introduction: Language and the Communication of Social Identity." Pages 1–21 in *Language and Social Identity*, edited by J. J. Gumperz. Studies in Interactional Sociolinguistics 2. Cambridge: Cambridge University Press.

Habermas, J. 1987. *Lifeworld and System: A Critique of Functionalist Reason*. Vol. 2 of *The Theory of Communicative Action*. Boston: Beacon.

Hafemann, S. 1986. *Suffering and the Spirit: An Exegetical Study of II Cor 2:14—3:3 Within the Context of the Corinthian Correspondence*. WUNT 2, 19. Tübingen: Mohr Siebeck.

———. 2000. "The Role of Suffering in the Mission of Paul." Pages 165–84 in *The Mission of the Early Church to Jews and Gentiles*, edited by J. Ådna, and H. Kvalbein. WUNT 127. Tübingen: Mohr Siebeck.

Hagedorn, A. C., Z. A. Crook, and E. Stewart, editors. 2007. *In Other Words: Essays on Social Science Methods and the New Testament in Honor of Jerome H. Neyrey*. Social Word of Biblical Antiquity 2/1. Sheffield: Sheffield Phoenix.

Halbwachs, M. 1992. *On Collective Memory*. Translated by L. A. Coser. The Heritage of Sociology. Chicago: University of Chicago Press.

Hales, S. 2003. *The Roman House and Social Identity*. Cambridge: Cambridge University Press.

Hall, D. R. 2003. *The Unity of the Corinthian Correspondence*. JSNTSup 251. London: T. & T. Clark.

Hall, J. M. 1997. *Ethnic Identity in Greek Antiquity*. Cambridge: Cambridge University Press.

Hall, S. 1996. "Introduction: Who Needs 'Identity'?" Pages 1–17 in *Questions of Cultural Identity*, edited by S. Hall, and P. Du Gay. London: Sage.

———. 2000. "Conclusion: the Multi-cultural Question." Pages 209–41 in *Un/Settled Multiculturalisms: Diasporas, Entanglements, 'Transruptions,'* edited by B. Hesse. London: Zed.

Hanges, J. C. 1998. "1 Corinthians 4:6 and the Possibility of Written Bylaws in the Corinthian Church." *JBL* 117:275–98.

Hansen, B. 2007. "'All of You are One': The Social Vision of Gal 3:28, 1 Cor 12:13 and Col 3:11." PhD diss., University of St. Andrews.

Hanson, K. C. 1996. "Kinship." Pages 62–79 in *The Social Sciences and New Testament Interpretation*, edited by R. L. Rohrbaugh. Peabody, MA: Hendrickson.

Hanson, K. C., and D. E. Oakman. 1998. *Palestine in the Time of Jesus: Social Structures and Social Conflicts*. Minneapolis: Fortress.

Hanson, P. D. 1975. *The Dawn of Apocalyptic: The Historical and Sociological Roots of Jewish Apocalyptic Eschatology*. Philadelphia: Fortress.

Hardin, J. 2008. *Galatians and the Imperial Cult An Analysis of the First-century Social Context of Paul's Letter*. WUNT II, 237. Tübingen: Mohr Siebeck.

Hardwick, L. 2000. "Essay Twelve: Concepts of Peace." Pages 335–68 in *Experiencing Rome: Culture, Identity and Power in the Roman Empire*, edited by J. Huskinson. London: Routledge 2000.

Harink, D. 2005. "Paul and Israel: An Apocalyptic Reading." Paper presented at SBL Annual Meeting, Philadelphia, PA.

Harland, P. A. 2005. "Familial Dimensions of Group Identity: 'Brothers' (ΑΔΕΛΦΟΙ) in Associations of the Greek East." *JBL* 124:491–513.

———. 2009. *Dynamics of Identity in the World of the Early Christians*. New York: T. & T. Clark.

Harré, R. 1980. *Social Being: A Theory for Social Psychology*. Totowa, NJ: Rowman and Littlefield.

Harré, R., and L. Van Langenhove. 1998a. "The Dynamics of Social Episodes." Pages 1–13 in *Positioning Theory: Moral Contexts of International Action*, edited by R. Harré, and L. Van Langenhove. Oxford: Blackwell.

———. 1998b. "Reflexive Positioning: Autobiography." Pages 60–73 in *Positioning Theory: Moral Contexts of International Action*, edited by R. Harré, and L. Van Langenhove. Oxford: Blackwell.

Harré, R., and L. Van Langenhove, editors. 1998. *Positioning Theory: Moral Contexts of International Action*. Oxford: Blackwell.

Harrison, J. R. 2003. *Paul's Language of Grace in Its Graeco-Roman Context*. WUNT 172. Tübingen: Mohr Siebeck.

Harvey, J. D. 1998. *Listening to the Text: Oral Patterning in Paul's Letters*. ETS Studies 1. Grand Rapids: Baker.

Hays, R. B. 1997. *First Corinthians*. Interpretation. Louisville: John Knox.

———. 1999. "Wisdom according to Paul." Pages 111–23 in *Where Shall Wisdom Be Found?*, edited by S. C. Barton. Edinburgh: T. & T. Clark.

———. 2005. *The Conversion of the Imagination: Paul as Interpreter of Israel's Scripture*. Grand Rapids: Eerdmans.

Heater, D. B. 2004. *Citizenship: The Civic Ideal in World History, Politics, and Education*. 3rd ed. Manchester: Manchester University Press.

Heil, J. P. 2005. *The Rhetorical Role of Scripture in 1 Corinthians*. SBL Studies in Biblical Literature. Atlanta: Society of Biblical Literature.

Hellerman, J. H. 2005. *Reconstructing Honor in Roman Philippi: Carmen Christi as Cursus Pudorum.* SNTSMS 132. New York: Cambridge University Press.

Hengel, M. 1977. *Crucifixion in the Ancient World and the Folly of the Message of the Cross.* Philadelphia: Fortress.

Henriques, J. 1998. "Social Psychology and the Politics of Racism." Pages 60–89 in *Changing the Subject: Psychology, Social Regulation, and Subjectivity,* edited by J. Henriques, et al. London: Routledge.

Héring, J. 1949. *La Première Epître de Saint Paul aux Corinthiens.* Commentaire du Nouveau Testament 7. Neuchatel: Delachaux & Niestlé.

Hill, B. H. 1964. *The Springs: Peirene, Sacred Spring, Glauke.* Corinth 1.6. Princeton: ASCSA.

Hock, R. F. 1978. "Paul's Tentmaking and the Problem of His Social Class." *JBL* 97:555–64.

———. 1980. *The Social Context of Paul's Ministry: Tentmaking and Apostleship.* Philadelphia: Fortress.

———. 2003. "Paul and Greco-Roman Education." Pages 198–227 in *Paul in the Greco-Roman World: A Handbook,* edited by J. P. Sampley. Harrisburg, PA: Trinity.

Hogeterp, A. L. A. 2006. *Paul and God's Temple: A Historical Interpretation of Cultic Imagery in the Corinthian Correspondence.* Biblical Tools and Studies 2. Leuven: Peeters.

Hogg, M. A. 2004. "Social Categorization, Depersonalization, and Group Behavior." Pages 203–231 in *Self and Social Identity,* edited by M. Hewstone, and M. B. Brewer. Oxford: Blackwell.

———. 2006. "Social Identity Theory." Pages 111–36 in *Contemporary Social Psychological Theories,* edited by P. J. Burke. Stanford: Stanford University Press.

Hogg, M. A., and D. Abrams. 1988. *Social Identifications: A Social Psychology of Intergroup Relations and Group Processes.* London: Routledge.

———. 2003. "Intergroup Behavior and Social Identity." Pages 407–31 in *The SAGE Handbook of Social Psychology,* edited by M. A. Hogg, and J. Cooper. London: Sage.

Hogg, M. A., D. J. Terry, and K. M. White. 1995. "A Tale of Two Theories: A Critical Comparison of Identity Theory with Social Identity Theory." *Social Psychology Quarterly* 58:255–69.

Holland, G. S. 1999. "The Self Against the Self in Romans 7:7–25." Pages 260–71 in *The Rhetorical Interpretation of Scripture: Essays from the 1996 Malibu Conference,* edited by D. L. Stamps, and S. E. Porter. JSNTSup 180. Sheffield: Sheffield Academic.

Hollander, H. W. 1998. "The Meaning of the Term 'Law' νόμος in 1 Corinthians." *NovT* 40:117–35.

Holmberg, B. 1980. *Paul and Power: The Structure of Authority in the Primitive Church as Reflected in the Pauline Epistles.* Philadelphia: Fortress.

———. 1990. *Sociology and the New Testament: An Appraisal.* Minneapolis: Fortress.

———. 1998. "Jewish *Versus* Christian Identity in the Early Church." *RB* 105:397–425.

———. 2004. "The Methods of Historical Reconstruction in the Scholarly 'Recovery' of Corinthian Christianity." Pages 255–71 in *Christianity at Corinth: The Quest for the Pauline Church,* edited by E. Adams and D. G. Horrell. Louisville: Westminster John Knox.

———. 2008a. "Early Christian Identity—Some Conclusions." Pages 173–78 in *Exploring Early Christian Identity,* edited by B. Holmberg. WUNT 226. Tübingen: Mohr Siebeck.

————. 2008b. "Understanding the First Hundred Years of Christian Identity." Pages 1–32 in *Exploring Early Christian Identity*, edited by B. Holmberg. WUNT 226. Tübingen: Mohr Siebeck.

Holmberg, B., editor. 2008. *Exploring Early Christian Identity*. WUNT 226. Tübingen: Mohr Siebeck.

Holmberg, B., and M. Winninge, editors. 2008. *Identity Formation in the New Testament*. WUNT 227. Tübingen: Mohr Siebeck.

Hooker, M. D., and S. G. Wilson, editors. 1982. *Paul and Paulinism: Essays in Honour of C. K. Barrett*. London: SPCK.

Hope, V. M. 1998. "Negotiating Identity and Status: The Gladiators of Roman Nîmes." Pages 179–95 in *Cultural Identity in the Roman Empire*, edited by R. Laurence and J. Berry. London: Routledge.

Horrell, D. G. 1993. "Converging Ideologies: Berger and Luckmann and the Pastoral Epistles." *JSNT* 50:85–103.

————. 1996. *The Social Ethos of the Corinthians Correspondence: Interests and Ideology from 1 Corinthians to 1 Clement*. SNTW. Edinburgh: T. & T. Clark.

————. 1999. "Social Scientific Interpretation of the New Testament: Retrospect and Prospect." Pages 3–27 in *Social-scientific Approaches to New Testament Interpretation*, edited by D. G. Horrell. Edinburgh: T. & T. Clark.

————. 2000a. "'No Longer Jew or Greek': Paul's Corporate Christology and the Construction of Christian Community." Pages 321–44 in *Christology, Controversy, and Community: New Testament Essays in Honour of David R. Catchpole*, edited by D. G. Horrell, and C. M. Tuckett. NovTSup 99. Leiden, Brill.

————. 2000b. "Models and Methods in Social-scientific Interpretation: A Response to Philip Esler." *JSNT* 78:83–105.

————. 2001. "Berger and New Testament Studies." Pages 142–53 in *Peter Berger and the Study of Religion*, edited by L. Woodhead, P. Heelas, and D. Martin. London: Routledge.

————. 2002a. "'Becoming Christian': Solidifying Christian Identity and Content." Pages 309–335 in *Handbook of Early Christianity: Social Science Approaches*, edited by A. J. Blasi, P. A. Turcotte, and J. Duhaime. Walnut Creek, CA: AltaMira.

————. 2002b. "Paul." Pages 258–83 in *The Biblical World*, edited by J. Barton. London, Routledge.

————. 2002c. "Social Sciences Studying Formative Christian Phenomena: A Creative Movement." Pages 3–28 in *Handbook of Early Christianity: Social Science Approaches*, edited by A. J. Blasi, P. A. Turcotte, and J. Duhaime. Walnut Creek, CA: AltaMira.

————. 2002d. "Paul's Narratives or Narrative Substructure? The Significance of 'Paul's Story.'" Pages 157–71 in *Narrative Dynamics in Paul: A Critical Assessment*, edited by B. W. Longenecker. Louisville: Westminster John Knox.

————. 2004. "Domestic Space and Christian Meetings at Corinth: Imagining New Contexts and the Buildings East of the Theatre." *NTS* 50:349–69.

————. 2005. *Solidarity and Difference: A Contemporary Reading of Paul's Ethics*. London: T. & T. Clark.

————. 2006. *An Introduction to the Study of St Paul*. 2nd ed. New York: Continuum.

————. 2007. "The Label Χριστιανός: 1 Peter 4:16 and the Formation of Christian Identity." *JBL* 126:361–81.

————. 2008. "Pauline Churches or Early Christian Churches? Unity, Disagreement, and the Eucharist." Pages 185–203 in *Einheit der Kirche im Neuen Testament*, edited by A. Alexeev et. al. WUNT 218. Tübingen: Mohr Siebeck.

————. 2009. "Whither Social-Scientific Approaches to New Testament Interpretation? Reflections on Contested Methodologies and the Future." Pages 6–20 in *After the First Urban Christians*, edited by T. Still and D. Horrell. New York: T. & T. Clark.

Horsley, R. A. 1997. "1 Corinthians: A Case Study of Paul's Assembly as an Alternative Society." Pages 242–52 in *Paul and Empire: Religion and Power in Roman Imperial Society* edited by R. A. Horsley. Harrisburg, PA: Trinity.

————. 1998. *1 Corinthians*. ANTC. Nashville: Abingdon.

————. 2000. "Rhetoric and Empire—and 1 Corinthians." Pages 72–102 in *Paul and Politics: Ekklesia, Israel, Imperium, Interpretation; Essays in Honor of Krister Stendahl*, edited by R. A. Horsely. Harrisburg, PA: Trinity.

————. 2004. "Introduction." Pages 1–23 in *Paul and the Roman Imperial Order*, edited by R. A. Horsley. Harrisburg, PA: Trinity.

————. 2007. *Scribes, Visionaries, and the Politics of Second Temple Judea*. Louisville: Westminster John Knox.

————. 2008. *Wisdom and Spiritual Transcendence at Corinth: Studies in First Corinthians*. Eugene, OR: Cascade.

Horsley, R. A., editor. 1997. *Paul and Empire: Religion and Power in Roman Imperial Society*. Harrisburg, PA: Trinity.

————. 2000. *Paul and Politics: Ekklesia, Israel, Imperium, Interpretation; Essays in Honor of Krister Stendahl*. Harrisburg, PA: Trinity.

————. 2004a. *Paul and the Roman Imperial Order*. Harrisburg, PA: Trinity.

————. 2004b. *Hidden Transcripts and the Arts of Resistance: Applying the Work of James C. Scott to Jesus and Paul*. Semeia Studies 48. Leiden: Brill.

————. 2005. *Christian Origins: A People's History of Christianity*. Vol. 1. Minneapolis: Fortress.

Huang, W. Y. 2003. "Ancient Elitism and 1 Corinthians 1–7." PhD diss., University of Sheffield.

Hunt, A. R. 1996. *The Inspired Body: Paul, the Corinthians, and Divine Inspiration*. Macon, GA: Mercer University Press.

Hurd, J. C. 1983. *The Origin of 1 Corinthians*. Macon, GA: Mercer.

Huskinson, J. 2000. "Essay One: Looking for Culture, Identity and Power." Pages 3–27 in *Experiencing Rome: Culture, Identity and Power in the Roman Empire*, edited by J. Huskinson. London: Routledge.

Huskinson, J., editor. 2000. *Experiencing Rome: Culture, Identity and Power in the Roman Empire*. London: Routledge.

Hvalvik, R. 2005. "'All Those Who in Every Place Call on the Name of Our Lord Jesus Christ': The Unity of the Pauline Churches." Pages 123–43 in *The Formation of the Early Church*. WUNT 183, edited by J. Ådna. Tübingen: Mohr Siebeck.

Ivarsson, F. 2008. "A Man Has to Do What a Man Has to Do: Protocols of Masculine Sexual Behaviour and 1 Corinthians 5–7." Pages 183–98 in *Identity Formation in the New Testament*, edited by B. Holmberg and M. Winninge. WUNT 227. Tübingen: Mohr Siebeck.

James, W. 1890. *The Principles of Psychology*. New York: Holt.

Jaquette, J. 1995. *Discerning What Counts: The Function of the Adiaphora Topos in Paul's Letters*. SBLDS 146. Atlanta: Scholars.

Jenkins, R. 1996. *Social Identity*. Key Ideas. London: Routledge.

———. 2000. "Categorization: Identity, Social Process and Epistemology." *Current Sociology* 48:7–25.

Jewett, R. 1971. *Paul's Anthropological Terms: A Study of Their Use in Conflict Settings.* AGJU 10. Leiden: Brill.

———. 1978. "The Redaction of 1 Corinthians and the Trajectory of the Pauline School." *Journal of the American Academy of Religion Supplements* 46:389–444.

———. 1993. "Tenement Churches and Communal Meals in the Early Church: The Implications of a Form-critical Analysis of 2 Thess 3:10." *Biblical Research: Journal of the Chicago Society of Biblical Research* 38:23–43.

———. 2003. "Paul, Shame, and Honor." Pages 551–74 in *Paul in the Greco-Roman World: A Handbook*, edited by J. P. Sampley. Harrisburg, PA: Trinity.

———. 2007. *Romans: A Commentary*. Hermeneia. Minneapolis: Fortress.

Johnson Hodge, C. E. 2007. "*If Sons, Then Heirs*": A Study of Kinship and Ethnicity in the Letters of Paul. Oxford: Oxford University Press.

Jones, F. L. 1935. "Martial, the Client." *Classical Journal* 30:355–61.

Jongkind, D. 2001. "Corinth in the First Century A.D.: The Search for Another Class." *TynBul* 52:139–48.

Jossa, G. 2006. *Jews or Christians? The Followers of Jesus in Search of Their Own Identity.* WUNT 202. Tübingen: Mohr Siebeck.

Jost, J. T., and A. W. Kruglanski. 2002. "The Estrangement of Social Constructionism and Experimental Social Psychology: History of the Rift and Prospects for Reconciliation." *Personality and Social Psychology Review* 6:168–87.

Joubert, S. J. 1995. "Managing the Household: Paul as *Paterfamilias* of the Christian Household Group in Corinth." Pages 213–23 in *Modelling Early Christianity: Social-scientific Studies of the New Testament in Its Context,* edited by P. F. Esler. London: Routledge.

———. 2000. *Paul as Benefactor: Reciprocity, Strategy and Theological Reflection in Paul's Collection.* WUNT124. Tübingen: Mohr Siebeck.

———. 2001. "One Form of Social Exchange or Two? 'Euergetism,' Patronage, and Testament Studies." *BTB* 31:17–25.

Judge, E. A. 1960. *The Social Pattern of the Christian Groups in the First Century.* London: Tyndale.

———. 1980. "The Social Identity of the First Christians: A Question of Method in Religious History." *Journal of Religious History* 11:201–17.

———. 2008. "Cultural Conformity and Innovation in Paul: Some Clues from Contemporary Documents." Pages 157–74 in *Social Distinctives of the Christians in the First Century: Pivotal Essays by E. A. Judge,* edited by D. M. Scholer. Peabody: Hendrickson.

Kamler, B., and P. Thomson. 2006. *Helping Doctoral Students Write: Pedagogies for Supervision.* London: Routledge.

Käsemann, E. 1942. "Die Legitimität des Apostels." *ZNW* 41:33–71.

———. 1960. *Exegetische Versuche und Besinnungen.* Göttingen: Vandenhoeck & Ruprecht.

———. 1969. *New Testament Questions of Today.* Translated by W. J. Montague. Philadelphia: Fortress.

———. 1971. *Perspectives on Paul.* Translated by Margaret Kohl. London: SCM.

Kazen, T. 2008. "Son of Man and Early Christian Identity Formation." Pages 97–122 in *Identity Formation in the New Testament*, edited by B. Holmberg and M. Winninge. WUNT 227. Tübingen: Mohr Siebeck.

Kee, H. C. 1989. *Knowing the Truth: A Sociological Approach to New Testament Interpretation*. Minneapolis: Fortress.

Keener, C. S. 2005. *1–2 Corinthians*. New Cambridge Bible Commentary. Cambridge: Cambridge University Press.

Kent, J. H. 1966. *The Inscriptions, 1926–1950*. Corinth 8.3. Princeton: ASCSA.

Ker, D. P. 2000. "Paul and Apollos—Colleagues or Rivals?" *JSNT* 77:75–97.

Kiecolt, K. J. 1994. "Stress and the Decision to Change Oneself: A Theoretical Model." *Social Psychology Quarterly* 57:49–63.

Kim, C.-H. 2004. *The Significance of Clothing Imagery in the Pauline Corpus*. JSNTSup 268. London: T. & T. Clark.

Kim, S. 2008. *Christ and Caesar: The Gospel and the Roman Empire in the Writings of Paul and Luke*. Grand Rapids: Eerdmans.

Kim, Y. S. 2008. *Christ's Body in Corinth: The Politics of a Metaphor*. Minneapolis: Fortress.

Kirk, A. K. 2005. "Social and Cultural Memory." Pages 1–24 in *Memory, Tradition, and Text: Uses of the Past in Early Christianity*, edited by A. K. Kirk and T. Thatcher. Semeia Studies 52. Atlanta: Society of Biblical Literature.

Kitchin, R., and S. Freundschuh. 2000. *Cognitive Mapping: Past, Present, and Future*. Routledge Frontiers of Cognitive Science 4. London: Routledge.

Klauck, H.-J. 2006. *Ancient Letters and the New Testament: A Guide to Context and Exegesis*. Waco, TX: Baylor University Press.

Kloppenborg, J. S., and S. G. Wilson, editors. 1996. *Voluntary Associations in the Graeco-Roman World*. London: Routledge.

Knauer, G. N. 1964. "Vergil's *Aeneid* and Homer." *GRBS* 5:61–84.

Koenig, J. 2001. "Favorinus' 'Corinthian Oration' in its Corinthian context." *PCPS* 47:141–71.

Koester, C. R. 1990. "'The Savior of the World': John 4:42." *JBL* 109:665–80.

Koester, H. 1992. "Jesus the Victim." *JBL* 111:3–15.

———. 1998. "The Memory of Jesus' Death and the Worship of the Risen Lord." *HTR* 91:335–50.

König, J., and T. Whitmarsh. 2007. "Ordering Knowledge." Pages 3–39 in *Ordering Knowledge in the Roman Empire*, edited by J. König and T. Whitmarsh. Cambridge: Cambridge University Press.

Konradt, M. 2003. "Die korinthische Weisheit und das Wort vom Kreuz: Erwägungen zur korinthischen Problemkonstellation und paulinischen Intention in 1 Kor 1–4." *ZNW* 94:181–214.

Konstan, D. 1995. "Patrons and Friends." *Classical Philology* 90:328–42.

Kovacs, J. L. 1989. "The Archons, the Spirit, and the Death of Christ: Do We Need the Hypothesis of Gnostic Opponents to Explain 1 Corinthians 2:6–16?" Pages 217–36 in *Apocalyptic and the New Testament: Essays in Honor of J. Louis Martyn*, edited by J. Marcus and M. Soards. JSNTSup 24. Sheffield: Sheffield Academic.

Kreitzer, L. J. 2005. "The Messianic Man of Peace as Temple Builder: Solomonic Imagery in Ephesians 2:13–22." Pages 484–512 in *Temple and Worship in Biblical Israel*, edited by J. Day. Library of Hebrew Bible/Old Testament Studies 422. London: T. & T. Clark.

Kuck, D. W. 1992. *Judgment and Community Conflict: Paul's Use of Apocalyptic Judgment Language in 1 Corinthians 3:5—4:5*. NovTSup, 66. Leiden: Brill.

Kyle, D. G. 1998. *Spectacles of Death in Ancient Rome*. London: Routledge.

Lackoff, G., and M. Johnson. 1980. *Metaphors We Live By*. Chicago: University of Chicago Press.

Lamp, J. S. 2000. *First Corinthians 1—4 in Light of Jewish Wisdom Traditions: Christ, Wisdom and Spirituality*. Lewiston, NY: Mellen.

Lampe, P. 2003. "Paul, Patrons, and Clients." Pages 488–523 in *Paul in the Greco-Roman World: A Handbook*, edited by J. P. Sampley. Harrisburg, PA: Trinity.

Lanci, J. R. 1992. "Roman Eschatology in First-century Corinth." Paper presented at SBL Annual Meeting, San Francisco, CA.

———. 1997. *A New Temple for Corinth: Rhetorical and Archaeological Approaches to Pauline Imagery*. Studies in Biblical Literature 1. New York: Lang.

Lang, M. L. 1977. *Cure and Cult in Ancient Corinth: A Guide to the Asklepieion*. Princeton: ASCSA.

Lassen, E. M. 1991. "The Use of the Father Image in Imperial Propaganda and 1 Cor 4:14–21." *TynBul* 42:127–36.

Laurence, R., and J. Berry, editors. 1998. *Cultural Identity in the Roman Empire*. London: Routledge.

Lawler, S. 2008. *Identity: Sociological Perspectives*. London: Polity.

Lawrence, L. J. 2005. *Reading with Anthropology: Exhibiting Aspects of New Testament Religion*. Milton Keynes, UK: Paternoster.

Leander, H. 2008. "Parousia as Medicine: A Postcolonial Perspective on Mark and Christian Identity Construction." Pages 223–45 in *Identity Formation in the New Testament*, edited by B. Holmberg and M. Winninge. WUNT 227. Tübingen: Mohr Siebeck.

Legault, A. 1972. "'Beyond the Things Which are Written' (1 Cor 4:6)." *NTS* 18:227–31.

Lémonon, J. -P. 2001. "Le discernement dans les lettres pauliniennes." *Lumière et Vie* 252:23–31.

Lesher, J. H. 1992. *Xenophanes of Colophon: Fragments; A Text and Translation with a Commentary*. Toronto: University of Toronto Press.

Levine, A. J. 1991. "Tobit: Teaching Jews How to Live in the Diaspora." *Bible Review* 8:42–51, 64.

Lieu, J. 2002a. "'Impregnable Ramparts and Walls of Iron': Boundary and Identity in 'Judaism' and 'Christianity.'" *NTS* 48:297–313.

———. 2002b. *Neither Jew nor Greek?: Constructing Early Christianity*. SNTW. Edinburgh: T. & T. Clark.

———. 2004. *Christian Identity in the Jewish and Graeco-Roman World*. Oxford, Oxford University Press.

Lim, K. -Y. 2007. "'The Sufferings of Christ are Abundant in Us' (2 Corinthians 1:5): A Narrative Dynamics Investigation of Paul's Sufferings in 2 Corinthians." PhD diss., University of Wales, Lampeter.

Litfin, A. D. 1994. *St. Paul's Theology of Proclamation 1 Corinthians 1–4 and Greco-Roman Rhetoric*. Cambridge: Cambridge University Press.

Longenecker, B. W. 2002. "Narrative Interest in the Study of Paul: Retrospective and Prospective." Pages 3–16 in *Narrative Dynamics in Paul: A Critical Assessment*, edited by B. W. Longenecker. Louisville: Westminster John Knox.

———. 2009. "Exposing the Economic Middle: A Revised Economy Scale for the Study of Early Urban Christianity." *JSNT* 31:243–78.

Longenecker, R. N. 1982. "The Pedagogical Nature of the Law in Galatians 3:19—4:7." *JETS* 25:53–61.

Lopez, D. C. 2008. *Apostle to the Conquered: Reimaging Paul's Mission*. Minneapolis: Fortress.

Luomanen, P. 2007. "The Sociology of Knowledge, the Social Identity Approach and the Cognitive Science of Religion." Pages 199–229 in *Explaining Christian Origins and Early Judaism: Contributions from Cognitive and Social Science*, edited by P. Luomanen, I. Pyysiäinen, and R. Uro. BIS 89. Leiden: Brill.

Lütgert, W. 1908. *Freiheitspredigt und Schwarmgeister in Korinth: ein Beitrag zur Charakteristik der Christuspartei*. Gütersloh: Bertelsmann.

MacDonald, D. R. 2001. *Mimesis and Intertextuality in Antiquity and Christianity*. Studies in Antiquity and Christianity. Harrisburg, PA: Trinity.

MacDonald, M. Y. 1988. *The Pauline Churches: A Socio-historical Study of Institutionalization in the Pauline and Deutero-Pauline Writings*. SNTSMS 60. Cambridge: Cambridge University Press.

Malešević, S. 2006. *Identity as Ideology: Understanding Ethnicity and Nationalism*. Basingstoke: Palgrave Macmillan.

Malherbe, A. J. 1983. *Social Aspects of Early Christianity*. Philadelphia: Fortress.

———. 1989. *Paul and the Popular Philosophers*. Minneapolis: Fortress.

Malina, B. J. 2001. *The New Testament World: Insights from Cultural Anthropology*. 3rd ed. Louisville: Westminster John Knox.

Malina, B. J., and J. H. Neyrey. 1996. *Portraits of Paul: An Archaeology of Ancient Personality*. Louisville: Westminster John Knox.

Malina, B. J., and J. J. Pilch. 2006. *Social-science Commentary on the Letters of Paul*. Minneapolis: Augsburg Fortress.

Mandel, P. 2007. "Scriptural Exegesis and the Pharisees in Josephus." *Journal of Jewish Studies* 58:19–32.

Marchal, J. A. 2006. *Hierarchy, Unity, and Imitation: A Feminist Rhetorical Analysis of Power Dynamics in Paul's Letter to the Philippians*. SBL Academia Biblica 24. Atlanta: Society of Biblical Literature.

———. 2008. *The Politics of Heaven: Women, Gender, and Empire in the Study of Paul*. Minneapolis: Fortress.

Marohl, M. J. 2007. *Faithfulness and the Purpose of Hebrews: A Social Identity Approach*. PTMS. Eugene, OR: Pickwick.

Marshall, P. 1987. *Enmity in Corinth: Social Conventions in Paul's Relations with the Corinthians*. WUNT 23. Tübingen: J. C. B. Mohr.

Martin, D. B. 1990. *Slavery As Salvation: The Metaphor of Slavery in Pauline Christianity*. New Haven: Yale University Press.

———. 1995. *The Corinthian Body*. New Haven: Yale University Press.

———. 1999. "Social-scientific Criticism." Pages 125–41 in *To Each Its Own Meaning*, edited by S. L. McKenzie, and S. R. Haynes. Louisville: Westminster John Knox.

———. 2001. "Paul and the Judaism/Hellenism Dichotomy: Towards a Social History of the Question." In T. Engberg-Pedersen, editor. 2001:29–61.

Martin Jr., H. M. 1997. "Plutarch." In S. E. Porter, editor. 1997b: 715–36.

Martin, J. R., and D. Rose. 2003. *Working with Discourse Meaning Beyond the Clause*. Open Linguistics Series. London: Continuum.

Martyn, J. L. 1967. "Epistemology at the Turn of the Ages: 2 Corinthians 5:16." Pages 269–87 in *Christian History and Interpretation: Studies Presented to John Knox*, edited by W. R. Farmer, C. F. D. Moule, and R. R. Niebuhr. Cambridge: Cambridge University Press.

———. 2002. "De-apocalypticizing Paul: An Essay Focused on *Paul and the Stoics* by Troels Engberg-Pedersen." *JSNT* 96:61–102.

Matsuo, H. 1992. "Identificational Assimilation of Japanese Americans: A Reassessment of Primordialism and Circumstantialism." *Sociological Perspectives* 35:505–523.

Mauss, M. 1938. "Une catégorie de l'esprit humain: La notion de personne, celle de 'moi.'" *Journal of the Royal Anthropological Institute* 68:263-81.

May, A. S. 2004. *The Body for the Lord: Sex and Identity in 1 Corinthians 5–7*. JSNTSup 278. London: T. & T. Clark International.

McCall, G. L. 2003. "The Me and the Not-Me: Positive and Negative Poles of Identity." Pages 11–26 in *Advances in Identity Theory and Research*, edited by P. J. Burke, et al. New York: Kluwer Academic/Plenum.

McCall, G. L., and J. L. Simmons. 1978. *Identities and Interactions*. New York: Free Press.

McClendon, J. W. 1966. "Baptism as a Performative Sign." *Theology Today* 23:403-16.

McCready, W. O. 1996. "EKKLĒSIA and Voluntary Associations." Pages 59–73 in *Voluntary Associations in the Graeco-Roman World*, edited by J. S. Kloppenborg, and S. G. Wilson. London: Routledge.

McDonnell, M. 2006. *Roman Manliness: Virtus and the Roman Republic*. Cambridge: Cambridge University Press.

McNamara, T. 1997. "Theorizing Social Identity: What Do We Mean by Social Identity? Competing Frameworks, Competing Discourses." *TESOL Quarterly* 31:561-67.

Mead, G. H., and C. W. Morris. 1934. *Mind, Self & Society from the Standpoint of a Social Behaviorist*. Chicago: University of Chicago Press.

Meeks, W. A. 1983a [2003] *The First Urban Christians: The Social World of the Apostle Paul*. New Haven: Yale University Press.

———. 1983b. "Social Functions of Apocalyptic Language in Pauline Christianity." Pages 687–705 in *Apocalypticism in the Mediterranean World and the Near East*, edited by D. Hellhom. Tübingen: Mohr Siebeck.

———. 2001. "Corinthian Christians as Artificial Aliens." Pages 129–38 in *Paul Beyond the Judaism/Hellenism Divide*, edited by T. Engberg-Pedersen. Louisville: Westminster John Knox.

———. 2005. "Why Study the New Testament?." *NTS* 51:155-70.

———. 2007. "Introduction." In Schütz 2007: xiii–xxiv.

———. 2009. "Taking Stock and Moving On." Pages 134–46 in *After the First Urban Christians*, edited by T. D. Still, and D. G. Horrell. New York: T. & T. Clark.

Meggitt, J. J. 1998. *Paul, Poverty and Survival*. SNTW. Edinburgh: T. & T. Clark.

———. 2004. "The Social Status of Erastus: Rom 16:23." Pages 219–25 in *Christianity at Corinth: The Quest for the Pauline Church*, edited by E. Adams, and D. G. Horrell. Louisville: Westminster John Knox.

Meritt, B. D. 1931. *Greek Inscriptions, 1896–1927*. Corinth 8.1. Cambridge: Harvard University Press.

Meyer, B. F. 1986. *The Early Christians: Their World Mission and Self-discovery*. Good News Studies 16. Wilmington, DE: Michael Glazier.

————. 1987. "The World Mission and the Emergent Realization of Christian Identity." Pages 243–64 in *Jesus, the Gospels, and the Church: Essays in Honor of W. R. Farmer*, edited by E. P. Sanders. Macon, GA: Mercer University Press.

————. 1989. *Critical Realism and the New Testament*. PTMS 17. San Jose, CA: Pickwick.

————. 1992. *Christus Faber: The Master-builder and the House of God*. PrTMS 29. Allison Park, PA: Pickwick.

Middleton, P. 2006. *Radical Martyrdom and Cosmic Conflict in Early Christianity*. LNTS 307. London: T. & T. Clark.

Mihaila, C. 2006. "The Paul-Apollos Relationship and Paul's Stance Toward Greco-Roman Rhetoric: An Exegetical and Socio-historical Study." PhD diss., Southeastern Baptist Theological Seminary.

Miles, G. B. 1995. *Livy: Reconstructing Early Rome*. Ithaca: Cornell University Press.

Misztal, B. A. 2003. *Theories of Social Remembering*. Philadelphia: Open University Press.

Mitchell, M. M. 1991. *Paul and the Rhetoric of Reconciliation: An Exegetical Investigation of the Language and Composition of 1 Corinthians*. Louisville: Westminster John Knox Press.

Moghaddam, F., E. Hanley, and R. Harré. 2003. "Sustaining Intergroup Harmony: An Analysis of the Kissinger Papers Through Positioning Theory." Pages 137–55 in *The Self and Others: Positioning Individuals and Groups in Personal, Political, and Cultural Contexts*, edited by R. Harré, and F. M. Moghaddam. Westport, CT: Praeger.

Moore-Gilbert, B. 2003. "Homi Bhabha." Pages 71–76 in *Key Contemporary Social Theorists*, edited by A. Elliott, and L. Ray. Oxford: Blackwell.

Moretti, G. 1948. *Ara Pacis Augustae*. Roma: La Libreria dello Stato.

Morris, L. 1987. *The First Epistle of Paul to the Corinthians: An Introduction and Commentary*. Tyndale New Testament Commentaries 7. Leicester: InterVarsity.

Moscovici, S., and M. Zavalloni. 1969. "The Group as a Polarizer of Attitudes." *Journal of Personality and Social Psychology* 12:125–35.

Moule, C. F. D. 1977. *The Origin of Christology*. Cambridge: Cambridge University Press.

Mount, C. N. 2005. "1 Corinthians 11:3–16: Spirit Possession and Authority in a Non-Pauline Interpolation." *JBL* 124:313–40.

Mountford, R. 2001. "On Gender and Rhetorical Space." *Rhetoric Society Quarterly* 31:41–48.

Moxnes, H. 1991. "Patron-client Relations and the New Community in Luke-Acts." Pages 241–68 in *The Social World of Luke-Acts*, edited by J. H. Neyrey. Peabody: Hendrickson.

————. 1996. "Honor and Shame." Pages 19–40 in *The Social Sciences and New Testament Interpretation*, edited by R. L. Rohrbaugh. Peabody, MA: Hendrickson.

————. 2003. "Asceticism and Christian Identity in Antiquity: A Dialogue with Foucault and Paul." *JSNT* 26:3–29.

————. 2005. "From Theology to Identity: The Problem of Constructing Early Christianity." Pages 264–81 in *Moving Beyond New Testament Theology? Essays in Conversation with Heikki Räisänen*, edited by T. Penner, and C. Vander Stichele. Helsinki: Finnish Exegetical Society.

———. 2008. "Body, Gender, and Social Space." Pages 163–81 in *Identity Formation in the New Testament*, edited by B. Holmberg and M. Winninge. WUNT 227. Tübingen: Mohr Siebeck.

Munck, J. 1959. *Paul and the Salvation of Mankind*. Richmond: John Knox.

Munzinger, A. 2007. *Discerning the Spirits Theological and Ethical Hermeneutics in Paul*. Cambridge: Cambridge University Press.

Murphy-O'Connor, J. 1986. "Interpolations in 1 Corinthians." *CBQ* 48:81–94.

———. 1993. "Co-authorship in the Corinthian Correspondence." *RB* 100:562–79.

———. 1996. *Paul: A Critical Life*. Oxford: Clarendon.

———. 2002. *St. Paul's Corinth: Texts and Archaeology*. Collegeville, MN: Liturgical.

Nanos, M. D. 1996. *The Mystery of Romans: The Jewish Context of Paul's Letter*. Minneapolis: Fortress.

———. 2002a. *The Irony of Galatians Paul's Letter in First-century Context*. Minneapolis: Fortress.

———. 2002b. "The Inter- and Intra-Jewish Political Context of Paul's Letter to the Galatians." Pages 396–407 in *The Galatians Debate*, edited by M. Nanos. Peabody: Hendrickson.

———. 2002c. "What Was at Stake in Peter's 'Eating with Gentiles' at Antioch?" Pages 282–318 in *The Galatians Debate*, edited by M. Nanos. Peabody: Hendrickson.

———. 2005a. "How Inter-Christian Approaches to Paul's Rhetoric Can Perpetuate Negative Valuations of Jewishness—Although Proposing to Avoid That Outcome." *BibInt* 13:255–69.

———. 2005b. "Intruding 'Spies' and 'Pseudo-brethren.'" Pages 59–97 in *Paul and His Opponents*, edited by S. E. Porter. Pauline Studies 2. Leiden: Brill.

Nanos, M., editor. 2002. *The Galatians Debate*. Peabody: Hendrickson.

Newsom, C. A. 2004. *The Self as Symbolic Space: Constructing Identity and Community at Qumran*. Leiden: Brill.

Neyrey, J. H. 1990. *Paul, In Other Words: A Cultural Reading of His Letters*. Louisville: Westminster John Knox.

———. 1998. *Honor and Shame in the Gospel of Matthew*. Louisville: Westminster John Knox.

———. 2005. "God, Benefactor and Patron: The Major Cultural Model for Interpreting the Deity in Greco-Roman Antiquity." *JSNT* 27:465–92.

Nguyen, V. H. T. 2007. "The Identification of Paul's Spectacle of Death Metaphor in 1 Corinthians 4:9." *NTS* 53:489–501.

———. 2008a. *Christian Identity in Corinth: A Comparative Study of 2 Corinthians, Epictetus and Valerius Maximus*. WUNT 243. Tübingen: Mohr Siebeck.

———. 2008b. "God's Execution of His Condemned Apostles." *ZNW* 99:33–48.

Nolland, J. 2005. *The Gospel of Matthew: A Commentary on the Greek Text*. NIGTC. Grand Rapids: Eerdmans.

Oakes, P. 2001. *Philippians: From People to Letter*. SNTSMS 110. Cambridge: Cambridge University Press.

———. 2005. "Re-mapping the Universe: Paul and the Emperor in 1 Thessalonians and Philippians." *JSNT* 27:301–22.

———. 2008. "Urban Structure and Patronage." Paper presented at SBL Annual Meeting, Boston, MA.

———. 2009. *Reading Romans in Pompeii: Paul's Letter at Ground Level*. Minneapolis: Fortress.

Oakes, P., editor. 2002. *Rome in the Bible and the Early Church*. Grand Rapids: Baker.

O'Brien, P. T. 1977. *Introductory Thanksgivings in the Letters of Paul*. NovTSup 49. Leiden: Brill.

O'Day, G. R. 1990. "Jeremiah 9:22–23 and 1 Corinthians 1:26–31: A Study in Intertextuality." *JBL* 109:259–67.

Odell-Scott, D. 2003. *Paul's Critique of Theocracy: A/Theocracy in Corinthians and Galatians*. JSNTSup 250. London: T. & T. Clark International.

Økland, J. 2004. *Women in their Place: Paul and the Corinthian Discourse of Gender and Sanctuary Space*. JSNT 269. London: T. & T. Clark.

———. 2007. "The Transformation of Corinthian Goddesses." Pages 72–76 in *Complexity: Interdisciplinary Communications 2006/2007*, edited by W. Østreng. Oslo: Norwegian Academy of Science and Letters.

Ollrog, W. -H. 1979. *Paulus und seine Mitarbeiter: Untersuchungen zu Theorie und Praxis der paulinischen Mission*. Wissenschaftliche Monographien zum Alten und Neuen Testament 50. Neukirchen-Vluyn: Neukirchener Verlag.

Orr, W. F., and J. A. Walther. 1976. *I Corinthians: A New Translation*. Garden City, NY: Doubleday.

Osiek, C., and D. L. Balch. 1997. *Families in the New World: Households and House Churches*. Louisville: Westminster John Knox.

Osiek, C., M. Y. MacDonald, and J. H. Tulloch. 2006. *A Woman's Place: House Churches in Earliest Christianity*. Minneapolis: Fortress.

Ostenfeld, E. N., K. Blomqvist, and L. C. Nevett, editors. 2002. *Greek Romans and Roman Greeks: Studies in Cultural Interaction*. Aarhus Studies in Mediterranean Antiquity 3. Aarhus: Aarhus University Press.

Paden, J. N. 1970. "Urban Pluralism, Integration, and Adaptation of Communal Identity in Kano, Nigeria." Pages 242–70 in *From Tribe to Nation in Africa: Studies in Incorporation Processes*, edited by R. Cohen, and J. Middleton. Scranton, NJ: Chandler.

Paige, T. 1992. "Stoicism, ἐλευθερία and Community at Corinth." Pages 180–93 in *Worship, Theology and Ministry in the Early Church: Essays in Honor of Ralph P. Martin*, edited by M. J. Wilkins and T. Paige. JSNTSup 87. Sheffield: JSOT.

Paolo, C. 1997. "The Argument from Knowing and Not Knowing in Plato's *Theaetetus*. 187e5–188c8." *Proceedings of the Aristotelian Society* 96:177–96.

Parsons, T. 1951. *The Social System*. Glencoe, IL: Free Press.

Partridge, M. 2007. "Performing Faiths . . . Patterns, Pluralities, and Problems in the Lives of Religious Traditions." Pages 75–90 in *Faithful Performances Enacting Christian Tradition, edited* by T. Hart, and S. Guthrie. Aldershot, UK: Ashgate.

Pascal, N. R. 1984. "The Legacy of Roman Education in the Forum." *Classical Journal* 79:351–55.

Pearson, B. A. 1973. *The Pneumatikos-Psychikos Terminology in 1 Corinthians: A Study in the Theology of the Corinthian Opponents of Paul and Its Relation to Gnosticism*. SBLDS 12. Missoula, MT: Published by Society of Biblical Literature for the Nag Hammadi Seminar.

Peirce, B. N. 1995. "Social Identity, Investment, and Language Learning" *TESOL Quarterly* 29:9–31.

Perdue, L. G. 2008. *The Sword and the Stylus: An Introduction to Wisdom in the Age of Empires*. Grand Rapids: Eerdmans.

Perelman, C., and L. Olbrechts-Tyteca. 1969. *The New Rhetoric: A Treatise on Argumentation.* Notre Dame: University of Notre Dame Press.

Peterson, J. 2007. "Christ our Pasch: Shaping Christian Identity in Corinth." Pages 133–45 in *Renewing Tradition: Studies in Texts and Contexts in Honor of James W. Thompson.* edited by M. W. Hamilton, T. H. Olbricht, and J. Peterson. PTMS 65. Eugene, OR: Pickwick.

Pfaff, C. A. 2003. "Archaic Corinthian Architecture, ca. 600 to 480 B.C." Pages 95–140 in *Corinth, the Centenary, 1896–1996,* edited by C. K. Williams II and N. Bookidis. Corinth 20. Princeton: ASCSA.

Phillips, T. E., editor. 2009. *Roman Imperialism and Local Identities.* Cambridge: Cambridge University Press.

Pickett, R. 1997. *The Cross in Corinth: The Social Significance of the Death of Jesus.* JSNTSup 143. Sheffield: Sheffield Academic.

———. 2005. "Conflicts in Corinth." Pages 113–37 in *Christian Origins: A People's History of Christianity,* vol. 1, edited by R. A. Horsley. Minneapolis: Fortress.

Piérart, M. 1998. "Panthéon et hellénisation dans la colonie romaine de Corinthe: la 'redécouverte' du culte de Palaimon à l'Isthme." *Kernos* 11:85–109.

Pilch, J. J., editor. 2001. *Social Scientific Models for Interpreting the Bible.* BIS 53. Leiden: Brill.

Pitt-Rivers, J. A. 1977. *The Fate of Shechem or The Politics of Sex: Essays in the Anthropology of the Mediterranean.* Cambridge: Cambridge University Press.

Pogoloff, S. M. 1992. *Logos and Sophia: The Rhetorical Situation of 1 Corinthians.* Atlanta: Scholars.

Porter, S. E. 1997. "Paul of Tarsus and His Letters." Pages 533–85 in *Handbook of Classical Rhetoric in the Hellenistic Period, 330 B.C.—A.D. 400,* edited by S. E. Porter. Leiden: Brill.

Porter, S. E., editor. 1997a. *Handbook to the Exegesis of the New Testament.* New Testament Tools and Studies 25. Leiden: Brill.

———. 1997b. *Handbook of Classical Rhetoric in the Hellenistic Period, 330 B.C.—A.D. 400.* Leiden: Brill.

———. 2005. *Paul and His Opponents.* Pauline Studies 2. Leiden: Brill.

———. 2006. *Paul and His Theology.* Pauline Studies 3. Leiden: Brill.

———. 2008. *Paul's World.* Pauline Studies 4. Leiden: Brill.

Prabhu, A. 2007. *Hybridity Limits, Transformations, Prospects.* SUNY Series, Explorations in Postcolonial Studies. Albany: State University of New York Press.

Pratt, M. L. 2008. *Imperial Eyes: Travel Writing and Transculturation.* 2nd ed. London: Routledge.

Preisker, H. 1967. "μισθός κτλ." Pages 695–728 in vol. 4 of *Theological Dictionary of the New Testament,* edited by G. Kittel, and G. Friedrich. Translated by G. W. Bromiley. Grand Rapids: Eerdmans.

Preston, R. 2006. "Roman Questions, Greek Answers: Plutarch and the Construction of Identity." Pages 86–119 in *Being Greek Under Rome: Cultural Identity, The Second Sophistic and The Development of Empire,* edited by S. Goldhill. Cambridge: Cambridge University Press.

Price, S. R. F. 1984. *Rituals and Power: The Roman Imperial Cult in Asia Minor.* Cambridge: Cambridge University Press.

Pyysiäinen, I. 2001. *How Religion Works: Towards a New Cognitive Science of Religion.* Cognition and Culture Book Series 1. Leiden: Brill.

Ramsaran, R. A. 2004. "Resisting Imperial Domination and Influence: Paul's Apocalyptic Rhetoric in 1 Corinthians." Pages 89–101 in *Paul and the Roman Imperial Order*, edited by R. A. Horsley. Harrisburg, PA: Trinity.

Reitzenstein, R. 1927. *Die hellenistischen Mysterienreligionen nach ihren Grundgedanken und Wirkungen*. Leipzig: Teubner.

———. 1978. *Hellenistic Mystery Religions: Their Basic Ideas and Significance*. Translated by J. E. Steely. PTMS, 15. Pittsburg: Pickwick.

Restum, J. 1993. "Selected Demographic Variables as Predictors of Ego-identity Status among George Fox College Students." PsyD thesis, George Fox College.

Revell, L. 2009. *Roman Imperialism and Local Identities*. Cambridge: Cambridge University Press.

Reydams-Schils, G. J. 2005. *The Roman Stoics: Self, Responsibility, and Affection*. Chicago: University of Chicago Press.

Rhee, H. 2005. *Early Christian Literature: Christ and Culture in the Second and Third Centuries*. Routledge Early Church Monographs. London: Routledge.

Richards, E. R. 2004. *Paul and First-century Letter Writing: Secretaries, Composition, and Collection*. Downers Grove, IL: InterVarsity.

Ricoeur, P. 1991. "Life in Quest of Narrative." Pages 20–33 in *On Paul Ricoeur: Narrative and Interpretation*, edited by D. Wood. London: Routledge.

Rives, J. B. 1995. *Religion and Authority in Roman Carthage from Augustus to Constantine*. Oxford: Clarendon.

———. 2000. "Religion in the Roman Empire." Pages 245–75 in *Experiencing Rome: Culture, Identity and Power in the Roman Empire*, edited by J. Huskinson. London: Routledge 2000.

———. 2007. *Religion in the Roman Empire*. Oxford: Blackwell.

Robertson, A., and A. Plummer. 1911. *A Critical and Exegetical Commentary on the First Epistle of St. Paul to the Corinthians*. ICC 33. Edinburgh: T. & T. Clark.

Robertson, C. K. 2001. *Conflict in Corinth: Redefining the System*. Studies in Biblical Literature, 42. New York: Lang.

Robinson, B. A. 2005. "Fountains and the Formation of Cultural Identity at Roman Corinth." Pages 111–40 in *Urban Religion in Roman Corinth: Interdisciplinary Approaches*, edited by D. N. Schowalter and S. J. Friesen. Harvard Theological Studies 53. Cambridge: Harvard University Press.

Roebuck, C. 1951. *The Asklepieion and Lerna*. Corinth 14. Princeton: ASCSA.

Rohrbaugh, R. L., editor. 1996. *The Social Sciences and New Testament Interpretation*. Peabody, MA: Hendrickson.

Roitto, R. 2008a. "Behaving Like a Christ-believer: A Cognitive Perspective on Identity and Behavior Norms in the Early Christ-movement." Pages 93–114 in *Exploring Early Christian Identity*, edited by B. Homberg. WUNT 226. Tübingen: Mohr Siebeck.

———. 2008b. "Act as a Christ-believer, as a Household Member or as Both?—A Cognitive Perspective on the Relationship Between the Social Identity in Christ and Household Identities in Pauline and Deutero-Pauline Texts." Pages 141–61 in *Identity Formation in the New Testament*, edited by B. Holmberg and M. Winninge. WUNT 227. Tübingen: Mohr Siebeck.

Romano, D. G. 2003. "City Planning, Centuriation and Land Division in Roman Corinth, Colonia Laus Iulia Corinthiensis and Colonia Iulia Flavia Augusta Corinthiensis."

Pages 279–301 in *Corinth, the Centenary, 1896–1996*, edited by C. K. Williams II and N. Bookidis. Corinth 20. Princeton: ASCSA.

———. 2005a. "A New Fragment of an Inscription From the Julian Basilica at Roman Corinth." *Hesperia* 74:95–100.

———. 2005b. "A Roman Circus in Corinth." *Hesperia* 74:585–611.

———. 2006. "Roman Surveyors in Corinth." *Proceedings of the American Philosophical Society* 150:62–85.

Ross, J. M. 1971. "Not Above What is Written." *ExpTim* 82:215–17.

Rossini, O. 2007. *Ara Pacis*. Milan: Electa.

Rothaus, R. M. 2000. *Corinth, the First City of Greece: An Urban History of Late Antique Cult and Religion*. Religions in the Graeco-Roman World 139. Leiden: Brill.

Rudolph, D. J. 2006. "A Jew to the Jews: Jewish Contours of Pauline Flexibility in 1 Corinthians 9:19–23." PhD diss., University of Cambridge.

Runesson, A. 2000. "Particularistic Judaism and Universalistic Christianity? Some Critical Remarks on Terminology and Theology." *Journal of Greco-Roman Christianity and Judaism* 1:120–44.

———. 2008. "Inventing Christian Identity: Paul, Ignatius, and Theodosius I." Pages 59–92 in *Exploring Early Christian Identity*, edited by B. Homberg. WUNT 226. Tübingen: Mohr Siebeck.

Runnalls, D. R. 1997. "The Rhetoric of Josephus." Pages 737–54 in *Handbook of Classical Rhetoric in the Hellenistic Period, 330 B.C.—A.D. 400*, edited by S. E. Porter. Leiden: Brill.

Saddington, D. 2007. "A Note on the Rhetoric of Four Speeches in Josephus." *Journal of Jewish Studies* 58:228–35.

Said, E. W. 1978. *Orientalism*. New York: Pantheon.

Saller, R. P. 1982. *Personal Patronage under the Early Empire*. Cambridge: Cambridge University Press.

Sampley, J. P. 1991. *Walking Between the Times: Paul's Moral Reasoning*. Minneapolis: Fortress.

———. 2002. *First Corinthians*. New Interpreter's Bible Commentary 10. Nashville: Abingdon.

Sampley, J. P., editor. 2003. *Paul in the Greco-Roman World: A Handbook*. Harrisburg, PA: Trinity.

Samra, J. G. 2006. *Being Conformed to Christ in Community: A Study of Maturity, Maturation, and the Local Church in the Undisputed Pauline Epistles*. LNTS 320. London: T. & T. Clark.

Sanders, E. P. 1977. *Paul and Palestinian Judaism: A Comparison of Patterns of Religion*. Philadelphia: Fortress.

———. 1999. "Common Judaism and the Synagogue in the First Century." Pages 1–17 in *Jews, Christians, and Polytheists in the Ancient Synagogue: Cultural Interaction during the Greco-Roman Period*, edited by S. Fine. London: Routledge.

Sandnes, K. O. 1991. *Paul, One of the Prophets? A Contribution to the Apostle's Self-understanding*. WUNT 43. Tübingen: Mohr Siebeck.

Sardiello, R. 1998. "Identity and Status: Stratification in Deadhead Subculture." Pages 118–47 in *Youth Culture: Identity in a Postmodern World*, edited by J. S. Epstein. Malden, MA: Blackwell.

Saunders, R. 2005. "Paul and the Imperial Cult." Pages 227–38 in *Paul and His Opponents*, edited by S. E. Porter. Pauline Studies 2. Leiden: Brill.

Sawyer, J. F. A. 1999. *Sacred Languages and Sacred Texts*. Religion in the First Christian Centuries. London: Routledge.

Schlatter, A. 1914. *Die korinthische Theologie*. Beiträge zur Förderung Christlicher Theologie, 18. Gütersloh: Bertelsmann.

———. 1969 [1934]. *Paulus, der Bote Jesu: eine deutung seiner briefe an die Korinther*. Stuttgart: Calwer.

Schmidt, T. E. 1989. "Sociology and New Testament Exegesis." Pages 115–32 in *Introducing New Testament Interpretation*, edited by S. McKnight. Grand Rapids: Baker.

Schmithals, W. 1971. *Gnosticism in Corinth: An Investigation of the Letters to the Corinthians*. Nashville: Abingdon.

Schnabel, E. J. 2004. *Early Christian Mission*. Downers Grove, IL: InterVarsity.

———. 2005. "The Objectives of Change, Factors of Transformation, and the Causes of Results: The Evidence of Paul's Corinthian Correspondence." *Trinity Journal* 26 NS: 179–204

———. 2006. *Der erste Brief des Paulus an die Korinther*. HistorischTheologische Auslegung. Wuppertal: R. Brockhaus.

Schneider, J. 1971. "Of Vigilance and Virgins—Honor, Shame and Access to Resources in Mediterranean Societies." *Ethnology* 10:1–24.

Schowalter, D. N., and S. J. Friesen, editors. 2005. *Urban Religion in Roman Corinth: Interdisciplinary Approaches*. Harvard Theological Studies 53. Cambridge: Harvard University Press.

Schrage, W. 1991. *Der erste Brief an die Korinther*. Evangelisch-katholischer Kommentar zum Neuen Testament 7. Zürich: Benziger.

———. 2007. *Studien zur Theologie im 1 Korintherbrief*. Neukirchen-Vluyn: Neukirchener.

Schreiner, T. R. 2001. *Paul, Apostle of God's Glory in Christ: A Pauline Theology*. Leicester: Apollos.

Schubert, P. 1939. *Form and Function of the Pauline Thanksgivings*. Beihefte zur Zeitschrift für die neutestamentliche Wissenschaft 20. Berlin: Töpelmann.

Schüssler Fiorenza, E. 1994. *In Memory of Her: A Feminist Theological Reconstruction of Christian Origins*. New York: Crossroad.

———. 1999. *Rhetoric and Ethic: The Politics of Biblical Studies*. Minneapolis: Fortress.

Schütz, J. H. 2007. *Paul and the Anatomy of Apostolic Authority, New Introduction by Wayne A. Meeks*. Louisville and London: Westminster John Knox and Cambridge University Press.

Schwartz, D. R. 2007. "'Judaean' or 'Jew'? How Should We Translate *Ioudaios* In Josephus?" Pages 3–27 in *Jewish Identity in the Greco-Roman World: Jüdische Identität in der griechisch-römischen Welt*, edited by J. Frey, D. R. Schwartz, and S. Gripentrog. Ancient Judaism and Early Christianity 71. Leiden: Brill.

Scott, I. W. 2006. *Implicit Epistemology in the Letters of Paul: Story, Experience and the Spirit*. WUNT 2, 205. Tübingen: Mohr Siebeck.

Scott, J. M. 1995. *Paul and the Nations: The Old Testament and Jewish Background of Paul's Mission to the Nations with Special Reference to the Destination of Galatians*. WUNT 84. Tübingen: Mohr Siebeck.

Scranton, R. L. 1951. *Monuments in the Lower Agora and North of the Archaic Temple*. Corinth 1.3. Princeton: ASCSA.

Scroggs, R. A. 1967–68. "Paul: Σοφὸς καὶ πνευματικός." *NTS* 14:33–55.

————. 1980. "The Sociological Interpretation of the New Testament: The Present State of Research." *NTS* 26:164–79.

Segal, A. 1990. *Paul the Convert: The Apostolate and Apostasy of Saul the Pharisee*. New Haven: Yale University Press.

Senft, C. 1979. *La première épître de Saint-Paul aux Corinthiens*. CNT 2/7. Paris: Delachaux & Niestlé.

Serpe, R.T. 1987. "Stability and Change in Self: A Structural Symbolic Interactionist Explanation." *Social Psychology Quarterly* 50:44–55.

Severy, B. 2003. *Augustus and the Family at the Birth of the Roman Empire*. New York: Routledge.

Shanor, J. 1988. "Paul as Master Builder: Construction Terms in First Corinthians." *NTS* 34:461–71.

Sharpley, H. 1906. *A Realist of the Aegean, Being a Verse-translation of the Mimes of Herodas*. London: Nutt.

Shaw, C. R., and E. W. Burgess. 1930. *The Jack-Roller, A Delinquent Boy's Own Story*. Chicago: University of Chicago Press.

Shear, T. L. 1930. *The Roman Villa*. Corinth 5. Cambridge: ASCSA.

Sherif, M. 1961. *Intergroup Conflict and Cooperation: The Robbers Cave Experiment*. Norman: University Book Exchange.

Shkul, M. 2005. "Deutero-Pauline Construction of Distinctive Social Identity & Community Boundaries in Ephesians." Paper presented at SBL Annual Meeting, Philadelphia, PA.

————. 2007. "Reading Ephesians: Exploring Social Entrepreneurship in the Text." PhD diss., University of Sheffield.

Sibilio, P. M. 2005. "A Mystery Once More: Re-examining the Influence of Mystery Cults in 1 Corinthians 1–4." PhD diss., Loyola University.

Silk, M. S. 1974. *Interaction in Poetic Imagery with Special Reference to Early Greek Poetry*. Cambridge: Cambridge University Press.

————. 1996. "Metaphor." Pages 966–8 in *The Oxford Classical Dictionary*, edited by S. Hornblower, and A. Spawforth. 3rd ed. Oxford: Oxford University Press.

Simpson, J. A., and E. S. C. Weiner, editors. 1989. *The Oxford English Dictionary*. Oxford: Clarendon.

Smith, A. S. 2005. *The Primacy of Vision in Virgil's Aeneid*. Austin: University of Texas Press.

Smith-Lovin, L. 2003. "The Self, Identity, and Interaction in an Ecology of Identities." Pages 167–78 in *Advances in Identity Theory and Research*, edited by P. J. Burke, et al. New York: Kluwer Academic/Plenum.

Soards, M. L. 1999. *1 Corinthians*. Peabody, MA: Hendrickson.

Sollors, W. 1986. *Beyond Ethnicity: Consent and Descent in American Culture*. New York: Oxford University Press.

Spawforth, A. J. S. 1994. "Corinth, Argos, and the Imperial Cult: Pseudo-Julian, Letters 198." *Hesperia* 63:211–232.

————. 1995. "The Achaean Federal Cult Part I: Pseudo-Julian, Letters 198." *TynBul* 46:151–68.

————. 1996. "Roman Corinth: the Formation of a Colonial Elite." Pages 167–82 in *Roman Onomastics in the Greek East*, edited by A. D. Rizakis. Meletemata 21. Athens: Research Centre for Greek and Roman Antiquity, National Hellenic Research Foundation.

————. 2007. "'Kapetōleia Olympia': Roman Emperors and Greek Agōnes." Pages 377–90 in *Pindar's Poetry, Patrons, and Festivals From Archaic Greece to the Roman Empire,* edited by S. Hornblower, and C. Morgan. Oxford: Oxford University Press.

Spivak, G. 1990. *The Post-colonial Critic: Interviews, Strategies, Dialogues.* London: Routledge.

Stack, J., editor. 1986. *The Primordial Challenge: Ethnicity in the Contemporary World.* New York: Greenwood.

Stackhouse, M. L. 1995. *On Moral Business: Classical and Contemporary Resources for Ethics in Economic Life.* Grand Rapids: Eerdmans.

Stanley, C. D. 1992. *Paul and the Language of Scripture: Citation Technique in the Pauline Epistles and Contemporary Literature.* SNTSMS 69. Cambridge: Cambridge University Press.

————. 2004. *Arguing with Scripture: The Rhetoric of Quotations in the Letters of Paul.* New York: T. & T. Clark.

Stansbury-O'Donnell, M. D. 2006. *Vase Painting, Gender, and Social Identity in Archaic Athens.* Cambridge: Cambridge University Press.

Steedman, C. 1996. "About Ends: On the Ways in which the End is Different from an Ending." *History of the Human Sciences* 9:99–114.

Stegemann, E., and W. Stegemann. 1999. *The Jesus Movement: A Social History of Its First Century.* Minneapolis: Fortress.

Stets, J. E. 2006. "Identity Theory." Pages 88–110 in *Contemporary Social Psychological Theories,* edited by P. J. Burke. Stanford: Stanford University Press.

Stets, J. E., and P. J. Burke. 2000. "Identity Theory and Social Identity Theory." *Social Psychology Quarterly* 63:224–37.

Stets, J. E., and M. J. Carter. 2006. "The Moral Identity: A Principle Level Identity." Pages 293–313 in *Purpose, Meaning, and Action: Control Systems Theories in Sociology,* edited by K. McClelland and T. J. Fararo. New York: Palgrave-MacMillan.

Still, T. D. 2006. "Did Paul Loathe Manual Labor? Revisiting the Work of Ronald F. Hock on the Apostle's Tentmaking and Social Class." *JBL* 125:781–95.

Still, T. D., and D. G. Horrell, editors. 2009. *After the First Urban Christians.* New York: T. & T. Clark.

Stillwell, R. 1952. *The Theatre.* Corinth 2. Princeton: ASCSA.

Stillwell, R., R. L. Scranton, and S. E. Freeman. 1941. *Architecture.* Corinth 1.2. Princeton: ASCSA.

Stiver, D. R. 2001. *Theology After Ricoeur: New Directions in Hermeneutical Theology.* Louisville: Westminster John Knox.

Stommel, E. 1959. "Christliche Taufriten und antike Badesitten." *Jahrbuch für Antike und Christentum* 2:5–14.

Stone, D. L. 2007. "Burial, Identity, and Local Culture in North Africa." Pages 126–44 in *Articulating Local Cultures: Power and Identity Under the Expanding Roman Republic.* edited by P. Dommelen, and N. Terrenato. Journal of Roman Archaeology Supplementary Series 63. Portsmouth, RI: Journal of Roman Archaeology.

Stowers, S. 2003. "Paul and Self-mastery." Pages 524–50 in *Paul in the Greco-Roman World: A Handbook,* edited by J. P. Sampley. Harrisburg, PA: Trinity.

Strauss, A. L. 1969. *Mirrors and Masks: The Search for Identity.* San Francisco: Sociology.

Strecker, C. 1999. *Die liminale Theologie des Paulus: Zugänge zur paulinischen Theologie aus kulturanthropologischer Perspektive.* FRLANT 185. Göttingen: Vandenhoeck & Ruprecht.

Strüder, C. W. 2003. "Preferences Not Parties the Background of 1 Cor 1:12." *Ephemerides Theologicae Lovanienses* 79:431–55.

———. 2005. *Paulus und die Gesinnung Christi Identität und Entscheidungsfindung aus der Mitte von 1 Kor 1–4*. BETL 190. Leuven: Leuven University Press.

Stryker, S. 1968. "Identity Theory and Role Performance." *Journal of Marriage and the Family* 30:558–64.

———. 1980. *Symbolic Interactionism: A Social Structural Version*. Menlo Park, CA: Benjamin Cummings.

Stryker, S., and P. J. Burke. 2000. "The Past, Present, and Future of an Identity Theory." *Social Psychology Quarterly* 63:284–97.

Stryker, S., and R. T. Serpe.1982. "Commitment, Identity Salience, and Role Behavior: A Theory and Research Example." Pages 199–218 in *Personality, Roles, and Social Behavior*, edited by W. Ickes, and E. S. Knowles. New York: Springer.

———. 1994. "Identity Salience and Psychological Centrality: Equivalent, Overlapping, or Complementary Concepts?" *Social Psychology Quarterly* 57:16–35.

Stuhlmacher, P. 1987. "The Hermeneutical Significance of 1 Cor 2:6–16." Pages 328–47 in *Tradition and Interpretation in the New Testament: Essays in Honor of E. Earle Ellis*, edited by G. F. Hawthorne, and O. Betz. Grand Rapids: Eerdmans.

Sugirtharajah, R. S. 2002. *Postcolonial Criticism and Biblical Interpretation*. Oxford: Oxford University Press.

Sumney, J. 2008. *Colossians: A Commentary*. New Testament Library. Louisville: Westminster John Knox.

Sutherland, C. H. V. 1940. "The Historical Evidence of Greek and Roman Coins." *GR* 9:65–80.

———. 1984. *The Roman Imperial Coinage*. Vol. 6, *From Diocletian's Reform A.D. 294 to the Death of Maximinus A.D. 313*. London: Spink.

Swancutt, D. 2001. "*Pax Christi*: Romans as Protrepsis to Live as Kings." PhD diss., Duke University.

———. 2003. "Christian 'Rock' Music in Corinth?" Pages 125–43 in *Psalms in Community: Jewish and Christian Textual, Liturgical, and Artistic Traditions*, edited by H. W. Attridge, and M. Fassler. SBL Symposium 25. Atlanta: Society of Biblical Literature.

———. 2006. "Scripture 'Reading' and Identity Formation in Paul: *Paideia* among Believing Greeks." Paul and Scripture Seminar—SBL November.

Syed, Y. 2005. *Vergil's Aeneid and the Roman Self: Subject and Nation in Literary Discourse*. Ann Arbor: University of Michigan Press.

Tajfel, H. 1972. "La catégorisation sociale." Pages 272–302 in *Introduction à la psychologie sociale, edited* by S. Moscovici. Paris: Librairie Larousse.

———. 1978a. "Interindividual Behaviour and Intergroup Behaviour." Pages 27–60 in *Differentiation Between Social Groups: Studies in the Social Psychology of Intergroup Relations*, edited by J. Tajfel. European Monographs in Social Psychology 14. London: Published in cooperation with European Association of Experimental Social Psychology by Academic Press.

———. 1978b. "Social Categorization, Social Identity and Social Comparison." Pages 61–76 in *Differentiation Between Social Groups: Studies in the Social Psychology of Intergroup Relations*, edited by J. Tajfel. European Monographs in Social Psychology 14. London: Published in cooperation with European Association of Experimental Social Psychology by Academic Press.

———. 1981. "Social Stereotypes and Social Groups." 144–67 in *Intergroup Behavior*, edited by J. C. Turner and H. Giles. Chicago: University of Chicago Press.

Tajfel, H., editor. 1978. *Differentiation Between Social Groups: Studies in the Social Psychology of Intergroup Relations*. European Monographs in Social Psychology 14. London: Published in cooperation with European Association of Experimental Social Psychology by Academic Press.

Tajfel, H., and J. C. Turner. 1979. "An Integrative Theory of Group Conflict." Pages 33–47 in *The Social Psychology of Intergroup Relations*, edited by W. C. Austin and S. Worschel. Monterey, CA: Brooks/Cole.

———. 1986. "The Social Identity Theory of Intergroup Behavior." Pages 7–24 in *The Social Psychology of Intergroup Relations*, 2nd ed., edited by S. Worschel and W. Austin. Chicago: Nelson-Hall.

Tan, S. L., and F. M. Moghaddam. 1998. "Positioning in Intergroup Relations." Pages 178–94 *Positioning Theory: Moral Contexts of International Action*, edited by R. Harré, and L. Van Langenhove. Oxford: Blackwell.

Taylor, N. H. 2005. "Apostolic Identity and the Conflicts in Corinth and Galatia." Pages 99–123 in *Paul and His Opponents*, edited by S. E. Porter. Pauline Studies 2. Leiden: Brill.

Tellbe, M. 2001. *Paul between Synagogue and State: Christians, Jews, and Civic Authorities in 1 Thessalonians, Romans, and Philippians*. Coniectanea Biblica 34. Stockholm: Almqvist & Wiksell.

———. 2008. "The Prototypical Christ-believer: Early Christian Identity Formation in Ephesus." Pages 115–38 in *Exploring Early Christian Identity*, edited by B. Holmberg. WUNT 226. Tübingen: Mohr Siebeck.

———. 2009. *Christ-Believers in Ephesus*. WUNT 242. Tübingen: Mohr Siebeck.

Theis, J. 1991. *Paulus als Weisheitslehrer der Gekreuzigte und die Weisheit Gottes in 1 Kor 1–4*. Biblische Untersuchungen 22. Regensburg: Pustet.

Theissen, G. 1982. *The Social Setting of Pauline Christianity: Essays on Corinth*. Philadelphia: Fortress.

———. 1987. *Psychological Aspects of Pauline Theology*. Philadelphia: Fortress.

———. 1999. *A Theory of Primitive Christian Religion*. London: SCM.

———. 2007. "Urchristliche Gemeinden und antike Vereine: Sozialdynamik im Urchristentum durch Widersprüche zwischen Selbstverständnis und Sozialstruktur." Pages 221–47 in *In Other Words: Essays on Social Science Methods and the New Testament in Honor of Jerome H. Neyrey*, edited by A. C. Hagedorn, Z. A. Crook, and E. Stewart. Social World of Biblical Antiquity 2/1. Sheffield: Sheffield Phoenix.

Thiselton, A. C. 1978. "Realized Eschatology at Corinth." *NTS* 24:510–26.

———. 2000. *The First Epistle to the Corinthians: A Commentary on the Greek Text*. NIGTC. Grand Rapids: Eerdmans.

———. 2006a. "The Significance of Recent Research on 1 Corinthians for Hermeneutical Appropriation of this Epistle Today." *Neot* 40:320–52.

———. 2006b. *Thiselton on Hermeneutics: Collected Works with New Essays*. Grand Rapids: Eerdmans.

———. 2007. *The Hermeneutics of Doctrine*. Grand Rapids: Eerdmans.

Thoits, P. A. 1983. "Multiple Identities and Psychological Well-being: A Reformulation and Test of the Social Isolation Hypothesis." *American Sociological Review* 49:174–87.

Thomas, W. I., and F. Znaniecki. 1918. *The Polish Peasant in Europe and America: Monograph of an Immigrant Group.* Chicago: University of Chicago Press.

Thrall, M. E. 2002. "The Initial Attraction of Paul's Mission in Corinth and of the Church He Founded There." Pages 59–73 in *Luke and the Graeco-Roman World: Essays in Honour of Alexander J. M. Wedderburn,* edited by A. Christophersen, et al. JSNTSup 217. New York: Sheffield Academic.

Tidball, D. 1984. *The Social Context of the New Testament: A Sociological Analysis.* Grand Rapids: Zondervan.

Tigay, J. H. 1996. *Deuteronomy.* JPS Torah Commentary. Philadelphia: Jewish Publication Society.

Tomlin, G. 1997. "Christians and Epicureans in 1 Corinthians." *JSNT* 68:51–72.

Tomson, P. J. 1990. *Paul and the Jewish Law: Halakha in the Letters of the Apostle to the Gentiles.* Minneapolis: Fortress.

Torelli, M. 2001. "Reflections in Context." Pages 53–56 in *Pausanias: Travel and Memory in Roman Greece,* edited by S. E. Alcock, J. F. Cherry, and J. Elsner. Oxford: Oxford University Press.

Trapp, M. B. 2007. *Philosophy in the Roman Empire: Ethics, Politics and Society.* Ashgate Ancient Philosophy Series. Aldershot, UK: Ashgate.

Trebilco, P. 2005. "Naming Ourselves and Naming Others in the Corinthian Letters." Paper presented at the British New Testament Conference, Liverpool, England.

Tucker, J. B. 2008. "The Role of Civic Identity on the Pauline Mission in Corinth." *Didaskalia: The Journal of Providence College and Seminary* 19:72–91.

———. 2009a. "Christian Identity—Created or Construed?" *JBV* 30:71–77.

———. 2009b. "*'You Belong to Christ': Paul and the Formation of Social Identity in 1 Corinthians 1–4.*" PhD diss., University of Wales, Lampeter.

———. 2010a. "Baths, Baptism, and Patronage: The Continuing Role of Roman Social Identity in Corinth." In *Reading Paul in Context,* edited by K. Ehrensperger and J. B. Tucker, 173–88.

———. 2010b. "Paul and the Formation of the Urban Christ-Movement." *JBV* 31: 97–106.

Tuckett, C. 1994. "Jewish Christian Wisdom in 1 Corinthians?" Pages 201–19 in *Crossing the Boundaries: Essays in Biblical Interpretation in Honour of Michael D. Goulder,* edited by S. E. Porter, P. Joyce, and D. E. Orton. Leiden: Brill.

———. 2000. "Paul, Scripture and Ethics: Some Reflections." *NTS* 46:403–24.

Turner, J. C. 1985. "Social Categorization and the Self-concept: A Social Cognitive Theory of Group Behavior." Pages 77–121 in vol. 2 of *Advances in Group Processes,* edited by E. J. Lawler. Greenwich, CT: JAI Press.

———. 1987. "A Self-categorization Theory." Pages 42–67 in *Rediscovering the Social Group: A Self-categorization Theory,* edited by J. C. Turner, et al. Oxford: Blackwell.

———. 1999. "Some Current Issues in Research on Social Identity and Self-Categorization Theories." Pages 6–34 in *Social Identity: Context, Commitment, Content,* edited by N. Ellemers, R. Spears, and B. Doosje. Oxford: Blackwell.

Turner, J. C., and H. Giles. 1981. *Intergroup Behavior.* Chicago: University of Chicago Press.

Turner, J. C., and K. J. Reynolds. 2001. "The Social Identity Perspective in Intergroup Relations: Theories, Themes, and Controversies." Pages 133–52 in *Blackwell Handbook of Social Psychology: Intergroup Processes,* edited by R. Brown, and S. L. Gaertner. Oxford: Blackwell.

Turner, V. 1967. *The Forest of Symbols: Aspects of Ndembu Ritual*. Ithaca, NY: Cornell University Press.

Tyler, R. L. 2001. "The History of the Interpretation of τὸ μὴ ὑπὲρ ἃ γέγραπται in 1 Corinthians 4:6." *Restoration Quarterly* 43:243–52.

Van Dijk, T. A. 2001. "Critical Discourse Analysis." Pages 352–71 in *The Handbook of Discourse Analysis*, edited by D. Schiffrin, D. Tannen, and H. E. Hamilton. Blackwell Handbooks in Linguistics. Malden, MA: Blackwell.

VandenBos, G. R. 2007. *APA Dictionary of Psychology*. Washington, DC: American Psychological Association.

Van der Watt, J. G., editor. 2006. *Identity, Ethics, and Ethos in the New Testament*. Zeitschrift für die neutestamentliche Wissenschaft und die Kunde der älteren Kirche 141. Berlin: de Gruyter.

VanLandingham, C. 2006. *Judgment and Justification in Early Judaism and the Apostle Paul*. Peabody: Hendrickson.

Vollenweider, S. 2002. "Weisheit am Kreuzweg: Zum theologischen Programm von 1 Kor 1 und 2." Pages 43–58 in *Kreuzestheologie im Neuen Testament*, edited by A. Dettwiler, and J. Zumstein. WUNT 151. Tübingen: Mohr Siebeck.

Vos, J. S. 1996. "Die Argumentation des Paulus in 1 Kor 1:10—3:4." Pages 87–119 in *The Corinthian Correspondence*, edited by R. Bieringer. BETL 125. Leuven: Leuven University Press.

Walbank, M. E. H. 1989. "Pausanias, Octavia and Temple E at Corinth." *Annual of the British School at Athens* 84:361–94.

———. 1996. "Evidence for the Imperial Cult in Julio-Claudian Corinth." *Journal of Roman Archaeology Supplementary Series* 17:201–214.

———. 1997. "The Foundation and Planning of Early Roman Corinth." *Journal of Roman Archaeology* 10:95–130.

———. 2003. "Aspects of Corinthian Coinage in the Late 1st and Early 2nd Centuries A.C." 337–49 in *Corinth, the Centenary, 1896–1996*, edited by C. K. Williams II and N. Bookidis. Corinth 20. Princeton: ASCSA.

Walker Jr., W. O. 1992. "1 Corinthians 2:6–16: A Non-Pauline Interpolation?" *JSNT* 47:75–94.

Wallace, D. B. 1996. *Greek Grammar Beyond the Basics: An Exegetical Syntax of the New Testament*. Grand Rapids: Zondervan.

Wallace, D. R. 2005. "The Gospel of God: Romans as Paul's Aeneid." PhD diss., Southwestern Baptist Theological Seminary.

Wallace-Hadrill, A. 1989. "Patronage in Roman Society: From Republic to Empire." Pages 63–88 in *Patronage in Ancient Society*, edited by A. Wallace-Hadrill. London: Routledge.

Walters, J. C. 2005. "Civic Identity in Roman Corinth and its Impact on the Early Christians." Pages 397–417 in *Urban Religion in Roman Corinth: Interdisciplinary Approaches*, edited by D. N. Schowalter and S. J. Friesen. Harvard Theological Studies 53. Cambridge: Harvard University Press.

Wanamaker, C. 2002. "Apocalyptic Discourse, Paraenesis and Identity Maintenance in 1 Thessalonians." *Neot* 36:131–45.

———. 2003. "A Rhetoric of Power: Ideology and 1 Corinthians 1–4." Pages 115–37 in *Paul and the Corinthians: Studies on a Community in Conflict: Essays in Honour of Margaret Thrall*, edited by T. J. Burke, and J. K. Elliott. NovTSup 109. Leiden: Brill.

————. 2005. "Metaphor and Morality: Examples of Paul's Moral Thinking in 1 Corinthians 1–5." *Neot* 39:409–33.

————. 2006. "The Power of the Absent Father: A Socio-rhetorical Analysis of 1 Corinthians 4:14—5:13." Pages 339–64 in *The New Testament Interpreted Essays in Honor of Bernard C. Lategan*, edited by C. Breytenbach, J. C. Thom, and J. Punt. NovTSup 124. Leiden: Brill.

Watson, F. 2006. "Constructing an Antithesis: Pauline and Other Jewish Perspectives on Divine and Human Agency." Pages 99–116 in *Divine and Human Agency in Paul and His Cultural Environment*, edited by J. M. G. Barclay, and S. J. Gathercole. London: T. & T. Clark.

————. 2007. *Paul, Judaism, and the Gentiles: Beyond the New Perspective.* Grand Rapids: Eerdmans.

Weber, M. 1947. *The Theory of Social and Economic Organization.* New York: Free Press.

Weinberg, S. S. 1960. *The Southeast Building, the Twin Basilicas, the Mosaic House.* Corinth 1.5. Princeton: ASCSA.

Weiss, J. 1910. *Der erste Korintherbrief.* Kritisch-exegetischer Kommentar über das Neue Testament 5. Göttingen: Vandenhoeck & Ruprecht.

————. 1937. *Earliest Christianity: A History of the Period A.D. 30–150.* Translated by F. C. Grant. New York: Harper & Row.

Welborn, L. L. 1987a. "A Conciliatory Principle in 1 Cor 4:6." *NovT* 29:320–46.

————. 1987b. "On the Discord in Corinth." *JBL* 106:85–111.

————. 1997. *Politics and Rhetoric in the Corinthian Epistles.* Macon, GA: Mercer University Press.

————. 2002. "Μωρὸς γένεσθω: Paul's Appropriation of the Role of the Fool in 1 Cor 1–4." *BibInt* 10:420–35.

————. 2005. *Paul, the Fool of Christ: A Study of 1 Corinthians 1–4 in the Comic-philosophic Tradition.* London: T. & T. Clark.

Wenham, D. 1997. "Whatever Went Wrong in Corinth?" *ExpTim* 108:137–41.

West, A. B. 1931. *Latin Inscriptions, 1896–1926.* Corinth, 8.2. Cambridge: Harvard University Press.

West, D. A. 1997. *Horace: The Complete Odes and Epodes.* Oxford: Oxford University Press.

————. 2002. *Horace Odes: Dulce Periculum III.* Oxford: Oxford University Press.

Wetherell, M. 1987. "Social Identity and Group Polarization." Pages 142-70 in *Rediscovering the Social Group: A Self-categorization Theory*, edited by J. C. Turner, et al. Oxford: Blackwell.

————. 2008. "Subjectivity or Psycho-discursive Practices? Investigating Complex Intersectional Identities." *Subjectivity* 22:73–81.

White, L. M. 2005. "Favorinus's 'Corinthian Oration': A Piqued Panorama of the Hadrianic Forum." Pages 61–110 in *Urban Religion in Roman Corinth: Interdisciplinary Approaches*, edited by D. N. Schowalter and S. J. Friesen. Harvard Theological Studies 53. Cambridge: Harvard University Press.

Whitmarsh, T. 2001. *Greek Literature and the Roman Empire: The Politics of Imitation.* Oxford: Oxford University Press.

————. 2004. *Ancient Greek Literature.* Cultural History of Literature. Cambridge: Polity Press.

Widmann, M. 1979. "1 Kor 2:6–16: Ein Einspruch gegen Paulus." *ZNW* 70:44–53.

Wilckens, U. 1959. *Weisheit und Torheit: eine exegetisch-religions-geschichtliche Untersuchung zu 1 Kor 1 und 2.* Beiträge zur historischen Theologie, 26. Tübingen: Mohr Siebeck.

———. 1979. "Zu 1 Kor 2:6–16." Pages 501–537 in *Theologia Crucis-Signum Crucis, Festschrift für Erich Dinkler zum 70 Geburtstag,* edited by C. Andresen, and G. Klein. Tübingen: Mohr Siebeck.

———. 1997. *Der Brief an die Römer.* Evangelisch-katholischer Kommentar zum Neuen Testament 6. Zürich: Benziger.

Wilk, F. 1998. *Die Bedeutung des Jesajabuches für Paulus.* Forschungen zur Religion und Literatur des Alten und Neuen Testaments 179. Göttingen: Vandenhoeck & Ruprecht.

———. 2005. "Isaiah in 1 and 2 Corinthians." Pages 133–58 in *Isaiah in the New Testament.* The New Testament and the Scriptures of Israel, edited by S. Moyise, and M. J. J. Menken. London: T. & T. Clark.

Williams II, C. K. 1987. "The Refounding of Corinth: Some Roman Religious Attitudes." Pages 26–37 in *Roman Architecture in the Greek World,* edited by S. Macready, and F. H. Thompson. London: The Society of Antiquaries.

———. 1989. "A Re-evaluation of Temple E and the West End of the Forum of Corinth." Pages 156–62 in *The Greek Renaissance in the Roman Empire,* edited by S. Walker, and A. Cameron. London: Institute of Classical Studies.

———. 1994. "Roman Corinth as a Commercial Center." In T. E. Gregory, editor. 1994:31–46.

Williams II, C. K., and O. H. Zervos. 1990. "Excavations at Corinth, 1989: The Temenos of Temple E." *Hesperia* 59:325–69.

Williams II, C. K., and N. Bookidis, editors. 2003. *Corinth, the Centenary, 1896–1996.* Corinth 20. Princeton: ASCSA.

Williams, D. K. 2000. "Paul's Anti-imperial 'Discourse of the Cross': The Cross and Power in 1 Corinthians 1–4." Pages 796–823 in *Society of Biblical Literature 2000 Seminar Papers.* Atlanta: Society of Biblical Literature.

Williams, G. 1992. *Sociolinguistics: A Sociological Critique.* London: Routledge.

Williams III, H. H. D. 2001. *The Wisdom of the Wise: The Presence and Function of Scripture Within 1 Cor 1:18—3:23.* Leiden: Brill.

Williams, M. S. 2007. "Nonterritorial Boundaries of Citizenship." Pages 226–56 in *Identities, Affiliations, and Allegiances,* edited by S. Benhabib, I. Shapiro, and D. Petranovic. Cambridge: Cambridge University Press.

Williams, R. H. 2006. *Stewards, Prophets, Keepers of the Word: Leadership in the Early Church.* Peabody, MA: Hendrickson.

Willis, W. 1989. "The 'Mind of Christ' In 1 Corinthians 2:16." *Bib* 70:110–22.

Wilson, R. M. 1972. "How Gnostic were the Corinthians?" *NTS* 19:65–74.

———. 1982. "Gnosis at Corinth." Pages 102–19 in *Paul and Paulinism: Essays in Honour of C. K. Barrett,* edited by M. D. Hooker and S. G. Wilson. London: SPCK.

Winter, B. W. 1989. "'If a Man Does Not Wish to Work . . .': A Cultural and Historical Setting for 2 Thessalonians 3:6–16." *TynBul* 40:303–315.

———. 1995. "The Achaean Federal Imperial Cult II: The Corinthian Church." *TynBul* 169–78.

———. 2001. *After Paul Left Corinth: The Influence of Secular Ethics and Social Change.* Grand Rapids: Eerdmans.

————. 2002a. *Philo and Paul Among the Sophists: Alexandrian and Corinthian Responses to a Julio-Claudian Movement.* Grand Rapids: Eerdmans.

————. 2002b. "Roman Law and Society in Romans 12–15." Pages 67–102 in *Rome in the Bible and the Early Church*, edited by P. Oakes. Grand Rapids: Baker.

————. 2003a. *Roman Wives, Roman Widows: The Appearance of New Women and the Pauline Communities.* Grand Rapids: Eerdmans.

————. 2003b. "The Toppling of Favorinus and Paul by the Corinthians." Pages 291–306 in *Early Christianity and Classical Culture Comparative Studies in Honor of Abraham J. Malherbe*, edited by J. T. Fitzgerald, T. H. Olbricht, and L. M. White. NovTSup 110. Leiden: Brill.

Winter, M. 1975. *Pneumatiker und Psychiker in Korinth zum religionsgeschichtlichen Hintergrund von 1 Kor 2:6—3:4.* Marburger Theologische Studien 12. Marburg: Elwert.

Wire, A. C. 1990. *The Corinthian Women Prophets: A Reconstruction Through Paul's Rhetoric.* Minneapolis: Fortress.

Wiseman, J. 1972. "The Gymnasium Area at Corinth, 1969–1970." *Hesperia* 41:1–42.

————. 1979. "Corinth and Rome I: 228 B.C.—A.D. 267." In *ANRW* 7:438–548.

Witherington, B., III. 1995. *Conflict and Community in Corinth: A Socio-rhetorical Commentary on 1 and 2 Corinthians.* Grand Rapids: Eerdmans.

————. 1998. *Grace in Galatia: A Commentary on St. Paul's Letter to the Galatians.* Grand Rapids: Eerdmans.

Wolff, C. 1996. *Der erste Brief des Paulus an die Korinther.* Theologischer Handkommentar zum Neuen Testament 7. Leipzig: Evangelische Verlagsanstalt.

Wolter, M. 1997. "Ethos und Identität in Paulinischen Gemeinden." *NTS* 43:430–44.

————. 2006. "'Let No One Seek His Own, but Each One the Other's' (1 Corinthians 10:24): Pauline Ethics According to 1 Corinthians." Pages 199–217 in *Identity, Ethics, and Ethos in the New Testament*, edited by J. G. Van der Watt. Beihefte zur Zeitschrift für die neutestamentliche Wissenschaft 141. Berlin: de Gruyter.

Woolf, G. 1994. "Becoming Roman, Staying Greek: Culture, Identity, and the Civilizing Process in the Roman East." *PCPS* 40:116–43.

————. 2003. "*Polis*-religion and Its Alternatives in the Roman Provinces." Pages 39–54 in *Roman Religion*, edited by C. Ando. Edinburgh: Edinburgh University Press.

Worchel, S., and W. G. Austin, editors. 1986. *Psychology of Intergroup Relations.* Nelson-Hall Series in Psychology. Chicago: Nelson-Hall.

Wortham, R. A. 1999. *Social-scientific Approaches in Biblical Literature.* Texts and Studies in Religion 81. Lewiston, NY: Mellen.

Wright, N. T. 2000. "Paul's Gospel and Caesar's Empire." Pages 160–83 in *Paul and Politics: Ekklesia, Israel, Imperium, Interpretation; Essays in Honor of Krister Stendahl*, edited by R. A. Horsley. Harrisburg, PA: Trinity.

————. 2003. *The Resurrection and the Son of God.* Christian Origins and the Question of God 3. Minneapolis: Fortress.

————. 2005. *Paul in Fresh Perspective.* Minneapolis: Fortress.

Wuellner, W. 1979. "Greek Rhetoric and Pauline Argumentation." Pages 177–88 in *Early Christian Literature and the Classical Intellectual Tradition: In Honorem Robert M. Grant.*, edited by W. R. Schoedel and R. L. Wilkin. Théologique Historique 53. Paris: Beauchesne.

————. 1987. "Where is Rhetorical Criticism Taking Us?" *CBQ* 49:448–63.

Yarbrough, O. L. 1997. "Review: *Paul on Marriage and Celibacy: The Hellenistic Background of 1 Corinthians 7* by Will Deming." *JBL* 116:155–56.

Yeo, K. K. 2008. *Musing with Confucius and Paul: Toward a Chinese Christian Theology.* Eugene, OR: Cascade.

Yinger, K. L. 1999. *Paul, Judaism, and Judgment According to Deeds.* Cambridge: Cambridge University Press.

Young, N. H. 1987. "Paidagogos: The Social Setting of a Pauline Metaphor." *NovT* 29:150–76.

Zahn, T., et al. 1909. *Introduction to the New Testament.* Edinburgh: T. & T. Clark.

Zanker, P. 1988. *The Power of Images in the Age of Augustus.* Ann Arbor: University of Michigan Press.

Zetterholm, M. 2009. *Approaches to Paul: A Student's Guide to Recent Scholarship.* Minneapolis: Fortress.

Index of Ancient Sources

Index of Modern Authors